Microsoft Cybersecurity Architect SC-100 Exam Guide

Design and implement secure solutions for the SC-100 exam

Steve Miles

www.bpbonline.com

First Edition 2026

ISBN: 978-93-65897-197

LIMITS OF LIABILITY AND DISCLAIMER OF WARRANTY

The information contained in this book is true and correct to the best of author's and publisher's knowledge. The author has made every effort to ensure the accuracy of these publications, but the publisher cannot be held responsible for any loss or damage arising from any information in this book.

All trademarks referred to in the book are acknowledged as properties of their respective owners but BPB Publications cannot guarantee the accuracy of this information.

Distributors:

BPB PUBLICATIONS
20, Ansari Road, Darya Ganj
New Delhi-110002
Ph: 23254990/23254991

DECCAN AGENCIES
4-3-329, Bank Street,
Hyderabad-500195
Ph: 24756967/24756400

MICRO MEDIA
Shop No. 5, Mahendra Chambers,
150 DN Rd. Next to Capital Cinema,
V.T. (C.S.T.) Station, MUMBAI-400 001
Ph: 22078296/22078297

To View Complete BPB Publications Catalogue Scan the QR Code:

Published by Manish Jain for BPB Publications, 20 Ansari Road, Darya Ganj, New Delhi-110002 and Printed by him at Repro India Ltd., Rewari.

www.bpbonline.com

Dedicated to

To those responsible for securing systems, data, and identities, making difficult decisions that often go unseen but always have an impact

About the Author

Steve Miles works in a senior technology role for the cloud practice of a multi-billion turnover European IT distributor.

He is a Microsoft **Most Valuable Professional** (MVP), **Microsoft Certified Trainer** (MCT), and an Alibaba Cloud MVP. He has 25+ years of technology experience in hosted datacenter services, hybrid, and multi-cloud platforms, and a previous military career in engineering, signals, and communications.

Steve is the author of many books on Microsoft technologies with a focus on Azure, AI, and data, as well as security.

About the Reviewers

- **Chinedu Ozulumba** is a risk management and cybersecurity professional with experience spanning **enterprise risk management** (**ERM**), **governance, risk, and compliance** (**GRC**), and cybersecurity architecture. His work focuses on helping organizations understand, quantify, and manage risk in complex, regulated, and technology-driven environments.

  Chinedu has contributed to enterprise-level risk and cybersecurity initiatives and has been honored to serve as a peer reviewer for a RiskTech enterprise application. He currently serves as a technical reviewer for cybersecurity and risk-focused publications, providing feedback on topics such as Zero Trust architecture, identity-first security, **business continuity and disaster recovery** (**BCDR**), and Microsoft security best practices. His reviews emphasize clarity, practical applicability, and alignment with real-world organizational challenges.

  With a strong interest in translating complex risk concepts into accessible, decision-ready insights, Chinedu is passionate about bridging the gap between technical teams and executive leadership. Outside of professional work, he enjoys continuous learning, reflective writing, and exploring how risk principles apply to everyday decision-making.

- **Bahadir Sahin**, Ph.D., is a dynamic cybersecurity professional and interdisciplinary scholar with over a decade of applied experience across government and financial sectors. He is currently a senior cybersecurity consultant focused on architecting cloud-native security programs and enterprise-level defense strategies using the Microsoft Security stack—including Microsoft Sentinel and Defender—as well as Splunk and IBM Security SOAR. Bahadir specializes in risk management frameworks such as NIST and ISO 27001 as an active researcher and academic with an extensive peer-reviewed publication record in cybersecurity governance, security architecture and emergency management operations.

Acknowledgement

Thanks to the editorial team for the opportunity to bring this book together and for supporting it through to publication.

Appreciation also goes to the technical reviewers for validating the content against the SC-100 skills measured and keeping it accurate and aligned.

Knowledge is rarely developed in isolation, and the ability to write this book has come from years of working with others across the technology community, building an understanding of security concepts and how they are applied in practice. This book is, in part, a way of passing that on.

Preface

Security architecture is rarely one big decision. It is usually the result of a long series of smaller ones—how identities are handled, how access is granted (and just as importantly, revoked), how data is protected, and how signals are interpreted when something does not look right. Over time, those decisions either hold together or they do not. The SC-100 exam reflects that reality. It does not focus on individual features in isolation. You are expected to understand how those pieces fit, and where they do not.

In most environments, the real issues are not caused by something being completely missing. They tend to come from things not quite lining up—policies that do not reflect how access is actually used, identity controls that drift over time, or data protection that does not follow the data far enough. Those gaps are easy to miss at first, until they start causing issues. Often, they only show up when something breaks or when someone asks a question that does not have a clean answer.

This book focuses on those kinds of situations. It does not treat security as a checklist. Instead, it looks at what actually happens when different controls meet real usage—where things hold, where they break, and why. Some of that comes from design, and some of it just comes from seeing the same patterns play out again and again.

As you work through the chapters, the focus shifts away from configuration steps and toward decisions. It is not just about how something is setup. It is about why it exists in the first place, and what problem it is really trying to solve. Identity, endpoints, data, and cloud services do not really sit in isolation, even if they are often built that way. The risk usually shows up where those areas start to overlap.

In practice, environments do not evolve in a controlled way. New services get adopted quickly, usage patterns shift, and governance often plays catch-up. That is where design decisions start to matter, because retrofitting control is always harder than getting it right early on.

If you are working toward the SC-100 exam, the aim here is to help you recognize those patterns so you are not relying on memorization alone. If you are already working in a security role, much of this should feel familiar, either from things you have already dealt with or from situations you will likely run into soon enough.

Chapter 1: Design a Resiliency Strategy for Attacks – Starts with what needs to be in place before anything goes wrong. It works through backup design, recovery expectations, and how services like Defender XDR, Entra ID, and Sentinel support keeping systems available under attack.

Chapter 2: Design Security Solutions with Microsoft Security Benchmarks – Works through how Microsoft reference architectures and security benchmarks are applied in real environments, including where they fit cleanly and where interpretation is needed.

Chapter 3: Design Security Solutions with Microsoft Cloud Frameworks – Steps through how CAF and the Well-Architected Framework translate into actual design choices, especially around landing zones, governance, and long-term maintainability.

Chapter 4: Design Security Operations Solutions – Covers how security operations are structured using Sentinel and Defender XDR, focusing on detection, investigation, and response that can be sustained over time.

Chapter 5: Design Identity and Access Control Solutions – Looks at identity design across authentication, Conditional Access, and authorization, and how those controls need to adapt as environments grow and change.

Chapter 6: Design Privileged Access Management Solutions – Focuses on administrative access, including how PIM, just-in-time access, and privileged access models are used to limit exposure and maintain control.

Chapter 7: Design Regulatory Compliance and Data Governance Solutions – Works through how compliance requirements are translated into technical controls using tools like Purview and Compliance Manager, with an emphasis on validation and reporting.

Chapter 8: Design Cloud and Hybrid Security Solutions – Covers how security posture is assessed and maintained across cloud and hybrid environments using Defender for Cloud, Secure Score, and related capabilities.

Chapter 9: Design Endpoint and Device Security Solutions – Looks at securing endpoints across servers, clients, and devices, using Defender for Endpoint and Intune to enforce consistent protection and compliance.

Chapter 10: Design Workload and Platform Protection Solutions – Explores how workloads are secured across SaaS, PaaS, and IaaS, including how responsibility is shared and where gaps typically appear.

Chapter 11: Design Network Security Architecture Solutions – Covers how network security is designed across modern environments, including segmentation, access control, and secure connectivity patterns.

Chapter 12: Design Microsoft 365 Security Solutions – Focuses on protecting Microsoft 365 workloads, including email, collaboration, and data, and how those protections are applied consistently across services.

Chapter 13: Design Application and API Security Solutions – Works through application security across the lifecycle, including identity, API protection, and integration with development practices.

Chapter 14: Design Data Protection and Governance Solutions – Looks at how data is protected across its lifecycle using classification, labeling, encryption, and governance controls.

Chapter 15: Practice Exams – Provides scenario-based questions that test how design decisions are applied across the full set of SC-100 domains.

Coloured Images

Please follow the link to download the
Coloured Images of the book:

https://rebrand.ly/09db7b

We have code bundles from our rich catalogue of books and videos available at https://github.com/bpbpublications. Check them out!

Errata

We take immense pride in our work at BPB Publications and follow best practices to ensure the accuracy of our content to provide an indulging reading experience to our subscribers. Our readers are our mirrors, and we use their inputs to reflect and improve upon human errors, if any, that may have occurred during the publishing processes involved. To let us maintain the quality and help us reach out to any readers who might be having difficulties due to any unforeseen errors, please write to us at:

errata@bpbonline.com

Your support, suggestions and feedback are highly appreciated by the BPB Publications' Family.

Instagram

Facebook

LinkedIn

YouTube

Piracy

If you come across any illegal copies of our works in any form on the internet, we would be grateful if you would provide us with the location address or website name. Please contact us at business@bpbonline.com with a link to the material.

If you are interested in becoming an author

If there is a topic that you have expertise in, and you are interested in either writing or contributing to a book, please visit www.bpbonline.com. We have worked with thousands of developers and tech professionals, just like you, to help them share their insights with the global tech community. You can make a general application, apply for a specific hot topic that we are recruiting an author for, or submit your own idea.

Reviews

Please leave a review. Once you have read and used this book, why not leave a review on the site that you purchased it from? Potential readers can then see and use your unbiased opinion to make purchase decisions. We at BPB can understand what you think about our products, and our authors can see your feedback on their book. Thank you!

For more information about BPB, please visit www.bpbonline.com.

Join our Discord space

Join our Discord workspace for latest updates, offers, tech happenings around the world, new releases, and sessions with the authors:

https://discord.bpbonline.com

Table of Contents

CHAPTER 1
Design a Resiliency Strategy for Attacks

Introduction

This chapter presents approaches to building attack-resilient architectures that are based on *Microsoft* security best practices. It discusses the integration of Microsoft technologies for resilience, recovery, and continuity, and the concepts of immutable storage, privileged access separation, and recovery plan validation.

Readers will learn about following the principles of layered defense and Zero Trust with an application in the identity, data, and infrastructure, creating a detection, containment, and recovery strategy for advanced attacks focused on identity, data, and infrastructure.

Structure

This chapter covers the following topics:

- Designing a security strategy for business resiliency
- Designing BCDR for hybrid multi-cloud
- Ransomware mitigation with BCDR and PAM
- Evaluating secure update management strategies

Objectives

This chapter gives readers the confidence to be able to make design judgments to build defenses against ransomware and other attacks, and any other evolving threats, end-to-end.

This chapter's content directly maps to and is also in full alignment with the *SC-100* skills measured update, that can be accessed in the official Microsoft study can be found within the official Microsoft study guide for *Exam SC-100: Microsoft Cybersecurity Architect*[1].

---

1 **https://learn.microsoft.com/en-us/credentials/certifications/resources/study-guides/sc-100**

This chapter covers the official SC-100 skills measured that focus on designing security strategies aligned with business resiliency objectives. It examines how security architects identify and prioritize threats to business-critical assets, design **business continuity and disaster recovery** (**BCDR**) solutions that support secure backup and restore across hybrid and multi-cloud environments, and implement mitigation strategies for ransomware attacks with particular emphasis on BCDR readiness and privileged access protection.

These skills are covered under the exam section: *Design solutions that align with security best practices and priorities,* which make up 20-25% of the total exam skills measured.

Designing a security strategy for business resiliency

A strong security strategy to support business resilience aims not only to prevent attacks but to sustain the organization and keep it operating through disruption and when things go wrong.

Effective resiliency thinking requires moving beyond abstract and theoretical categories of risk. It requires a certain depth of knowledge about the organization: what systems are central to providing services, what are the foundational dependencies from those systems, and what are the administrative pathways that need to remain open even when things become worse. The objective is not to be totally secure, but durable; to ensure that the business is kept running while enemies/failures attempt to take it down.

This section explains how the workloads can be classified based on their business impact, how the threats can be prioritized based on their relevance to business operations, and how access patterns can be designed that allow administrators to take fast and safe actions during accompanying incidents. This content maps to the official SC-100 skills measured topic: *Design a security strategy to support business resiliency goals, including identifying and prioritizing threats to business-critical assets.*

Identifying and prioritizing critical assets

Resiliency begins by acknowledging that not all workloads are as crucial as others to business operations. Some systems may be mission-critical and the operational core of the enterprise, and others maintain productivity or analytics tools that may be important, yet not core.

This differing importance is recognized by a good strategy that adjusts the protection; accordingly, Prioritizing allows the business to invest in the right controls, not the most controls, and recover systems in order of greatest continuity.

Business impact and workload tiering

Workload tiering is an effective yet easy method for determining which systems require the most robust defense. Organizations categorize systems according to the level of seriousness that would occur if the system is not available or compromised.

Tier 0 systems, such as identity services, certificate authorities, and access policy engines, control everything. If they fail, no admin can sign in, no system can validate permissions, and recovery actions cannot safely take place.

Tier 1 systems represent major business systems that provide direct support to day-to-day operations: financial systems, booking platforms, logistics applications, point of sale environments, and other mission-critical workloads. Tier 2 systems are important too, but the impact on daily operations is less direct in nature.

This categorization allows security architects to target their efforts on the most important systems. Since the Tier 0 failures spread to every other layer, they require not only tight controls around access, but stricter monitoring and recovery processes that focus on getting them back online first. The following figure illustrates a simple workload tiering model that shows how systems are grouped by business impact and dependency, and how those tiers influence recovery priority during incidents:

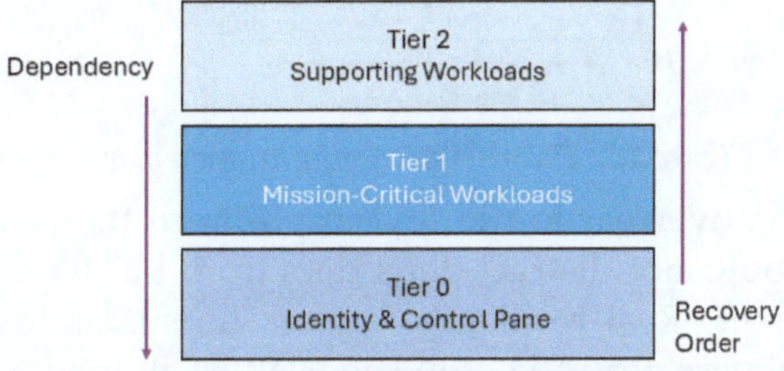

Figure 1.1: *Workload tiering model for cybersecurity resilience*

Organizations prevent having to expend efforts on homogeneous models of protection that compromise security where it really matters by matching resources to business value to be protected.

Tiering has also made it easier to communicate with the senior people in the business. Instead of technical descriptions of clusters of servers, architects can describe protection priorities in business terms, like *this system needs to be restored within minutes because it maintains identity*, or *this workload improves internal productivity but does not stop the operations*. When business leaders are aligned with the impact, they are clear and confident in their support for resilient design decisions.

Prioritizing threats to business-critical assets

After identifying high-value systems, the next task is prioritizing which threats could disrupt them in meaningful ways. A threat's true severity is not based on how technically interesting it is, but how much harm it causes to the systems that uphold business continuity.

For Tier 0 systems, threats involving credential theft, lateral movement, privilege escalation, and identity manipulation are the most dangerous. These attacks can disable the organization's ability to authenticate users or authorize recovery actions. Threat prioritization, therefore, becomes an exercise in mapping adversary techniques to workload importance. An outage affecting a Tier 2 reporting system is inconvenient; an outage affecting a Tier 0 domain controller is existential.

By analyzing threats through the lens of operational dependency, architects ensure that controls, whether monitoring, hardening, or access restrictions, are concentrated where they will produce real resiliency gains. The following figure is a 2x2 matrix showing how threat severity increases when high-impact assets intersect with high-impact threats:

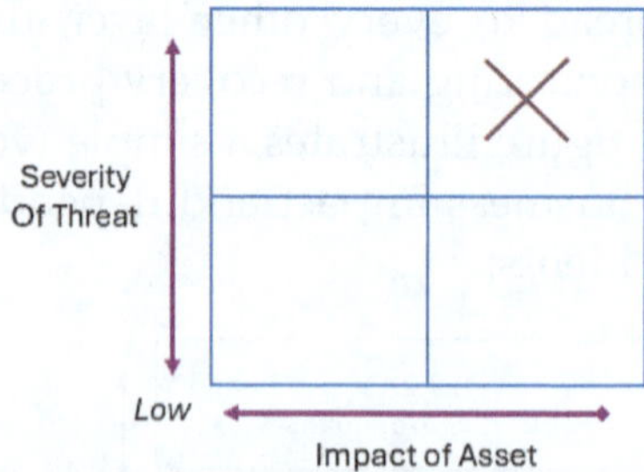

Figure 1.2: Threat-to-asset prioritization map

This approach also prevents overreaction to low-importance threats. A minor vulnerability in a non-critical system should not distract defenders from hardening identity platforms or improving recovery processes. Real resiliency focuses on sustaining the organization, not chasing every possible weakness. Prioritization keeps effort aligned with impact.

Securing and maintaining administrative access

Even a very well-engineered resiliency plan will fail if administrators are unable to intervene during an incident; security controls should not be barriers to operational agility.

Administrators require secure work areas, well-defined access sequences, and backups in the event of identity system failures. In this section, we look at how privileged approaches to accessing provide resilience and secure paths that remain usable in high-stress conditions.

Privileged access foundations

Privileged Access Workstation (**PAWs**), **Privileged Identity Management** (**PIM**), and break-glass accounts can be considered the backbone of administrative control resilience.

The PAWs remove administrative tasks from their day-to-day computing environments. Isolating admin credentials from email, surfing the web, and normal applications slashes the danger of credential theft enormously.

In an incident, admins log in from clean and controlled devices, preventing breach of trust and affected device endpoints; two paths are available: a *normal path* and an *emergency path*.

The following figure is an illustration that aims to show the normal path, i.e., PAW I PIM I Privileged Role, and the emergency path, i.e., PAW I Break Glass Account I Privileged Role:

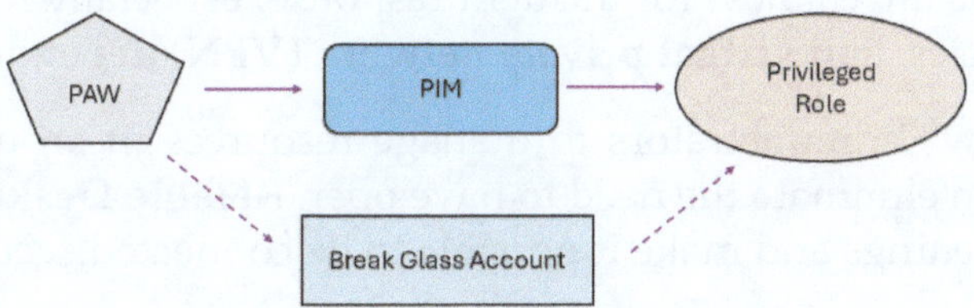

Figure 1.3: Resilient privileged access paths

The **just-in-time** (**JIT**) access through PIM decreases standing privilege. Instead of permanent admin roles, with PIM, the elevation is only temporary and only for the required amount of time. This reduces the attack surface and ensures that even if the users' credentials are obtained by the attackers, they do not have high-privileges unless an elevation has been actively allowed. It also allows the use of fine-grained auditing and conditional access controls to evaluate the risk prior to elevation.

Break-glass accounts provide an added level of assurance. They are used as emergency points of entry when identity systems fail, or PIM is unavailable, or policy tools fail. These accounts are not used very often as they are very restricted; they have storage, and they are routinely tested. In a degraded environment, particularly in response to ransomware, break-glass access is important to make sure that administrators can still access systems they need to restore. A more detailed explanation of the three foundational privileged approaches is as follows:

- **PAWs**: They are secure enclaves for the sensitive task; they decrease the hazard of omitting productivity software, blocking internet browsing, and restricting access to trusted administrative interfaces. It is this setup that guarantees resilience. Even in the event of a large-scale compromise, administrators can rely on a known-clean device to use safely and confidently.
- **JIT privilege via PIM**: PIM's temporary elevation model, therefore, helps build resilience by eliminating the old privileges that can be exploited by attackers.

  In the event of an incident response, PIM provides a structured and audited elevation request to ensure that only authorized administrators gain access, and only for the required duration. This way, there is less confusion and privilege sprawl when under pressure.
- **Emergency break-glass access**: Break-glass accounts serve in the role of a backstop to the degradation of primary identity means. They must be offline accessible, stored securely, in tamper-proof locations, and tested regularly. Their existence will ensure that recovery efforts are not delayed because the normal identity plane has not been available, which is so critical for resiliency planning.

Together, these parts combine to control incidents.

Resilient administrative access pathways

Administrative access is a weakness for incident response, especially if the network filtering, conditional access policies, and **virtual private network** (**VPN**) dependencies are degraded.

A resilient design allows administrators to manage resources in an unstable environment. Tools like Azure Bastion eliminate the need to have open **Remote Desktop Protocol** (**RDP**) or **Secure Shell** (**SSH**) openings and make it possible to be connected securely without opening up your firewall.

When network segmentation is tight and / or identity trust is being reviewed, Bastion provides a path of control and isolation to access critical servers. The following figure shows a secure administrative access pathway that illustrates how privileged roles, PAWs, Azure Bastion, and JIT access combine to provide a controlled and isolated route to critical workloads:

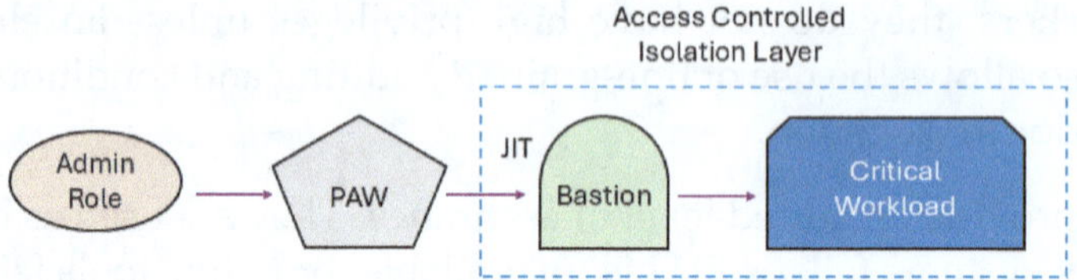

***Figure 1.4**: Secure admin access pathway*

This is complemented by JIT access to the **virtual machine** (**VM**) that only opens up the necessary openings at the right time. Unlike permanently exposed management ports, JIT only grants port access to short and auditable windows. This balances down the attack surface with operational agility. During disruptions, admins are still able to access important workloads without having to loosen security policies.

Resilient administrative access is not about making it convenient; however, it is more about mitigating friction during the recovery. A predictable and secure access path allows administrators to take action as quickly as possible, reducing downtime and being positive to the organization.

Balancing strong security with operational agility

Security controls that prevent administrators from accessing at the wrong time can help improve resiliency. The challenge lies in these cries: to find a balance between protecting the environment from misuse and, in particular, having the opportunity to recover legitimately. This calls for intelligent management of PIM policies, secure workstations, conditional access policies, and emergency protocols.

Overly rigid controls that may delay or even prevent response activities. The problem with too-permissive controls, however, is that they increase the risk of compromise at the worst possible time. Good resiliency design requires an approach that recognizes that the controls must be robust but flexible. Administrators need the tools and pathways they need, but the environment should have robust guardrails in place to prevent opportunistic attacks.

This balance is a delicate one; however, it is essential. Without it, the security architecture is too narrow for responding or too loose for staying out of the way of escalation. The best resilient designs expect disruption and prepare administrators to operate under pressure from the change.

Designing BCDR for hybrid multi-cloud

BCDR nurtures an organization to operate despite system failure, infrastructure availability, or detrimental events to its continuity.

In the context of the SC-100 exam, BCDR focuses much more on the practical and architectural aspects of the process, addressing the need to secure backup paths for your isolated environments, using retention policies that meet the long-term needs, using region-to-region redundancy as the default resiliency model, and testing your recovery plans to ensure they work reliably under duress.

This section, as such, avoids general theory and instead gets into the exam-relevant skills, focusing on how to create resilient services using Azure natively available tools, allowing the hybrid environment to recover cleanly and predictably.

This content maps to the official SC-100 skills measured topic: *Design solutions for BCDR, including secure backup and restore for hybrid and multi-cloud environments.*

Designing backup and retention for hybrid estates

Backup design is often the most practical way of expressing a BCDR strategy. If the data of a workload is not available, or if it is corrupted or tampered with, it cannot be recovered. Hybrid environments present certain problems; some servers are in isolated networks, while others have no internet access at all, and some will have stringent **long-term retention** (**LTR**) needs. In this context, Azure Backup and other components all allow the architect to unify retention policies, enhance recoverability, and integrate on-premises systems into cloud-based backup workflows.

Backing up in a hybrid estate is basically a process of closing the gaps between the isolated networks and the cloud instance, between short-term operational backups and the compliance requirement of multiple years, and between local recovery processes and centralized governance. The following topics cover the exam skills measured for this topic, which form the backbone of Azure's hybrid BCDR strategy.

Backup for isolated or offline servers

Some servers run in environments where there is no means or no desire to establish direct outbound connectivity to Azure. These situations can include regulated workloads, OT environments, highly segmented networks, or systems that have strict firewall policies. In such cases, the recommended solution for the cloud backup is **Microsoft Azure Backup Server (MABS)**.

The MABS is a proxy between the protected servers and Azure. Instead of each workload contacting Azure Backup directly, the server sends backup data to MABS, which in turn sends the data to the Azure Recovery Services vault. The following flow helps to visualize why MABS, not the Azure Backup agent, is the appropriate mechanism for air-gapped or offline workloads:

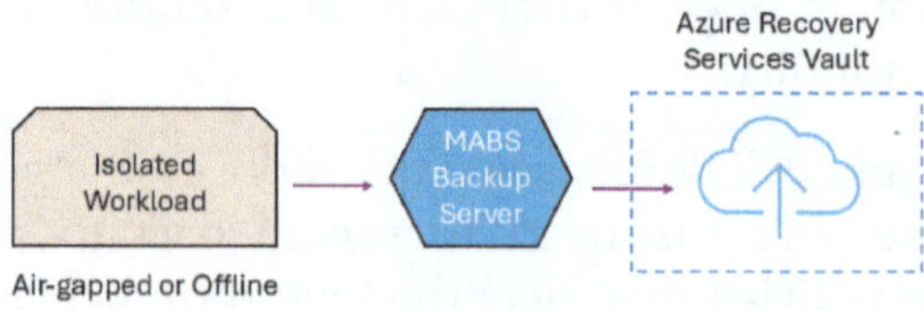

Figure 1.5: MABS hybrid backup path

This setup maintains the separation of isolation in a way that provides durability, off-site protection, and centralized management with cloud-based retention.

The design also increases resiliency by facilitating the management of the backup across different network segments. Rather than having to use separate backup solutions for each individual server that is isolated from the rest of the servers on the network and those that are connected to the internet, MABS allows the enterprise to have a unified backup architecture in hybrid environments. As a result, the process of recovery is easier to predict and validate.

Server to MABS to Azure Backup flow

The backup chain is a relatively simple one: firstly, the protected server sends data to MABS; then, MABS maintains a local copy for a quick restore, and on some scheduled basis, sends recovery points to Azure.

This two-step flow ensures continuity even with intermittent and unreliable local connectivity. It also ensures that recovery can be done in offline scenarios. MABS keeps recent snapshots locally, and hence you can quickly recover without any outside need for infrastructure.

Scenarios where MABS is used instead of agents

The exam covers the knowledge of a very important principle: the standard Azure Backup agent only functions when the server can communicate with Azure with the help of outbound connectivity.

In isolated networks, where egress is limited or restricted, the agent cannot communicate with Azure services, and as such, the MAB is the right choice for the solution architecture design.

It is important for the exam to remember this distinction that anytime a workload cannot get directly to Azure, the answer is always to MABS.

Long-term retention for compliance

Organizations often have retention obligations that are outside the typical time frame of operational recovery. Records such as financial information, healthcare information, legal evidence, and regulatory audit materials may have to be retained for a very long time. In your dataset, the requirement was for multi-year retention, hence the correct solution was Azure Backup LTR.

LTR enables organizations to retain snapshots on a monthly or annual basis for a longer duration using policies to automate the time that data is kept and when it is retired. This approach avoids the requirement for manual archiving and ensures consistency in the whole environment. Instead of making backups available for export or relying on ad hoc scripts, LTR puts a well-structured and policy-driven retention strategy in place, which is a fit for compliance requirements. The following figure is a clean timeline diagram with daily, weekly, monthly, and yearly retention checkpoints:

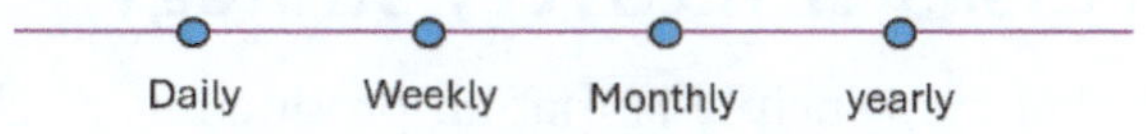

***Figure 1.6**: Azure Backup LTR timeline*

The preceding visual helps readers understand how LTR builds a layered retention structure that grows over time. Another benefit of LTR is that the data is still under the control of the Recovery Services vault. This has the advantage of simplification in monitoring, auditing, and retention validation. The benefits include durability, predictability, and a transparent audit trail necessary for regulatory compliance for the organization.

Retention cycles by time interval

The flexibility that LTR brings is due to its layering retention scheme. Daily snapshots for your immediate recovery of operation, weekly snapshots allow you to go back in time for more recent snapshots to make medium-term fixes, and monthly and yearly snapshots facilitate compliance on a long-term horizon.

Since the cycles are policy-controlled, and since the admins do not need to manually select the restore points that will be retained, this approach works. The fact that the cadence is clear means that the process is predictable and well governed.

Choosing between LTR and archive tier

The distinction between storage datasets needs to be maintained. LTR is explicitly used for backup retention, and the archive tier is for data that is not frequently accessed and is not part of the backup lifecycle. Archive storage cannot be used in place of backups since it does not have snapshot semantics and recovery-oriented metadata. In a solution requirement situation that involves multi-year backup retention requirements, the correct selection is always LTR, not archive.

Building disaster recovery architectures

Backup is for protection, while DR is making sure you have services available again, but on a quick and predictable basis. The skills assessed for the exam do not test complex multi-cloud failover scenarios or advanced workload portability, and it is all about having a region-to-region resiliency model in Azure and having documented, tested recovery plans.

Azure architects Azure regions in structured pairs, and its replication guarantees make DR planning easy. Most organizations are based on warm-standby deployment and cross-regional replication for fast rebuild of service availability. These practices come about from a drive to have data integrity and have operational continuity as the priority over other measures and outcomes.

Region-to-region disaster recovery strategy

In Azure, an important resiliency principle is that all production workloads should have a recovery strategy that relies upon region-to-region failover. Azure paired regions ensure that, if one region is hit by a catastrophic failure, a second region is available to receive replicated data or stage determined workloads. For many organizations, this warm-standby approach is the right balance of cost and continuity.

Region-to-region DR is not only about data replication; it is more than a replication exercise, but actually an architectural commitment of designing for all the inter-dependent components; systems must be designed to failover safely with policies and designs of appropriate **Domain Name System** (**DNS**) updates, data synchronization, and dependencies for identity and security in place.

It should be reinforced that whilst other more complex scenarios are available, the region-to-region DR is for many the expected and best practice solution, unless law, regulation, or other requirements dictate otherwise. The following figure demonstrates Microsoft's preferred resiliency path:

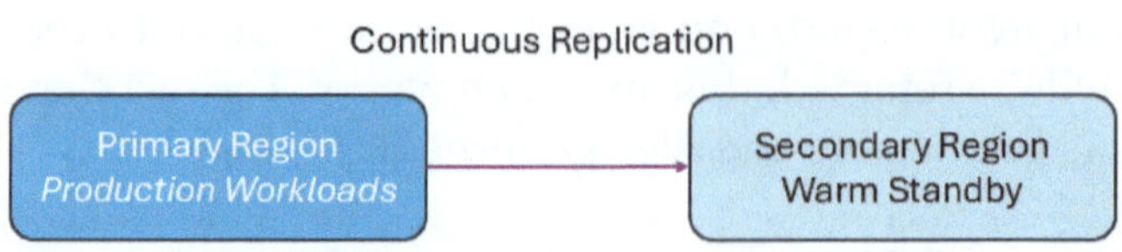

Figure 1.7: *Region-to-region DR model*

This strategy is less complicated (and more cost-effective) than multi-cloud DR. Rather than having to coordinate identity, networking, and data replication across different platforms, a region-to-region DR approach helps keep the architecture coherent and easy to manage and govern.

Creating and validating recovery plans

A solid DR design can break down if the steps to recover from a disaster are ill-defined, never tested, or are dependent too much on internal system knowledge. Recovery plans are the backbone of the continuance; they spell out who does what, when, and what is needed. When a plan comes into play, the theoretical design becomes a real-world activity.

Your data indicates that testing recovery plans is very important. Testing reveals that there are missing permissions, incorrect assumptions concerning dependences, obsolete scripts, and configuration drift that only exist in a real incident. A tested plan provides a sense of direction and confidence in action to administrators when the pressure is greatest.

Testing is not optional, but is the only way to ensure backups are recovered in line with recovery expectations, workloads can be brought back in the correct order, and that the environment behaves predictably when stressed. A resilient organization incorporates validation of its recovery plan into its daily operations and does not see validation as a checkbox for compliance.

Ransomware mitigation with BCDR and PAM

Ransomware is highly disruptive because it attacks data and the ability to recover it. Modern attackers have a methodical plan and have focused on the following in their attacks:

- Attack privileged accounts.
- Sabotage/corrupt backups.
- Break identity systems so admins cannot respond.

In fact, during an event, the main question is not *how to decrypt the files* but *whether we can still recover*.

Parts of ransomware resilience covered in this section are dataset validated. It focuses on protecting the backup integrity, helps to restore the identity before the workloads, helps to follow a structured recovery sequence, and helps to block reinfection through cloud sync services. Trusted privileged access is critical since a recovery requires admin paths to be efficient solutions. The aim is to explain precisely the architectural patterns that ensure that an organization is in a state to rebuild, rather than describing all the ransomware tactics.

This section's content maps to the official SC-100 skills measured topic: *Design solutions for mitigating ransomware attacks, including prioritization of BCDR and privileged access.*

Protecting and preserving recoverability

Recovery is the key to ransomware resiliency. Even in the worst-case scenario, usually the one where the attackers have prized positions or destroy some components of the infrastructure, the attack's upper hand will always be with organizations that have intact and trustworthy backups. Each exam skillset-mapped concept in this area reflects the concept that recovery must be protected prior to an attack, and not after.

Protecting backups from compromised admins

After gaining administrative privileges by attackers, the storage of backups is often deleted. This is deliberate; if the backups are damaged or tampered with, the primary recovery pathway for the organization has been destroyed. Your data provides validation to two defenses that are built into Azure to offset this tactic: Soft Delete and **multi-user authorization** (**MUA**).

These two mechanisms combined make for significantly increased survivability of backup data, as shown in the following figure:

Figure 1.8: *Backup protection layers*

Soft Delete preserves deleted backup items for a specified amount of time, even if a malicious or hacked administrator tries to remove the items. It creates a valuable cushion in situations where attackers have some limited control but have not taken full control of the environment yet. Soft Delete is a safety net around the recovery points for an organization. When deleting the backup items, whether intentionally or accidentally, Soft Delete prevents them from being immediately deleted. This gives administrators a brief, crucial window to bail themselves out of malicious or accidental actions. As a result, the difference that can be made by Soft Delete is often the difference between having a viable recovery path and being unable to recover the data at all.

MUA, which is powered by Resource Guard, also imposes an additional layer of security by requiring a second independent approval for destructive backup operations. Even if someone compromises a vault administrator, they cannot undo backup protection or delete retention points without a second authorization held outside the compromised blast radius. MUA helps by enabling the risks of one compromised administrator to be mitigated, preventing unacceptable damage from occurring. It does so by requiring an external authorization source (for example, a separate security team or a vault secured by a different subscription) for Azure Backup to impose dual control over high-impact operations. This requirement is reminiscent of the traditional separation-of-duties, but applied to cloud-native backup workflows.

Immutable or isolated backups

Attackers and threats evolve rapidly, with some ransomware campaigns aimed at complete metadata of backups or retention policies, or storage fabric. Immutable storage and air-gapped copies are countermeasures to these threats by ensuring that no alteration of the content of backup can be accomplished regardless of the attacker's privilege.

The nature of immutable backups is such that they cannot be altered after they are written. They provide a non-editable record of the state of the system that is being backed-up. When recovering from a ransomware event, the architects must be sure that the backed-up data that is being restored is safe from attacker tampering. Immutable storage ensures this integrity so that the organization can rebuild with certainty.

Isolated backups (for example, sometimes kept in an environment with limited access or physically separated from each other) give extra insurance. Even if attackers break into production systems, there is much less they can do to reach stores that are isolated.

The result is a robust layered defense approach, so that backups are kept reliable, even in the face of a worst-case privilege escalation mechanism. The backup options are as follows:

- **Immutable storage snapshots**: Immutable snapshots have a write-once model that prevents malware and administrators from modifying recovery points, either maliciously or accidentally. As the data cannot be changed, it is impossible for attackers to corrupt backups prior to encryption. This ensures that a version of the system is always available that is known to be clean with integrity.

- **Air-gapped backup patterns**: Air-gapped backups can be implemented in an environment that, by definition, is intentionally disconnected from production systems and networks. They cannot be accessed with default network access or standard system or administrative access and credentials, which makes it difficult for attackers to compromise and access. Despite being more complex and complicated to operate, this approach provides unmatched protection, particularly to highly regulated workloads.

Testing and validating clean recovery points

A backup that has not even been tested cannot be trusted. Testing is the only way to make sure that the backup process took all of the necessary data, that the restoration path will work under pressure, and that the restored system will behave properly. With respect to the recovery aspects associated with ransomware, the purpose of testing is supplemented by ensuring that the restore point is older than the compromise.

Organizations that do not test restoration workflows at the appropriate time are often left to find out at the worst time. Missing dependencies, incorrect permissions, outdated scripts, or incomplete data capture on a backup may render a backup unusable. Regular and structured testing removes these uncertainties and creates a level of confidence when it comes to recovery plans.

Testing also informs decision-makers during an incident, and if administrators are aware of what recovery points have been vetted and can be brought back clean, then they can be assured they are not loading contamination back into the environment. This makes the recovery period much shorter and safer.

Restoring operational trust after ransomware

Modern ransomware attacks also aim to destroy operational trust, not merely company data. When authentication, authorization, or administrative boundaries are broken, environments become unpredictable.

This requires that recovery be started by re-establishing identity and administrative pathway trust before the return of workload data and / or facilitating cloud services.

Restoring identity infrastructure first

Identity is used as an authoritative source for access decisions. If an **identity document** (**ID**) is compromised, all restoration activities are unsafe because the administrators cannot recognize who is signing in or what permissions are from a legitimate authority. Best practice guidance suggests that recovery starts with restoring the identity infrastructure, typically domain controllers, Entra ID aspects, and supporting Tier 0 systems.

The following figure shows the recommended identity-first recovery sequence, starting with Tier 0 systems and progressing through core workloads and endpoints:

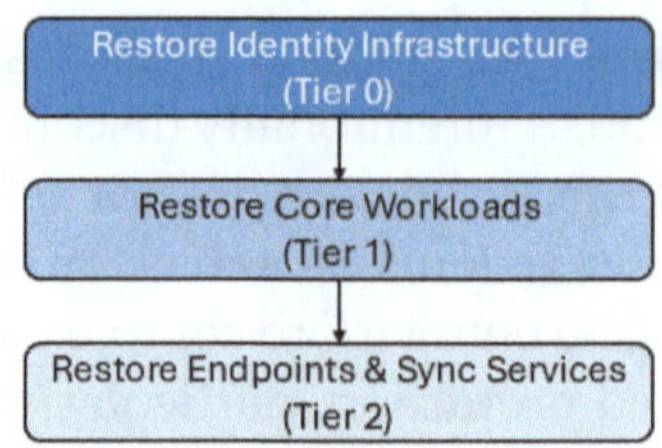

***Figure 1.9**: Identity-first recovery sequence*

In a ransomware attack, attackers frequently change the settings on directories, add malicious accounts, or change group memberships. Recovery should then reverse these changes, propagate the integrity of the restored identity environment, and prove that administrative actions are from trusted credentials; only after this is it likely safe to consider rebuilding application layers and data services.

The following points describe the key identity components that must be restored first to establish a trusted recovery foundation:

- **Tier 0 domain controllers**: Domain controllers need to be restored first since they manage the logins and privileges of the users. If they remain compromised or offline, then subsequent recovery steps cannot be collaborated on with confidence afterwards.

It is by restoring Tier 0 identity assets that we are restoring the basic foundation that the entire environment is built upon.

- **Entra ID components and sync paths**: Hybrid identity environments rely on connecting and interfacing between Entra ID and Active Directory. If these connections are disabled or tampered with by attackers, identities and policies can then fail to flow between primary and on-premises systems, incorrectly positioning the hybrid identity plane. Restoring and validating the sync paths allows the hybrid identity environment to get back on track.

Halting sync and restoring clean cloud data

In the case of Microsoft 365 environments, ransomware propagation often carries on through the synchronization services. Infected files can repeatedly sync between compromised endpoints and repositories in the cloud, making the containment process challenging. In order to break this loop, the administrators should temporarily stop sync operations and clean the content before restoring it, and restart sync only if endpoints are checked.

This process demands an approach that is aligned with a disciplined approach. Administrators are faced with the challenge of restoring file versions predating the attack, ensuring devices are not producing malicious content, and validating that sync relationships will not introduce uncorrupted files. When done correctly, it prevents reinfection and ensures that users gain access to health data again.

The following actions describe the steps used to stop cloud synchronization and restore clean data in Microsoft 365 environments during ransomware recovery:

- **OneDrive sync disablement**: OneDrive is a continuous sync mechanism and sometimes can propagate corrupted content across devices. Temporarily disabling sync promotes engaging app replication and genuine administrators' time to restore clean versions of files. This break in propagation is necessary when user devices are devices that cannot be thought to be trusted.

- **Exchange ActiveSync isolation for mobile devices**: ActiveSync has the ability to synchronize harmful attachments, corrupted emails, or harmful file content to mobile devices. Disabling/restricting ActiveSync should be implemented while recovery is done to ensure that the containment boundary is preserved and the number of affected devices is reduced.

Ransomware-resilient privileged access

Privileged access must be working and trusted during incident response. PAWs provide clean administrative workspaces, PIM provides temporary elevation, and break-glass accounts for fallback access when identity services are impaired. Such controls aid in recovery by ensuring that administrators can work safely, even in completely untrusted environments, in most cases.

Ransomware recovery is a time-sensitive situation. If administrators are unable to elevate at the correct time, underneath the sign-in systems, or restricted infrastructure, recovery becomes slow or stopped. Privileged access resilience helps to facilitate rapid and controlled intervention and avoid administrative bottlenecks at the worst possible time. Ransomware incidents are handled through a structured sequence that begins with containment, continues with investigation, and concludes with recovery.

Ransomware recovery goes through a very purposeful and structured process. Skipping steps takes on risk, followed by increased downtime, or will result in re-encryption. Your dataset affirmed the significance of this sequence, especially its stress on identity and simple recovery points. The sequence explanation is as follows:

- **Containment**: It means isolation of compromised systems, stopping sync paths, and account blockage of account(s) that show signs of misuse. This step prevents this from also spreading and stabilizes the environment.
- **Investigation**: It is focused on figuring out which systems and who are affected by compromised systems, which restore points are reliable, and what residual risk is present in the environment. With the help of an investigation, it also checks whether attackers tampered with the metadata of backups or directory objects.
- **Recovery**: It can only occur once the containment and investigation process is complete. It begins with the Tier 0 identity systems, then moves on to application workloads, and then returns the user access. Following this structure is what guarantees that restored systems run in a secure, stable environment.

The following figure displays the sequence flow:

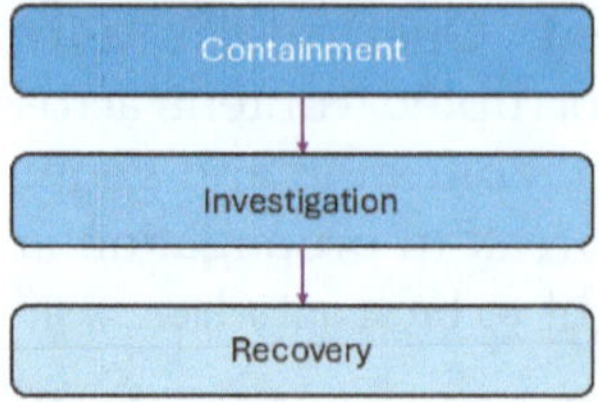

***Figure 1.10**: Containment, investigation, and recovery flow*

The following actions describe how containment, investigation, and recovery are carried out in sequence during a ransomware incident:

- **Containment actions**: Containment is one of the methods to contain the impact of ransomware. It includes making sync disabled, preventing accounts, separating systems from the network, and stopping further encryption of files. If this first step is not undertaken, recovery actions could potentially spread the attack.
- **Investigation actions**: Investigation verifies what is compromised, what is clean, and what can be trusted. Before data is restored, it will validate restore points, look for abuse of privilege, and make sure that the identity infrastructure is ready for controlled recovery.

- **Recovery actions**: Recovery is based on the idea of restoring trust first. Identity is reconstituted, administrative units are fixed, and workloads are restored in an organized manner. This works to ensure predictable and safe restoration.

Evaluating secure update management strategies

Security updates are one of the most reliable and cost-effective means of protection against attack. Most intrusions, even high-profile ransomware attacks, exploit the vulnerabilities for which patches are available. This section focuses on the Azure Update Manager, Azure Arc for hybrid servers, and update rings to stage rollout. These features are some of the most significant for hybrid enterprise environments.

Although prevention and detection do take greater attention, patching often offers the greatest return in security investment. A good update strategy can increase resilience by eliminating the weak points that attackers exploit (instead of actually blocking attacks). Evaluating secure update management involves consistent coverage, disruption reduction, and reducing exposure times, especially in diverse hybrid environments. This content maps to the official SC-100 skills measured topic: *Evaluate solutions for security updates.*

Unified patch governance

Patches in many organizations are fragmented. Cloud VMs use one process, on-premise servers use a different one, and multi-cloud workloads use a third one. This fragmentation results in inconsistent compliance, risk unpredictability, and duplicated administrative efforts.

Azure Update Manager fills this gap as a central patch orchestration across all of the environments. Combined with Azure Arc, it will provide a unified control plane for patch management, no matter where the workload is.

Azure Update Manager for hybrid patching

Azure Update Manager provides a unified interface to schedule the updates, review the compliance, and enforce the consistent patching policies of all the servers across an environment.

In the exam skills that are being measured, Update Manager is the strategic solution for transferring orchestration of patches in scale, especially when organizations require visibility for both Azure and on-premises workloads.

Update Manager works by combining with the monitoring and automation in Azure. It gathers the status of each patch from servers, identifies missing patches, and allows administrators to setup deployments that will avoid disruptions to business. Its automation capabilities are a critical element of resiliency, given that patching manually, especially in a large environment, is error-prone and not standard.

Another feature of Update Manager that is useful is that it emphasizes ease of use. Instead of having many different tools or scripts to deal with and manage patch status, organizations can view and respond to patch status in one place. This reduces the operational overhead while also increasing audit readiness. Update Manager also works with log analytics, providing clear details of patch events, failures, and times of patch deployment.

The following areas highlight the core patch management capabilities provided by Update Manager that support controlled deployment and compliance visibility:

- **Patch scheduling and orchestration**: Scheduling updates is more than the functionality of when to let patches install; it also requires the structuring of waves of updates in order to minimize risk and be appropriate for the respective operational demands. Update Manager provides fine-grained control over timing, reboot behavior, maintenance windows, and workload groupings. These capabilities allow organizations to implement updates with little impact and ensure mission-critical essential systems are patched through a controlled pattern.
- **Compliance and reporting basics**: Visibility plays a huge role in security governance. Update Manager's compliance reporting provides information about which systems are up to date, which are not, and which failed their prior deployments. This information allows security teams to focus on apparent critical remediation and maintain patch compliance within the policies. Not only that, it helps audits because you can get clear evidence of patch activities.

Azure Arc for on-premises and multi-cloud servers

Azure Arc extends Azure's management plane to any server, whether on-premises, in some other cloud provider, or at the edge. In the presence of patching, Arc is the enabling technology that can make Update Manager relevant across the hybrid and multi-cloud environments. Without Arc, on-premises servers would not be included in Azure's governance capabilities.

Arc-enabled servers send telemetry back to Azure and are included in Update Manager schedules, as well as providing compliance data as if Arc-enabled VMs were native Azure ones. This consistency is a major plus for enterprises which are spanning across multiple hosting environments. Instead of keeping isolated patching solutions, Arc centralizes the control and consolidates personalized enforcement of policy.

Arc also strengthens resiliency, ensuring that patch processes are the same between environments. Attackers like to take advantage of the weak link, a neglected on-premises server, a forgotten VM in a secondary cloud account, an unmanaged appliance, etc. Organizations can reduce fragmentation and knock down the attack surface to a fraction of its size by bringing all the servers into the Azure Arc.

Reducing update risk

Patching reduces the exploitation, but can also lead to operational instability if it is being patched without testing. Systems may behave in unexpected ways, applications may fail, or dependencies may be changing in unpredictable ways. To avoid this danger, organizations employ staged deployment strategies.

Update rings for staged deployments

A structured ring structure is added to patch deployment via update rings. Instead of making a mass update, where systems will be down for a while, organizations first update a small pilot group. This pilot group ensures the stability before the updates are rolled out to larger-lots pre-production and production cohorts.

The operational risk can be mitigated, and the patch schedule can remain on track with the use of update rings. When a patch causes some issue in the pilot ring, administrators can halt the rollout of the patch and fix it before it reaches mission-critical systems. This approach ensures that the environment is resilient, ensuring that security upgrades will never decrease service availability.

Staged deployment is especially helpful in the case of hybrid environments. Since workloads are so variable, there is a bigger probability for hidden dependencies. The paths of roll-out are controlled, consistent with the various roles and levels of risk associated with each workload on the estate.

Conclusion

In this chapter, we looked at how business resiliency is accomplished not by a single discipline, but by the intersection of several interconnected capabilities.

A business resiliency strategy establishes which systems and services must survive disruption, providing the context for all recovery decisions. Based on those priorities, BCDR design defines how services are restored in a predictable and repeatable way.

Ransomware mitigation then protects that recovery capability by ensuring attackers cannot erase, encrypt, or corrupt the mechanisms required to restore operations. Secure update management underpins each of these areas by reducing the vulnerability surface that attackers rely on to initiate disruption in the first place.

As a result, each pillar helps to strengthen others. For example, recovery plans are based on having secure access to administration, ransomware response begins with identity restoration, and update strategies counteract exploits that may bring downtime.

The skills assessed in the exam focus on practical use of resilience, where backup is located away from administrative compromise, or DR choices are made region-based over complex multi-cloud solutions; solutions for the privileged access patterns achieving usable backups under stress; solutions for centralized patch governance for hybrid estates are the focus of this exam.

A security architect's job requires the application of these principles into predictable operationally-aligned solution architecture designs that ensure continuity of business in the face of failures of systems or failures of attackers to a system. Resiliency does not prevent us from being disrupted by things; it makes sure disruption does not evolve into catastrophic business-impacting events.

The next chapter builds on these resiliency principles by focusing on how identity, access, and control planes are secured to prevent disruptions from escalating into broader security incidents.

Questions

Success in any exam requires a real understanding of the technologies, concepts, and principles, and not simply memorizing them. These questions allow the readers to determine whether they can apply the concepts of this chapter, which include tiering, privileged access, BCDR, ransomware recovery, and update governance, in the way the SC-100 exam expects.

1. **Which workload tier should be restored first during a major attack, and why?**
   a. Tier 2, because user productivity systems must be restored first
   b. Tier 1, because they host critical business operations
   c. Tier 0, because identity and control plane services underpin every other recovery action
   d. Whichever system has the largest dataset
2. **An organization has a set of servers in a highly isolated network with no outbound internet access. Which backup architecture should be used?**
   a. Azure Backup agent installed on each server
   b. Exporting VHDs to cold storage
   c. MABS acting as the proxy
   d. Azure Site Recovery directly from each server
3. **Which control prevents a compromised backup administrator from deleting recovery points?**
   a. Update rings
   b. Azure Firewall

c. MUA (Resource Guard)

d. Azure Monitor alerts

4. **What is the purpose of Soft Delete in Azure Backup?**

a. Reduce backup storage costs

b. Retain deleted backup items for a recovery safety window

c. Encrypt all backup metadata

d. Move backups to the Archive tier automatically

5. **An enterprise needs multi-year retention for compliance. Which mechanism should be used?**

a. Archive tier storage

b. LTR in Recovery Services vault

c. Snapshot copies in Blob Storage

d. Local disk backups

6. **Which privileged access control guarantees administrators can still operate during identity outages?**

a. Update Manager

b. Break-glass accounts stored securely and tested regularly

c. Arc-enabled servers

d. Defender for Cloud

7. **During ransomware recovery, why must administrators disable OneDrive or ActiveSync sync temporarily?**

a. It reduces storage consumption

b. It improves network performance during recovery

c. It prevents the re-propagation of corrupted data back into the cloud

d. It enforces Conditional Access

8. **Which is the correct high-level sequence for ransomware response?**

a. Restore | Investigate | Contain

b. Contain | Investigate | Recover

  c. Investigate | Contain | Recover

  d. Recover | Contain | Investigate

9. **What is the main advantage of update rings when evaluating secure update strategies?**

   a. They reduce storage costs for patches

   b. They automate backup before every update

   c. They reduce operational risk by validating patches on pilot systems first

   d. They eliminate the need for maintenance windows

10. **Why is region-to-region DR favored over multi-cloud DR for most Azure workloads?**

    a. It is less secure but easier to configure

    b. It avoids dependency on identity systems

    c. It provides a coherent architecture aligned with Azure's native replication and pairing model

    d. It guarantees zero downtime during failover

Answers

1. c: Tier 0, because identity and control plane services underpin every other recovery action.

   Tier 0 systems (domain controllers, identity services, certificate authorities) must be restored first. If identity is compromised or offline, no administrator can authenticate, elevate, or perform controlled recovery of any other system.

2. c: MABS.

   MABS is designed explicitly for isolated, offline, or no-egress servers, acting as the proxy that sends backups to an Azure Recovery Services vault. The Azure Backup agent cannot function without direct outbound connectivity.

3. c: MUA (Resource Guard).

   MUA provides dual authorization for destructive backup operations, preventing even a compromised admin account from removing retention points without a second independent approver.

4. b: Retain deleted backup items for a recovery safety window.

   Soft Delete keeps deleted recovery points for a fixed retention period, allowing quick recovery if attackers or admins attempt malicious/accidental deletion.

5. b: LTR.

   LTR provides structured, policy-driven multi-year retention (monthly/annual snapshots). Archive tier is not a backup mechanism and does not preserve recovery metadata.

6. b: Break-glass accounts stored securely and tested regularly.

   Break-glass accounts provide emergency administrative access when identity services or PIM are unavailable. They are foundational to ransomware and BCDR resilience.

7. c: Prevents re-propagation of corrupted data back into the cloud.

   During ransomware incidents, sync channels (OneDrive, ActiveSync) can push encrypted or infected files back into the cloud, overwriting clean versions. Temporarily halting sync prevents reinfection loops.

8. b: Contain | Investigate | Recover.

   The SC-100 and Microsoft best-practice sequence always follows this order:

   a. **Contain:** Stop spread, disable sync, isolate devices.

   b. **Investigate:** Determine clean restore points, assess blast radius.

   c. **Recover:** Restore identity | workloads | endpoints

9. c: They reduce operational risk by validating patches on pilot systems first.

   Update rings allow organizations to:

   a. Test patches on a small pilot group.

   b. Pause rollout if issues arise.

   c. Protect Tier 0 and Tier 1 systems from untested updates.

10. c: It provides a coherent architecture aligned with Azure's native replication and pairing model.

    Azure paired regions support predictable, governed DR replication. Multi-cloud DR introduces unnecessary complexity in identity, networking, replication, and governance unless explicitly required by regulation.

CHAPTER 2
Design Security Solutions with Microsoft Security Benchmarks

Introduction

The evolving state of modern cloud environments requires a security design that is consistent, repeatable, and defensible at scale. As organizations look to adopt Microsoft Azure and Microsoft 365 as cloud-only and increasingly hybrid architectures, security controls must align with architectural patterns that manage identity, workloads, data, infrastructure, and operations.

This chapter shows how Microsoft's security reference models, the **Microsoft Cybersecurity Reference Architectures** (**MCRA**) and the **Microsoft cloud security benchmark** (**MCSB**), provide a foundational structure for developing secure enterprise environments.

When architects base design decisions on these Microsoft-aligned reference models, they create environments where protection and governance are inherited by default, risks are evaluated, and security outcomes remain predictable as platforms evolve. This chapter focuses more on architectural reasoning than on configuring products and services, helping the reader justify design decisions that balance security, resiliency, governance, and operational practicality.

Structure

The chapter covers the following topics:

- Cybersecurity capabilities and controls alignment
- Protecting against insider, external, and supply-chain attacks
- Zero Trust security and RaMP alignment

Objectives

This chapter addresses the fundamental security design skills required of a Microsoft cybersecurity architect. It focuses on designing solutions that fit best practices for cybersecurity capabilities and controls in order to ensure security is implemented as a form of deliberate, consistent architecture, as opposed to a collection of isolated methodologies and tools. This chapter's content maps directly to the SC-100 skills measured published in the official Microsoft study guide for Exam SC-100: Microsoft Cybersecurity Architect[1].

The chapter also addresses the design of protection against insider threats, external attackers, and supply-chain compromise, recognizing that modern risk often stems from trusted access, lateral movement, shadow **artificial intelligence** (**AI**), exposed services, or third-party dependencies.

In addition, it examines how these design decisions align with Zero Trust security principles, including the Zero Trust **Rapid Modernization Plan** (**RaMP**), illustrating how Zero Trust concepts translate into practical architectural decisions that reduce explicit trust while supporting phased modernization.

These skills are covered under the exam section: *Design solutions that align with security best practices and priorities,* which represents approximately 20-25% of the overall SC-100 skills measured.

Cybersecurity capabilities and controls alignment

Cloud security does not fail because organizations lack controls; it fails because controls are applied inconsistently, interpreted differently across teams, or disconnected from architectural intent.

As cloud environments scale, informal security decisions quickly accumulate into systemic risk; a capability-driven approach to security design establishes a shared foundation, one that defines not only which controls exist, but how they integrate and operate together, how they are enforced, and how they evolve as the environment grows. Cloud security fundamentally relies on implementing enforceable controls that operate consistently across environments.

Security features like identity governance, data protection, secure configuration, platform, and workload isolation are only effective when structured as architectural guardrails and measured against standards.

In large-scale cloud environments, inconsistent deployment and interpretation can cause drift, so controls should be embedded into landing zones, policy frameworks, configuration baselines, and ongoing assessments to ensure predictable, scalable protection. This section's content maps to the official SC-100 skills measured topic: *Design solutions that align with best practices for cybersecurity capabilities and controls.*

---

1 **https://learn.microsoft.com/en-us/credentials/certifications/resources/study-guides/sc-100**

Aligning cloud security architecture with MCSB controls

The MCSB sets standards for secure cloud architecture as enforceable controls. Building landing zones on MCSB ensures all workloads receive consistent protection, regardless of the deployment team.

Designing landing zones directly from MCSB establishes a predictable architecture; identity flows enforce the use of managed identities and privilege boundaries; network designs implement segmentation, private endpoints, and constrained ingress; data controls define encryption and access boundaries; and logging requirements ensure detectable and monitorable behavior across all resource layers.

This direct benchmark-to-architecture mapping is essential because it embeds security expectations into the very foundation and fabric of the cloud platform, rather than relying on downstream post-implementation configuration.

Architecturally, aligning to MCSB means treating the benchmark as the design input for landing zone standards rather than a compliance checklist applied after deployment.

This includes defining mandatory identity patterns (managed identity-first), network patterns (segmentation and private endpoints), data patterns (encryption and access boundaries), and logging patterns (centralized collection and retention), then enforcing them through policy initiatives and repeatable deployment templates. This approach ensures MCSB controls are inherited by default by every workload deployed into the platform.

In practice, inheritance only remains reliable when the enforcement scope is explicit and centrally governed. Policy assignments must be bound at the management group or subscription boundary used for landing zones, and exemptions must be rare, time-bound, and centrally approved. Landing zones apply these controls through management group hierarchies and policy initiatives that encode benchmark requirements as enforceable standards; policy effects determine how controls behave, from preventing risky configurations to deploying missing protections. Without a clear scope and exemption discipline, benchmark controls degrade into optional guidance, and security outcomes become inconsistent at scale.

Continuous validation is achieved by enabling the relevant Defender for Cloud plans, which surface configuration deviations and missing protections. These signals allow architects to refine templates, policies, and deployment processes so that future workloads conform automatically. In this model, posture assessment is not a periodic audit but an architectural feedback loop, ensuring ongoing alignment to MCSB and driving platform improvements and operational efficiency and excellence as cloud services evolve.

The MCSB also aligns naturally with the **Cloud Adoption Framework** (**CAF**) operating model by translating *how we run the cloud* into cloud-native control areas.

In practice, CAF operational responsibilities (govern, secure, manage, and operate) map cleanly to MCSB control families such as identity, network, data, logging, and posture management. This connection matters because it shifts security from one-off configuration decisions to a repeatable operating model where landing zones, policy, and monitoring consistently enforce the same control expectations across every workload and every environment.

Secure Score, hardening, and posture improvement

Secure Score provides a quantified representation of configuration hardening across identity, devices, workloads, and platforms. Its recommendations are prioritized according to the risk reduction associated with each control, enabling architects to focus first on the most impactful issues; for example, exposed management ports, missing **multi-factor authentication** (**MFA**) requirements, or unprotected workloads carry high weight because they materially increase the likelihood of compromise.

Posture evaluation is also scope-specific, as device compliance and endpoint posture are assessed through Microsoft Intune (device compliance policies and health signals), while cloud resource posture for services such as virtual machines and storage accounts is assessed through Microsoft Defender for Cloud (recommendations, secure configuration signals, and workload protection status). Designing a repeatable posture program, therefore, requires using the right evaluation plane for each surface rather than assuming one tool covers everything.

When posture signals repeatedly identify the same types of misconfiguration, such as unencrypted storage, missing agents, or misaligned access boundaries, it indicates structural gaps rather than isolated errors. Architects respond by refining landing zones, updating templates, adjusting deployment patterns, and strengthening guardrails so that future workloads inherently comply with expected standards. In this way, posture becomes a continuous architectural feedback loop; signals drive design refinement, and design refinement improves posture consistency over time.

Hardened baselines are enforced through repeatable landing zone components, policy initiatives, and **infrastructure as code** (**IaC**) modules. When workload posture deviates, such as unsecured endpoints, missing updates, or disabled logging, the architectural response is to update templates, adjust guardrails, or strengthen mandatory controls so that the misconfiguration cannot recur in future deployments. This turns Secure Score findings into sustainable architectural improvements rather than one-time operational tasks.

When security posture must be evaluated against recognized frameworks (for example, NIST CSF), Microsoft Defender for Cloud provides the practical assessment mechanism through its regulatory compliance and standards-based evaluations. Architects can measure control coverage, identify gaps, and track remediation progress in a way that supports CAF-style continuous improvement and audit-ready reporting by enabling the appropriate Defender for Cloud plans and reviewing compliance dashboards.

Hardening management ports and privileged pathways

Management surfaces are among the most exploited cloud entry points. Hardening begins with eliminating public **Remote Desktop Protocol** (**RDP**)/**Secure Shell** (**SSH**) access and routing administrative actions through isolated control paths. These include Azure Bastion, **just-in-time** (**JIT**) access enforced through identity controls, private management networks, and devices restricted by Conditional Access. This ensures that privileged operations occur only within controlled pathways that do not expose administrative interfaces to the internet.

The architectural objective is elimination, not mitigation. Reducing exposure through **Internet Protocol** (**IP**) allowlists or adaptive rules still leaves management surfaces reachable and exploitable. Secure management is achieved only when direct administrative connectivity is removed entirely, and all privileged access is forced through identity-validated, monitored control paths.

Strengthening privileged pathways limits lateral movement opportunities, reduces the availability of high-value targets, and ensures that administrators interact with workloads through constrained channels designed for security rather than convenience. It is essential to distinguish between **reducing exposure** and **meeting the secure management port's objective**. Controls such as adaptive network hardening can help reduce inbound risk, but they do not replace architectural removal of direct management access.

The secure management ports outcome is achieved by eliminating public RDP / SSH and forcing administrative access through controlled paths such as Azure Bastion, private management connectivity, and JIT workflows enforced by identity policy.

Workload posture through the defender plan onboarding

Workloads must be enrolled in the appropriate Defender plans to obtain visibility into vulnerabilities, misconfigurations, and identity risks. For platforms like **Azure Kubernetes Service** (**AKS**), onboarding activates image scanning, cluster posture checks, and workload identity assessments; without onboarding, posture cannot be evaluated, and critical security gaps remain undetected. Onboarding is therefore an architectural requirement: workloads are designed to integrate with platform protections from day one, enabling automated posture evaluation.

When workloads are not onboarded by default, security visibility becomes conditional on deployment behavior, creating blind spots that scale with the environment. Architecturally, onboarding must be mandatory and embedded into workload provisioning so that protection and assessment cannot be bypassed, delayed, or selectively applied.

For container platforms such as AKS, posture scoring and recommendations depend on enabling the correct Microsoft Defender for Cloud plan(s) for the resource type; if AKS posture appears missing or excluded from Secure Score, the architectural remediation is to enable the relevant Defender plan for containers and ensure the required onboarding settings are configured so protections and assessments are applied automatically to new clusters. This ensures AKS resources are evaluated consistently alongside other landing zone workloads rather than remaining outside the posture baseline.

Posture signals as architectural feedback

Posture signals only create value when they are used to validate enforcement quality rather than to drive isolated remediation. A small number of findings may reflect deployment error, but repeated findings across unrelated workloads indicate that a control is mis-scoped, optional, or bypassable; in these cases, posture acts as a validation mechanism for architectural intent, confirming whether landing zone standards, policy scope, and deployment pipelines are actually enforcing the expected security outcome.

Benchmark-aligned data protection and encryption standards

Data protection in cloud environments depends on consistent enforcement of encryption controls, key management, and access boundaries. Many Azure services encrypt data by default using **Advanced Encryption Standard** (**AES**)-256, but organizations may require **customer-managed keys** (**CMKs**) to meet compliance or regulatory requirements; CMKs provide enhanced control by allowing explicit management of key creation, access, rotation, and auditability.

Architectural alignment ensures that encryption standards are applied predictably across storage, compute, container, and database platforms. Policy-based enforcement mandates CMK usage where required, while automation handles regular key rotation and re-encryption workflows. This ensures that encryption behavior does not drift over time and that the organization maintains cryptographic assurance aligned to its risk posture.

Encryption architecture must assume key rotation and revocation will occur. Workloads that fail during rotation expose hidden coupling between applications and cryptographic material. Designing for key change tolerance is therefore a prerequisite for treating customer-managed encryption as a reliable control rather than a fragile compliance feature.

Key rotation and compliance enforcement

Key rotation protects against long-term exposure and strengthens the overall resilience of encrypted data. Architecturally, rotation is automated to reduce operational overhead and maintain consistency across environments. Workloads must be designed to tolerate rotation without service disruption, ensuring that encryption remains continuously enforceable.

Where benchmark or regulatory requirements mandate customer-managed keys, key rotation should be enforced as an explicit compliance standard rather than an informal operational practice. For example, a monthly CMK rotation requirement can be implemented through automated key rotation processes and validated through policy-driven compliance checks. Workloads must be designed to tolerate rotation without downtime, ensuring encryption remains continuously enforceable while meeting the expected rotation cadence.

Encryption alignment is effective only when paired with structured governance, regular key rotation, and ongoing validation by posture tools.

Identity, device, and endpoint baseline alignment

Identity and device trust form the core of secure cloud operation. Weaknesses in identity governance, excessive privilege assignment, unmanaged endpoints, or unmonitored administrative paths frequently lead to compromise. Architectural patterns, therefore, integrate identity lifecycle management, device compliance, privilege enforcement, and endpoint protection into a cohesive baseline; this ensures that access to cloud workloads is constrained not only by identity but by the state and trustworthiness of the device, and that privilege is tightly scoped and elevated only when required.

Endpoint trust is what makes identity controls enforceable in practice. Without device compliance and endpoint integrity checks, privileged identities can be exercised from compromised environments, collapsing the effectiveness of role scoping and approval workflows. Architectural identity governance, therefore, depends on endpoint state as an input to every privileged action.

Identity and endpoint baselines also determine how effectively an organization can execute post-breach response for ransomware. The **Detection and Response Team** (DART)-aligned expectation is that response begins by isolating affected assets and revoking compromised access paths, then using centralized telemetry to scope impact before initiating recovery. Architectures with strong identity governance, segmented admin paths, and reliable logging enable responders to act quickly without expanding blast radius or losing investigative visibility.

Lessons from identity and endpoint weaknesses

Compromise commonly occurs through predictable weaknesses: standing local admin rights, unmanaged endpoints, stale credentials, excessive global privileges, or gaps in logging.

Addressing these patterns requires structural enforcement of identity controls, including routine access reviews, Conditional Access policies governing device posture, and segmentation of high-privilege identities into secure tiers. These measures reduce the ease with which attackers can pivot from a compromised endpoint into privileged cloud operations.

Zero Trust endpoint administration and local admin removal

Eliminating standing local administrator privileges is a key security measure because it stops attackers from disabling protections or stealing credentials. Instead, access is granted when needed through secure options like **Privileged Identity Management** (**PIM**), **Local Administrator Password Solution** (**LAPS**)-controlled local accounts, and **Privileged Access Workstation** (**PAWs**). To ensure safety, Conditional Access makes sure that administrative tasks only come from protected devices. Strong endpoint management is essential for reliable privileged operations, lowering risks and promoting consistent administrator actions.

However, endpoint controls determine where privileged actions can execute, while identity governance determines who can perform them and for how long, which is why Zero Trust endpoint administration must be paired with lifecycle-driven privilege control.

Identity governance as architecture

Identity lifecycle processes should function as core architectural controls that both define and restrict the assignment of privileges. By automating joiner, mover, and leaver workflows; enforcing entitlement reviews; and establishing structured approval procedures, organizations ensure that privileges remain aligned with operational duties. This approach creates consistent privilege boundaries and mitigates the risk of unauthorized or excessive access accumulating over time.

Protecting against insider, external, and supply-chain attacks

Security incidents rarely originate from a single technical failure; they emerge from combinations of human behavior, architectural assumptions, and inherited trust. Insider threats exploit excessive access, external attackers exploit exposed surfaces and lateral pathways, and supply-chain attacks exploit implicit trust in software and partners. A resilient security design must therefore assume that compromise is possible and focus on limiting how far, how fast, and how silently an attacker can move. Threats exploit weaknesses across identities, workloads, networks, and operational processes. External actors probe exposed surfaces and escalate privileges; insiders misuse legitimate access; supply-chain vulnerabilities introduce risk through dependencies.

Architectural controls must therefore reduce exposure, constrain movement, detect misuse, and maintain visibility across all threat pathways. This section's content maps to the official SC-100 skills measured topic: *Design solutions that align with best practices for protecting against insider, external, and supply-chain attacks*. It focuses on controls needed to address the threat-model expectations.

Attack chain defense

Attackers follow a predictable progression: reconnaissance, entry, escalation, movement, and exfiltration. Architectural controls must disrupt each stage by reducing discoverability, enforcing segmentation, isolating privileged operations, and validating dependencies; each control strengthens the environment's ability to resist, contain, or detect threat activity before it escalates into wider compromise.

Limiting reconnaissance exposure

Limiting reconnaissance exposure reduces an attacker's ability to discover, profile, and target cloud workloads before exploitation occurs.

Reconnaissance activity typically precedes intrusion and relies on identifying exposed endpoints, predictable naming patterns, and unfiltered ingress paths; architectural controls, therefore, focus on minimizing externally visible surfaces and constraining how traffic reaches applications.

Typical architectural protections include:

- Removing public exposure through private endpoints.
- Restricting inbound access using network security groups and firewalls.
- Routing application traffic exclusively through controlled ingress services such as Azure Front Door or Application Gateway.
- Enforcing **web application firewall** (**WAF**) inspection to block scanning and probing behavior.
- Using neutral naming conventions that avoid revealing workload purpose and environment.

Beyond reducing exposed surfaces, the architecture must detect reconnaissance when it occurs; WAF and gateway telemetry highlights scanning patterns such as repeated path enumeration, malformed requests, abnormal request rates, and authentication probing. These signals enable early identification and correction of unintended exposure before attackers can escalate activity.

Separately from runtime detection, the architecture must detect when newly deployed applications are unintentionally exposed or deployed with known weaknesses. Posture and vulnerability signals from platform security tooling surface high-risk conditions early in the deployment lifecycle, such as public exposure, missing WAF coverage, or vulnerable configurations, so teams can correct misconfigurations immediately, before reconnaissance escalates into exploitation.

Early exposure signals are architectural feedback, not deployment noise; repeated detection of public endpoints, missing WAF coverage, or insecure defaults indicates that application ingress patterns or landing zone standards are misaligned with intended exposure models and must be corrected at design time.

Constraining lateral movement through segmentation

Lateral movement is enabled when workloads share flat networks, overbroad privileges, or unsegmented identity pathways; segmentation limits an attacker's ability to pivot by enforcing boundaries between identities, workloads, and administrative paths.

Architectural controls include:

- Identity boundary separation using tiered administrative models.
- Network segmentation across VNets, subnets, and firewalled zones.
- Isolation of privileged access through PAWs, Azure Bastion, and identity controls.
- Use of workload identities to prevent credential reuse.
- End-to-end encryption to prevent credential interception.

These controls ensure that compromise of one workload does not automatically enable access to others.

Segmentation also improves detection by creating clear trust boundaries where unexpected access attempts are anomalous. Lateral movement attempts trigger alerts when identities cross-tiers, workloads communicate outside approved paths, or privileged access occurs from untrusted environments. This allows defenders to detect and contain movement before it escalates into full environment compromise.

Preventing exfiltration with restricted outbound paths

When attackers are unable to traverse and progress internally, they often attempt to exfiltrate data directly from those already compromised resources they have access to; outbound controls are therefore required to ensure data cannot leave through unintended channels.

Architectural safeguards include:

- Firewall-enforced egress restrictions.
- Private Link to enforce internal-only service access.
- SaaS monitoring for unauthorized uploads or sharing.
- Data loss prevention applied to sensitive data paths.
- Traffic inspection through approved proxy services.

These measures ensure that compromised workloads cannot freely transmit data to external destinations. Outbound restrictions also create high-signal detection opportunities; attempts to bypass egress controls, upload protected data, or establish unauthorized outbound connections generate alerts that surface exfiltration activity early; this enables rapid containment before sensitive data is lost.

Supply-chain and dependency defense

Supply-chain and dependency defense addresses risks introduced through third-party components such as container images, libraries, runtimes, and external agents. Vulnerabilities embedded in these dependencies frequently provide attackers with initial access or execution pathways, even when core platform controls are correctly implemented.

Typical architectural protections include:

- Continuous vulnerability scanning of deployed workloads.
- Identification of outdated libraries, vulnerable base images, and insecure runtime packages.
- Detection of unsigned or unverified artifacts.

These assessments are surfaced through integrated vulnerability management and posture tooling. Architectural enforcement requires hardened image baselines, **continuous integration / continuous deployment** (**CI/CD**) integrated scanning, artifact signing, and security gates that prevent noncomplaint builds from deployment; this ensures dependency risk is addressed proactively as part of the delivery pipeline rather than reactively after compromise.

For server and workload vulnerability assessment, Microsoft Defender for Cloud surfaces integrated vulnerability scanning used by Defender for Servers; this provides continuous identification of known vulnerabilities and exposure conditions across supported workloads, enabling architects to standardize vulnerability assessment as part of the platform baseline rather than relying on periodic manual scans.

Ransomware investigation, response, and recovery

Ransomware attacks exploit weak identity boundaries, broad privileges, unmonitored endpoints, and unprotected backups. The environment must be designed so that containment is possible, telemetry is available, and recovery points remain intact; architectural preparation directly determines how effectively an organization can investigate and recover.

Correct sequence for ransomware response

An effective ransomware response is sequence-dependent; actions taken out of order can destroy evidence, allow reinfection, or reintroduce attacker persistence. Azure security best practices and DART guidance, therefore, emphasize a strict, architectural response order:

- **Isolate affected systems to stop propagation**: Immediate isolation prevents ransomware from spreading laterally or encrypting additional assets. Isolation targets compromised devices, workloads, and identities, not just networks, and must occur before investigation or recovery begins.

- **Determine entry method and scope using telemetry**: Once the spread is halted, responders use centralized logs and alerts to identify how the attacker gained access and which assets, identities, and workloads are affected. This establishes blast radius and prevents incomplete remediation.
- **Assess identity compromise and privilege escalation**: Identity compromise is often the persistence mechanism. Tokens, service principals, credentials, and privileged roles must be invalidated to remove persistence. Recovery must not proceed until compromised access paths are revoked.
- **Validate backup integrity before restoration**: Backups are validated to ensure they are clean, intact, and not tampered with. Restoring from compromised or attacker-accessible backups can reintroduce malware or enable immediate reinfection.
- **Execute controlled recovery only after persistence is removed**: Restoration occurs only once attacker access has been eliminated. Recovery is performed in a controlled manner, often using clean environments, to ensure systems return to a trusted state.

This ordered sequence ensures containment precedes investigation, investigation precedes recovery, and recovery does not reintroduce risk.

Architectural prerequisites for effective ransomware response

Effective ransomware response depends on architectural readiness rather than reactive tooling. Environments must support rapid containment, forensic investigation, and clean recovery without reintroducing attacker persistence.

Foundational architectural requirements include:

- Immutable and centralized logging.
- Segmented workloads to prevent uncontrolled lateral spread.
- Restricted administrative access paths.
- Strong identity governance minimizes standing privilege.
- Backup isolation to prevent tampering.

Post-breach response design must distinguish between isolation and containment. Isolation halts active spread, while containment preserves evidence and prevents reinfection. Architectures that support both enable decisive response without destroying investigative context.

Resilient recovery design

Resilient recovery design assumes that attackers will target backups deliberately—attempting to delete, encrypt, or corrupt them to block recovery; recovery architectures must therefore treat backups as protected assets, not passive storage. Key architectural elements include the following measures:

- **Immutable storage with soft-delete protections**: Backups must be protected against modification and deletion, even by privileged accounts. Immutability and soft-delete ensure recovery points remain available if attacker credentials are abused.
- **Dedicated backup identities and networks**: Backup operations use isolated identities and network paths that are separate from production workloads; this prevents attackers who compromise workloads or admins from accessing backup infrastructure.
- **Geo-redundant backup storage**: Backups are replicated across regions to protect against regional failure, destructive attacks, or deliberate deletion attempts within a single location.
- **Clean-room restoration environments**: Recovery is performed in isolated environments that are not connected to the compromised production estate; this prevents reinfection and allows validation before systems are reintroduced.
- **Automated backup integrity validation**: Backup integrity is continuously tested, so recovery points are known to be usable before an incident occurs; this removes uncertainty during high-pressure response scenarios.

Together, these measures ensure recovery remains possible, reliable, and attacker-resistant, even when privileged access is compromised, aligning directly with expectations for ransomware resilience and secure **business continuity and disaster recovery** (**BCDR**) design.

Insider risk mitigation and application misuse controls

Insider threats bypass perimeter defenses by operating within trusted access boundaries, making architectural controls essential; effective mitigation focuses on limiting misuse capability, enforcing contextual verification, and detecting abuse with high-confidence signals rather than attempting blanket prevention.

Misuse potential is reduced by constraining privilege and execution paths; least privilege access, removal of standing administrative rights, and strict application execution controls ensure legitimate access cannot be easily repurposed for malicious activity or post-compromise tooling.

Contextual verification is applied at moments of elevated risk; step-up authentication and session controls require renewed trust for sensitive actions such as large data downloads, privilege elevation, or abnormal access patterns, preventing silent abuse during valid sessions.

Detection is embedded through high-signal mechanisms such as behavioral analytics and honeytokens; because these artifacts have no legitimate use, interaction provides immediate indication of insider reconnaissance, privilege probing, or misuse, enabling rapid investigation with minimal false positives. Together, these controls align to ensure insider activity is constrained by design, continuously verified, and detected early, even when actions originate from authorized identities.

Restricting application execution

Restricting application execution is a critical control for limiting the ability of insiders or compromised identities to introduce malicious tools into cloud workloads.

Unauthorized executables are commonly used for data theft, credential extraction, privilege escalation, and covert communication; by constraining workloads to run only approved applications, architects ensure that system behavior remains predictable and enforceable.

Typical architectural protections include:

- Locking down server roles to a defined set of approved binaries.
- Blocking unknown or unsanctioned tools from executing.
- Preventing the use of scripting utilities commonly abused for exploitation.
- Enforcing application allow-listing at scale using adaptive controls.

Microsoft Defender for Cloud supports this pattern through adaptive application controls, which learns observed application behavior and enable policy-driven blocking of unapproved executables. This reduces insider misuse and also limits post-compromise attacker capability by preventing common tooling from running inside trusted environments.

Step-up authentication for sensitive actions

Insider misuse and post-compromise activity often occur during otherwise legitimate sessions, making static authentication insufficient. Step-up authentication enforces dynamic re-verification of trust when risk increases, rather than relying solely on the original sign-in decision.

Additional verification is triggered for high-risk actions such as accessing sensitive data, downloading large volumes of information, connecting from anomalous locations, or performing behavior that deviates from established usage patterns; this ensures that sensitive operations cannot proceed based on outdated or weakened trust signals. Step-up controls balance security and usability by applying additional authentication only at critical moments, while ensuring access remains context-aware, risk-driven, and continuously enforced across identities and sessions.

Using honeytokens to detect malicious exploration

Honeytokens are deliberate decoys placed in locations where no legitimate access should occur; they are designed to detect reconnaissance, privilege probing, and unauthorized exploration by insiders or compromised identities. Architectural use of honeytokens includes:

- Placement within sensitive data paths, administrative locations, or high-value resource hierarchies.
- Classification as high-value entities within security analytics platforms.

Any interaction with a honeytoken generates a high-fidelity alert because no valid business process should access it; this allows security teams to detect malicious internal activity early, with minimal false positives and immediate investigative confidence.

SaaS, multi-cloud visibility, and behavioral analytics

A modern cloud security architecture must provide continuous, unified visibility across **software as a service** (**SaaS**) platforms, Azure resources, multi-cloud services, and hybrid environments. Threat actors do not respect platform boundaries, and meaningful detection depends on correlating identity, network, workload, and application activity across all environments rather than analyzing each in isolation. Architecturally, this requires centralized ingestion of security-relevant telemetry and the use of behavioral analytics to detect deviations from normal patterns of use.

Behavioral signals such as anomalous access locations, unusual data access volumes, unexpected privilege usage, or abnormal application behavior surface high-confidence indicators of compromise that static rules often miss; by designing visibility as a first-class architectural requirement, rather than an operational afterthought. Organizations ensure that misuse, lateral movement, and cross-platform attacks can be detected and investigated before they escalate into broader compromise.

Behavioural analytics in SaaS environments

Behavioral analytics detect misuse and compromise in SaaS environments by evaluating activity patterns rather than relying solely on static rules. As SaaS platforms are accessed remotely and continuously, abnormal behavior is often the earliest indicator of risk.

Architectural signals evaluated include:

- Unusual access locations or impossible travel patterns.
- Anomalous download volumes or data access behavior.
- Risky OAuth consent grants.
- Excessive external sharing or shadow IT activity.

These analytics surface high-confidence alerts in near real-time, enabling rapid investigation or automated response while the impact is still limited.

In Microsoft environments, real-time detection of risky SaaS behavior is delivered through Microsoft Defender for Cloud Apps, which analyzes session and activity patterns across connected SaaS services. It can surface high-confidence alerts for abnormal downloads, risky OAuth consent grants, suspicious access locations, and anomalous sharing behavior as events occur, enabling rapid investigation or automated response while the impact is still limited.

Cross-cloud visibility through log integration

Cross-cloud visibility ensures threats spanning SaaS, Azure, multi-cloud, and hybrid environments can be detected and correlated. Isolated logging prevents identification of coordinated or lateral activity across platforms.

Architectural visibility requires:

- Central ingestion of firewall, gateway, and network flow logs.
- Correlation with identity, workload, and SaaS telemetry.
- Normalization of events within a centralized analytics platform.

This unified view enables detection of lateral movement, cross-environment access anomalies, and coordinated attack activity that would remain invisible if logs were analyzed in isolation.

Microsoft Sentinel is the practical consolidation layer for this visibility model; non-native firewall and gateway logs from third-party or multi-cloud control planes are ingested into Sentinel and normalized so they can be correlated with identity events, workload telemetry, and SaaS signals. This enables detection and reaction to cross-environment attack patterns, such as credential misuse followed by unusual egress paths, that would not be visible when each platform's logs are ingested and investigated separately.

Visibility as architecture, not monitoring

Visibility must be designed into the architecture from the outset rather than added later as an operational overlay. Visibility gaps expand as environments grow. If logging, retention, and normalization are not defined at the architectural level, each new workload introduces uncertainty into detection and investigation. Designing observability into landing zones ensures security insight scales predictably with the platform. Security-relevant signals identity activity, network flows, workload behavior, and application events must be generated, retained, and correlated consistently across all environments so that detection remains reliable as platforms scale and change; architectural visibility requires deliberate decisions around what is logged, how long it is retained, and how events are normalized and correlated across trust boundaries.

When these decisions are embedded into landing zones, network design, and workload standards, the environment remains observable by default; this ensures that security investigations are not limited by missing telemetry, inconsistent retention, or fragmented data sources, even as new services and architectures are introduced.

Zero Trust security and RaMP alignment

Zero Trust is often described as a destination, but in practice, it is a design discipline that reshapes how trust is granted, validated, and revoked across an environment. Organizations rarely implement Zero Trust in a single motion; they evolve toward it as legacy assumptions are replaced with identity-centric controls and continuous verification. The challenge lies not in understanding the principles, but in sequencing change in a way that delivers immediate risk reduction while supporting long-term transformation.

Zero Trust shifts security design away from implicit network trust and toward continuous, identity-driven verification across users, devices, applications, and workloads. Rather than assuming that access is safe once granted, Zero Trust architectures continuously evaluate context, enforce least privilege, and constrain lateral movement by design; these principles fundamentally reshape how cloud platforms are secured, particularly in large, distributed, and hybrid environments.

The Zero Trust RaMP provides a structured approach for adopting these principles incrementally. By prioritizing foundational controls, such as identity governance, device trust, privileged access isolation, and workload segmentation, RaMP helps organizations modernize security without attempting disruptive, all-at-once transformations.

This section translates Zero Trust principles and RaMP guidance into concrete architectural patterns that can be applied consistently across cloud workloads, administrative access paths, and enterprise environments. This section's content maps to the official SC-100 skills measured topic: *Design solutions that align with best practices for Zero Trust security, including the RaMP.*

Zero Trust principles from MCRA

Zero Trust becomes actionable when its principles: verify explicitly, use least privilege, and Assume breach are applied consistently across identity, device, network, and workload layers. Each principle defines an architectural stance that shapes how access is granted, how boundaries are enforced, and how the environment reacts to changing risk.

In practice, the three Zero Trust principles map directly to enforceable mechanisms as follows:

- Verify explicitly is implemented through Conditional Access, risk evaluation, and continuous policy checks (identity, device, location, and session signals).
- Use of least privilege is implemented through role-based access, scoped permissions, and JIT elevation with PIM.

- Assume breach is implemented through segmentation, encryption, containment boundaries, and forensic-ready logging so that compromise is detected and constrained rather than allowed to spread.

This is where the architecture becomes visible, as shown in the following figure, how Zero Trust principles extend consistently across identity, endpoints, data, applications, infrastructure, and network to enforce security as an integrated system rather than isolated controls:

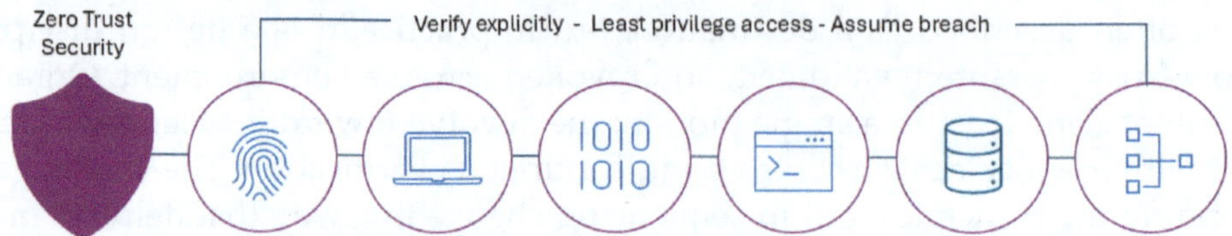

Figure 2.1: Zero Trust architecture across identity, endpoints, data, apps, infrastructure, and networks

This architecture illustrates how Zero Trust principles are enforced across each technology layer, with identity, device state, data sensitivity, and network context continuously evaluated to control access and limit the impact of potential compromise.

With this foundation in place, the next section explores how these principles are applied in practice, starting with how verify explicitly is enforced across security controls.

Applying verify explicitly across all security control planes

Verification is not a single moment but a continuous process; access decisions must incorporate identity context, device posture, workload behavior, risk signals, and environmental conditions. Controls such as Conditional Access, device compliance checks, workload identity validation, and continuous session evaluation ensure that access is granted only when the complete context meets policy requirements. This principle ensures every layer independently validates trust, reducing reliance on any single control surface.

Zero Trust access rules are expressed as explicit policy outcomes, not general intent. Common baseline rules include blocking access from unknown or untrusted locations and requiring compliant (managed and healthy) devices for sensitive access. These decisions are enforced through Conditional Access using identity risk, location conditions, and device compliance state so that access is continuously bounded by verified context.

Implementing least privilege access as architectural rule

Least privilege must be enforced as a structural property of the architecture, not as a discretionary operational practice. Access paths are deliberately narrowed so that users, workloads, and automated processes receive only the permissions required for a specific task, and only for the duration that the task is performed. This eliminates broad, persistent permissions that silently expand the attack surface over time.

Architectural enforcement of least privilege relies on clear role boundaries, workload-specific identities, segmented access paths, and the removal of standing administrative rights. Privilege elevation is controlled, time-bound, and auditable, ensuring that sensitive actions occur only within approved contexts. By constraining privilege in this way, the architecture limits lateral movement opportunities and ensures that abnormal access patterns stand out clearly against a tightly defined baseline of expected behavior.

Continuous access enforcement and dynamic trust adjustments

Continuous access evaluation (CAE) and adaptive policies allow sessions to react immediately to changes in risk, such as credential theft signals, device non-compliance, location anomalies, or revoked privileges. These mechanisms prevent long-lived sessions from remaining trusted after conditions change.

CAE is designed to make access decisions react in near real-time when conditions change. When risk increases, such as token revocation, password reset, disabled account, or device compliance failure, CAE-supported sessions can be re-evaluated, and access can be interrupted without waiting for a long session lifetime to expire. This prevents *still-valid* sessions from persisting after trust signals have changed.

Applying the Assume breach as a design principle

Assume breach requires the architecture to operate under the expectation that an attacker will eventually gain initial access, regardless of preventative controls. Design decisions therefore emphasize containment over prevention, ensuring that compromise of one identity, workload, or network segment does not automatically enable access to others. This principle directly shapes segmentation strategy, identity isolation, and encryption of internal traffic, so trust is never implicit.

Architectural enforcement of Assume breach results in tightly scoped trust boundaries, isolated privileged paths, and continuous visibility across those boundaries. Workloads are segmented to prevent lateral movement, administrative access is tiered and constrained, and telemetry is designed to support investigation from the outset.

The environment limits blast radius, preserves forensic evidence, and enables rapid detection and response when compromise occurs by embedding these assumptions into the platform design.

Zero Trust for workload and application access

Zero Trust workload access replaces network location-based trust with explicit identity and access validation at every hop. Rather than assuming traffic is trusted once it enters the network, the architecture ensures that each request to a workload is authenticated, authorized, and evaluated against policy. In this model, segmentation and controlled ingress are not optimizations but prerequisites, preventing direct connectivity to backend services and eliminating implicit trust between application tiers.

Backend workloads are designed to be unreachable except through approved, identity-aware access paths. Ingress components enforce inspection and routing, while backend services accept traffic only from validated sources using tightly scoped network rules, private connectivity, and workload identities. This approach ensures that applications cannot be bypassed, probed directly, or accessed laterally, establishing enforceable trust boundaries that align workload communication with Zero Trust principles rather than perimeter-based assumptions.

Limitations of ingress proxies as trust boundaries

Using Azure Front Door or Application Gateway provides routing, **Transport Layer Security (TLS)** termination, load balancing, and WAF inspection. However, these services alone do not establish a Zero Trust boundary; they control ingress but do not validate the identity of backend callers or enforce workload-level trust. A Zero Trust boundary requires:

- Backend services are reachable only via private endpoints.
- Identity-validated access tokens between services.
- Segmented network paths prevent direct exposure.
- Request evaluation based on identity, device posture, and policy.

Ingress gateways are part of the boundary, not the boundary itself. A practical Zero Trust pattern is to make backend services unreachable except through the approved ingress path.

This is achieved by restricting backend access to only the Azure Front Door (or gateway) source using service tags and tightly scoped network rules, while keeping the backend private through private endpoints or internal addressing. Combined with identity-based authorization between services, this ensures the proxy is an enforced boundary rather than simply a routing convenience.

Enforcing identity-aware perimeters for backend workloads

Identity-aware perimeters ensure backend workloads are not merely hidden from the internet but are explicitly unreachable except through validated trust channels.

Network isolation alone is insufficient; access must be constrained so that only approved platform services and authenticated workloads can initiate communication; this shifts the security boundary from IP reachability to identity and policy, eliminating implicit trust inside the environment.

Architectural enforcement includes:

- Allowing inbound traffic only from approved service sources (for example, Azure Front Door or gateway service tags).
- Keeping backend services private using private endpoints or internal addressing.
- Requiring managed identity tokens for service-to-service access.
- Restricting network paths with tightly scoped **network security groups** (**NSGs**) and routing rules.
- Rejecting any request that is not identity-validated or platform-verified.

Together, these controls ensure backend workloads cannot be contacted directly, prevent lateral probing, and enforce Zero Trust boundaries at the application layer rather than relying on network placement alone.

Application isolation as a Zero Trust requirement

Each application service must be treated as a discrete trust domain rather than a trusted internal component. Trust is never implied by network location or shared infrastructure; it is established explicitly for every interaction. By enforcing authentication, authorization, and validation on every service-to-service request, the architecture prevents a single compromised component from becoming a pivot point into adjacent applications. This internal isolation ensures that compromise is contained, observable, and unable to spread laterally across the application landscape.

Architectural enforcement of application isolation includes:

- Requiring authenticated service identities for all inter-service communication.
- Authorizing requests using scoped, service-specific permissions.
- Encrypting traffic between application components, even within private networks.
- Preventing implicit trust between services sharing the same network or platform.
- Designing applications so that failure or compromise of one component does not grant access to others.

This approach transforms application boundaries into active security controls, ensuring that internal communication paths are continuously validated and resilient to breach conditions.

Zero Trust privileged access strategy

Privileged access represents the highest-value attack target. RaMP provides a structured path for modernizing privileged access by prioritizing early adoption of identity governance, conditional enforcement, privileged elevation workflows, and isolation of administrative operations. This section covers the architectural requirements needed to meet the privilege-related requirements covered in this chapter.

Privileged access modernization priorities in RaMP

Privileged identities represent the highest-value attack surface in any cloud environment, which is why RaMP prioritizes their modernization early; if privileged access is weak, all other controls can be bypassed or disabled. The initial RaMP wave focuses on eliminating implicit trust and replacing it with controlled, time-bound, and observable privilege activation.

Core architectural priorities include:

- Enforcing strong authentication and Conditional Access on all privileged roles to ensure access is continuously validated.
- Removing standing administrative rights so privilege exists only when explicitly approved and required.
- Using PIM to govern elevation through JIT activation, approval, and auditing.
- Segmenting privileged accounts into dedicated roles aligned to specific administrative scopes and trust levels.

Together, these measures ensure privileged access is no longer persistent or implicit. Instead, elevation is deliberate, temporary, and constrained to known trust paths, reducing blast radius and preventing privileged identities from becoming a persistent foothold for attackers.

Preventative controls for landing zones and privileged operations

Privileged pathways must be isolated from general-purpose user environments to prevent credential theft, session hijacking, and lateral movement into administrative control planes. Architectural isolation ensures that even if a standard user or device is compromised, privileged operations cannot be executed from that context.

Core safeguards include:

- PAWs for high-assurance administrative tasks, providing hardened devices with minimal attack surface and dedicated trust boundaries.
- Azure Bastion or similarly isolated ingress paths to eliminate direct exposure of management ports and enforce controlled administrative connectivity.

- Strong Conditional Access policies that require compliant, trusted devices and enforce step-up authentication for administrative roles.
- Centralized monitoring of privileged activity using Microsoft Sentinel to detect anomalous elevation, access patterns, and misuse.
- Mandatory PIM workflows to ensure elevation is JIT, approved, time-bound, and fully audited.

These controls prevent administrative credentials from being used opportunistically and ensure privileged operations are executed only through verified, monitored, and tightly governed pathways by isolating how and where privileged access occurs.

Role alignment to security levels

Job roles must be mapped explicitly to MCRA security levels, where each level represents a distinct trust boundary with different operational sensitivity. Privileged roles are assigned only the minimum access required to perform approved tasks within that boundary, and elevation workflows are designed to match the security level of the action being taken. Organizations reduce privilege sprawl, enforce separation of duties, and ensure privileged access paths remain consistent with Microsoft's reference architecture guidance by aligning job functions to MCRA security levels.

Architectural alignment includes:

- Assigning job functions to least privilege access sets.
- Separating identities across security tiers.
- Enforcing elevation workflows appropriate to role sensitivity.
- Preventing privilege overlap that enables escalation.

This approach prevents privilege sprawl, enforces separation of duties, and ensures access paths are consistent with Microsoft reference architecture guidance.

External access governance without guest accounts

External access requires strict governance to avoid unmanaged or persistent privilege exposure; rather than creating long-lived guest identities, access is controlled through entitlement workflows.

Architectural controls include:

- Time-bound access assignments.
- Approval-based onboarding.
- Policy-driven access packages.

- Automatic expiration and review.

This model enables controlled external collaboration while ensuring access remains auditable, temporary, and aligned with internal governance standards.

In Microsoft environments, this pattern is implemented with entitlement management access packages, which provide time-bound, approval-based access to specific groups, apps, and SharePoint resources without requiring persistent guest accounts to be created and left behind. Access packages enforce assignment policy, automatic expiration, and periodic review, ensuring external access remains governed, auditable, and consistently revoked when no longer required.

Privileged access stability through device and identity assurance

Privileged access is only trustworthy when both the identity and the device are verified at the moment of use. Most cloud compromises succeed not by breaking platform controls, but by abusing standing privilege or launching administrative actions from compromised endpoints; architecture must therefore enforce device trust and identity assurance as prerequisites for any privileged operation.

Key architectural protections include:

- Removal of standing local administrator rights to prevent attackers from inheriting or escalating privilege from compromised endpoints.
- PAWs to ensure privileged sessions originate only from hardened, isolated devices.
- Conditional Access on admin accounts requires strong authentication, compliant devices, and risk-aware sign-in enforcement.
- Managed identities for workloads to eliminate embedded credentials and secret reuse in automation.
- JIT elevation with auditing to ensure privilege is temporary, scoped, and observable.

Together, these controls ensure privileged actions can occur only from verified identities on trusted devices, and that privilege cannot persist silently or be reused after trust conditions change. This stability is essential for limiting blast radius, detecting misuse, and maintaining control of the environment during both normal operations and post-compromise response.

Zero Trust endpoint and access administration

Zero Trust endpoint administration guarantees that privileged actions are executed exclusively via authorized, secured devices and rigorously regulated identity workflows.

This approach enhances the enforcement framework by preventing administrative operations from being initiated on compromised or unmanaged endpoints.

Admin path isolation through PAWs and Azure Bastion

Privileged access is a primary attack target, so administrative actions must occur only through isolated, high-trust paths rather than from general-purpose user devices. Zero Trust architectures, therefore, treat the admin path itself as a protected workload.

PAWs provide a hardened execution environment for administrative tasks. They are purpose-built to reduce attack surface and prevent credential exposure by enforcing:

- No email, web browsing, or productivity apps.
- Minimal installed software and hardened configuration.
- Enhanced logging and monitoring of privileged activity.
- Conditional Access enforces compliant, trusted devices.
- Network segmentation restricting access to admin-only endpoints.

PAWs prevent phishing, malware, and token theft from becoming privilege escalation paths by separating admin activity from daily user activity. In cases where dedicated PAWs are not operationally viable, Azure Bastion provides a controlled alternative by enabling browser-based RDP / SSH access without exposing management ports. Bastion removes public inbound access to VMs while enforcing authenticated, audited administrative sessions over a protected control plane.

In both models, the architectural goal is the same: administrative credentials are never used from unmanaged devices, never traverse exposed network paths, and never rely on implicit trust. This isolation is essential to limiting lateral movement and meeting Zero Trust privileged access requirements in Microsoft-aligned security architecture guidance.

Reducing administrative attack surface through JIT and PIM

Persistent administrative privileges increase the risk of privilege escalation; implementing PIM ensures that elevated access is granted only temporarily, is fully auditable, and requires appropriate approvals.

When combined with Conditional Access policies and device compliance checks, this approach significantly decreases the likelihood of unauthorized administrative actions and minimizes the impact in the event of credential compromise.

Endpoint state determining administrative trust

Zero Trust mandates validation of device status prior to authorizing administrative access. Factors such as compliance, device health, encryption state, and threat indicators directly determine whether privileged operations are permitted. This approach ensures that endpoint posture remains consistently aligned with privileged access decisions.

Conclusion

This chapter examined how Microsoft security benchmarks and reference architectures can be used to design consistent, resilient, and auditable security solutions across modern cloud environments. By aligning cybersecurity capabilities to enforceable controls, architects can ensure that identity, configuration, data protection, and posture management behave predictably at scale.

The chapter demonstrated how structured benchmarks such as the MCSB support landing zone design and continuous posture validation, how architectural controls disrupt insider, external, and supply-chain attack paths, and how ransomware resilience depends on strong identity governance, segmentation, and recovery-ready design.

Finally, the chapter explored how Zero Trust principles and the RaMP guide the evolution of privileged access, workload isolation, and endpoint administration, ensuring security controls remain effective as environments grow and threats evolve.

The next chapter builds on these security foundations by examining how the Microsoft CAF and the Azure WAF are used to design secure, governed cloud environments at scale. It focuses on translating organizational strategy into landing zones, governance guardrails, and operational baselines, showing how security, reliability, and operational excellence are embedded into cloud architectures through Microsoft-aligned frameworks.

Questions

Success in any exam requires a real understanding of the technologies, concepts, and principles, and not simply memorizing them. These questions allow the readers to determine whether they can apply the concepts of this chapter, which include security benchmarks, architectural control inheritance, posture management, attack-path disruption, Zero Trust design, and privileged access modernization, in the way the SC-100 exam expects.

1. **An organization wants all new Azure workloads to inherit identity, network, and logging controls automatically. Which architectural approach best achieves this outcome?**

    a. Manual configuration by workload owners

    b. Applying security controls after deployment

c. Designing landing zones directly from MCSB requirements

d. Enabling Secure Score recommendations individually

2. **Why is treating the MCSB as a design input more effective than using it as a compliance checklist?**

a. It reduces audit scope

b. It allows teams to ignore non-applicable controls

c. It embeds security expectations into the platform architecture

d. It replaces the need for monitoring

3. **Which signal most strongly indicates a structural architectural weakness rather than an isolated configuration error?**

a. A single failed policy evaluation

b. A recurring posture recommendation across multiple workloads

c. A temporary Secure Score drop

d. A missing alert rule

4. **Which architectural control most effectively limits lateral movement after initial compromise?**

a. Endpoint antivirus

b. Flat network routing

c. Segmentation across identity, network, and administrative paths

d. Public service endpoints

5. **Why does Secure Score function as an architectural feedback mechanism rather than a one-time assessment?**

a. It measures user productivity

b. It replaces penetration testing

c. It surfaces recurring design gaps that must be corrected in templates and guardrails

d. It automatically remediates all findings

6. **Which Zero Trust principle directly justifies eliminating standing administrative privileges?**

a. Verify explicitly

b. Assume breach

   c. Use least privilege
   d. Trust but verify

7. **Why are ingress proxies such as Azure Front Door insufficient on their own to establish a Zero Trust boundary?**
   a. They do not support TLS
   b. They increase latency
   c. They do not enforce identity-based authorization for backend workloads
   d. They cannot scale globally

8. **Which architectural outcome is RaMP primarily designed to deliver in its earliest phases?**
   a. Full automation of all security controls
   b. Immediate Zero Trust maturity across all workloads
   c. Reduction of risk through early modernization of privileged access
   d. Replacement of legacy identity platforms

9. **During ransomware response planning, why must containment occur before investigation or recovery?**
   a. It simplifies reporting
   b. It reduces the compliance scope
   c. It prevents continued spread and evidence destruction
   d. It accelerates system restoration

10. **Why are posture and vulnerability signals considered architectural inputs rather than operational alerts?**
    a. They are generated automatically
    b. They are only relevant to compliance teams
    c. They indicate where platform standards must be redesigned to prevent recurrence
    d. They replace logging and monitoring

Answers

1. c: Designing landing zones directly from MCSB requirements.

   When MCSB is used as the architectural baseline for landing zones, identity, network, logging, and posture controls are inherited by default. This ensures consistent protection across all workloads without relying on manual configuration.

2. c: It embeds security expectations into the platform architecture.

   Treating MCSB as a design input ensures controls are enforced structurally through templates, policy, and guardrails, rather than applied inconsistently after deployment.

3. b: A recurring posture recommendation across multiple workloads.

   Repeated findings indicate architectural gaps in landing zones or templates, not isolated errors. These signals require design correction rather than individual remediation.

4. c: Segmentation across identity, network, and administrative paths.

   Lateral movement is constrained by enforcing trust boundaries that prevent compromised identities or workloads from accessing adjacent resources.

5. c: It surfaces recurring design gaps that must be corrected in templates and guardrails.

   Secure Score highlights patterns of misconfiguration that inform architectural refinement, making it a continuous feedback loop rather than a snapshot.

6. c: Use least privilege.

   Eliminating standing administrative access ensures privilege is granted only when required, reducing blast radius and limiting attacker persistence.

7. c: They do not enforce identity-based authorization for backend workloads.

   Ingress proxies manage traffic flow but do not validate backend caller identity or enforce workload-level trust, which is required for Zero Trust boundaries.

8. c: Reduction of risk through early modernization of privileged access.

   RaMP prioritizes identity governance, privileged isolation, and JIT access early because compromise of privileged identities undermines all other controls.

9. c: It prevents continued spread and evidence destruction.

   Containment halts attacker activity and preserves forensic data, enabling accurate investigation and safe recovery.

10. c: They indicate where platform standards must be redesigned to prevent recurrence.

    Posture and vulnerability signals inform architectural improvements so misconfigurations cannot reappear in future deployments.

CHAPTER 3
Design Security Solutions with Microsoft Cloud Frameworks

Introduction

This chapter examines how to design secure, governed, and operationally resilient cloud environments using the Microsoft **Cloud Adoption Framework** (**CAF**) and the Azure **Well-Architected Framework** (**WAF**). It explains how organizational strategy is translated into secure landing zones, governance models, and operational baselines that support consistent security outcomes at scale.

The reader will learn about the five pillars of the WAF: cost optimization, operational excellence, performance efficiency, reliability, and security, and how these principles influence architectural decisions across governance, platform design, and workload evaluation. By applying CAF guidance alongside WAF principles, readers gain a structured approach to planning cloud adoption, enforcing guardrails, and assessing workload design against Microsoft-recommended best practices.

Structure

This chapter covers the following topics:

- Security and governance strategy with CAF and WAF
- Recommending CAF and WAF security governance solutions
- Implementing security with Azure landing zones
- DevSecOps processes aligned with CAF guidance

Objectives

This chapter covers the skills required to design new security and governance strategies, as well as to evaluate existing approaches, using the Microsoft CAF for Azure and the Microsoft

Azure WAF. It examines how to recommend security and governance solutions that align with these frameworks, ensuring architectural decisions are consistent, defensible, and scalable.

The chapter also addresses how to design solutions for implementing and governing security through Azure landing zones, establishing standardized foundations that enforce controls by default. Finally, it explores how to design a DevSecOps process that aligns with best practices defined in the Microsoft CAF, integrating security and governance into the software delivery lifecycle.

These skills fall under the exam section: *Design solutions that align with security best practices and priorities,* which represents approximately 20-25% of the overall SC-100 skills measured.

Security and governance strategy with CAF and WAF

Security and governance strategy in Azure begins with two foundational Microsoft frameworks: the CAF and the WAF. CAF provides the organizational, governance, and operational model that defines how cloud adoption should occur. At the same time, WAF offers the architectural principles used to evaluate whether workloads are reliable, secure, performant, and cost-effective.

The CAF Secure methodology defines how security is embedded across the entire cloud adoption lifecycle, ensuring that protection, resilience, and governance are applied from initial strategy through ongoing operations.

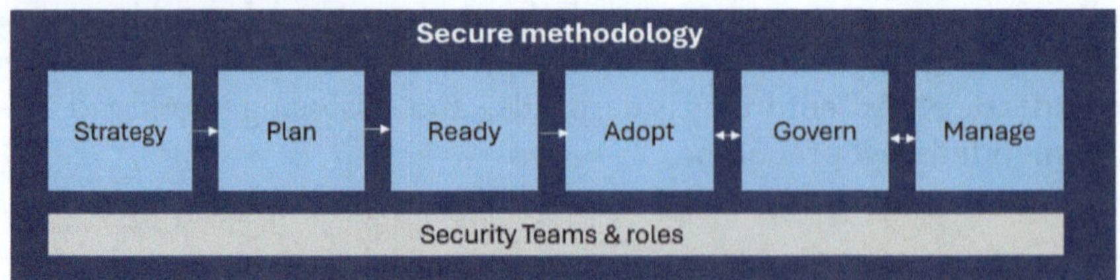

***Figure 3.1:** The CAF Secure methodology*

The CAF Secure methodology brings together a set of core security capabilities that operate across the entire cloud adoption lifecycle. It begins with modernizing security posture to align with Zero Trust principles, ensuring that identity, access, and protection mechanisms are designed for today's threat landscape. It also establishes preparedness by embedding incident response capabilities that reduce impact and support rapid recovery. At its foundation, the methodology enforces the principles of confidentiality, integrity, and availability to protect both data and services. Over time, this approach is sustained through continuous improvement, ensuring that security posture evolves alongside emerging risks and operational demands.

Without a strategic foundation, cloud environments drift rapidly. Teams deploy resources inconsistently, permissions accumulate, networks become fragmented, and compliance controls cannot be enforced reliably. CAF and WAF counter this drift by defining the governance hierarchy, landing zone topology, policy boundaries, and operational guardrails that shape how security decisions are applied across an enterprise. When correctly applied, these frameworks establish the structure in which identity, networking, resource organization, compliance, and monitoring can operate predictably at scale.

Security and governance strategy establishes architectural intent and enforcement boundaries; services and tooling are selected later to implement that intent rather than to define it. This section's content maps to the official SC-100 skills measured topic: *Design a new or evaluate an existing strategy for security and governance based on the Microsoft CAF for Azure and the Microsoft Azure WAF.*

This section explains how these frameworks guide governance strategy and architectural consistency across large cloud estates.

Designing governance architecture with CAF

CAF requires organizations to articulate and design their operating model and governance structure before any workloads are deployed; this aligns security with business structure and prevents retrofitted governance later in the cloud journey. Establishing governance early ensures that platform decisions scale predictably and at the same pace as adoption accelerates.

CAF prescribes a layered model including platform, landing zone, and application scopes, each with its own policy, identity, networking, and compliance boundaries. This structure ensures that governance is inherited consistently: policies flow downward, monitoring configurations propagate, and identity and network segmentation operate at predictable boundaries. The role of the architect is to ensure each segment of the hierarchy reflects the organization's security, compliance, and operational needs.

CAF requires governance structures to align not only with organizational ownership but also with how workloads progress through their lifecycle. In enterprise environments, this commonly means aligning management group hierarchy beneath the landing zone level to **software development lifecycle** (**SDLC**) stages, such as development, test, and production.

This alignment allows governance controls to vary appropriately by lifecycle stage while maintaining a consistent platform foundation. Development environments may permit broader experimentation and relaxed change controls, while production environments enforce stricter policy, access restrictions, and monitoring requirements. By anchoring management group structure to SDLC stages, architects ensure that policy inheritance, compliance enforcement, and operational oversight reflect the risk profile of each environment.

CAF treats SDLC alignment as a core architectural decision rather than an operational convenience. Governance structures that ignore lifecycle boundaries often result in either over-restrictive development environments or under-protected production workloads.

A misaligned hierarchy leads to inconsistent guardrails, duplicated policy assignments, and fragmented operational oversight. By grounding the hierarchy in CAF archetypes, such as enterprise-scale, regulated, or multitenant models, the cloud platform inherits standardization that eliminates ambiguity in security and governance decisions.

Management group hierarchy and governance boundaries

Management group hierarchy defines how governance is enforced at scale. In CAF-aligned designs, management groups act as architectural control planes rather than organizational conveniences; their primary function is to enforce policy inheritance, access boundaries, and compliance consistently across the platform.

The hierarchy must enforce:

- Separation of platform operations (identity, networking, management) from landing zone workloads.
- Dedicated policy scopes for regulated or high-risk environments.
- Predictable inheritance of policies and role-based access assignments.
- Clear isolation between internal, partner-managed, and externally exposed environments.

When designed correctly, the management group hierarchy determines where policies are assigned, how access is scoped, and how governance standards are inherited across subscriptions. Misaligned hierarchies result in inconsistent guardrails and fragmented oversight, while CAF-aligned hierarchies provide centralized enforcement with workload-level autonomy.

Applying WAF pillars to cloud governance decisions

WAF provides the principles required to evaluate whether an environment is well-architected. While commonly associated with workload reviews, WAF also influences strategy at the governance layer by defining the quality attributes that platforms and workloads are expected to meet.

When applied to cloud governance, each WAF pillar influences how policies, controls, and operational practices are defined and enforced across the platform:

- **Security pillar**: Establishes requirements for identity, access control, data protection, posture management, and threat mitigation within governance decisions.
- **Reliability pillar**: Influences how governance accounts for resource dependencies, fault domains, business continuity, and hybrid resiliency.
- **Operational excellence pillar**: Shapes how monitoring, observability, automation, and DevOps practices are integrated into governance models.

- **Performance efficiency and cost optimization pillars**: Guide resource selection and scaling policies, indirectly strengthening security by limiting unmanaged growth and reducing operational risk.

Since WAF is both evaluative and prescriptive, architects use it to validate whether governance decisions, such as network segmentation, key management requirements, or monitoring baselines, will produce secure and resilient outcomes. When CAF provides the structure, WAF provides the quality lens used to assess that structure.

Using WAF security and reliability pillars

WAF pillars define the quality requirements that platforms and landing zones must enforce by default. Rather than being applied only during workload reviews, these principles shape governance controls at the platform-level.

WAF pillars drive governance decisions when:

- Evaluating whether observability, logging, and monitoring are enforced consistently across landing zones.
- Validating that identity and access controls enforce least privilege and eliminate standing administrative access.
- Assessing whether network segmentation establishes clear trust boundaries and limits blast radius.
- Ensuring availability, resiliency, and recovery requirements are embedded into the platform and landing zone design.

When applied correctly, the security and reliability pillars become governance requirements, guiding how landing zones are structured, which controls are enforced centrally, and how architectural quality standards are inherited before workloads are deployed.

Resource placement strategy in landing zones

Correct resource placement is essential for consistent governance. Enterprise-scale landing zones rely on predictable placement of **Domain Name Service** (**DNS**), networking, identity-aligned access boundaries, logging, and policy enforcement so that all workloads inherit the same foundational capabilities.

Landing zones are intentionally prescriptive; networking is typically centralized within a platform zone to enforce routing, inspection, and segmentation. Logging and monitoring are centralized to enable correlation and consistent operational oversight. DNS is commonly hosted as a shared service and linked through defined network patterns to support private connectivity and reliable name resolution. These patterns prevent teams from creating fragmented architectures that bypass governance controls.

Canonical resource assignments in enterprise-scale architecture

Enterprise-scale architectures rely on consistent resource placement to ensure governance controls are inherited, enforced, and observable across all landing zones. These placement patterns define how shared services and workload environments interact within a governed cloud platform.

Canonical placement patterns include the following:

- DNS is hosted in a centralized platform or shared services zones rather than distributed across workloads.
- Centralized monitoring workspaces at the platform layer to provide consistent visibility and correlation.
- Network topology is defined before workload deployment to enforce routing, inspection, and segmentation.
- Application landing zones inheriting policy and compliance guardrails uniformly.
- Identity is treated as a platform-level control plane that anchors role assignment and governance.

In CAF-aligned designs, shared platform services, such as DNS resolution, logging, network connectivity, and security management, are deployed into dedicated platforms or shared services landing zones. Workload landing zones are reserved exclusively for application resources and inherit platform controls through policy assignment and network integration.

For example, private DNS zones that support private endpoints are commonly hosted centrally and linked to spoke networks to ensure consistent name resolution and governance. Centralized monitoring workspaces aggregate telemetry from all landing zones, enabling cross-environment visibility and governance oversight. Network components responsible for routing and inspection are placed in platform zones to prevent workload teams from bypassing security controls.

In some enterprise-scale designs, private DNS zones are deployed per landing zone to ensure clear ownership, isolation, and predictable policy inheritance, while still integrating with centralized governance and monitoring. These placement decisions are architectural requirements, not preferences. Incorrect placement breaks policy inheritance, fragments visibility, and weakens the enforcement model that CAF is designed to establish; resource placement, therefore, directly determines how effectively governance and security controls operate across the platform.

Recommending CAF and WAF security governance solutions

Security governance in Azure is implemented through controls that enforce consistency, compliance, and operational discipline across large cloud estates. CAF provides the model for organizing governance at scale, defining how policies, identity structures, network boundaries, and management groups apply across the platform.

WAF ensures that these governance mechanisms meet architectural quality expectations, particularly within the security and operational excellence pillars. Together, they provide the blueprint for shaping how guardrails are defined, implemented, and validated.

Without structured governance, cloud environments become patchworks of individually configured workloads, each with its own interpretation of security requirements; policies drift, compliance becomes reactive, visibility is fragmented, and operational teams struggle to maintain consistent protection.

CAF and WAF counter these effects by prescribing how governance tools, Azure Policy, Defender for Cloud, management groups, identity models, and cross-cloud controls interact to create predictable security outcomes. This section's content maps to the official SC-100 skills-measured topic: *Recommend solutions for security and governance based on the Microsoft CAF for Azure and the Azure WAF.*

Enforcing governance guardrails with Azure Policy

Azure Policy is the central mechanism for enforcing governance in Azure environments. It enables organizations to define and apply configuration standards consistently across subscriptions and management groups, ensuring that platform and workload deployments align with architectural expectations.

CAF prescribes the use of Azure Policy to enforce governance guardrails that prevent insecure or noncomplaint configurations from being deployed; policies define not only what configurations are allowed, but also how deviations are detected, reported, and remediated. In mature environments, policy assignments are applied at the management group scope so that all landing zones and workloads inherit the same baseline controls.

Common examples include restricting public access to services, enforcing private connectivity, mandating encryption standards, and requiring diagnostic logging. WAF reinforces this approach by treating governance as a quality bar. Secure and well-operated workloads must meet baseline configuration requirements, and operational excellence depends on these requirements being automated, observable, and repeatable. Azure Policy provides both preventative enforcement and auditability at scale.

CAF-aligned Azure Policy constructs

CAF-aligned governance relies on Azure Policy constructs to translate architectural intent into enforceable platform controls. Understanding how these constructs work together is essential for applying consistent guardrails across enterprise environments; effective governance relies on continuous enforcement to maintain required configurations over time, rather than on periodic detection and manual correction.

Key policy constructs include:

- **Policies**: They define individual configuration rules, such as preventing public IP creation.
- **Initiatives**: They group related policies into standardized security or compliance baselines.
- **Assignments**: They apply initiatives at the management group scope to ensure uniform inheritance.
- **Effects**: They control enforcement behaviour, including deny, audit, and **`deployIfNotExists`**.

CAF emphasizes the use of **`deployIfNotExists`** to shift governance from reactive enforcement to automated configuration.

Rather than identifying misconfigurations after deployment, this approach ensures required settings are applied consistently and continuously across all landing zones without manual intervention.

Governance through compliance standards and benchmark alignment

Compliance frameworks such as ISO 27001, SOC 2, NIST, and industry-specific regulations introduce structured security expectations that cloud architectures must meet. Governance solutions must translate these expectations into enforceable technical controls rather than relying on periodic assessments; CAF treats compliance as a governance capability that must be embedded into platform design.

In practice, governance-driven compliance is achieved by translating standards and benchmarks into platform-level controls, continuous assessment, and architectural quality attributes:

- Compliance controls are applied at platform and landing zone scopes so that all workloads inherit required protections.
- Azure Policy initiatives aligned to regulatory standards provide a measurable link between compliance objectives and Azure resource configurations.

- Defender for Cloud surfaces compliance posture through continuous assessment, highlighting deviations and configuration gaps.
- WAF supports compliance alignment by embedding security and operational quality into architectural design.
- The security pillar focuses on confidentiality, integrity, and availability through identity controls, network segmentation, encryption, and monitoring.
- The operational excellence pillar ensures compliance is sustained through automation, visibility, and integration into operational processes.

Using Azure Policy and Defender for Cloud

Enterprise compliance governance depends on translating regulatory requirements into enforceable, continuously assessed platform controls; Azure Policy and Defender for Cloud work together to provide this enforcement at scale.

Effective compliance governance includes:

- Assigning compliance initiatives at the management group scope so all workloads inherit mandatory requirements.
- Using Defender for Cloud dashboards to validate implementation and surface configuration deviations.
- Defining remediation workflows that align with the severity and business impact of findings.
- Ensuring policy definitions reflect organizational interpretations of regulatory and industry standards.

Together, Azure Policy and Defender for Cloud establish a continuous compliance governance model that enables consistent enforcement, measurable posture, and ongoing validation across enterprise-scale cloud environments.

Extending governance across multi-cloud with Azure Lighthouse

Organizations increasingly operate across hybrid and multi-cloud environments, which introduces additional governance complexity. Governance solutions must extend beyond individual subscriptions and tenants to provide centralized oversight and consistent control.

Azure Lighthouse enables delegated resource management across multiple tenants and environments. It allows centralized teams to apply governance, monitor posture, and review access consistently without requiring direct ownership of every subscription. When combined with Defender for Cloud and Azure Arc, Lighthouse supports governance across Azure, on-premises, and other cloud platforms.

CAF positions Lighthouse as a key enabler for scalable governance in federated or service-provider operating models; it allows platform teams to maintain visibility and enforce standards across distributed environments while preserving clear ownership boundaries. WAF reinforces this approach by emphasizing consistent observability, access control, and operational quality regardless of where workloads run.

Role assignment visibility and distributed governance

In this model, Lighthouse provides the architectural mechanism for consistent governance across complex estates, rather than serving as a simple remote access tool.

Effective distributed governance includes:

- Defining delegated access at appropriate scopes for governance and security teams.
- Ensuring distributed workloads report telemetry and posture data into centralized views.
- Onboarding cross-cloud and on-premises resources through Azure Arc to enable consistent governance.
- Reviewing role assignments across tenants and environments to maintain least privilege access.

Distributed and multi-cloud environments require governance controls that extend beyond individual subscriptions and tenants. Azure Lighthouse enables centralized oversight while preserving clear ownership boundaries.

Implementing security with Azure landing zones

Azure landing zones are not simply pre-packaged or out-of-the-box environments; they are structured, policy-driven platforms that enforce architectural decisions at scale. Azure landing zones execute the governance, security, and operational expectations defined by the CAF; they ensure that every workload, regardless of the team deploying it, inherits consistent identity boundaries, network segmentation, policy guardrails, monitoring configurations, security measures, and compliance controls.

Controls defined at the landing zone level are enforced by the platform and are not left to workload-level discretion. When implemented correctly, landing zones eliminate the guesswork behind protecting and securing cloud workloads; network designs become standardized, privileged access follows known pathways, encryption is enforced uniformly, and posture assessments apply consistently across environments.

Protection and security are not added after deployment, but embedded into the structure of the landing zone design itself, requiring architects to select mechanisms, design patterns, and controls into the platform architecture. This section's content maps to the official SC-100 skills-measured topic: *Design solutions for implementing and governing security by using Azure landing zones.*

Privileged access governance in landing zones

Privileged access determines how administrative actions interact with the platform and therefore represents one of the most critical security surfaces in any landing zone. Effective landing zone design requires preventative controls that ensure privileged operations are performed through secure, monitored, and isolated pathways. Landing zones must enforce strict separation between privileged and non-privileged activities. Administrative sessions should originate from approved devices, traverse restricted network paths, and be subject to conditional enforcement.

Privileged Identity Management (PIM) enables just-in-time elevation, ensuring administrative privileges are temporary, auditable, and constrained to authorized tasks. Monitoring systems capture privileged operations and highlight anomalous or risky behaviour. These controls are part of the landing zone baseline rather than optional add-ons.

CAF requires platform teams to embed these controls at the management group level so that all workloads and operational teams inherit consistent privileged access expectations. This includes enforcing multi-factor authentication, restricting privileged actions to hardened devices, and ensuring elevation workflows cannot be bypassed by workload teams. Privileged operations are treated as governed interactions rather than discretionary administrator actions. Preventive controls are those that stop insecure actions from occurring, rather than detecting them after the fact.

Within landing zones, the most impactful preventative controls focus on eliminating standing privilege and enforcing controlled administrative pathways. Just-in-time privilege elevation through PIM prevents permanent administrative access and reduces exposure time for high-risk roles. Conditional Access policies tied to compliant or hardened devices ensure that privileged actions can only be performed from approved environments. Together, these controls prevent unauthorized or risky administrative activity before it can affect the platform. Detective controls such as monitoring and alerting remain important, but preventative measures form the foundation of governance by constraining what actions are possible in the first place.

PIM, Conditional Access, and administrative path isolation

Privileged access within a landing zone must follow controlled, auditable pathways that reduce exposure to misuse or compromise. Governance requires preventative controls that limit when, where, and how administrative actions can occur.

Effective privileged pathway design includes:

- Mandatory PIM elevation to eliminate standing administrative privileges.
- Conditional Access policies enforcing compliant or hardened administrative devices.
- **Privileged Access Workstation** (**PAWs**), or equivalent secure endpoints, for high-value operations.

- Azure Bastion to provide controlled administrative virtual machine access and prevent direct **Remote Desktop Protocol** (**RDP**) or **Secure Socket Shell** (**SSH**) exposure.
- Centralized monitoring of privileged operations with governance-focused alerts.

Together, these measures reduce attack surface and ensure privileged activity follows predictable, enforceable, and auditable patterns within the landing zone.

Network security governance and administrative isolation

Network segmentation is foundational to a secure landing zone; effective governance requires that administrative and workload traffic follow approved paths that cannot be bypassed by local configuration changes within individual subscriptions or virtual networks.

Landing zones typically use centralized network topologies, such as hub-and-spoke designs, to host shared services, including firewalls, routing, DNS, and secure admin and management access. Administrative traffic is routed through controlled entry points rather than connecting directly to workloads. Governance-level network rules enforce these patterns even when workload teams attempt to modify local network security groups or routing tables.

CAF views centralized network control as essential for preventing configuration drift, limiting lateral movement, and ensuring consistent enforcement of protection and security boundaries. Predictable ingress and egress patterns also support reliability and operational monitoring across the platform.

Using VNet manager security admin rules

Network governance in landing zones requires controls that cannot be bypassed by local configuration changes. VNet manager security admin rules provide centralized enforcement of administrative and workload traffic patterns across the platform.

Security admin rules enable platform teams to:

- Restrict direct RDP or SSH connectivity from workload networks.
- Enforce Azure Bastion-only administrative access across all landing zones.
- Apply governance-level network rules that cannot be overridden locally.
- Standardize segmentation patterns across subscriptions.
- Ensure administrative and workload traffic follows monitored, controlled routes.

These capabilities deliver governance-grade network enforcement, ensuring that network access policies are applied consistently and predictably across enterprise-scale environments rather than relying on workload-level configuration.

Data security and encryption governance in landing zones

Data protection is a core expectation of a secure cloud platform. Landing zones must define uniform requirements for encryption at rest, key management, secret storage, and boundary protection to prevent inconsistent security decisions across workloads.

Azure services provide platform-managed encryption by default, but many organizations require customer-managed keys to satisfy regulatory or internal governance requirements. Landing zones specify when such keys are required, how they are rotated, where they are stored, and how they integrate with identity and access governance; these decisions must be applied consistently across storage accounts, databases, managed disks, and application components.

Governance also includes enforcing boundary protections such as private connectivity, encryption in transit, and **Transport Layer Security (TLS)** requirements. CAF treats encryption as a secure-by-default platform capability rather than a workload-specific configuration choice.

Applying key management decisions across workloads

Encryption governance in landing zones requires consistent enforcement of key management decisions across all workloads. Rather than allowing teams to define their own approaches, these controls must be embedded into the platform architecture.

Effective key management governance includes:

- Enforcing customer-managed key usage through policy rather than leaving it to workload discretion.
- Applying automated, consistent key rotation cycles.
- Placing key vaults in platform zones with strict access boundaries.
- Using private endpoints to prevent exposure of encrypted data over public networks.
- Enforcing TLS to protect data in transit.

These practices embed encryption governance directly into landing zone architecture, ensuring data protection controls are applied uniformly and predictably across the platform.

Multi-cloud posture and landing zone operational baseline

As organizations adopt hybrid and multi-cloud strategies, landing zones must extend governance and security controls beyond the first-party cloud vendor and cloud-native workloads; a unified operational baseline is required to prevent visibility gaps and inconsistent enforcement across environments.

Landing zones define mandatory onboarding requirements so that workloads, whether running in Azure, on-premises, or other cloud platforms, are integrated into centralized governance and monitoring. This enables consistent vulnerability assessment, compliance evaluation, threat detection, and configuration monitoring across the entire estate.

CAF positions unified posture management as an operational governance capability; by extending platform standards across environments, organizations maintain consistent security expectations regardless of where workloads run.

Defender for Cloud and Arc as CAF operational controls

A multi-cloud landing zone requires a consistent operational baseline that extends governance controls, protection, and security measures across all environments; centralized onboarding and enforcement prevent visibility gaps and inconsistent protection.

An effective multi-cloud landing zone ensures:

- Workloads are onboarded into centralized governance and protection before entering production.
- Security management plans are enabled consistently across environments.
- Compliance checks run uniformly regardless of execution location.
- Threat detection signals aggregate into centralized monitoring platforms.
- Policy-driven governance applies through configuration and extension-based controls.

This approach ensures that protection, compliance, and posture remain visible, enforceable, and measurable across cloud, hybrid, and multi-cloud environments.

DevSecOps processes aligned with CAF guidance

DevSecOps within the Microsoft CAF embeds security as a continuous practice across planning, development, build, test, release, and operational phases. Rather than treating security as a post-deployment activity, CAF positions it as a core design and engineering discipline; this ensures threats are modeled early, secrets are handled correctly, protection is enforced, code and dependencies are validated, and deployments follow governed, auditable pipelines.

Without structured DevSecOps alignment, cloud workloads inherit an inconsistent protection, compliance, and security posture; pipelines may run with excessive permissions, threat models may not reflect architectural risks, and vulnerabilities introduced during development can surface only after production deployment.

CAF counters this by prescribing threat modeling methodologies, identity governance for pipelines, security scanning across **continuous integration/continuous delivery** (**CI/CD**) stages, and enforcement of guardrails that prevent insecure code paths from reaching production. This section's content maps to the official SC-100 skills-measured topic: *Design a DevSecOps process that aligns with best practices in the Microsoft CAF.*

Threat modeling and security scanning in CAF DevSecOps

A CAF-aligned approach requires threats to be identified and addressed during design, before code is written or infrastructure is deployed; this enables architects and development teams to reason about attack surfaces, trust boundaries, misuse cases, and failure modes while design changes are still low-cost.

CAF reinforces that threat modeling is an architectural process rather than a development checklist item; standardized methodologies break applications into predictable components, allowing teams to document threats consistently and design mitigations that align with enterprise security controls.

Dynamic application security testing (**DAST**) complements this approach by validating running applications and deployed components; runtime and dependency testing identify vulnerabilities that static analysis alone cannot detect, such as insecure configurations, dependency weaknesses, and runtime exposure paths.

These activities are embedded into the build and test stages to prevent vulnerable code from progressing through the pipeline.

OWASP threat modelling for CAF

CAF-aligned threat modeling, as defined by the **Open Web Application Security Project** (**OWASP**), identifies architectural risks early, before code or infrastructure is deployed. A top-down approach ensures that security considerations are embedded into design decisions rather than discovered after implementation.

Effective threat modeling includes:

- Enumerating user flows and application components.
- Identifying trust boundaries and interaction points.
- Documenting potential misuse and abuse cases.
- Prioritizing threats using standardized risk scoring.
- Recommending mitigations aligned with enterprise security controls.

Early identification of architectural weaknesses and vulnerabilities ensures security risks are addressed during design, reducing operational exposure and remediation effort later in the lifecycle.

DAST and dependency testing requirements

DAST validates application behavior under realistic runtime conditions to identify vulnerabilities that static analysis alone cannot detect; these checks are integrated into the build and test stages to prevent insecure components from progressing through the pipeline.

Effective dynamic testing evaluates:

- Runtime behavior under adversarial conditions.
- Dependencies retrieved through package managers.
- API responses and exposed attack surfaces.
- Authentication and session management behavior.
- Misconfigurations in container images or platform services.

These practices ensure that vulnerabilities introduced through code, configuration, or third-party components are identified and addressed before deployment.

Identity governance for CI/CD pipelines

Identity management in DevOps environments is a frequent point of failure; pipelines historically relied on long-lived secrets or broadly scoped service principals, increasing the risk of credential compromise and privilege misuse. CAF-aligned DevSecOps replaces these patterns with identity mechanisms that are short-lived, auditable, and governed, as follows:

- Pipeline identities are governed in the same way as human identities, with precisely scoped permissions and centrally enforced lifecycle control.
- Workload identity federation enables pipelines to authenticate using token-based trust relationships rather than stored secrets.
- Managed identities provide stable, centrally governed identities with precisely scoped permissions.

Together, these approaches eliminate secret sprawl, simplify credential lifecycle management, and enforce least privilege access across deployment workflows.

CAF emphasizes that identity governance must apply equally to human and non-human actors. Automated pipelines are treated as first-class identities subject to the same access controls, auditing, and separation-of-duties requirements as administrators and application workloads.

Implementing workload identity federation and managed identities

Secure CI/CD pipelines require identity mechanisms that are short-lived, auditable, and governed. Workload identity federation and managed identities replace long-lived credentials with token-based trust and centrally controlled access.

Effective pipeline identity governance includes:

- Authenticating pipelines using token-based trust rather than stored credentials.
- Mapping managed identities precisely to required permissions.
- Applying role assignments that follow least privilege patterns aligned with platform governance.
- Requiring auditable, scoped permissions for sensitive operations.
- Eliminating secrets from repositories, variable groups, and build agents.

These identity practices reduce operational risk while strengthening governance, auditability, and traceability across delivery pipelines.

Integrating security tasks across CI/CD stages

Security in DevSecOps is implemented as a sequence of embedded controls aligned to each stage of the delivery pipeline. Rather than relying on a single security gate, CAF promotes distributing security checks throughout the build, test, release, and deployment phases. This ensures architectural and governance requirements are enforced continuously as changes progress through the delivery lifecycle.

In practice, this approach results in distinct security responsibilities being applied at each stage of the CI/CD pipeline:

- Build stages focus on identifying insecure code patterns, vulnerable dependencies, and exposed secrets.
- Test stages validate runtime behaviour and configuration under controlled conditions.
- Release stages enforce policy compliance and governance checks.
- Deployment stages validate infrastructure configuration and detect drift after release.

Together, these controls create a layered security model that reduces the likelihood of vulnerable workloads reaching production.

Applying security controls to pipeline stages

CAF-aligned DevSecOps distributes security controls across the delivery pipeline so that risks are identified and blocked as early as possible; rather than relying on a single security gate, controls are embedded into each stage of the pipeline.

Security controls are applied as follows:

- **Build stage**:
  - Static application security testing
  - Dependency and package version scanning
  - Container image analysis
  - Secret discovery and blocking
- **Test stage**:
  - DAST
  - Integration testing against secure configurations
  - Automated penetration testing is supported
- **Release stage**:
  - Policy validation and compliance checks
  - Verification of deployment templates
  - Governance gate enforcement
- **Deployment stage**:
  - Infrastructure configuration validation
  - Drift detection
  - Post-deployment vulnerability scanning

This staged approach ensures that security failures are detected early and that governance requirements are enforced consistently throughout the delivery lifecycle.

DevSecOps as an extension of CAF governance

DevSecOps is not a tooling decision but an extension of governance into the software delivery lifecycle. Pipeline identities align with platform **role-based access controls** (**RBACs**), threat modeling aligns with architectural standards, and scanning aligns with compliance and security baselines. Deployments inherit landing zone guardrails rather than bypassing them.

When DevSecOps practices are embedded into governance, security outcomes become predictable and repeatable; when they are applied inconsistently or manually, risk increases and operational confidence erodes. CAF frames DevSecOps as the mechanism that connects architectural intent with day-to-day delivery operations, ensuring security is sustained from design through deployment and into runtime rather than enforced retrospectively.

Conclusion

This chapter examined how Microsoft's cloud architecture frameworks provide a structured foundation for designing secure, protected, governed, and operationally resilient cloud environments. By applying the CAF and the Azure WAF together, architects can translate organizational strategy into enforceable governance models, standardized landing zones, and repeatable operational practices that scale across complex environments.

The chapter demonstrated how CAF defines the organizational structure, governance boundaries, and operational responsibilities required for cloud adoption, while WAF provides the evaluative lens used to assess architectural quality across security, reliability, performance, cost, and operational excellence. Together, these frameworks ensure that security controls are not applied in isolation but are embedded into platform design and workload lifecycle decisions.

Through landing zones, governance policies, and DevSecOps practices, the chapter showed how architectural intent is enforced consistently across identity, networking, data protection, monitoring, and deployment pipelines. Rather than relying on manual configuration or post-deployment remediation, these patterns establish security and governance as inherited platform capabilities that guide workload teams toward compliant and well-managed designs. By grounding cloud security decisions in Microsoft's endorsed frameworks, organizations can reduce architectural drift, improve operational predictability, and ensure that security requirements are applied uniformly across cloud, hybrid, and multi-cloud environments.

The next chapter builds on these framework-driven foundations by examining how security architecture is validated, monitored, and improved over time through continuous posture management and threat-driven insights. It explores how organizations assess the effectiveness of their security controls, identify exposure and attack paths across cloud environments, and use posture and threat signals to guide architectural decisions. By focusing on visibility, evaluation, and prioritization, the chapter shows how security design evolves from static architecture into an adaptive, continuously improving security practice.

Questions

Success on any assessment depends on understanding the underlying technologies, concepts, and principles rather than memorizing facts. These questions help readers confirm that they can apply this chapter's ideas in realistic design scenarios, including security benchmarks, architectural control inheritance, posture management, attack-path disruption, Zero Trust design, and privileged access modernization.

1. **An organization wants all new Azure workloads to inherit identity, network, and logging controls automatically. Which architectural approach best achieves this outcome?**
    a. Manual configuration by workload owners
    b. Applying security controls after deployment
    c. Designing landing zones directly from **Microsoft cloud security benchmark (MCSB)** requirements
    d. Enabling Secure Score recommendations individually
2. **Why is treating the MCSB as a design input more effective than using it as a compliance checklist?**
    a. It reduces audit scope
    b. It allows teams to ignore non-applicable controls
    c. It embeds security expectations into the platform architecture
    d. It replaces the need for monitoring
3. **Which signal most strongly indicates a structural architectural weakness rather than an isolated configuration error?**
    a. A single failed policy evaluation
    b. A recurring posture recommendation across multiple workloads
    c. A temporary Secure Score drop
    d. A missing alert rule
4. **Which architectural control most effectively limits lateral movement after an initial compromise?**
    a. Endpoint antivirus
    b. Flat network routing
    c. Segmentation across identity, network, and administrative paths
    d. Public service endpoints
5. **Why does Secure Score function as an architectural feedback mechanism rather than a one-time assessment?**
    a. It measures user productivity
    b. It replaces penetration testing
    c. It surfaces recurring design gaps that must be corrected in templates and guardrails
    d. It automatically remediates all findings

6. **Which Zero Trust principle directly justifies eliminating standing administrative privileges?**
    a. Verify explicitly
    b. Assume breach
    c. Use least privilege
    d. Trust but verify
7. **Why are ingress proxies such as Azure Front Door insufficient on their own to establish a Zero Trust boundary?**
    a. They do not support TLS
    b. They increase latency
    c. They do not enforce identity-based authorization for backend workloads
    d. They cannot scale globally
8. **Which architectural outcome is RaMP primarily designed to deliver in its earliest phases?**
    a. Full automation of all security controls
    b. Immediate Zero Trust maturity across all workloads
    c. Reduction of risk through early modernization of privileged access
    d. Replacement of legacy identity platforms
9. **During ransomware response planning, why must containment occur before investigation or recovery?**
    a. It simplifies reporting
    b. It reduces the compliance scope
    c. It prevents continued spread and evidence destruction
    d. It accelerates system restoration
10. **Why are posture and vulnerability signals considered architectural inputs rather than operational alerts?**
    a. They are generated automatically
    b. They are only relevant to compliance teams
    c. They indicate where platform standards must be redesigned to prevent recurrence
    d. They replace logging and monitoring

Answers

1. c: Designing landing zones directly from MCSB requirements.

   When MCSB is used as the baseline for landing zone design, identity, network, logging, and posture controls are inherited by default, removing reliance on manual configuration.

2. c: It embeds security expectations into the platform architecture.

   Using MCSB as a design input ensures controls are enforced structurally through guardrails and standardized deployment patterns rather than applied inconsistently after deployment.

3. b: A recurring posture recommendation across multiple workloads.

   Repeated findings across workloads usually indicate a systemic design gap in templates, standards, or inherited controls, not a single misconfiguration.

4. c: Segmentation across identity, network, and administrative paths.

   Lateral movement is most effectively constrained by enforced trust boundaries that reduce blast radius and limit what compromised identities or workloads can reach.

5. c: It surfaces recurring design gaps that must be corrected in templates and guardrails.

   Secure Score highlights patterns that should drive architectural refinement, making it a continuous feedback loop rather than a snapshot.

6. c: Use least privilege.

   Eliminating standing administrative access ensures privileges exist only when needed, reducing exposure time and limiting attacker persistence.

7. c: They do not enforce identity-based authorization for backend workloads.

   Ingress proxies manage traffic flow and front-door exposure, but they do not inherently prove caller identity and enforce workload-level authorization for downstream services.

8. c: Reduction of risk through early modernization of privileged access.

   Early phases prioritize privileged access isolation and modernization because privileged compromise can undermine all other controls.

9. c: It prevents continued spread and evidence destruction.

   Containment stops attacker activity, limits propagation, and preserves forensic evidence so investigation and recovery can proceed safely.

10. c: They indicate where platform standards must be redesigned to prevent recurrence.

    Posture and vulnerability signals should drive changes to baseline standards and inherited controls so issues do not reappear in future deployments.

Chapter 4
Design Security Operations Solutions

Introduction

This chapter examines how to design integrated, scalable, and governed security operations solutions across Microsoft's cloud ecosystem. Rather than treating security operations as a collection of tools, this chapter frames SecOps as an architectural capability that must be intentionally designed to support consistent outcomes at scale. It focuses on building end-to-end detection, investigation, and response architectures that unify signals from identities, endpoints, workloads, applications, and infrastructure into a coherent operational model.

The chapter explores how Microsoft Sentinel, Microsoft Defender **extended detection and response** (**XDR**), Microsoft Purview, and supporting monitoring services work together to provide centralized visibility, threat detection, and automated response across hybrid and multi-cloud environments. It explains how telemetry ingestion, correlation, and orchestration enable security teams to move from isolated alerts to structured incident narratives and governed response workflows.

The chapter shows how organizations can evaluate detection coverage, identify gaps, and continuously improve their security posture by grounding operational design decisions in threat-informed models such as MITRE ATT&CK.

Structure

This chapter covers the following topics:

- XDR and SIEM solutions
- Centralized logging and auditing with Purview
- Monitoring for hybrid and multi-cloud environments
- SOAR with Sentinel and Defender XDR
- Designing and evaluating SOC security workflows
- Threat detection coverage with MITRE ATT&CK

Objectives

This chapter covers the skills required to design comprehensive detection and response solutions that incorporate XDR and **security information and event management** (**SIEM**) capabilities; it examines how to design centralized logging and auditing strategies, including the use of Microsoft Purview Audit, to ensure security-relevant activity is consistently captured, retained, and reviewable across the environment.

The chapter also explores how to design monitoring solutions that support hybrid and multi-cloud environments, ensuring visibility is maintained across cloud-native, on-premises, and third-party platforms; it addresses the design of **security orchestration and automated response** (**SOAR**) solutions through Microsoft Sentinel to enable coordinated threat response at scale.

Finally, the chapter examines how to design and evaluate end-to-end security workflows, including incident response, threat hunting, and incident management processes; it also covers how to assess and improve threat detection coverage using MITRE ATT&CK matrices, ensuring architectural detection strategies align with real-world adversary techniques.

By the end of this chapter, readers will understand how to design modern Microsoft-aligned security operations architectures that reduce alert fatigue, improve **mean time to respond** (**MTTR**), and support resilient, auditable incident handling across complex enterprise environments.

These skills fall under the exam domain: *Design security operations, identity, and compliance capabilities*, which represent approximately 25-30 % of the overall SC-100 skills[1] measured.

XDR and SIEM solutions

Modern security operations, SecOps, depend on the coordinated behavior of two complementary layers: a centralized incident and event management SIEM solution that unifies signals, investigations, and governance across the entire digital estate, and an XDR platform that provides deep, context-aware analytics.

Microsoft's security architecture reflects this separation of responsibility clearly; Defender's XDR capabilities specialize in understanding the behavior of identities, endpoints, email, **Software as a service** (**SaaS**), and **infrastructure as a service** (**IaaS**)/**platform as a service** (**PaaS**) workloads, while Microsoft Sentinel provides the SIEM foundation that correlates signals from Defender and other signal sources into coherent, end-to-end incident narratives.

Defender XDR supplies domain-specific behavioral detections and response, Sentinel governs cross-platform correlation and the incident lifecycle, and Microsoft Purview Audit provides authoritative Microsoft 365-scoped user and administrator activity records for investigation and compliance.

1 **https://learn.microsoft.com/en-us/credentials/certifications/resources/study-guides/sc-100**

An effective detection and response strategy must therefore treat these layers as a single operating fabric rather than isolated tools. XDR supplies depth and behavioral insight, while SIEM provides operational structure and scale; when either layer is missing, organizations experience fragmented detection or uncoordinated investigations; together, they form the architectural foundation required to support security operations across hybrid and multi-cloud environments.

This relationship is illustrated in the following architecture, where XDR signals are aggregated and correlated within the SIEM layer:

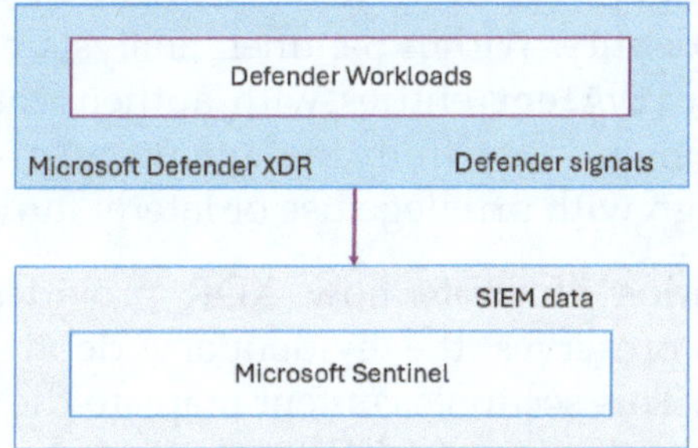

Figure 4.1: *XDR signals from multiple security domains correlated within Microsoft Sentinel as the SIEM layer*

Each Defender workload generates detection signals within its domain, which are then consolidated in Microsoft Sentinel to support cross-domain investigation and incident management.

XDR and SIEM integration succeeds only when telemetry is treated as a structured set of evidence types rather than a single stream of security data; behavioral detections and incidents represent analytic conclusions (what the platform believes is suspicious), while logs and audit records represent evidence (what actually occurred).

In Microsoft's ecosystem, Defender XDR primarily contributes high-fidelity detections, correlated incidents, and entity context across identities, endpoints, email, SaaS, and cloud workloads. Sentinel, by contrast, provides the correlation plane and operational record that links detections to the wider estate by querying retained telemetry and normalizing activity across multiple sources. Architecturally, design decisions must therefore separate detection signals from evidence sources.

Detections and incidents drive triage and response, but investigations and compliance depend on raw telemetry, such as Azure Activity Logs, resource diagnostics, identity logs, and audit trails, because these provide time-ordered, reviewable records. Treating these as distinct layers prevents a common failure mode in security operations design: assuming that alerts alone are sufficient for reconstruction, governance, or auditability.

This distinction between detection signals and underlying evidence becomes clearer when examined through concrete incident scenarios.

For example, a Defender XDR incident may be generated when suspicious credential access behavior is detected on an endpoint by Microsoft Defender for Endpoint. When this incident appears in Microsoft Sentinel, analysts can pivot from the incident to the underlying telemetry by reviewing records in the **SecurityAlert** table to understand the detection context, the **DeviceEvents** table to examine process creation and file activity on the affected device, and the **IdentityInfo** table to identify the user and device relationships involved. This enables the SOC to reconstruct how endpoint behavior and identity context combine into a single incident narrative rather than treating the alert as an isolated signal.

In a separate scenario, Defender XDR may raise an incident based on anomalous sign-in activity associated with an identity. Within Sentinel, analysts can validate and expand this incident by correlating **SecurityAlert** entries with authentication activity captured in the **SigninLogs** table and enrichment data from the **IdentityInfo** table, confirming whether suspicious access patterns align with privilege use or lateral movement.

Taken together, these scenarios illustrate how XDR provides high-confidence detection outcomes, while the SIEM preserves the evidentiary depth required for investigation, governance, and auditability. This section's content maps to the official SC-100 skill: *Design a solution for detection and response that includes XDR and SIEM.*

Integrating XDR analytics with cloud-scale SIEM visibility

XDR thrives on a deep understanding of what is happening inside workloads, devices, identities, and cloud platforms; these analytics detect behavioral anomalies, uncover suspicious lateral movement, and reveal misconfigurations or vulnerabilities that attackers routinely exploit. However, XDR on its own is limited by its domain: it provides depth, not breadth; a SIEM system complements this by providing the broad, organization-wide visibility that XDR cannot offer. Platform logs, network flow data, identity activity, SaaS usage, and multi-cloud infrastructure telemetry converge into a SIEM workspace. When integrated properly, the SIEM becomes the correlation surface through which an organization interprets seemingly isolated alerts as parts of larger attack chains; signals from XDR tools enrich those correlations with behavioral context, allowing the **security operations center** (**SOC**) to interpret events not just as technical anomalies but as evidence of attacker goals and progression.

In practice, this depth-and-breadth model also depends on consistent ingestion patterns for telemetry that originates outside Microsoft-native services; the perimeter devices forward events using formats such as **Common Event Format** (**CEF**) and Syslog to collect and forward them into Microsoft Sentinel. This allows firewall and network activity to be correlated directly with identity, endpoint, and cloud workload signals inside a single incident narrative, avoiding brittle point integrations and ensuring perimeter telemetry is treated as first-class security data, and not just log noise or clutter.

When these systems operate together, detection becomes an architectural capability rather than a by-product of disparate tools; workloads are onboard with consistent posture and telemetry requirements. Security signals follow predictable ingestion paths. Investigation and response occur in a shared operational plane. Integration is therefore foundational, not optional.

Sentinel as operational center for investigation

A successful detection strategy must be paired with equally strong investigative capabilities. The SIEM acts as a workspace where analysts observe, explore, and understand incidents; rather than pivoting across multiple product consoles, analysts rely on the SIEM to surface timelines, entities, relationships, and contextual enrichment drawn from all integrated sources, including Defender's XDR insights.

Sentinel's investigation model is built around incident-centric workflows; each incident pulls together alerts, entities, logs, and activity sequences into a structured representation of what occurred. Analysts can examine lateral movement patterns, correlate identity behavior with endpoint events, and reconstruct the operational impact of an attack surface shift; this avoids the fragmentation that occurs when investigations are distributed across isolated portals and ensures the SOC operates from a unified view of reality.

For hybrid environments, identity changes within Active Directory can be as operationally significant as native cloud workload alerts, particularly when privileged groups are modified. Onboarding domain controllers into Microsoft Defender for Identity and streaming those identity security signals into Sentinel allows sensitive events, such as changes to high-value security groups, to raise actionable incidents with minimal administrative effort; this ensures identity-centric attacks are detected and investigated within the same operational context as cloud and endpoint activity.

The SIEM's enrichment capabilities, including threat intelligence, behavioral baselines, and visualized relationships, provide the grounding analysts need to move beyond surface-level alert handling. Investigation becomes an evidence-driven process that integrates telemetry from across the organization, enabling analysts to determine not only what happened, but why, how, and what must occur next.

Endpoint behavior and automated response

Endpoints form a critical part of the detection ecosystem. Compromise frequently begins at the device level, where attackers exploit vulnerabilities, harvest credentials, escalate privileges, or initiate lateral movement; an XDR-aligned endpoint protection layer supplies the behavioral analytics required to detect such activity early. When endpoint insights are integrated into the broader SIEM environment, the SOC gains visibility into device actions as part of the organization's holistic threat story.

Automation further strengthens this fabric. Manual response cannot keep pace with the velocity or complexity of attacks, and inconsistency in analyst behavior introduces risk; automated playbooks triggered from SIEM incidents enforce predictable, governed responses. Actions such as isolating devices, disabling accounts, resetting tokens, enriching events, or notifying operational teams occur rapidly and consistently, following predefined security workflows that reflect organizational policy rather than individual analyst judgment.

This integration ensures that detection does not end with awareness; it evolves smoothly into an orchestrated response, automated actions operate near the workload where immediacy matters, while the SIEM coordinates the broader response across teams, processes, and systems. Response becomes part of the architecture rather than an ad-hoc activity.

Establishing SIEM as the enterprise incident platform

To function effectively, a SOC requires a single location where all meaningful security activity converges. A central SIEM provides the incident management surface that unifies logs, alerts, investigations, and response actions; it becomes the authoritative system of record for security operations, governing how incidents are detected, escalated, analyzed, and resolved.

This centralization ensures that operational processes remain coherent across teams and technologies; identity compromise, endpoint alerts, cloud workload anomalies, SaaS misuse, and network deviations all surface in a common incident queue. Analysts develop muscle memory in a shared toolsets process for escalation, containment, forensic evidence preservation, and communication remain consistent regardless of the source of the signal.

Organizations avoid the fragmentation that arises when security tools operate in isolation by positioning the SIEM as the operational hub. Defender XDR continues to play its crucial role as the analytics engine, but the SIEM shapes the workflows, governance, and lifecycle of incidents. This division of responsibility scales across hybrid and multi-cloud estates and ensures organizational security posture remains coordinated and manageable.

Finally, enabling endpoint detection and automated response is a deliberate architectural decision rather than a default outcome. Endpoint detection capability depends on onboarding endpoints and servers so behavioral telemetry is continuously available, while automated response capability depends on configuring Sentinel automation rules and playbooks to act on incidents in a governed manner. Treating EDR and SOAR as explicit enablement steps ensures the SOC gains both high-fidelity detections and predictable, auditable response outcomes.

Together, XDR and SIEM define how threats are detected, correlated, and managed across the enterprise. Yet alerts and incidents only describe *interpretations* of activity; Long-term investigation, accountability, and assurance depend on whether the underlying actions themselves are reliably recorded and preserved.

Centralized logging and auditing with Purview

Effective security operations rely on the ability to reconstruct events accurately and consistently across identities, workloads, applications, and platforms. In modern cloud environments, activity is distributed across services, tenants, and providers, making fragmented logging a major operational risk. Without a centralized logging and auditing architecture, security teams struggle to correlate events, validate incidents, or meet compliance and forensic requirements.

Microsoft's approach to centralized telemetry combines service-level diagnostic logs, Microsoft Purview Audit for Microsoft 365 activity, and Microsoft Sentinel as the unified operational and investigative surface. Each layer contributes a distinct type of visibility: diagnostics describe how systems behave, audit logs capture how users and administrators interact with services, and the SIEM correlates these signals into meaningful security narratives.

This section examines how to design a logging and auditing architecture that supports detection, investigation, governance, and compliance across hybrid and multi-cloud environments. The content maps to the official SC-100 skill: *Design a solution for centralized logging and auditing, including Microsoft Purview Audit.*

Establishing unified log architecture across cloud services

A centralized log architecture begins with defining which telemetry must be collected and where it should be stored. Azure services emit multiple categories of logs, including activity logs that record control plane operations, resource diagnostics that describe workload behavior, and platform metrics that support operational monitoring. Ingestion into Microsoft Sentinel is implemented using native data connectors, the Azure Monitor agent with data collection rules, or standardized formats such as CEF, depending on the telemetry source and platform.

These signals must be streamed into a small number of well-governed Log Analytics workspaces where they can be queried, correlated, and retained consistently. Microsoft 365 workloads introduce an additional dimension of telemetry that cannot be captured through Azure diagnostics alone. User actions, administrative changes, and data access events across Exchange, SharePoint, Teams, and Entra ID require a separate audit pipeline. Consolidating these diverse signals into a unified logging strategy ensures that security investigations are not limited by platform boundaries and that analysts can correlate system behavior with human activity.

A mature design also recognizes that not all logs serve the same purpose. Some telemetry is required for real-time detection, while other data supports forensic reconstruction, compliance validation, or operational troubleshooting. Assigning retention periods based on purpose, regulatory obligations, and cost considerations ensures that critical evidence remains available without creating unnecessary storage overhead.

Retention is an architectural decision because different telemetry types serve different operational purposes. High-volume logs used primarily for near-real-time detection and operational troubleshooting often require shorter **hot** retention to control cost, while evidence required for forensic reconstruction and compliance typically demands longer **cold** retention and stricter governance. The design must therefore assign retention based on investigation requirements, regulatory obligations, and the business impact of losing historical visibility, rather than applying a single blanket policy across all telemetry.

In globally distributed environments, the retention strategy must also respect data residency. While regulations require telemetry to remain within specific geographies, regional workspaces, and controlled data movement becomes part of the logging architecture; this approach allows organizations to preserve investigative effectiveness while remaining compliant, and prevents the false choice between *centralize everything* and *fragment visibility*, both of which degrade security outcomes in different ways.

Integrating Microsoft Purview Audit into telemetry fabric

Microsoft Purview Audit provides authoritative visibility into user and administrator activity across Microsoft 365 services. It records actions such as file access, sharing, mailbox operations, permission changes, and administrative configuration updates. In many scenarios, Purview Audit is the only reliable source for reconstructing user-driven timelines during investigations involving data exposure, insider risk, or account compromise. This capability depends on required audit events being enabled, retained for the necessary duration, and accessible to the SOC at investigation time.

Since audit capability and retention behavior can vary by organizational configuration, architects must treat audit readiness as a design constraint rather than an assumption. In practice, this means validating that the environment can capture the required audit events, retain them for the necessary duration, and make them accessible to the SOC under least privilege controls. This capability check prevents a common failure mode where an organization designs incident reconstruction workflows that depend on audit evidence that is not retained long enough or is not available at the time of investigation.

Integrating Purview Audit into the broader telemetry fabric ensures that Microsoft 365 activity is analyzed alongside infrastructure, identity, and endpoint signals. When audit events are correlated with cloud resource logs and identity telemetry in Sentinel, security teams gain a more complete understanding of intent and impact. Suspicious workload behavior can be evaluated in the context of user actions, and anomalous access patterns can be traced across services rather than investigated in isolation.

This integration transforms auditing from a compliance-only function into a core component of security operations. Audit data becomes actionable intelligence that enriches investigations, supports detection engineering, and strengthens the organization's ability to explain what happened during complex incidents.

Designing workspaces for security, operations, and governance

Centralization does not imply unrestricted access. Different teams require different views of telemetry, and the logging architecture must enforce appropriate boundaries while preserving investigative effectiveness. Log Analytics workspaces, therefore, serve a dual role: they are both telemetry repositories and access control boundaries where least privilege principles must be applied deliberately. Workspace boundaries define governance scope, access isolation, and compliance boundaries, not just data storage location, and may align to region, business unit, or regulatory requirement.

In many environments, the logging design must explicitly separate security and operations consumption without duplicating the entire monitoring stack. Two mechanisms make this practical at scale; first, resource-based access control within Sentinel and Log Analytics determines which teams can query which data sets, and second, the Azure Monitor agent can be configured so that specific server event logs are sent to the appropriate workspace or workspaces; allowing operational logs to be visible to **information technology** (IT) operations teams while security teams retain visibility across both operational and security telemetry when investigations require it.

Security teams typically require broad visibility across identity, audit, workload, and infrastructure logs to investigate incidents effectively; operations teams, by contrast, may only need access to performance metrics, service health data, or specific application diagnostics. Designing workspace boundaries and access policies with these consumption patterns in mind ensures that each team can perform its role without exposing sensitive data unnecessarily or weakening investigative capability.

This model extends naturally to hybrid environments. Logs from on-premises systems may be collected through agents or gateways before being forwarded to cloud workspaces. Maintaining a consistent workspace strategy across cloud and on-premises sources ensures telemetry remains coherent and investigations are not disrupted by environmental boundaries.

Integrating application and edge telemetry into Sentinel

Critical security insights often originate at the application boundary, where attackers probe for weaknesses long before deeper compromise occurs. **Web application firewalls (WAFs)**, reverse proxies, content delivery networks, and network gateways generate telemetry that reveals reconnaissance activity, exploitation attempts, and anomalous access patterns. Treating this telemetry as optional creates blind spots that attackers can exploit.

Integrating application and edge logs into Sentinel allows the SOC to correlate boundary activity with identity events, endpoint behavior, and cloud workload signals; for example, unusual request patterns detected by a WAF may align with suspicious sign-ins, privilege escalation attempts, or unexpected data transfers. When these signals are analyzed together, investigations begin with a more complete picture of attacker behavior.

Organizations ensure that detection and investigation extend beyond core workloads to include the full attack surface through the incorporation of application and edge telemetry into the centralized logging architecture.

Supporting external SIEMs and multiplatform requirements

Many organizations operate federated security models where Microsoft Sentinel is part of a broader monitoring ecosystem rather than the sole destination for telemetry. Regulatory requirements, legacy tooling, or enterprise-wide SOC consolidation may require selected logs or incident summaries to be shared with external platforms.

A well-designed architecture avoids duplicating ingestion pipelines or creating unmanaged data flows. Instead, Sentinel workspaces can export curated telemetry or incident data through supported mechanisms such as event streaming; this preserves a unified operational model while allowing external SIEMs or analytics platforms to receive only the data they require in a controlled and auditable manner.

The same discipline applies inside Sentinel itself. Visualization and response serve different operational purposes and must be governed separately. Dashboards that help SOC leaders and analysts understand incident flow, workload distribution, or detection trends should be implemented as workbooks. Automated responses to analytics-generated incidents should be implemented through automation rules and playbooks. Keeping these concerns distinct ensures operational insight does not become entangled with response logic and remains easier to review, audit, and evolve.

This flexibility reinforces a key architectural principle: centralized logging and auditing must remain adaptable. Whether telemetry feeds Sentinel alone or multiple downstream systems, value is maximized when data flow is intentional, traceable, and governed by clear design decisions.

Centralized logging establishes trust in what occurred, but that trust is only as strong as the scope of what is observed. As environments extend beyond a single cloud boundary, the challenge shifts from record-keeping to ensuring that no part of the estate operates outside consistent visibility.

Monitoring for hybrid and multi-cloud environments

Modern organizations rarely operate within the boundaries of a single cloud platform. Most environments span Azure, on-premises datacenters, SaaS platforms, and additional public cloud providers such as **Amazon Web Services** (**AWS**) or Google Cloud; this distribution increases operational flexibility but also introduces monitoring challenges, as each platform exposes telemetry through different control planes, formats, and native tools. Without a deliberate monitoring strategy, visibility becomes inconsistent, creating blind spots that attackers can exploit.

Microsoft's monitoring approach addresses this complexity by extending Azure-native governance and visibility beyond Azure itself. Azure Arc enables non-Azure resources to participate in Azure management and monitoring, while Defender for Cloud provides unified posture management and threat detection across hybrid and multi-cloud estates. Microsoft Sentinel then acts as the centralized operational layer that correlates telemetry from all environments into a single investigative and response surface. Effective hybrid and multi-cloud monitoring requires control plane logs, identity activity, workload telemetry, and network or perimeter data to be collected and correlated together into a centralized investigation surface.

This role clarity prevents a common design error of expecting a SIEM to provide security posture management or expecting a management projection service to replace detection and investigation. When Arc, Defender for Cloud, and Sentinel are designed as complementary layers, hybrid and multi-cloud environments become first-class citizens in governance, monitoring, and response instead of exceptions that create blind spots.

This section examines how to design a monitoring architecture that maintains consistent visibility, governance, and detection across diverse environments. The section's content maps to the official SC-100 skill: *Design monitoring to support hybrid and multi-cloud environments*.

Unified monitoring with Azure Arc and Defender

Azure Arc provides the foundational capability for extending Azure monitoring and governance beyond native Azure resources. By projecting servers, Kubernetes clusters, and data services running outside Azure into the Azure Resource Manager control plane, Arc enables consistent policy assignment, configuration assessment, and telemetry collection regardless of where workloads reside.

Defender for Cloud builds on this foundation by delivering unified security posture management and threat detection across Azure, Arc-enabled on-premises systems, and supported multi-cloud platforms. Integrations with providers such as AWS and Google Cloud allow Defender for Cloud to ingest platform-specific telemetry, including control plane activity, identity events, and network signals. These signals are normalized and evaluated using consistent security baselines, reducing the risk that secondary cloud environments operate with weaker monitoring or protection standards.

This unified monitoring fabric eliminates the artificial distinction between primary and secondary platforms. When all workloads emit telemetry into a common analytical model, security teams can reason about risk and attacker behavior consistently across environments rather than treating non-Azure systems as exceptions.

Designing workspace and resource topologies for global monitoring

Monitoring architectures must scale across geography, regulatory boundaries, and organizational structures. A single centralized workspace may be sufficient for smaller environments, but larger organizations often require multiple workspaces aligned to regions, business units, or compliance zones. These decisions influence data residency, ingestion performance, and operational ownership.

Regional or segmented workspaces allow telemetry to remain within required geographic boundaries while still supporting centralized investigation. Services such as Azure Lighthouse enable a global SOC to access and investigate incidents across multiple workspaces and tenants without collapsing governance boundaries or duplicating data. This approach preserves local autonomy while enabling cross-region correlation and coordinated response.

A deliberate workspace topology ensures that monitoring remains both compliant and operationally effective. Without this structure, organizations risk either over-centralizing data in ways that violate regulatory requirements or fragmenting visibility to the point where cross-environment attacks become difficult to detect.

Monitoring across hybrid and multi-cloud control planes

Hybrid and multi-cloud environments generate telemetry at multiple layers, including identity providers, cloud control planes, container orchestrators, network gateways, and workload runtimes. Each layer contributes critical signals that help security teams understand attacker behavior and environmental risk.

Effective monitoring design ensures that telemetry from these layers is collected, normalized, and made available for correlation. This includes ingesting cloud provider audit logs, network flow data, API activity, and workload diagnostics into Sentinel alongside Azure-native telemetry. When these signals are analyzed together, the SOC can detect attacks that traverse platform boundaries, such as compromised identities being reused across clouds or configuration drift enabling lateral movement between environments.

Centralizing this telemetry in Sentinel allows investigations to focus on attacker intent rather than platform-specific artifacts. Analysts can follow activity across clouds as part of a single narrative, reducing investigation time and improving detection accuracy.

Ensuring consistent monitoring standards across operational teams

Technology alone cannot guarantee effective monitoring. Inconsistent configuration practices, uneven logging standards, and ad-hoc onboarding of new platforms frequently undermine visibility. A mature monitoring architecture, therefore, defines clear standards that apply across all environments and teams.

These standards specify which log categories must always be enabled, how long telemetry must be retained, which alerts are mandatory, and who owns remediation when anomalies are detected. Embedding these requirements into policy, automation, and deployment templates ensures that monitoring is inherited by default rather than applied selectively.

Organizations eliminate gaps caused by human error or inconsistent operational practices by enforcing consistent monitoring standards. New workloads and platforms become observable from the moment they are deployed, enabling the SOC to maintain continuous visibility as the environment evolves.

With comprehensive monitoring in place across hybrid and multi-cloud environments, the organization gains consistent awareness of activity and risk. However, awareness alone is not sufficient to reduce impact. As environments grow more complex, responses must become faster and more predictable. This leads to the next architectural layer: SOAR.

SOAR with Sentinel and Defender XDR

As environments grow in scale and complexity, manual incident response becomes increasingly unreliable. Security teams face rising alert volumes, tighter response-time expectations, and greater regulatory scrutiny, all of which demand consistent and auditable handling of incidents. SOAR provides the mechanism for translating detection into timely, repeatable action while maintaining governance and operational control.

Within Microsoft's security ecosystem, Sentinel acts as the orchestration and coordination layer for automated response, while Defender XDR provides high-fidelity detection signals and workload-level response capabilities. Together, these services form an automation fabric that reduces MTTR, enforces consistent operational procedures, and ensures that response actions align with organizational policy rather than individual analyst discretion. This section explores how to design SOAR capabilities that are effective, governed, and scalable across hybrid and multi-cloud environments.

Designing SOAR in Sentinel requires distinguishing between detection logic, orchestration decisions, and execution steps; analytics rules generate alerts and incidents, automation rules control orchestration logic, and playbooks execute the response actions. Analytics rules define what constitutes suspicious behavior and create alerts or incidents when conditions are met. Automation rules determine what should happen next, such as routing incidents, assigning ownership, enriching context, or triggering response workflows based on severity, tactics, or affected entities. Playbooks, implemented with Logic Apps, execute the response actions themselves, such as disabling an account, isolating a device, enriching an incident with threat intelligence, or opening a ticket in an IT service management system.

Operational visibility must remain separate from operational action. Workbooks are the correct design choice for dashboards, reporting, and SOC performance visualization, but they do not provide response capability. Threat hunting queries, similarly, support proactive discovery and hypothesis testing, but they do not replace detection engineering. This separation ensures the SOC can evolve detection, reporting, and response independently while preserving a governed, auditable automation chain. This section's content maps to the official SC-100 skill: *Design a solution for security orchestration, automated response (SOAR), including Microsoft Sentinel and Microsoft Defender XDR.*

Integrating detection signals with automated response workflows

SOAR begins where detection ends. Alerts and incidents generated by Defender XDR, Azure platform services, and integrated third-party sources act as the entry points for automated workflows in Microsoft Sentinel. Analytics rules are responsible for identifying suspicious activity and creating incidents, while automation rules determine how Sentinel should respond when those incidents are raised. This separation allows detection logic and response logic to evolve independently while still producing predictable operational outcomes.

In Sentinel, automated response follows a clear and governed chain. Automation rules evaluate incident properties such as severity, tactics, or affected entities, and playbooks implemented with Logic Apps execute the response steps. This model ensures that automated actions are tied to incident context rather than raw alerts, reducing the risk of unnecessary or disruptive responses.

These automation capabilities are surfaced through Microsoft Sentinel in the unified Microsoft Defender portal, where automation rules define how alerts and incidents trigger orchestrated response actions, as shown in the following figure:

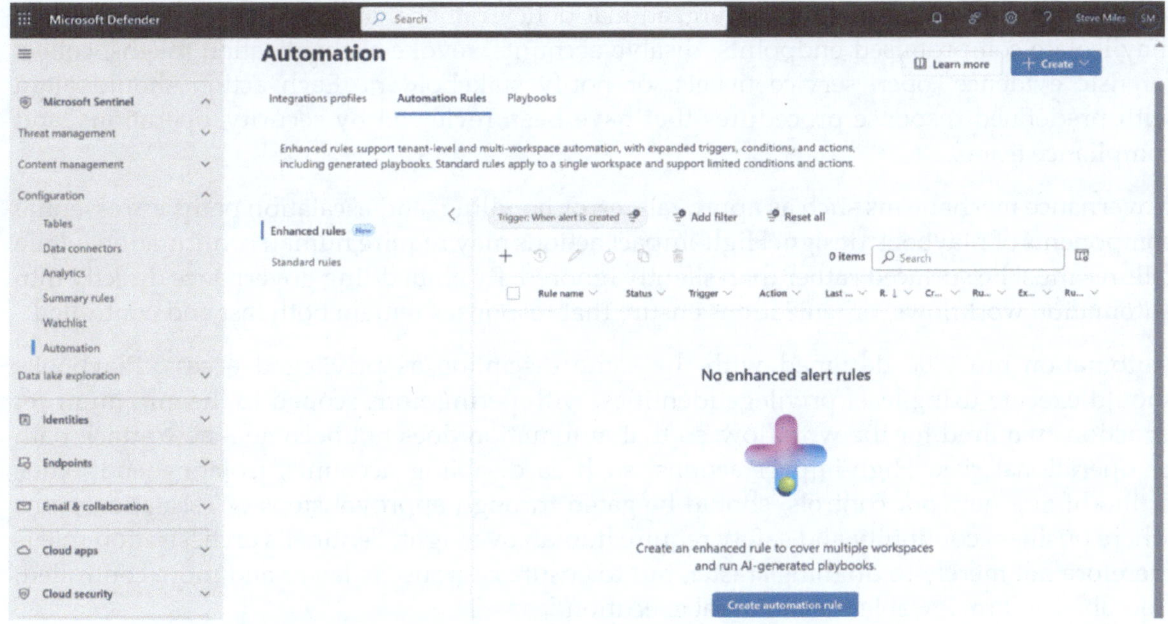

Figure 4.2: Unified automation capabilities in the Microsoft Defender

Although presented in a unified interface, these components serve distinct roles: analytics rules generate detections, automation rules define orchestration logic, and playbooks execute response actions.

Automation rules can be designed to invoke playbooks automatically, require approval for high-impact actions, or notify specific teams based on defined conditions. This allows organizations to apply automation selectively, ensuring that low-risk incidents are handled efficiently while higher-risk scenarios retain appropriate human oversight. The result is a faster response without sacrificing control or accountability.

Defender XDR contributes high-fidelity signals that are particularly well-suited for automation. Endpoint detections, identity risk events, cloud workload alerts, and SaaS anomalies provide reliable triggers for response workflows. By anchoring SOAR execution to these high-confidence detections, organizations ensure that automated response accelerates containment and coordination rather than amplifying noise.

Designing playbooks for consistent, governed response

Playbooks define the actions that occur when automation is triggered. Built on Azure Logic Apps, they can interact with Microsoft 365 services, Azure resources, identity platforms, IT service management systems, and custom applications. Their primary value lies in consistency: playbooks execute defined steps the same way every time, eliminating variability introduced by manual response.

Well-designed playbooks reflect organizational policy rather than ad-hoc remediation. They may isolate compromised endpoints, disable accounts, revoke authentication tokens, collect forensic evidence, open service tickets, or notify stakeholders. Each action should align with predefined response procedures that have been reviewed by security, operations, and compliance teams.

Governance mechanisms such as approvals, error handling, and escalation paths are essential components of playbook design. High-impact actions may require human confirmation, while failures must be surfaced rather than silently ignored. By embedding governance directly into automation workflows, organizations ensure that responses remain both fast and controlled.

Automation must be designed with the same discipline as privileged access. Playbooks should execute using least privilege identities, with permissions scoped to the minimum set of actions required for the workflow, so that automation does not become a new attack path or operational risk. High-impact actions, such as disabling accounts, isolating endpoints, or modifying network controls, should be gated through approval steps or escalation paths where business continuity and safety require human oversight. Sentinel's orchestration role is therefore not merely to do things faster, but to ensure response is faster and more controlled, traceable, and reviewable than manual execution.

Response near workloads, governed centrally

The SIEM itself should not execute all response actions. In many cases, the fastest and most effective containment occurs at the workload layer where the threat is detected. Defender XDR provides investigation and response capabilities that operate close to endpoints, identities, and cloud workloads, enabling rapid isolation, session termination, or policy enforcement.

The Sentinel's role is to coordinate these distributed actions rather than replace them. While Defender services execute localized response, Sentinel records those actions, enriches the incident context, and orchestrates broader workflows that may involve additional teams or systems. This coordination ensures that response actions are visible, auditable, and aligned with the overall incident lifecycle.

This architectural separation balances speed and governance. Response occurs where it is most effective, while Sentinel maintains a centralized view of what actions were taken, why they were taken, and how they fit into the broader incident narrative.

SOAR alignment with organizational and regulatory governance

Automation must operate within clearly defined governance boundaries. Response actions often involve privileged operations, access to sensitive data, or changes to production systems. Without appropriate controls, SOAR can introduce new risks even as it reduces response time.

Sentinel supports governance through role-based access control, managed identities, and audit logging. Playbooks can execute using least privilege identities, ensuring that automation has only the permissions required for its specific tasks. High-impact actions should require approval for high-risk scenarios, and all automated response activity must be auditable with execution context and outcome recorded. Regulatory and compliance considerations also shape SOAR design. Evidence collection, data handling, and notification procedures must align with legal obligations and internal policy. By integrating governance into automation from the outset, organizations ensure that SOAR strengthens security posture without undermining trust, accountability, or compliance.

With an automated response in place, the organization can react to incidents quickly and consistently. However, automation alone does not define operational maturity. Effective security operations also depend on well-designed human workflows that guide triage, investigation, escalation, and recovery. The next section focuses on designing and evaluating SOC security workflows that ensure incidents are handled predictably and effectively.

Designing and evaluating SOC security workflows

Security operations ultimately succeed or fail based on how effectively people, processes, and technology work together under pressure. Even with advanced detection and automation in place, poorly designed workflows lead to inconsistent outcomes, delayed responses, and missed escalation paths. A mature SOC relies on clearly defined workflows that guide analysts through investigation, containment, recovery, and post-incident improvement.

Well-designed SOC workflows ensure repeatability and accountability. They reduce uncertainty during incidents, preserve forensic integrity, and align operational actions with organizational and regulatory expectations. This section examines how to design and evaluate security workflows that support incident response, threat hunting, and ongoing incident management, ensuring that the SOC operates as a disciplined, resilient function rather than a reactive collection of tools. This section's content maps to the official SC-100 skill: *Design and evaluate security workflows, including incident response, threat hunting, and incident management.*

Establishing a clear incident lifecycle

Every security incident should follow a defined lifecycle that governs how it is identified, investigated, contained, and resolved. Without a structured lifecycle, analysts risk focusing on symptoms rather than root causes or taking actions that complicate recovery and investigation. A clear incident lifecycle provides the framework needed to make consistent, defensible decisions during high-pressure situations.

The lifecycle typically begins with triage, where alerts are validated and prioritized to separate genuine threats from noise. Confirmed incidents then progress to investigation, where analysts examine entities, timelines, and relationships to determine scope and impact. Containment actions limit further attacker activity, followed by eradication steps that remove persistence mechanisms. Recovery restores systems to a known-good state, and post-incident review captures lessons learned to improve future detection and response.

Operational efficiency improves fastest when lifecycle maturity is built-in a deliberate sequence. First, investigations must be supported by consistent, high-quality telemetry so analysts can establish scope without guesswork. Next, incident handling should be standardized, so triage, escalation, and evidence capture occur the same way every time. Only after these foundations are in place should automation be scaled, because automating an inconsistent workflow simply causes mistakes to happen faster. This sequencing ensures that process discipline precedes tooling acceleration. Organizations ensure incidents are handled methodically rather than reactively by enforcing this structured lifecycle and its order of operations. Each phase supports the next, reducing the risk of incomplete investigations, premature remediation, or loss of critical forensic evidence.

Operational maturity depends on clear handoffs as incidents move between triage, investigation, and specialized response. Tiered SOC models work only when responsibilities are explicit: initial triage validates alerts, confirms impact indicators, and gathers the first evidence package; deeper investigation expands scope, identifies affected entities, and determines containment strategy; specialized teams execute high-impact remediation and confirm recovery. Workflows should define the minimum evidence package that follows an incident, such as the incident timeline, affected identities and devices, key log references, containment actions taken, and any compliance-relevant indicators.

Where legal, compliance, or regulated data exposure may be involved, workflows must also define escalation triggers and early notification requirements. This prevents late-stage discovery of reporting obligations and ensures forensic integrity is maintained while decisions are made under pressure. The result is a SOC that behaves as a coordinated function rather than a collection of analysts responding in inconsistent ways.

Designing workflows that support coordinated analysis

Security incidents rarely involve a single signal or system. Effective investigations require analysts to correlate identity activity, endpoint behavior, application usage, cloud workload telemetry, and network data. SOC workflows must therefore support coordinated analysis across multiple domains rather than treating alerts in isolation.

A well-designed workflow encourages analysts to expand scope deliberately, identifying related accounts, affected resources, and potential lateral movement. Standardized investigation practices and shared tooling enable analysts to pivot efficiently between data sources without losing context. This coordination reduces duplication of effort and ensures that investigations reflect the full extent of an incident.

Clear ownership and escalation paths are also essential. When investigations cross functional boundaries, workflows define when and how to involve specialized teams such as identity governance, cloud operations, or legal and compliance. This prevents incidents from stalling due to unclear responsibilities and ensures timely decision-making.

Integrating threat hunting as a continuous practice

Threat hunting complements reactive incident response by proactively searching for adversary activity that has not yet triggered alerts. Rather than relying solely on automated detections, hunting activities explore hypotheses about how attackers might operate within the environment based on known tactics, emerging intelligence, or observed anomalies.

A mature SOC integrates threat hunting into its regular operations. Analysts develop hypotheses, query telemetry, and analyze patterns across identities, endpoints, applications, and workloads. Findings from hunting exercises feed directly into detection engineering, resulting in improved analytics and broader coverage over time. By embedding threat hunting into SOC workflows, organizations shift from a purely reactive posture to one that actively seeks out hidden threats. This continuous feedback loop strengthens detection capabilities and improves overall security maturity.

Sequencing response actions to preserve forensic integrity

Effective response depends not only on what actions are taken, but when they are taken. Immediate containment may prevent further damage, but it can also destroy volatile evidence if executed prematurely. Conversely, delaying containment may allow attackers to escalate privileges or exfiltrate data. SOC workflows must balance speed with forensic integrity.

A well-designed response sequence begins with stabilizing the environment and capturing relevant evidence, including logs, memory artifacts, and activity timelines. Containment actions such as account disablement, endpoint isolation, or network restriction should follow once sufficient evidence has been preserved. Eradication and recovery actions occur only after persistence mechanisms have been removed, and the environment is confirmed to be clean.

This disciplined sequencing supports both operational recovery and investigative requirements. It ensures that the organization can explain what occurred, satisfy regulatory obligations, and reduce the likelihood of recurrence.

Governing queue management, triage, and escalation

As alert volumes grow, effective queue management becomes critical to SOC performance. Workflows must define how alerts are classified, prioritized, and escalated to prevent analyst overload and ensure that critical incidents receive timely attention. Without clear triage rules, teams risk either overreacting to benign events or missing genuine threats.

Tiered SOC models support scalability by assigning responsibilities based on complexity and impact. Initial triage focuses on validating alerts and handling high-frequency, low-complexity events. More complex incidents are escalated to higher tiers with specialized expertise. Clear documentation and handover processes ensure continuity as incidents move through the pipeline. By governing queue management and escalation, organizations maintain a predictable operational rhythm. Incidents progress smoothly through investigation and resolution rather than accumulating in backlogs or being handled inconsistently.

Aligning investigation practices with organizational governance

SOC workflows must align with broader organizational governance, including legal, compliance, and regulatory requirements. Incidents involving sensitive data, regulated workloads, or legal exposure often require early involvement from oversight teams. Workflows should explicitly define when and how these stakeholders are engaged.

Governance also shapes evidence handling, data retention, and reporting obligations. Analysts must know which artifacts to preserve, how long to retain them, and how to document actions taken during an investigation. Aligning workflows with governance requirements reduces risk during audits and ensures that incident handling withstands external scrutiny. By embedding governance expectations directly into SOC workflows, organizations ensure that security operations remain consistent with policy and regulation even under pressure.

With disciplined workflows in place, the SOC can investigate and respond to incidents consistently. However, effective operations also depend on understanding whether detection coverage itself is sufficient. The final section examines how to evaluate and improve detection coverage using MITRE ATT&CK as a structured framework. Structured workflows ensure incidents are handled predictably, but their effectiveness assumes that meaningful threats are actually detected. Determining whether detection aligns with real adversary behavior, therefore, becomes the final test of operational maturity.

Threat detection coverage with MITRE ATT&CK

Effective security detection depends on understanding attacker behavior rather than reacting to isolated alerts. Modern adversaries move deliberately across identities, endpoints, applications, and infrastructure, adapting their techniques as they progress through an environment. Without a structured way to model this behavior, organizations struggle to assess whether their detection capabilities provide meaningful coverage or merely generate noise.

MITRE ATT&CK provides a common language for describing adversary tactics and techniques across different environments. By mapping detections and telemetry to ATT&CK matrices, security teams can evaluate coverage across the full attack lifecycle, identify blind spots, and prioritize improvements. Coverage is defensible only when required telemetry exists, detections are implemented, and techniques can be investigated and responded to reliably.

This section explores how ATT&CK can be used as a design and evaluation framework to ensure detection capabilities remain comprehensive across cloud, enterprise, mobile, and industrial environments. The section's content maps to the official SC-100 skill: *Design and evaluate threat detection coverage using MITRE ATT&CK matrices, including Cloud, Enterprise, Mobile, and industrial control systems (ICS).*

ATT&CK framework for evaluating detection coverage

MITRE ATT&CK organizes adversary behavior into tactics that represent phases of an attack and techniques that describe specific actions used to achieve those objectives. This structure allows security teams to reason about detection coverage in terms of attacker progression rather than individual alerts. Instead of asking whether a specific rule exists, teams evaluate whether they can observe and respond to behaviors associated with each phase of an intrusion.

Using ATT&CK as a framework shifts detection design from tool-centric to threat-centric. Telemetry sources are evaluated based on which tactics and techniques they can reveal, and gaps become visible when certain phases of the attack lifecycle lack reliable signals. This approach enables architects to assess whether detections align with real-world adversary behavior rather than theoretical threats.

ATT&CK becomes operationally useful when it is applied as a continuous improvement loop rather than a static mapping exercise. Architects begin by mapping required telemetry sources and existing detections to ATT&CK techniques, then identify coverage gaps where techniques cannot be observed reliably due to missing logs, incomplete onboarding, or insufficient analytics. Next, they close those gaps by enabling telemetry, standardizing ingestion, and implementing detections aligned to the techniques that matter most for the environment's threat profile. Finally, they validate coverage through threat hunting, incident retrospectives, and detection tuning, then repeat the cycle as the environment and adversary behaviors evolve. This approach makes coverage claims defensible. A technique is only covered when the required telemetry exists, is retained, and produces detection logic that reliably supports investigation and response. By tying ATT&CK mapping directly to telemetry enablement and detection engineering, organizations avoid paper coverage that collapses during real incidents.

Mapping cloud telemetry to ATT&CK tactics

Cloud environments introduce attack techniques that differ from traditional on-premises models. Control plane abuse, API misuse, token theft, and exploitation of misconfigured services are common paths for cloud-native attacks. Mapping cloud telemetry to ATT&CK cloud matrices ensures these behaviors are explicitly considered during detection design.

Effective mapping requires consistent ingestion of control plane logs, workload diagnostics, identity events, and network telemetry. Behavioral analytics from cloud-native protections enrich these signals by highlighting anomalies in authentication, privilege use, and resource interaction. When these signals are aligned to ATT&CK tactics, security teams can determine whether reconnaissance, persistence, lateral movement, or exfiltration attempts are observable within their environment.

This mapping process also highlights areas where additional instrumentation or configuration is required. If certain attacker behaviors cannot be detected due to missing logs or insufficient analytics, those gaps become clear inputs into architectural and operational improvements.

Coverage across identities, endpoints, applications, and infrastructure

Modern attacks rarely remain confined to a single layer. A compromised identity may be used to access applications, pivot to endpoints, and manipulate cloud infrastructure. Designing detection coverage, therefore, requires correlating telemetry across identities, devices, applications, and platforms rather than treating each domain independently.

Identity telemetry reveals authentication patterns, privilege escalation, and anomalous access. Endpoint signals expose process behavior, credential misuse, and lateral movement. Application and SaaS telemetry highlights data access anomalies and suspicious interactions, while infrastructure logs provide insight into configuration changes and network activity. Mapping these signals collectively to ATT&CK ensures that detections reflect how attackers actually move through environments. When detection logic aligns across these layers, security teams can evaluate not only whether a technique is detectable, but whether it is detectable with sufficient context to support investigation and response.

Identifying gaps and guiding detection engineering

Evaluating detection coverage against ATT&CK often reveals uneven visibility across tactics and techniques. Some phases of an attack may be well covered, while others lack reliable telemetry or analytics. These gaps are not failures; they are indicators of where detection engineering and architectural adjustments are needed.

Gap analysis guides decisions such as enabling additional logging, onboarding workloads into security monitoring platforms, refining analytics, or adjusting identity governance. By prioritizing gaps based on attacker impact and likelihood, organizations can improve detection maturity in a structured and measurable way. This continuous evaluation process ensures that detection capabilities evolve alongside attacker techniques rather than remaining static. ATT&CK becomes a living reference that informs ongoing improvement rather than a one-time assessment.

Applying ATT&CK to incident response and threat hunting

ATT&CK is not only a design time framework but also an operational tool. During incident response, analysts use ATT&CK to understand which phases of an attack have occurred and to anticipate likely next steps. This helps guide containment and eradication decisions by focusing on probable attacker behavior rather than isolated indicators.

In threat hunting, ATT&CK provides a hypothesis-driven approach. Analysts select specific techniques or tactics and search telemetry for evidence of those behaviors, even in the absence of alerts. Findings from these hunts inform detection improvements and strengthen coverage over time. By embedding ATT&CK into both response and hunting workflows, organizations ensure that detection remains aligned with real adversary tradecraft. This integration supports proactive defense and continuous improvement across all monitored environments.

Organizations gain a clear understanding of where their security operations are resilient and where gaps remain by evaluating detection against attacker tactics rather than isolated alerts. This threat-informed perspective ties operational design back to measurable defensive outcomes.

Conclusion

This chapter explained how modern security operations must be designed as an integrated architecture rather than assembled as disconnected tools. It showed how Microsoft Defender XDR provides deep behavioral analytics across identities, endpoints, email, SaaS, and cloud workloads, while Microsoft Sentinel provides the SIEM foundation that centralizes telemetry, correlates signals, and governs incident lifecycles across the wider environment. Together, these layers enable security teams to move from isolated alerts to coherent incident narratives, improving investigation quality and reducing operational fragmentation.

The chapter then established why centralized logging and auditing are foundational to both detection and accountability. It described how Azure diagnostic telemetry, workload logs, and Microsoft Purview Audit activity records must be collected, retained, and governed so investigations can reconstruct events reliably across Microsoft 365, Azure, and connected systems. By designing workspace boundaries, access controls, and ingestion strategies deliberately, organizations can preserve investigative effectiveness while maintaining least privilege and regulatory alignment.

Additionally, the chapter addressed monitoring design for hybrid and multi-cloud estates, where visibility gaps most often emerge. It explained how Azure Arc and Defender for Cloud extend monitoring and posture management beyond Azure, and how Sentinel provides a unified correlation and investigation surface across cloud providers and on-premises systems. This approach ensures monitoring standards remain consistent as environments scale across regions, tenants, and operational teams, preventing secondary platforms from becoming blind spots.

The chapter also examined how SOAR converts detection into predictable, governed action at scale. It clarified the roles of Sentinel automation rules and Logic Apps playbooks in orchestrating response workflows, and how Defender XDR enables workload-proximate containment actions while Sentinel coordinates incident governance and auditability. By embedding approvals, least privilege execution, and traceable run history into automation, organizations can reduce MTTR without sacrificing control.

Finally, the chapter positioned SOC workflows and MITRE ATT&CK coverage as the mechanisms that turn tooling into sustained operational maturity. It described how disciplined incident lifecycles, coordinated analysis practices, and continuous threat hunting create repeatable outcomes under pressure. By using MITRE ATT&CK to map telemetry and detections to adversary behavior, teams can identify coverage gaps, prioritize detection engineering, and continuously improve security operations across cloud, enterprise, mobile, and ICS environments.

The next chapter moves from detection, investigation, and response into the identity layer that underpins all secure access decisions. It examines how authentication, authorization, and policy-based access controls enforce Zero Trust, reduce attack paths, and limit blast radius across cloud, hybrid, and multi-cloud environments.

Questions

Success on any assessment depends on understanding the underlying technologies, concepts, and principles rather than memorizing facts. The following questions help readers confirm that they can apply this chapter's ideas in realistic design scenarios, including XDR and SIEM design, centralized logging and auditing, hybrid and multi-cloud monitoring, SOAR orchestration, SOC workflow maturity, and threat-informed detection coverage using MITRE ATT&CK.

1. **An organization wants deep behavioral detections across identities, endpoints, email, SaaS, and cloud workloads, while also maintaining a single incident management and correlation plane across the entire enterprise. Which design best achieves this outcome?**
   a. Use a SIEM only and disable XDR alerts to avoid duplicates
   b. Use Defender XDR for behavioral analytics and Sentinel as the centralized SIEM and incident platform
   c. Use endpoint EDR only and forward summary alerts by email to the SOC
   d. Use only native cloud provider tools in each environment to reduce integration effort
2. **Why is integrating XDR with a SIEM considered an architectural requirement rather than a tooling preference?**
   a. It eliminates the need for governance and compliance controls
   b. It ensures depth-and-breadth visibility, so alerts become correlated incident narratives instead of isolated signals

c. It prevents the need for log retention

d. It guarantees that all incidents can be remediated automatically without human review

3. **In a hybrid environment, which design choice best ensures identity-centric attacks originating from on-premises Active Directory are detected and investigated in the same operational plane as cloud and endpoint activity?**

a. Collect only firewall logs into the SIEM to reduce cost

b. Onboard domain controllers into Defender for Identity and integrate the resulting identity security signals into Sentinel

c. Disable identity alerts and rely on manual AD review

d. Use Microsoft Purview Audit as the primary source for AD changes

4. **An organization needs to ingest firewall and network device logs into Sentinel in a resilient, supportable way that avoids brittle point integrations. Which approach best fits?**

a. Copy device logs manually into CSV files for upload

b. Forward events using CEF to a Syslog collector and ingest into Sentinel

c. Send device logs only to local storage on the firewall

d. Use email forwarding of alerts to the SOC mailbox

5. **Why is centralized logging and auditing required for incident reconstruction and compliance, not just for detection?**

a. Because it reduces the need for investigations

b. Because it creates an authoritative, retained record of control plane actions and user/admin activity across the service

c. Because it replaces incident response procedures

d. Because it automatically prevents data loss

6. **Which statement best describes the role of Microsoft Purview Audit in a security operations architecture?**

a. It replaces SIEM correlation by generating incidents directly for all threats

b. It provides authoritative Microsoft 365 user and admin activity records that support investigations and accountability

c. It is primarily used to store endpoint telemetry for EDR detections

d. It is only relevant for performance monitoring

7. **An organization wants to centralize telemetry but must prevent unrestricted access to logs across teams while preserving SOC investigative effectiveness. What design principle best addresses this?**
   a. Store all logs in a single workspace and grant global reader access
   b. Use workspace boundaries and role-based access controls aligned to security vs operations consumption needs
   c. Disable audit logging and rely on alerts
   d. Send all logs only to the operations team to avoid SOC access
8. **Why is monitoring design for hybrid and multi-cloud environments a distinct architectural concern compared to monitoring Azure-only environments?**
   a. Because multi-cloud platforms do not generate security telemetry
   b. Because different control planes and log formats can create blind spots unless telemetry is normalized and correlated centrally
   c. Because SIEMs cannot ingest third-party logs
   d. Because XDR cannot detect threats outside Microsoft 365
9. **Which Microsoft capability most directly enables non-Azure servers and Kubernetes clusters to participate in Azure governance and monitoring patterns?**
   a. Azure Front Door
   b. Azure Arc
   c. Microsoft Purview Information Protection
   d. Microsoft Defender for Office 365
10. **What is the most accurate description of SOAR design within the Microsoft AWS security ecosystem?**
   a. SOAR is a feature of Defender XDR only and does not involve Sentinel
   b. Sentinel coordinates automation rules and playbooks, while Defender XDR contributes high-context detections and workload-level response actions
   c. SOAR replaces the need for incident response workflows
   d. SOAR should execute all responses automatically with no approvals to maximize speed

Answers

1. b: Use Defender XDR for behavioral analytics and Sentinel as the centralized SIEM and incident platform.

   Defender XDR provides depth across Microsoft security domains, while Sentinel provides the SIEM correlation and incident management plane that unifies signals into coherent investigations.

2. b: It ensures depth-and-breadth visibility, so alerts become correlated incident narratives instead of isolated signals.

   XDR provides deep behavioral detections, but SIEM correlation and governance are required to connect signals across the whole estate and run consistent incident workflows.

3. b: Onboard domain controllers into Defender for Identity and integrate the resulting identity security signals into Sentinel.

   This ensures on-premises identity attack indicators become part of the same incident queue and investigation context as cloud and endpoint activity.

4. b: Forward events using CEF to a Syslog collector and ingest into Sentinel.

   Using standard formats and a collector pattern provides resilient ingestion and avoids brittle, one-off integrations.

5. b: It is because it creates an authoritative, retained record of control plane actions and user/admin activity across services.

   Centralized logging and auditing ensure investigations can reconstruct timelines and meet compliance or forensic requirements beyond real-time detection needs.

6. b: It provides authoritative Microsoft 365 user and admin activity records that support investigations and accountability.

   Purview Audit captures activity that is often essential for reconstructing user-driven actions in Microsoft 365 during investigations.

7. b: Use workspace boundaries and role-based access controls aligned to security vs operations consumption needs.

   Centralization must still enforce least privilege; deliberate workspace and access design preserves SOC capability while limiting unnecessary exposure.

8. b: It is because different control planes and log formats can create blind spots unless telemetry is normalized and correlated centrally.

   Hybrid and multi-cloud environments introduce inconsistent telemetry sources; a designed approach is needed to maintain end-to-end visibility and correlation.

9. b: Azure Arc.

   Azure Arc projects non-Azure resources into the Azure control plane, enabling consistent governance, assessment, and monitoring patterns.

10. b: Sentinel coordinates automation rules and playbooks, while Defender XDR contributes high-context detections and workload-level response actions.

    This design balances centralized orchestration with fast, workload-proximate containment, while keeping response actions visible and auditable.

Chapter 5
Design Identity and Access Control Solutions

Introduction

Identity is the primary control plane of modern security architecture. As organizations adopt cloud services platforms, hybrid environments, and **artificial intelligence** (AI)-enabled workloads and tools, traditional network-based security models are no longer sufficient; access decisions must instead be driven by identity, context, device posture, and risk signals, enforced consistently across users, devices, and workloads.

This chapter focuses on designing secure, scalable **identity and access management** (**IAM**) solutions using Microsoft Entra ID as the foundation of a Zero Trust architecture. It explains how to control access to **software as a service** (**SaaS**), **platform as a service** (**PaaS**), **infrastructure as a service** (**IaaS**), hybrid, and multi-cloud resources using identity-centric policies rather than network trust. It also explores modern authentication and authorization strategies, including Conditional Access, **Continuous Access Evaluation** (**CAE**), and risk-based controls, and shows how these mechanisms enforce least privilege while remaining adaptive to changing threat conditions.

Readers will also learn how to design identity solutions for external users through **business-to-business** (**B2B**), **business-to-customer** (**B2C**), and decentralized identity models; harden **Active Directory Domain Services** (**AD DS**) in hybrid environments; and manage secrets, keys, and certificates securely using Azure-native services. Together, these capabilities enable organizations to protect identities, reduce attack surfaces, and enforce auditable, policy-driven access across the enterprise.

To reduce abstraction, the following sections include short design scenarios that contrast ineffective and effective access control patterns.

Structure

This chapter covers the following topics:

- Access control for cloud and hybrid resources
- Microsoft Entra ID for hybrid identity

- External identities and decentralized identity
- Modern authentication and authorization with Conditional Access
- Validating Conditional Access for Zero Trust
- Hardening AD DS
- Secrets, keys, and certificates management

Objectives

This chapter covers the skills required to design secure access solutions across SaaS, PaaS, IaaS, and hybrid or on-premises environments, as well as multi-cloud platforms. It examines how identity, networking, and application controls work together to enforce consistent access boundaries regardless of where resources are hosted.

The chapter explores how to design identity solutions using Microsoft Entra ID across cloud-native, hybrid, and multi-cloud environments, ensuring authentication and authorization decisions remain centralized and policy-driven. It also addresses how to design secure access for external identities, including B2B, B2C, and decentralized identity scenarios, while maintaining governance and visibility.

In addition, the chapter examines how to design a modern authentication and authorization strategy using Conditional Access, continuous access evaluation, risk scoring, and protected actions to adapt access decisions to user, device, and session risk. It evaluates how Conditional Access policies align with a Zero Trust strategy, ensuring access is continuously verified rather than implicitly trusted.

Finally, the chapter covers how to specify requirements to harden AD DS and how to design solutions for managing secrets, keys, and certificates, ensuring sensitive credentials are protected throughout their lifecycle and integrated securely into identity and access architectures.

These skills fall under the exam domain, *Design security operations, identity, and compliance capabilities,* which represent approximately 25-30 % of the overall SC-100 skills[1] measured.

Access control for cloud and hybrid resources

Access control is the point at which security architecture either coheres into an integrated system or fragments into exceptions and segmentation. In modern enterprises and organizations, users, applications, and administrators operate across SaaS platforms, public cloud infrastructure, and on-premises systems without regard for where a resource being accessed physically resides. When access is designed differently for each of these

1 **https://learn.microsoft.com/en-us/credentials/certifications/resources/study-guides/sc-100**

environments, enforcement becomes inconsistent, segmented, and isolated, with the weakest control becoming the effective security boundary.

Microsoft's Zero Trust model reframes access as a single, identity-driven decision process. Trust is no longer derived from network placement or infrastructure location, but from identity, device state, and contextual risk that is continuously evaluated.

Identity, therefore, becomes the primary control plane for access across public cloud and hybrid resources, while networking and application controls exist to support, not replace, that decision. While identity and Conditional Access form the primary enforcement layer for access decisions, effective access design must also account for permission sprawl within cloud platforms themselves.

Where organizations must govern permissions inside non-Microsoft cloud platforms, Microsoft Entra Permissions Management provides a **cloud infrastructure entitlements management** (**CIEM**) layer that continuously discovers, analyzes, and right-sizes cloud permissions. In this chapter, it is treated as a boundary-adjacent control that complements Entra ID and Conditional Access by reducing excessive cloud entitlements that identity policies alone cannot remediate.

This section maps to the following SC-100 skills measured: *Design a solution for access to SaaS, PaaS, IaaS, hybrid/on-premises, and multi-cloud resources, including identity, networking, and application controls.*

Identity-centric access across resource types

Access controls across SaaS, PaaS, and infrastructure evolved independently over time. SaaS platforms adopted identity early, platform services layered permissions on top, and infrastructure access remained anchored to networks and credentials. These parallel models introduce inconsistency and make it difficult to express security intent uniformly across computing models and environments.

Identity as the primary control plane

Fragmented access control is the defining weakness of hybrid environments. A common response is to extend network trust outward through **virtual private networks** (**VPNs**), trusted **Internet Protocol** (**IP**) ranges, or firewall exceptions. This approach scales poorly and ties trust to infrastructure topology that changes constantly; it also cannot evaluate modern security signals such as device state, user risk, or session integrity.

Centralizing access decisions in Microsoft Entra ID resolves this fragmentation. Conditional Access, role assignments, and session controls are defined once and enforced consistently across SaaS, PaaS, and infrastructure resources; networking remains relevant for traffic flow, but it no longer defines trust. Trust is established through identity.

The following diagram illustrates how Microsoft Entra ID acts as the central identity control plane across hybrid, SaaS, and multi-cloud environments:

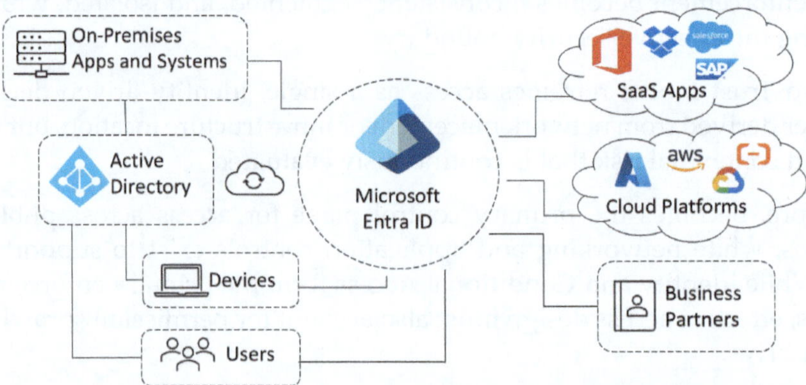

Figure 5.1: Microsoft Entra ID as the central identity control plane

By centralizing identity and access decisions, organizations ensure consistent policy enforcement regardless of where resources or users are located.

Firewalls, IP allowlists, and private endpoints still reduce exposure, but they cannot authenticate users or adapt to changing risk; they control where traffic can go, not who is allowed access or under what conditions. In a Zero Trust design, network controls are supporting safeguards, not primary access decisions.

Named locations fit into this model as a policy signal, not a trust boundary. A trusted location can reduce friction for known corporate networks, but it must never become an implicit allow rule. Location can contribute to risk evaluation, while identity and device controls remain the basis of authorization.

Removing network-based trust assumptions

Network location has traditionally implied trust; internal IP ranges, corporate offices, and private connectivity were assumed to reduce risk. In hybrid and multi-cloud environments, this assumption routinely fails. compromised systems often reside inside trusted networks, while legitimate users increasingly connect from unmanaged or external locations.

Zero Trust deliberately weakens the role of network location; location may contribute to risk evaluation, but it cannot grant access on its own. Instead, access is governed through a policy-driven model, where each request is evaluated against defined controls using identity signals, device posture, and contextual risk. This ensures that access decisions remain consistent and valid as users, devices, and environments change.

This policy-driven approach applies regardless of where workloads run. Whether applications are hosted in Azure, another public cloud, or a private datacenter, identity remains the core control plane through which these policies are enforced, even as network boundaries vary.

Enforcing secure access to infrastructure

Infrastructure access carries disproportionate risk because administrative actions can bypass application-level protections entirely. Securing this access depends on how administrative control is granted and where trust is enforced, rather than on network reachability alone.

Identity-based access to virtual machines and PaaS

Administrative access to infrastructure is inherently high-impact. Traditional approaches rely on exposed management ports, shared credentials, or static allowlists, controls that degrade over time and are difficult to audit.

In Azure environments, this design is expressed by preferring identity-based login mechanisms over workload-based or local credentials wherever supported. For users accessing cloud platforms and resources that authenticate using their Entra identities, access is governed by role assignments and Conditional Access policies, which enforce **multi-factor authentication (MFA)**, device compliance, and risk-based controls; this access then becomes a policy decision rather than a static configuration state.

Eliminating direct exposure of management endpoints

Exposed management endpoints such as **Remote Desktop Protocol (RDP)**, **Secure Shell (SSH)**, or administrative **application programming interfaces (APIs)** create a persistent attack surface. These endpoints are often opened temporarily and forgotten, leaving long-lived access paths guarded by brittle controls.

In practice, this means removing public exposure of management ports and brokering access through identity-aware entry points. Access is granted only after identity authentication and policy evaluation, ensuring that management connectivity is conditional, auditable, and time-bound. This approach reduces the attack surface while preserving administrative capability without relying on persistent network trust.

Secure access designs interpose identity-aware services between users and infrastructure. Authentication and policy evaluation occur before any connection is established, minimizing exposed ports and reducing reliance on firewall exceptions. Every access attempt is attributable to an identity and evaluated against the current policy.

Unified access to SaaS and internet resources

Once access is unified across platforms and resources, the remaining challenge is ensuring that all access decisions are made by authoritative identity systems.

As organizations adopt more SaaS and public internet-facing services, access control must extend beyond private infrastructure without creating parallel enforcement models that undermine consistency.

Controlling SaaS access with Entra-based enforcement

SaaS platforms often sit outside traditional security boundaries, leading organizations to treat them as exceptions rather than first-class resources. This creates uneven enforcement where externally hosted applications are less protected than internal systems.

Microsoft Entra ID enables centralized governance of SaaS access by enforcing Conditional Access at authentication time. Users must meet security requirements, such as MFA or a compliant device state, before accessing corporate data, regardless of where the application is hosted. This consistency prevents shadow access paths created when users choose less-protected applications to bypass controls.

Consistent internet and private apps access policies

Unified access requires distinguishing between internet-bound destinations and private enterprise applications while enforcing identity-based policy consistently across both; Microsoft **Global Secure Access** (**GSA**) makes this distinction explicit.

GSA's Entra Internet Access is used when the destination is a public SaaS application or web service, and the objective is to govern outbound access using identity and Conditional Access, while GSA's Entra Private Access is used when the destination is an internal application that must remain undiscoverable and not be exposed publicly; these capabilities are not interchangeable, and neither replaces the other.

Mature designs commonly require both. Entra Internet Access governs how identities reach SaaS and web destinations, while Entra Private Access brokers identity-based access to internal applications without traditional VPN dependency. The decision is driven by access intent, not network location.

A common design failure is securing cloud and on-premises resources differently based on where they are hosted, relying on VPNs, trusted networks, or bespoke controls for each platform. This fragments enforcement and makes the weakest environment the effective security boundary. A stronger design centralizes access decisions in the identity control plane, applying the same Conditional Access, role assignment, and session policies regardless of whether a resource is SaaS, PaaS, IaaS, or on-premises. This ensures access intent is expressed once and enforced consistently everywhere.

Microsoft Entra ID for hybrid identity

Hybrid identity rarely begins as a deliberate architectural choice; most organizations inherit Active Directory forests, legacy authentication protocols, and operational practices shaped by on-premises constraints. The security risk emerges when those inherited patterns are allowed to define modern access decisions. A secure hybrid identity design requires clear authority, deliberate containment of legacy dependencies, and consistent policy enforcement across environments.

Microsoft Entra ID is designed to serve as the authoritative identity control plane, even when on-premises directories continue to exist. Hybrid identity is therefore a managed condition, not an end state, and successful designs steadily reduce reliance on legacy systems while preserving operational continuity. This section maps to the SC-100 skills measured: *Design a solution for Microsoft Entra ID, including hybrid and multi-cloud environments.*

Core Entra ID architecture

Hybrid environments fail most often when identity authority is ambiguous. When authentication and authorization decisions are split across platforms, security controls behave inconsistently, and modern protections lose effectiveness. Establishing a single authoritative control plane is the prerequisite for applying Conditional Access, risk evaluation, and session enforcement consistently across public cloud and hybrid resources.

Entra ID as the central identity authority

A common design instinct is to retain Active Directory as the primary authority and treat Entra ID as an extension for cloud access. While familiar, this approach limits the organization's ability to apply modern security controls uniformly; access decisions depend on where authentication occurs, creating uneven enforcement and blind spots.

Microsoft's intended design is explicit; Entra ID becomes the authoritative source for authentication, authorization, and policy evaluation. Identities may originate on-premises, but access decisions occur in Entra ID. Synchronization exists to project identities forward, not to preserve parallel control planes. Once authority is centralized, Conditional Access and identity risk signals apply consistently across cloud and hybrid resources.

Cloud-native protections such as smart lockout strengthen this model by reducing password-spray and brute-force effectiveness at the identity control plane. Smart lockout is not a substitute for strong authentication, but it provides a resilient control that operates even when attackers target sign-in endpoints at scale.

Reducing dependence on legacy identity systems

A secure hybrid design contains legacy dependencies rather than extending them. Legacy identity systems persist because applications depend on them, not because they provide stronger security. Replicating these systems in cloud infrastructure recreates their risks while increasing operational complexity.

Modern authentication flows are absorbed into Entra ID, while legacy protocols are restricted to the smallest possible scope. Over time, this reduces the blast radius of legacy systems and prevents them from defining the organization's security posture.

Where identities and groups are synchronized from on-premises directories, governance must still be enforced at the Entra control plane. Synchronization can populate identities and attributes, but governance decisions, such as access assignment, review, and entitlement control, must remain deliberate and auditable in Entra to prevent inherited membership from becoming unmanaged privilege.

Supporting hybrid and legacy workloads

Hybrid identity introduces unavoidable trade-offs between compatibility, resilience, and attack surface. Decisions about synchronization models and legacy protocol support determine whether identity remains resilient during outages and whether modern controls can continue to function when parts of the environment are compromised.

Synchronization and hybrid identity considerations

Synchronization is not merely a connectivity decision; it defines where identity authority resides during failure conditions. Designs that rely heavily on on-premises components introduce dependencies that can disable cloud-based protections during outages or attacks. Architectures that minimize reliance on local infrastructure align more closely with Zero Trust principles. By keeping Entra ID authoritative even when on-premises systems are unavailable, access policies, risk evaluation, and enforcement continue to operate when they are most needed.

Where users must access private, on-premises applications, secure designs avoid expanding network trust simply to make the app reachable. Publishing apps through identity-aware access mechanisms (such as Microsoft GSA) enables Conditional Access, MFA, and session controls without requiring broad VPN connectivity; this preserves Zero Trust intent by making application access a policy decision rather than a network placement assumption.

Common hybrid sign-in patterns introduce different levels of dependency and resilience. Designs that minimize reliance on real-time on-premises authentication components reduce the risk of sign-in failure during outages and simplify the enforcement of modern controls. From a Zero Trust perspective, authentication paths that remain functional when on-premises infrastructure is unavailable provide stronger security continuity.

Entra Domain Services for legacy protocol support

A critical decision arises when legacy applications require **Lightweight Directory Access Protocol** (LDAP), Kerberos, or **New Technology Local Area Network Manager** (NTLM) authentication but must operate in cloud environments. Extending domain controllers into infrastructure preserves compatibility but recreates the full administrative and security burden of AD DS, including patching, privilege exposure, and lateral-movement risk.

Entra Domain Services provides a constrained alternative; it supports legacy authentication protocols without exposing domain controller administration and without re-establishing Active Directory as the primary authority.

The design intent is containment; Entra ID handles modern authentication, while Entra Domain Services absorbs unavoidable legacy dependencies. Infrastructure-based domain controllers should be deployed only when full domain control is explicitly required.

Identity threat detection in hybrid environments

Hybrid identity expands the attack surface by combining cloud authentication paths with on-premises credential exposure. Effective security depends on detecting identity threats wherever they originate and ensuring that detection directly influences access decisions.

Monitoring on-premises identity signals

Relying solely on cloud-based telemetry leaves blind spots when authentication still occurs on-premises. Credential theft, misconfiguration, and privilege abuse often originate in the directory layer before affecting cloud access.

Secure hybrid designs integrate on-premises identity telemetry with cloud-based risk evaluation so that suspicious activity detected locally can immediately influence access decisions. Signals originating from directory activity must feed into centralized risk assessment, ensuring that identity compromise detected on-premises results in enforced controls such as access restriction, reauthentication, or session revocation.

Detecting and responding to identity-based attacks

Detection without enforcement is insufficient. Identity risk signals must translate directly into access restrictions, challenges, or revocation. When compromise is suspected, access should degrade immediately, even for active sessions.

Effective response requires that detection outcomes directly affect authorization and session state. When identity compromise is suspected, enforcement mechanisms must reduce access immediately rather than waiting for manual intervention. This coupling ensures that detection shortens attacker dwell time instead of merely generating alerts.

A common hybrid identity failure is allowing the authentication authority to remain split between on-premises directories and cloud identity platforms. This creates inconsistent enforcement, limits the effectiveness of Conditional Access, and preserves legacy weaknesses as implicit trust anchors. A stronger design establishes Microsoft Entra ID as the authoritative control plane for authentication, authorization, and risk evaluation, while on-premises directories are limited to legacy compatibility roles. This ensures that modern identity protections apply consistently, even when parts of the environment are compromised or unavailable.

External identities and decentralized identity

External identities expand the security boundary beyond the organization's direct control; partners, suppliers, customers, and individual users authenticate from unmanaged environments, often using credentials issued by other identity providers. The architectural challenge is not enabling access, but governing access without importing external risk into the tenant. Poorly designed external identity solutions create long-lived guest accounts, inconsistent controls, and opaque access paths that are difficult to audit or revoke.

Microsoft Entra ID provides distinct models for external identity scenarios. Each model exists to solve a specific trust problem, and selecting the wrong one introduces either excessive friction or unnecessary exposure. This section maps to the SC-100 skills measured: *Design a solution for external identities, including B2B, B2C, and decentralized identity.*

B2B collaboration

B2B collaboration addresses scenarios where external users require access to internal resources such as applications, data, or administrative workflows. The design goal is to enable collaboration while ensuring that external users remain subject to the same governance expectations as internal identities.

Guest access vs. cross-tenant access

Traditional guest access creates local representations of external users inside the tenant. While simple to implement, unmanaged guest sprawl leads to stale accounts, excessive permissions, and weak lifecycle controls. Over time, guest identities become indistinguishable from internal users in terms of risk.

Cross-tenant access provides a more controlled alternative. Instead of creating unmanaged guests, access is governed through explicit trust relationships between tenants. Authentication occurs in the external tenant, while authorization is evaluated locally. This preserves identity ownership, enables consistent policy enforcement, and reduces the accumulation of unmanaged accounts.

The decision is clear: use guest access for small-scale or short-term collaboration, and use cross-tenant access when ongoing or large-scale partner relationships require governance, visibility, and lifecycle control.

When the scenario involves consuming a partner's multi-tenant application, access is established by creating an enterprise application (service principal) in the consuming tenant. The application registration remains owned by the publishing tenant, while the consuming tenant instantiates and governs its local service principal, applying Conditional Access, assignment, and lifecycle controls without taking ownership of the app itself.

Governing external access with entitlement management

External access without lifecycle governance inevitably becomes permanent. Entitlement management addresses this by making access time-bound, reviewable, and request-driven. Instead of granting direct permissions, access is packaged and assigned deliberately.

Access packages define what external users can access, how long access lasts, and who must approve it. Periodic access reviews ensure that access remains justified. This shifts external collaboration from an ad-hoc activity to a governed process, reducing both operational overhead and security risk.

B2C identity

Customer identity introduces fundamentally different requirements from workforce identity. Customers authenticate at scale, from unmanaged devices, and expect seamless experiences. Applying workforce identity controls directly to customer scenarios creates friction and limits scalability.

Separating workforce and customer identity

A critical architectural decision is whether to mix customer identities with workforce identities. Doing so blurs trust boundaries and complicates policy enforcement. Workforce controls such as Conditional Access, device compliance, and role assignment are not designed for anonymous or high-volume customer populations.

Microsoft Entra ID for customers provides a dedicated identity plane for external users who are not part of the organization's workforce. This separation preserves security boundaries, simplifies policy design, and prevents customer identities from inheriting internal privileges or access paths.

Federation and social identity providers

Customer identity systems often rely on federation with external identity providers, such as social platforms or consumer identity services. Federation reduces credential management overhead and improves user experience, but it also shifts part of the authentication trust outside the organization.

While federation simplifies authentication, it does not transfer responsibility for access control. Authentication assurance varies by provider, but authorization decisions remain local and must be enforced consistently through application and identity policy. This separation ensures that external authentication convenience does not dilute internal security requirements.

Decentralized identity

Decentralized identity introduces a different trust model. Instead of authenticating users through a central directory, users present verifiable credentials issued by trusted authorities. This model reduces reliance on shared identifiers and minimizes data disclosure.

While decentralized identity reduces data exposure in specific scenarios, most enterprise access still relies on directory-based identity, where authentication strength and continuous enforcement must be designed deliberately.

Using verifiable credentials for selective disclosure

Verifiable credentials enable users to prove specific attributes without revealing full identity details. This is particularly valuable in scenarios where privacy, regulatory constraints, or minimal disclosure requirements apply.

Decentralized identity is not a replacement for directory-based identity. It is a complementary model used where traditional authentication introduces unnecessary data exposure. The decision to use verifiable credentials should be driven by privacy requirements and the need to reduce stored identity data.

A common external identity design failure is treating all non-employees the same, using unmanaged guest accounts or workforce identity controls regardless of context. This leads to guest sprawl, weak lifecycle governance, and inappropriate policy inheritance. A stronger design selects the external identity model deliberately: cross-tenant access for governed partner collaboration, dedicated customer identity for consumer scenarios, and decentralized identity only where selective disclosure is required. This preserves clear trust boundaries while keeping access auditable, reviewable, and revocable.

Modern authentication and authorization with Conditional Access

Modern authentication assumes that compromise is possible at any time; credentials are stolen, devices drift out of compliance, and user behavior changes mid-session. Access models that treat authentication as a one-time event inevitably leave long windows of exposure. A modern strategy combines strong authentication with continuous evaluation and explicit control over sensitive actions.

Microsoft Entra ID implements this model by separating authentication, authorization, and session enforcement, allowing access decisions to evolve as risk changes rather than remaining fixed after sign-in. This section maps to the SC-100 skills measured: *Design a modern authentication and authorization strategy, including Conditional Access, continuous access evaluation, risk scoring, and protected actions.*

Conditional Access as the core policy engine

Conditional Access is the mechanism through which modern identity signals are translated into enforceable access decisions. It evaluates contextual information at sign-in and determines whether access should be allowed, denied, or constrained.

To understand how Conditional Access evaluates these signals during an access attempt, consider the following model:

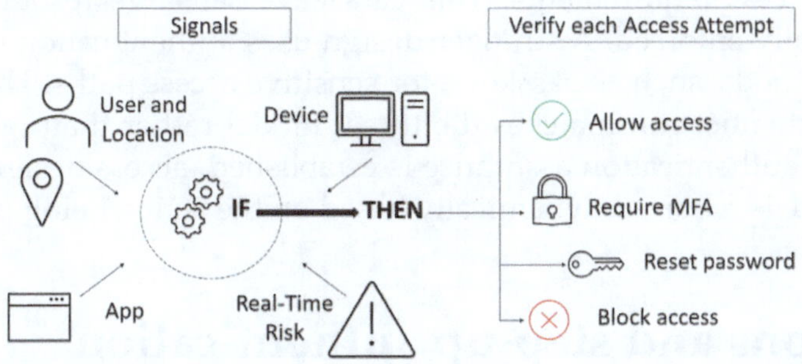

Figure 5.2: Conditional Access decision flow in Microsoft Entra ID

Conditional Access policies apply this evaluation in real-time, enforcing controls such as MFA, requiring compliant devices, or blocking access based on defined conditions.

Contextual and risk-based access decisions

Conditional Access policies evaluate signals such as user risk, device compliance, location, and application sensitivity. These signals allow access requirements to scale dynamically. Low-risk scenarios may permit seamless access, while elevated risk triggers additional verification or blocks access entirely. The architectural decision is to apply Conditional Access broadly rather than selectively. Limiting policies to high-risk applications creates inconsistent enforcement and predictable bypass paths. Modern designs establish baseline policies that apply to all access, with additional controls layered on where risk or sensitivity increases.

A common design mistake is applying Conditional Access only to a small set of high-risk applications while leaving broad access paths unprotected. This creates inconsistent enforcement and predictable bypass paths. A more effective design establishes baseline Conditional Access policies that apply to all access, with stronger requirements layered dynamically based on risk, sensitivity, or action being performed. This ensures access decisions are consistent, auditable, and resilient to changes in application usage or attacker behavior.

Strong authentication should be expressed as authentication strength, not as a generic require MFA statement. Different authentication methods provide different assurance levels, and sensitive access paths increasingly require phishing-resistant options. Using authentication strength ensures policies match the assurance required by the resource and the threat model, rather than accepting any method that happens to satisfy MFA.

This design direction aligns with the industry shift toward phishing-resistant authentication, including FIDO2-based passkeys. Using authentication strengths to require passkeys for sensitive access paths supports passwordless momentum while keeping requirements explicit, testable, and enforceable through Conditional Access.

An ineffective design treats all MFA methods as equivalent, allowing low-assurance factors to satisfy high-risk access requirements. This can leave sensitive resources exposed even when MFA is technically enforced. A stronger design uses authentication strength to require phishing-resistant methods, such as passkeys, for sensitive access paths. This ensures that the assurance level of authentication matches the threat model rather than relying on a generic MFA checkbox. Once authentication assurance is established, access design must also define when higher assurance is required dynamically based on the action being performed, not just the initial sign-in.

Protected actions and step-up authentication

Not all actions carry equal risk. Administrative operations, security configuration changes, and access to sensitive data require stronger assurance than routine application usage.

Step-up authentication is enforced by requiring higher authentication strength when users attempt protected actions, even if they already hold a valid session. This ensures that sensitive operations are gated by current assurance rather than inherited trust. The model limits escalation opportunities by making high-impact actions explicitly deliberate and verifiable.

Protected actions introduce step-up authentication for these scenarios. Even trusted users must re-verify when performing high-impact operations. This limits the damage caused by compromised sessions and prevents attackers from escalating privileges silently once initial access is obtained.

A weak design assumes that once a user is authenticated, all subsequent actions inherit the same level of trust for the duration of the session. This allows attackers to escalate privileges silently if a session is compromised. A stronger design treats high-impact actions as distinct risk events, enforcing step-up authentication at the moment those actions are performed. This ensures that sensitive operations remain deliberate, verifiable, and resistant to session abuse.

Continuous Access evaluation and session control

Authentication alone does not guarantee ongoing trust. Once an access token is issued, conditions may change without triggering reauthentication. Continuous session evaluation is therefore required to prevent stale trust from persisting.

Continuous Access evaluation and token revocation

CAE enables near real-time enforcement when identity conditions change. Events such as account disablement, password resets, or changes to MFA invalidate existing tokens and require reauthentication under the current policy.

Not all workloads support CAE equally. Microsoft 365 services natively honor CAE signals, enabling immediate session revocation, while other applications may rely on token lifetime expiry, requiring compensating controls. Designing secure access requires understanding which services support continuous evaluation and where additional safeguards are necessary. Where CAE is not supported, designs reduce exposure by tightening token lifetimes, applying session controls, and increasing the frequency of reauthentication for higher-risk access. These compensations do not replicate CAE behavior perfectly, but they narrow the window in which a stolen or stale session token remains useful.

The critical distinction is that Conditional Access governs access issuance, while CAE governs access persistence. Treating them as interchangeable leaves silent persistence paths that attackers exploit. Controlling session persistence addresses what happens after access is granted, but it does not determine how much assurance is required at sign-in. That question is answered by risk evaluation, which shapes the authentication strength and controls applied before access is issued.

Risk signals and adaptive enforcement

Risk signals determine how much trust an access request deserves at a given moment. Designing adaptive enforcement is not about reacting to alerts, but about deciding how authentication requirements and session constraints should change as confidence in an identity rises or falls. This section explains how risk scoring is translated into predictable, auditable access decisions.

User and sign-in risk evaluation

A common failure in risk-based design is assuming that elevated risk always requires blocking access, or that low-risk guarantees safety. Effective designs translate risk levels into predictable outcomes, such as requiring stronger authentication, limiting session capabilities, or denying access when confidence drops below an acceptable threshold.

Risk signals derived from anomalous behavior, credential exposure, or unfamiliar sign-in patterns inform access decisions dynamically. Elevated risk does not automatically imply denial; it may instead require stronger authentication or limit session capabilities.

Architectural clarity matters here. Risk-based controls should be deterministic and predictable. Users must understand why access requirements change, and security teams must be able to explain and audit those decisions.

Adaptive responses to changing risk

Risk is not static. A session that begins as low-risk may become high-risk due to downstream events. Adaptive enforcement ensures that access requirements escalate as risk increases, reducing the attacker's operational window.

This model reflects a Zero Trust assumption: trust is temporary and must be continually re-earned.

Authorization boundaries and least privilege

Authorization determines the blast radius of a compromised identity. Even when authentication is strong and continuously evaluated, excessive or permanent permissions turn successful sign-ins into high-impact failures. This section explains how modern authorization models limit scope and duration to reduce impact.

Modern identity systems treat authorization not as a static assignment, but as a continuously constrained control layer that defines what an identity can affect, for how long, and at what scope:

- **Role-based access and scope limitation**: Role-based access control enforces least privilege by limiting identities to only the permissions required for their role. Overly broad roles increase blast radius and obscure accountability.

  Designs should favor granular roles scoped to specific resources rather than broad, tenant-wide permissions. This reduces the impact of compromise and simplifies access reviews.

- **Just-in-time privilege activation**: Standing privilege creates persistent risk. Just-in-time activation limits elevation to deliberate, time-bound events that can be audited and approved. **Privileged Identity Management** (PIM) enables this model by requiring explicit activation and enforcing expiration.

  This approach assumes that even trusted administrators may be compromised and minimizes exposure accordingly.

Validating Conditional Access for Zero Trust

Conditional Access is only effective when it behaves as an enforcement mechanism rather than a policy catalog; poorly validated policies introduce blind spots, conflicting outcomes, or excessive friction that encourages users to seek workarounds.

In a Zero Trust model, validation is continuous and deliberate, ensuring that access decisions reflect current risk, apply consistently, and degrade safely when assumptions fail.

Validating Conditional Access requires more than confirming that policies exist. It demands assurance that policies are correctly scoped, ordered, and resilient to failure, and that they enforce Zero Trust principles under real-world conditions. This section maps directly to the SC-100 skill: *Validate the alignment of Conditional Access policies with a Zero Trust strategy.*

Establishing Zero Trust alignment

Zero Trust assumes no implicit trust and continuous verification. Conditional Access policies must therefore enforce explicit verification for all access scenarios, not just privileged or high-risk cases. Validation begins by confirming that baseline controls are applied universally and that no access paths bypass policy enforcement.

Baseline Conditional Access policies

Baseline policies establish minimum access requirements such as MFA, device trust, and session controls. These policies should apply broadly to all users and applications, with limited and well-justified exclusions.

Validation focuses on identifying gaps where users, service accounts, or applications are excluded unintentionally. Broad exclusions undermine Zero Trust by creating silent bypass paths. Effective designs minimize exclusions and document any that remain unavoidable.

Policy scope and exclusion management

Policy scope determines who and what a Conditional Access policy applies to. Overly narrow scopes create gaps, while overly broad scopes increase friction. Validation ensures that scopes reflect actual access patterns and that exclusions are intentional, reviewed, and time-bound.

Exclusions should be treated as temporary exceptions rather than permanent design elements. Regular review prevents policy drift and ensures that Zero Trust principles remain enforceable as environments evolve.

Policy evaluation order and outcome consistency

Conditional Access policies are evaluated collectively, not sequentially. Conflicting or overlapping policies can produce unintended outcomes if not carefully validated, as we will see in this section.

Understanding policy evaluation behaviour

Conditional Access evaluates all applicable policies and enforces the most restrictive outcome. Validation ensures that policies are designed with this behavior in mind and that no combination of policies results in weaker enforcement than intended.

Architects must verify that allow, require, and block decisions align across policies. A single misconfigured policy can negate the intent of others if evaluation behavior is misunderstood.

Preventing conflicting access outcomes

Conflicts arise when policies impose incompatible requirements or when exceptions in one policy undermine another. Validation involves testing representative access scenarios to confirm that outcomes match design intent.

This includes verifying that privileged access, external access, and service access behave as expected under normal and elevated risk conditions.

Continuous enforcement and failure handling

Zero Trust assumes that access conditions change over time and that enforcement must respond accordingly. Validation must therefore consider how Conditional Access behaves during identity changes, outages, and partial failures.

Validating Continuous Access evaluation

Continuous Access Evaluation ensures that changes such as account disablement, credential compromise, or MFA changes invalidate active sessions. Validation confirms that workloads supporting CAE respond correctly and that compensating controls exist where CAE is not supported.

Testing includes verifying token revocation behavior and ensuring that high-risk events result in immediate enforcement.

Safe failure and resilience design

Conditional Access failures can lock out users or unintentionally grant access. Validation ensures that policies fail safely, prioritizing security without causing widespread disruption. Emergency access accounts must be handled deliberately. They should be excluded only from controls that could cause tenant-wide lockout, while still being protected through strong authentication, restricted usage, and continuous monitoring. Their sign-ins should generate high-signal alerts, and their existence should be limited to the minimum required to recover from policy or identity failures.

This includes confirming that critical services remain accessible under defined conditions and that monitoring alerts administrators to policy failures promptly.

Monitoring, testing, and continuous improvement

Conditional Access validation is not a one-time exercise. Environments evolve, applications change, and new threats emerge. Ongoing monitoring and testing ensure that policies remain aligned with Zero Trust objectives.

Monitoring policy effectiveness

Logging and reporting provide visibility into how Conditional Access policies are applied. Validation relies on reviewing access outcomes rather than policy definitions. Sign-in activity must be examined to confirm that policies trigger as expected and that enforcement aligns with risk signals. Unexpected allow or block patterns often indicate scope gaps or conflicting conditions that require correction. Unexpected patterns may indicate misconfiguration or emerging attack techniques that require policy adjustment.

Iterative policy testing and refinement

Testing policies using controlled scenarios allows teams to validate changes before broad deployment. This reduces the risk of accidental lockouts and ensures that new policies integrate cleanly with existing controls.

Safe rollout practices prioritize visibility before enforcement. Policies should be evaluated using log-driven validation, targeted pilot groups, and staged expansion to broader populations. This approach confirms real-world impact, exposes unexpected exclusions, and ensures that enforcement outcomes match design intent before policies become mandatory.

A common validation failure is assuming that the presence of Conditional Access policies equates to effective enforcement, without testing how those policies behave together under real conditions. This often leaves silent exclusions, conflicting outcomes, or unintended allow paths that undermine Zero Trust intent. A stronger design validates Conditional Access by testing representative access scenarios, confirming evaluation behavior, and reviewing actual sign-in outcomes rather than policy definitions alone. This ensures that access decisions remain predictable, auditable, and resilient as environments evolve.

Hardening AD DS

AD DS remains a critical dependency in many organizations, even as identity authority shifts toward cloud-based controls. This identity provider's continued presence creates concentrated risk because compromise at the directory layer enables broad lateral movement, privilege escalation, and persistence. Hardening AD DS is therefore not about expanding its role, but about constraining its authority, reducing attack surface, and limiting the impact of inevitable compromise.

A modern design treats AD DS as a legacy system that must be tightly controlled, continuously monitored, and deliberately isolated from higher-trust identity planes. This section maps to the SC-100 skills measured: *Specify requirements to harden Active Directory Domain Services*.

Reducing the AD attack surface

AD DS exposes multiple authentication paths, administrative roles, and trust relationships that attackers routinely exploit. Reducing the attack surface requires narrowing where credentials can be used and minimizing the number of identities that can influence the directory state.

Limiting privileged account usage

Privileged accounts represent the highest-value targets in an AD DS environment. Standing administrative privileges create a persistent opportunity for misuse and increase the impact of credential theft.

Effective hardening limits the number of privileged accounts and restricts where those accounts can authenticate. High-privilege identities should not be used for routine activities or allowed to sign in from untrusted systems. Separating administrative identities from standard user identities reduces exposure and improves accountability.

Local Administrator Password Solution (**LAPS**) plays a specific role in this strategy by addressing lateral movement through local administrator accounts. By ensuring that local admin credentials are unique per device, LAPS prevents attackers from reusing credentials across systems. It does not protect domain administrator accounts and does not replace directory-level privilege controls.

Authentication policies and authentication policy silos

Authentication policies and silos restrict where privileged accounts can authenticate and which resources they can access. These controls prevent high-value credentials from being used on systems that are more likely to be compromised, such as user workstations or unmanaged servers.

By enforcing authentication boundaries, silos interrupt common attack paths such as pass-the-hash and credential replay. Privileged credentials are constrained to hardened systems, reducing the likelihood that compromise of a lower-trust asset leads to directory-wide impact.

Protecting authentication paths and trust relationships

Attackers rarely compromise AD DS directly. Instead, they exploit weak trust relationships and poorly protected authentication paths. Hardening focuses on preventing credential exposure and misuse across the environment.

Restricting interactive and delegated access

Interactive sign-in and delegation permissions increase the risk of credential theft. Privileged accounts should be restricted from interactive logon except where explicitly required, and delegation should be limited to controlled scenarios.

Reducing these access paths lowers the chance that credentials are exposed on systems outside the directory's security boundary. This containment approach aligns with Zero Trust assumptions by minimizing implicit trust between systems.

Securing service accounts and legacy dependencies

Service accounts and legacy applications often rely on static credentials and broad permissions. These identities become long-lived footholds if not carefully controlled.

Modern hardening efforts aim to reduce reliance on shared, static service credentials. Where possible, service identities should be uniquely scoped, lifecycle-managed, and monitored for abnormal behavior. This reduces persistence opportunities and limits the blast radius of credential compromise.

Hardening requires identifying service accounts, scoping their permissions tightly, and monitoring their usage. Where possible, legacy dependencies should be isolated or modernized to reduce reliance on directory-based authentication.

Monitoring and responding to directory-level threats

Even well-hardened directories are subject to attack. Continuous monitoring and rapid response are therefore essential components of AD DS security.

Detecting privilege abuse and lateral movement

Monitoring focuses on identifying anomalous behavior such as unusual authentication patterns, unexpected privilege changes, or access from atypical systems. Early detection reduces attacker dwell time and limits the scope of compromise.

Detection must prioritize high-value events that indicate potential directory-level impact rather than low-signal noise.

Containing impact during compromise

Zero Trust assumes that compromise will occur. Hardening strategies must therefore include containment mechanisms that limit impact when defenses fail.

By constraining where privileged credentials can be used and segmenting authentication paths, organizations reduce the ability of attackers to escalate privileges or move laterally, buying time for response and recovery.

A common directory hardening failure is attempting to modernize security by extending domain controllers into cloud infrastructure without reducing their authority or attack surface. This preserves legacy trust assumptions and creates high-impact compromise paths. A stronger design treats AD DS as a constrained legacy dependency, limiting privileged authentication paths, reducing standing privilege, and isolating directory influence from higher-trust identity planes. This approach assumes compromise is possible and focuses on containment rather than prevention alone.

Secrets, keys, and certificates management

Modern identity architectures extend beyond human users; applications, services, and automation authenticate continuously using secrets, keys, and certificates. When these non-human credentials are poorly managed, they silently bypass identity controls and persist long after their original purpose has ended. Effective secrets management treats non-human access as an identity problem, subject to the same governance expectations as user access.

Designing secure systems requires eliminating static credentials wherever possible, centralizing cryptographic material, and enforcing strict lifecycle controls so that access can be granted, audited, rotated, and revoked predictably. This section maps to the SC-100 skill: *Design a solution to manage secrets, keys, and certificates.*

Identity-based access to secrets

Secrets management begins with a fundamental design choice: whether access is granted based on possession of a secret or based on identity. Secret-based access introduces long-lived trust relationships that are difficult to monitor and revoke, while identity-based access enables policy enforcement and auditing.

Eliminating embedded credentials

Hardcoded secrets in applications, configuration files, or scripts represent one of the most persistent security weaknesses in modern environments. These credentials are often copied, reused, and rarely rotated, creating invisible access paths that bypass Conditional Access, risk evaluation, and access reviews.

Eliminating embedded credentials forces all access requests through the identity control plane. Instead of granting access because a secret is present, access is granted because an identity is authenticated and authorized. This shift enables the enforcement of least privilege, monitoring of usage, and immediate revocation when access is no longer required.

Using managed identities for non-human access

Managed identities provide the preferred authentication mechanism for applications and services. Rather than storing credentials, the platform authenticates the workload directly and issues tokens bound to the identity. There is nothing to distribute, rotate, or protect within the application itself.

When managed identities are unavailable, certificate-based service principals provide a more secure alternative to secret-based authentication. Certificates offer stronger assurance and clearer lifecycle management than shared secrets. Secret-based service principals should be avoided except where no other option exists, as they introduce static credentials that are difficult to govern.

For CI/CD pipelines and automation platforms, workload identity federation provides a modern alternative to stored credentials. Instead of maintaining secrets for pipeline identities, federated trust allows the pipeline to obtain tokens without persisting credentials, reducing both leakage risk and operational rotation burden.

Centralized key and certificate storage

Centralizing cryptographic material reduces sprawl and enforces consistent access controls. Distributed storage of keys and certificates across applications and infrastructure increases the likelihood of leakage, misconfiguration, and unmanaged access.

Key Vault and Managed HSM design decisions

Selecting between Azure Key Vault and Managed **Hardware Security Modules (HSMs)** depends on assurance requirements rather than scale. Standard Key Vault supports software-backed keys suitable for most application scenarios, offering centralized storage, access control, and auditing.

Managed HSMs provide hardware-backed key protection aligned with higher regulatory and compliance requirements. When cryptographic keys protect highly sensitive data or regulations mandate hardware isolation, Managed HSMs are appropriate. The decision is driven by risk and compliance posture, not by application architecture alone. Endpoint exposure is part of the same decision. Where organizations must prevent secret access over the public internet, Key Vault should be integrated through private connectivity and restricted network access, while workloads authenticate using managed identities. This pairs network isolation with identity-based authorization, ensuring that access remains auditable and least-privileged without relying on embedded credentials.

Enforcing least privilege and access boundaries

Access to keys and certificates should be tightly scoped. Broad access undermines the value of centralized storage and increases blast radius in the event of compromise.

Least privilege is enforced by granting identities access only to the specific keys or secrets required for their function. Access boundaries should be reviewed regularly, and unused permissions removed promptly. This approach ensures that non-human access remains more constrained than human access, reflecting the higher automation and persistence associated with service identities.

Lifecycle management and governance

Secrets, keys, and certificates have lifecycles that must be actively managed. Expired or overprivileged credentials introduce availability and security risks that often surface during incidents rather than routine operations.

Rotation, expiration, and revocation

Regular rotation limits the usefulness of compromised credentials and reduces the impact of accidental disclosure. Automated rotation mechanisms should be used wherever possible to avoid manual processes that are prone to error.

Rotation strategies must account for operational continuity as well as security. Certificate-based access should be designed with overlap periods to allow seamless rollover without outages, while compromised credentials must be revoked immediately. Effective designs ensure that revocation takes effect promptly and does not depend on manual redeployment or delayed updates.

Revocation must be immediate and reliable. When an identity is compromised or decommissioned, associated secrets and certificates must be invalidated without delay. Effective designs ensure that revocation propagates quickly and does not depend on application redeployment or manual intervention.

Auditing and monitoring non-human access

Visibility into non-human access is essential. Logs and monitoring should capture when secrets are accessed, by which identities, and from which contexts. Anomalous access patterns often indicate misconfiguration or compromise.

Auditing enables verification that access aligns with design intent and supports compliance requirements. Monitoring non-human identities with the same rigor as user identities closes a common blind spot in security operations.

A common secrets management failure is treating keys, certificates, and credentials as static configuration data rather than as identities with privileges and lifecycles. This leads to long-lived access paths that bypass Conditional Access, auditing, and revocation controls. A stronger design treats non-human access as an identity problem, enforcing managed identities, federated workload identity, centralized key storage, and deliberate rotation and revocation. This ensures that non-human access is governed, auditable, and constrained in the same way as human access.

Conclusion

This chapter explains how identity becomes the central enforcement plane for modern security, replacing network location as the basis of trust. It shows how to design consistent access control across SaaS, PaaS, IaaS, hybrid, and multi-cloud environments by centralizing authentication, authorization, and policy enforcement in Microsoft Entra ID.

Instead of relying on VPNs, trusted IP ranges, or static allowlists, the chapter frames access as a continuous, risk-aware decision driven by identity, device posture, and contextual signals.

The chapter then establishes how to design a hybrid identity in a way that preserves operational continuity while steadily reducing reliance on legacy systems. It positions Entra ID as the authoritative control plane for access decisions, with synchronization used to project identities into the cloud without fragmenting policy enforcement. It also addresses how to contain legacy dependencies using approaches such as Entra Domain Services for protocol compatibility, while integrating on-premises identity telemetry so that detection meaningfully influences access decisions.

External identity design is treated as an extension of the security boundary. The chapter distinguishes when to use guest access versus cross-tenant access for partner collaboration, how entitlement management reduces guest sprawl through time-bound and reviewable access, and why customer identity scenarios require separation from workforce identity. It also introduces decentralized identity as a selective disclosure model for privacy-driven use cases, rather than a replacement for directory-based identity.

Modern authentication and authorization strategy is presented through Conditional Access, CAE, and risk-based enforcement. The chapter explains how authentication strength, protected actions, and step-up controls reduce session abuse, while CAE and session governance reduce the risk of stale tokens persisting after conditions change. It also details how to validate Conditional Access alignment with Zero Trust by confirming scope coverage, minimizing exclusions, testing enforcement behavior, and ensuring safe failure patterns that avoid tenant-wide lockout.

Finally, the chapter covers hardening AD DS as a containment exercise rather than an expansion of authority, focusing on reducing attack surface, restricting privileged authentication paths, and limiting lateral movement. It closes by treating secrets, keys, and certificates as non-human identity credentials, emphasizing managed identities, workload identity federation, centralized key storage in Key Vault or Managed HSM, and lifecycle controls for rotation, revocation, auditing, and monitoring to prevent silent bypass of identity controls.

The next chapter builds on identity and access control by focusing on the elevated permissions that pose the greatest risk to cloud environments. It examines how privileged access must be tightly governed, time-bound, and continuously monitored, exploring design approaches that reduce standing privilege, limit lateral movement, and protect administrative operations across cloud, hybrid, and multi-cloud platforms.

Questions

Success on any assessment depends on understanding identity and access design decisions rather than memorizing individual features. The following questions help readers confirm that they can apply this chapter's concepts in realistic identity architecture scenarios, including Zero Trust access enforcement, hybrid identity authority, Conditional Access design, external identity governance, directory hardening, and non-human identity protection.

1. **An organization wants consistent access controls across SaaS, PaaS, IaaS, and on-premises resources without relying on VPN trust. Which architectural approach best achieves this outcome?**
   a. Extending trusted network locations
   b. Applying firewall rules per workload
   c. Centralizing access decisions in Microsoft Entra ID
   d. Using separate identity providers per platform
2. **Why is Microsoft Entra ID intended to be the authoritative control plane in hybrid identity designs rather than AD DS?**
   a. AD DS does not support synchronization
   b. Entra ID enables centralized policy enforcement and risk evaluation
   c. AD DS cannot authenticate cloud applications
   d. Entra ID eliminates the need for directories
3. **Which design choice most effectively prevents network location from becoming an implicit trust boundary?**
   a. Requiring VPN access for all users
   b. Using named locations as unconditional allow rules
   c. Treating network location as a Conditional Access signal
   d. Restricting access using IP allowlists only
4. **When designing administrative access to virtual machines, which approach best aligns with Zero Trust principles?**
   a. Shared local administrator accounts
   b. Permanent public RDP or SSH exposure
   c. Identity-based authentication governed by Conditional Access
   d. Static firewall exceptions for administrators
5. **Why should management endpoints such as RDP and SSH not be directly exposed to the internet?**
   a. They increase operational overhead
   b. They cannot be audited
   c. They create a persistent attack surface guarded by static controls
   d. They are incompatible with modern authentication

6. **Which scenario most strongly indicates the need for cross-tenant access rather than unmanaged guest accounts?**
    a. One-time document sharing
    b. Short-term contractor access
    c. Ongoing partner collaboration requiring governance
    d. Anonymous customer access
7. **Why should customer identities be separated from workforce identities?**
    a. Customer identities cannot use federation
    b. Workforce Conditional Access policies do not scale to consumer scenarios
    c. Customers require device compliance policies
    d. Workforce identities cannot access SaaS applications
8. **Which scenario best justifies using Entra Domain Services instead of deploying domain controllers in the infrastructure?**
    a. Full domain administration is required
    b. Legacy protocols are required without expanding AD DS authority
    c. On-premises synchronization is unavailable
    d. Password authentication must be disabled
9. **Why is CAE critical to modern authentication design?**
    a. It replaces Conditional Access
    b. It reduces authentication latency
    c. It invalidates sessions when identity conditions change
    d. It eliminates token lifetimes
10. **Why should secrets, keys, and certificates be treated as identities rather than configuration data?**
    a. They expire automatically
    b. They bypass governance when unmanaged
    c. They cannot be audited
    d. They are only used by legacy systems

Answers

1. c: Centralizing access decisions in Microsoft Entra ID.

   Identity-based access ensures consistent enforcement across cloud and hybrid environments without relying on network location as a trust boundary.

2. b: Entra ID enables centralized policy enforcement and risk evaluation.

   Hybrid identity designs require a single authoritative control plane where Conditional Access, risk signals, and session enforcement can be applied consistently.

3. c: Treating network location as a Conditional Access signal.

   Network location should inform risk evaluation, not implicitly grant access or bypass identity controls.

4. c: Identity-based authentication governed by Conditional Access.

   Administrative access should be mediated through identity, policy, and role assignment rather than static credentials or exposed endpoints.

5. c: They create a persistent attack surface guarded by static controls.

   Directly exposed management endpoints rely on brittle defenses that degrade over time and expand the attack surface.

6. c: Ongoing partner collaboration requiring governance.

   Cross-tenant access preserves identity ownership, enables lifecycle control, and prevents unmanaged guest sprawl.

7. b: Workforce Conditional Access policies do not scale to consumer scenarios.

   Customer identity requires a separate trust boundary to avoid friction, policy complexity, and privilege inheritance.

8. b: Legacy protocols are required without expanding AD DS authority.

   Entra ID Domain Services provides protocol compatibility while containing directory risk and administrative exposure.

9. c: It invalidates sessions when identity conditions change.

   CAE ensures access does not persist after compromise, configuration changes, or identity risk escalation.

10. b: They bypass governance when unmanaged.

    Uncontrolled secrets and keys create silent access paths that evade identity policy, auditing, and revocation.

CHAPTER 6
Design Privileged Access Management Solutions

Introduction

This chapter examines how to design secure, governed, and resilient privileged access architectures across cloud, hybrid, and multi-cloud environments. Privileged identities represent the highest-risk control plane in any organization. Poor role structure or weak governance can turn a minor compromise into tenant-wide or domain-wide control. This chapter explains how the enterprise access model, Microsoft Entra ID governance, and privileged endpoint isolation work together to keep administrative access scoped, time-bound, and defensible under Zero Trust assumptions.

Structure

This chapter covers the following topics:

- Privileged role assignment
- Entra ID governance
- Evaluating AD DS security and platforms
- Securing cloud tenant administration and platforms
- Cloud infrastructure entitlement management solutions
- Evaluating access review management solutions
- PAW design with remote access

Objectives

By the end of this chapter, you will be able to design solutions for assigning and delegating privileged roles by using the enterprise access model, evaluate Microsoft Entra ID governance controls such as **Privileged Identity Management** (**PIM**), entitlement management, and access reviews, and assess **Active Directory Domain Services** (**AD DS**) resilience to common escalation and credential theft techniques.

You will also be able to design secure administrative access for cloud tenants and multi-cloud platforms, apply **cloud infrastructure entitlement management** (**CIEM**) principles to reduce excess privilege (including non-human identities), evaluate access review management solutions, and design a **Privileged Access Workstation** (**PAW**) approach for high-risk administration.

These skills fall under the exam domain: *Design security operations, identity, and compliance capabilities*, which represent approximately 25-30 % of the overall SC-100 skills[1] measured.

Privileged role assignment

Privileged role design determines the blast radius of compromise. The enterprise access model provides the architectural framework for making those blast-radius decisions explicit and enforceable. It defines where privilege should exist, how elevation should occur, and how separation must be enforced. This section maps to the following SC-100 skills measured: *Design a solution for assigning and delegating privileged roles by using the enterprise access model.*

Enterprise access model and tiered administration

The foundation of the enterprise access model is tiered administration. Tiered administration recognizes that not all roles carry the same impact, and formalizes this through explicit security tiers, as shown in the following table:

Tier	Scope	Examples of roles and assets
Tier 0	Identity and security control plane	Entra ID Global Administrator, AD DS Domain Admins, security configuration
Tier 1	Server, application, and infrastructure management	Azure subscription administrators, VM administrators, SQL administrators, and application operators
Tier 2	User endpoints and low-impact systems	User workstations, kiosks, frontline devices, helpdesk tools

***Table 6.1**: Tiered administration overview*

A common failure occurs when tier boundaries are not enforced. An attacker compromises a Tier 2 workstation and extracts cached credentials using **pass-the-hash** (**PtH**) techniques. Since the same administrative account is also used for Tier 1 or Tier 0 access, the attacker moves laterally to a server and eventually escalates to domain-level control. Tiered administration prevents this escalation by ensuring credentials from lower tiers cannot be reused to access higher-impact control planes.

1 **https://learn.microsoft.com/en-us/credentials/certifications/resources/study-guides/sc-100**

Identity and security control plane roles belong in the highest tier because compromise at this level undermines all dependent systems. Infrastructure and workload roles belong in lower tiers where impact is narrower. The purpose of tiering is containment: compromise in a lower tier must not become an escalation path into a higher tier.

Role mapping must follow responsibility. Identity policy administrators should not manage workloads, and workload operators should not be able to modify identity governance or assign privileged roles. Assigning roles based on job function rather than seniority prevents privilege bleed across tiers.

Tier separation ensures that a compromise in one administrative layer cannot trivially expand into others. By constraining how far privilege extends, tiering converts catastrophic compromise into localized impact.

Role separation

After tiering, privileged access must be separated across planes: identity, platform, and workload. Standing privilege across multiple planes creates continuous high-impact exposure and shortens attacker paths from initial compromise to widespread control. Designs should discourage persistent cross-plane assignments and use deliberate, task-based elevation so administrators operate with only the authority needed for the current task.

Standing privilege creates ambient authority. Time-bound elevation ensures that privilege exists only when explicitly requested, making elevation events auditable and misuse easier to detect.

Cross-tier lateral movement occurs when compromise of a lower-impact role becomes a stepping-stone into higher-control planes. Prevention requires structural separation: distinct privileged identities per tier, sign-in restrictions aligned to tier boundaries, and administrative tooling that prevents credential reuse across tiers. Tier boundaries must be enforceable, not advisory.

Privileged role design

Zero Trust assumes privileged identities are never implicitly trusted. The **Rapid Modernization Plan** (**RaMP**) reflects modern cloud-first threats and replaces legacy **Enterprise Single Account Environment** (**ESAE**) models that relied on static network trust.

In modern designs, privileged access is deliberate, temporary, explicitly scoped, and constrained by identity-based controls rather than perimeter assumptions. To sustain those assumptions in practice, privileged access must be governed continuously rather than granted permanently.

Entra ID governance

Role design determines where privilege should exist. Governance determines how privilege is granted, activated, reviewed, and removed over time.

In cloud environments, unmanaged privilege accumulation is a common path to overexposure. Microsoft Entra ID governance shifts privileged access from static assignment to lifecycle control. This section maps to the following SC-100 skills measured: *Evaluate the security and governance of Microsoft Entra ID, including Microsoft Entra PIM, entitlement management, and access reviews.*

Privileged Identity Management

Even when privileged roles are correctly scoped and tiered, risk remains if those roles are held continuously. PIM reduces standing privilege by converting powerful roles into eligible assignments that must be activated when needed. Activation can require **multi-factor authentication** (**MFA**), justification, and approval, which makes elevation deliberate and time-bounded. PIM also strengthens auditing by recording who activated which role, when, and for how long.

Privileged Identity Management follows a structured lifecycle that governs how access is assigned, activated, approved, and audited, as follows:

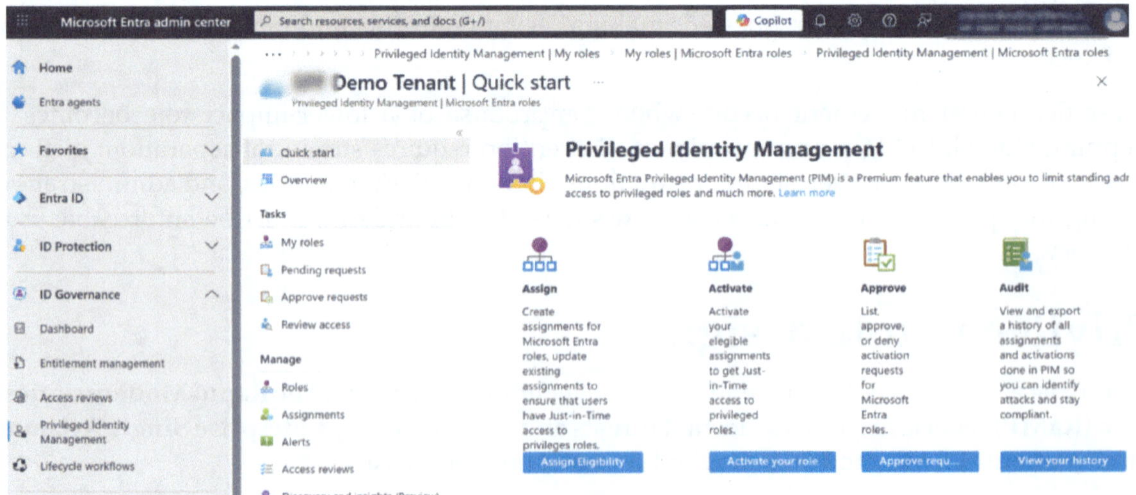

Figure 6.1:PIM lifecycle

These stages ensure that privileged access is not permanently assigned but instead controlled through governed workflows that enforce verification, oversight, and accountability.

PIM applies to both Microsoft Entra ID directory roles and Azure resource roles. This allows organizations to govern elevation consistently across identity control planes and cloud resource scopes, ensuring that administrative privilege is time-bound, whether it applies to tenant-wide configuration or subscription-level infrastructure management. Alerts for unusual elevation patterns add visibility and help detect misuse.

A common governance failure is assigning privileged roles correctly but allowing them to remain continuously eligible or permanently assigned, causing privilege to accumulate silently over time. A stronger design treats governance as a lifecycle control, ensuring privileged access is activated deliberately, expires automatically, and is continuously reviewed so that access reflects current responsibility rather than historical assignment.

Entitlement management

While PIM governs how elevated roles are activated, entitlement management governs who can request and obtain access, and under what conditions.

It uses access packages to bundle groups, applications, and roles into structured offerings aligned to job functions or projects, providing a centralized way to manage governed access across multiple resources. The following figure is an overview:

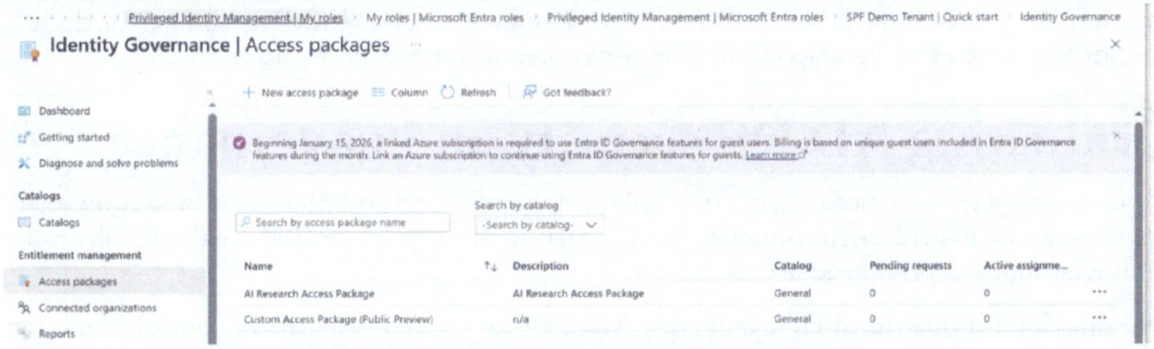

Figure 6.2: Access packages in Microsoft Entra ID

Access packages organize access into reusable units, enabling consistent assignment, approval, and lifecycle control across different roles and projects. Workflows enforce approvals, ownership, and time-bound access. Automatic removal at the end of entitlement periods prevents privilege from persisting after roles or projects change, reducing access creep without relying on manual cleanup.

Access reviews

Access reviews validate whether access remains appropriate as responsibilities change. Reviews should be scoped to high-risk access, such as privileged roles, sensitive applications, external users, and non-human identities, with a cadence aligned to risk.

Access reviews provide a structured way to regularly validate whether assigned access is still required across different parts of the environment.

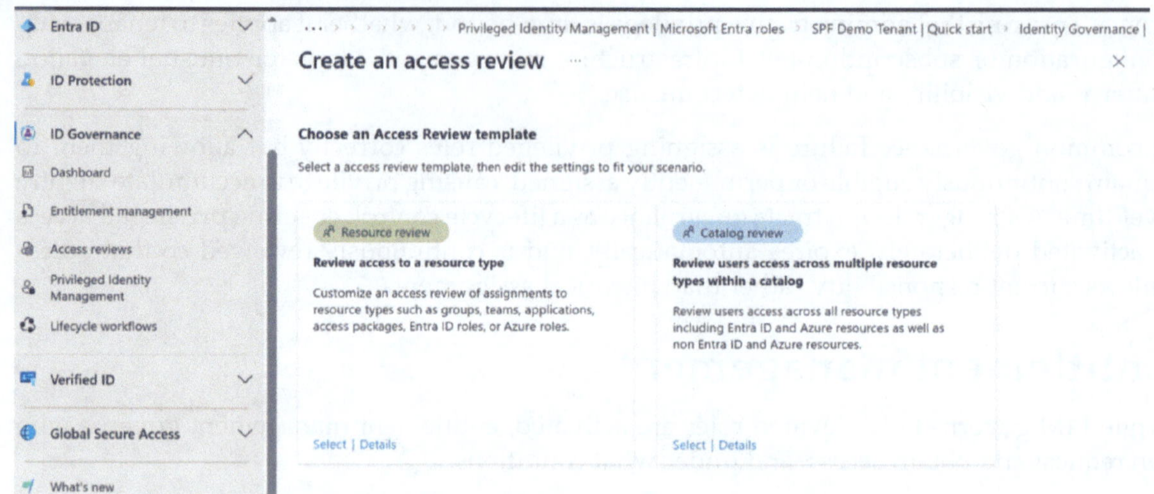

***Figure 6.3**: Access reviews in Microsoft Entra ID*

Reviews must be enforceable: automatic removal for denied access or non-response prevents inaction from becoming permanent privilege. Reviewers need sufficient context to decide confidently, such as ownership clarity and usage signals for sensitive app access.

Evaluating AD DS security and governance

Cloud identity governance reduces risk only if dependent control planes enforce equivalent constraints. In hybrid environments, AD DS frequently represents the weakest link in an otherwise modern privileged access design.

Even in cloud-modernized environments, AD DS often remains a critical control plane for legacy apps, infrastructure, and hybrid authentication paths. AD DS becomes a frequent escalation target because credential theft and lateral movement can convert a single compromise into domain-wide control. Effective governance constrains where privileged accounts can authenticate, limits credential exposure, and reduces lateral movement opportunities.

With identity governance established in Entra ID, attention now shifts to ensuring that the on-premises directory control plane does not undermine those protections through permissive authentication paths or poorly governed privileged identities. This section maps to the following SC-100 skills measured: *Evaluate the security and governance of AD DS, including resilience to common attacks.*

Hardening privileged accounts in AD

Privileged accounts in AD DS represent some of the highest-value targets in the environment because they often grant broad or complete control over authentication, authorization, and trust relationships. A single compromised domain-level account can bypass security controls, disable defenses, and establish persistence across both on-premises and hybrid environments.

These domain-level privileged accounts must be treated as exceptional identities. Their use should be rare, tightly scoped, and monitored. Allowing these accounts to sign in from general-purpose endpoints increases exposure to credential dumping and replay techniques such as PtH and pass-the-ticket. Restricting privileged usage paths reduces the attack surface and makes abnormal behavior easier to detect.

A common failure in hybrid environments is allowing domain-level privileged accounts to authenticate from general-purpose endpoints, assuming monitoring will compensate for exposure. A stronger design restricts where AD DS privileged identities can authenticate, ensuring credentials are processed only on hardened systems so that compromise of a user endpoint cannot escalate into directory-wide control.

Authentication policies and restricted admin usage

Authentication policies enforce where privileged identities can authenticate, turning tier boundaries into enforceable controls. Restricting high-tier accounts to domain controllers or designated administrative hosts prevents credentials from being processed on low-trust devices. This strengthens tier isolation and creates clear detection signals: authentication attempts outside approved paths become high-confidence indicators of misuse.

Reducing lateral movement and credential exposure

Lateral movement succeeds when credentials can be reused across systems. Reducing it requires eliminating shared secrets and limiting credential presence. Shared local administrator passwords enable rapid propagation after a single compromise. Using **Local Administrator Password Solution** (**LAPS**) assigns unique, rotating local admin passwords per device so stolen credentials cannot be reused elsewhere, reducing blast radius.

A common failure pattern occurs when tier boundaries are not enforced. An attacker compromises a standard workstation and extracts cached credentials, then uses PtH techniques to move laterally to another system where a higher-privilege account has signed in. From there, the attacker escalates into domain-level administration, gaining control over authentication and trust relationships.

Tiered administration breaks this chain by ensuring that Tier 0 credentials are never exposed on Tier 1 or Tier 2 systems. Privileged identities authenticate only from hardened administrative environments, and credential reuse across tiers is structurally prevented. The design confines compromise to a single tier instead of the full domain.

Each AD DS hardening control disrupts a specific escalation path. Authentication restrictions limit where credentials can be processed, reducing credential theft opportunities. LAPS prevents PtH-based lateral movement by eliminating shared local secrets. Privileged sign-in restrictions and hardened administrative hosts reduce exposure to pass-the-ticket attacks by ensuring high-value credentials are never presented on low-trust systems.

Identity protection for VDI and hybrid identity

Virtual desktop and hybrid identity environments introduce identity risks that do not exist in traditional, persistent endpoint models. Non-persistent and pooled **virtual desktop infrastructure** (**VDI**) environments can amplify credential exposure due to frequent sign-ins and shared hosts.

Hybrid identity environments also create trust transitions between Entra ID and AD DS that attackers can exploit. Privileged identities should authenticate only from approved, hardened systems aligned to security tiers. Allowing privileged sign-ins from pooled or low-trust environments weakens tier boundaries and increases credential exposure.

Securing cloud tenant administration and platforms

Cloud management planes are internet-reachable by design, so security must be identity-centric rather than perimeter-centric. Secure cloud administration reduces public exposure, uses controlled entry points, applies time-bound elevation, and maintains visibility across platforms.

Once identity governance and directory hardening are in place, the next design challenge is ensuring that cloud management planes do not reintroduce exposure through overly permissive access paths or persistent administrative reach. This section maps to the following SC-100 skills measured: *Design a solution for securing the administration of cloud tenants, including SaaS and multi-cloud infrastructure and platforms.*

Secure administrative access without public exposure

The first principle of securing cloud tenant administration is eliminating unnecessary exposure of management interfaces. In cloud environments, administrative control planes are reachable over the internet by default, which significantly increases the risk compared to traditional on-premises administration.

Publicly exposed **Remote Desktop Protocol** (**RDP**)/**Secure Shell** (**SSH**) or management endpoints create a persistent attack surface for scanning, brute-force attempts, and opportunistic exploitation. Secure designs remove direct exposure and use mediated access paths where authentication, authorization, and logging are applied consistently. Portal-based access centralizes enforcement through identity controls such as conditional access and device compliance checks.

A common failure in cloud administration design is exposing management interfaces directly to the internet and relying on static network controls or permanent administrator roles to reduce risk. A stronger design removes public exposure entirely and requires administrative access to pass through identity-governed entry points, ensuring every management action is authenticated, policy-evaluated, and auditable before a session is established.

Azure Bastion for portal-based remote administration

Azure Bastion addresses a recurring privileged access problem: how administrators securely reach **virtual machines** (**VMs**) without exposing those machines to the internet. Traditional remote administration relies on public **Internet Protocol** (**IP**) addresses, inbound firewall rules, or **virtual private network** (**VPN**) access, each of which expands the attack surface and weakens control over how administrative access occurs.

Azure Bastion enables RDP/SSH access to VMs without public IPs or inbound management ports. Sessions are launched through the Azure portal and traverse the Azure backbone, reducing exposure and enforcing identity controls before session establishment. Bastion should operate as a controlled gateway: sessions are scoped to target resources, and network segmentation behind Bastion must be preserved to prevent lateral movement.

JIT administrative access for cloud resources

Reducing administrative risk is not only about where access originates, but also about how long it exists. Persistent administrative privileges create continuous exposure: credentials can be abused at any time, misused accidentally, or exploited long after their original purpose has passed.

Just-in-time (**JIT**) access reduces continuous exposure by ensuring elevated privilege exists only for the time required to complete a task. Time-bound elevation makes privileged activity explicit and auditable, narrows the exploitation window for stolen credentials, and increases detection opportunities because elevation becomes a clear event rather than a background condition.

Governing administrative access in multi-cloud environments

As organizations adopt multiple cloud platforms, privileged access design becomes more complex and more fragile. Each provider introduces its own identity models, role definitions, and management interfaces. Without deliberate governance, administrative access fragments and privileges accumulate inconsistently.

Multi-cloud expands administrative complexity and increases the risk of fragmented privilege governance. Identity should be treated as the unifying control plane so that authentication, authorization, and monitoring remain consistent even when role models differ across providers. Effective governance focuses on shared principles: least privilege, explicit elevation, constrained access paths, and continuous visibility. Centralizing governance reduces blind spots and prevents attackers from exploiting weaker enforcement in one platform to compromise others.

Cloud infrastructure entitlement management solutions

Administrative roles are not the only source of excessive privilege in cloud environments. CIEM addresses a fundamental weakness in modern cloud environments: permissions tend to grow faster than governance. As subscriptions multiply, workloads evolve, and automation expands, entitlements accumulate in ways that are difficult to reason about using traditional role reviews alone. CIEM restores control by continuously analyzing what permissions exist, how they are used, and where they are excessive or unused.

PIM governs how privileged roles are activated through time-bound elevation, while access reviews govern whether access should continue based on reviewer decisions rather than observed usage. CIEM complements both by providing evidence-driven insight into *how permissions are actually used*, enabling safe right-sizing of entitlements for human and non-human identities across cloud platforms.

CIEM identifies overprivileged identities (human and non-human), highlights unused entitlements, and supports right-sizing access based on evidence rather than assumption. In multi-cloud environments, CIEM provides unified visibility across differing role and scope models.

By making entitlement usage visible and actionable, CIEM transforms access governance from a periodic cleanup exercise into a continuous control. Permissions are kept aligned with operational reality rather than historical assignment, directly reducing the attack surface created by excess privilege. While CIEM focuses on reducing excessive cloud entitlements, similar least-privilege principles apply within operating systems and administrative tooling. **Just Enough Administration** (**JEA**) limits what administrators can do within a privileged session by exposing only the specific commands or tasks required, rather than granting full administrative capability.

In this chapter, JEA is treated as a conceptual complement to CIEM: CIEM governs what access exists, while JEA constrains how that access can be exercised when legacy or OS-level administration is unavoidable. This section maps to the following SC-100 skills measured: Design a solution for cloud infrastructure entitlement management.

Managed identities for infrastructure and workloads

Managed identities are a cornerstone of secure cloud entitlement design because they eliminate one of the most persistent sources of entitlement risk: long-lived credentials.

In practice, this distinction becomes critical when automation identities are granted broad, static permissions simply to avoid deployment friction. Without visibility into how those permissions are actually exercised, excess access quietly accumulates over time. By pairing managed identities with CIEM insight, organizations can observe real permission usage and safely right-size workload access, ensuring automation identities retain only what they genuinely require.

Traditional service principals rely on secrets or certificates that must be created, stored, rotated, and eventually retired, processes that are frequently mismanaged in practice. Managed identities replace this fragile model with identities that are lifecycle-bound to the workload itself. The identity is created automatically when the resource is provisioned, exists only for the lifetime of that resource, and is removed when the resource is deleted. There are no secrets to distribute and no credentials that persist beyond the workload's existence.

The security value of managed identities is amplified by precise privilege scoping. Since the identity is purpose-built, permissions can be assigned narrowly, to a specific resource or operation, rather than broadly at subscription or tenant scope. This precision is essential in environments where automation runs continuously and at scale.

CIEM complements managed identities by observing how permissions are actually exercised. It can identify unused roles or scopes and support safe right-sizing without the operational risk associated with secret rotation. This makes least-privilege enforcement both more achievable and more sustainable over time.

In deployment pipelines and automation scenarios, managed identities also enforce a clean separation between human and workload access. Pipelines authenticate as workloads, not users, preventing the gradual accumulation of interactive administrative privileges in automation systems.

Using managed identities instead of service principals

Service principals require explicit credential management, whereas managed identities are platform-managed and lifecycle-bound. When workloads run in Azure, managed identities are the preferred choice because they eliminate credential handling and reduce operational overhead.

Selecting managed identities aligns entitlement governance with platform-native security controls and simplifies long-term management.

Reducing administrative overhead with platform-managed identities

Managed identities are created, rotated, and deleted automatically, which reduces the risk of orphaned credentials. CIEM visibility ensures these identities are assigned only the permissions they actively use and no more.

This combination of automation and governance keeps workload access aligned with least privilege over time.

Secure identity usage in pipelines

Automation pipelines are powerful force multipliers, but they are also common sources of excessive privilege. Pipelines often require elevated access to deploy or modify infrastructure, and without deliberate design, those permissions gradually expand far beyond their original purpose.

Pipelines often become overprivileged over time to avoid deployment failures. Secure pipeline design treats automation as a workload identity rather than a user identity, avoids long-lived secrets, and scopes permissions to the deployment surface only. CIEM evidence helps reduce unused pipeline permissions safely. Pipeline identities should be inventoried and decommissioned when projects end to prevent high-impact access from persisting indefinitely.

Evaluating access review management solutions

Access governance is only effective if access remains accurate over time; even with strong role design, entitlement management, and privileged access controls in place, permissions naturally drift as people change roles, projects end, and applications evolve. Access review management exists to counter this drift by introducing continuous validation into the identity lifecycle.

Rather than assuming that previously approved access remains appropriate, access reviews require explicit re-authorization. They shift governance from a one-time decision to an ongoing control, ensuring that access remains aligned with current business needs, ownership, and risk. In architectural terms, access reviews function as a corrective mechanism that addresses the inevitable entropy of large identity systems.

Once access is designed and granted deliberately, reviews ensure that it stays correct. Even perfectly governed privilege remains vulnerable if it is exercised from untrusted endpoints. This section maps to the following SC-100 skills measured: *Evaluate an access review management solution.*

Access review scoping and scheduling

Access reviews are most effective when they are intentional rather than exhaustive. Reviewing every permission with the same frequency is neither practical nor meaningful. Effective design focuses review effort on access that presents the greatest risk, while allowing lower-impact permissions to be validated less aggressively.

Reviews should focus on high-risk access such as privileged roles, sensitive applications, guest users, and non-human identities. Scope should match the sensitivity of the resource and the potential impact of misuse. Cadence must balance assurance with operational burden, and ownership must be assigned to reviewers who understand business intent, such as managers, application owners, or role sponsors.

A common design failure is treating access reviews as a uniform compliance exercise, applying the same scope and cadence to all permissions regardless of risk. This overwhelms reviewers and results in low-quality decisions or implicit approval. A stronger design prioritizes reviews for high-impact access, such as privileged roles, external users, and sensitive applications, while applying lighter-touch validation to low-risk access. This ensures review effort is proportional to risk and remains effective over time.

Automatic access removal and governance enforcement

Validation without enforcement does not meaningfully reduce risk. If access remains in place when reviews are missed or decisions are unclear, privilege persists by default, and governance becomes advisory rather than authoritative.

Review outcomes must be applied automatically. Automatic removal for non-response ensures inaction does not become implicit approval. Enforced removal prevents access creep and keeps privilege aligned with active responsibility rather than historical assignment.

Operational considerations for large-scale reviews

As environments grow, access reviews must scale without overwhelming administrators or reviewers. Large identity estates can contain thousands of groups, applications, and privileged roles. Without deliberate design, review processes collapse under their own weight and become ineffective.

At scale, the review success depends on prioritization, delegation, and automation. Reviewers need a clear decision context, and governance systems must support bulk processing and consistent enforcement. Sustainable review design balances security assurance with operational impact so the process remains achievable and meaningful.

PAW design with remote access

PAWs address a critical but often underestimated risk in identity security: the endpoint from which privileged actions are performed. Even the strongest identity governance and access controls can be undermined if administrative credentials are exposed on compromised devices. PAWs exist to ensure that high-impact administrative operations occur only from hardened, isolated environments designed to resist credential theft and lateral movement.

A PAW strategy does not replace role design, elevation controls, or access reviews. PAWs and remote access gateways address different risks. PAWs protect where privileged credentials are used by enforcing a hardened, trusted endpoint, while services such as Azure Bastion control how administrators reach target systems. Secure designs use both together: PAWs to protect credential execution and identity posture, and mediated access paths to constrain network exposure and session scope.

Together, these controls complete the privileged access architecture by anchoring administrative activity to a trusted execution environment. When privileged access is exercised, it must occur from a device whose configuration, network reach, and security posture reflect the sensitivity of the task being performed. This section maps to the following SC-100 skills measured: *Design a solution for PAW, including remote access.*

PAW security principles

PAWs are required for high-impact administrative roles that control identity systems, tenant-wide security configuration, or core infrastructure. These roles operate in the highest RaMP security tiers, and their compromise can undermine authentication, authorization, and enforcement systems.

A common privileged access design failure is enforcing strong identity governance while allowing administrators to perform high-impact actions from general-purpose user endpoints. Even when roles are time-bound and access is well governed, compromised endpoints can expose credentials, session tokens, or administrative tools, collapsing tier boundaries in practice. A stronger design treats the administrative endpoint as part of the trust boundary, requiring privileged actions to originate only from hardened, isolated PAWs. This ensures that identity controls are not undermined at the moment of execution.

PAWs isolate privileged credentials and tools from everyday user activity and reduce exposure to phishing, malware, and token replay.

PAWs are not required for non-privileged scenarios such as kiosks, frontline devices, call centers, or self-service terminals that do not perform high-risk administration. Applying PAWs where no privileged activity exists adds complexity without reducing privileged risk.

Remote administration should preserve identity-governed access paths rather than extending broad network reach. VPN-centric models expand lateral movement potential and reduce scoping. Strong designs prefer session paths that remain policy-driven and auditable, where access is evaluated per session and constrained to specific management surfaces rather than whole subnets.

PAWs require continuous compliance enforcement. As PAWs are constrained by design, deviation signals are meaningful; if a PAW falls out of compliance or shows compromise indicators, administrative access should be suspended until trust is restored through remediation or reprovisioning.

Conclusion

This chapter examined how to design privileged access management solutions that remain defensible across cloud, hybrid, and multi-cloud environments. It established the enterprise access model as the basis for structuring privileged roles through tiering, plane separation, and deliberate elevation to limit blast radius. It then showed how Microsoft Entra ID governance capabilities, such as PIM, entitlement management, and access reviews, control the lifecycle of privileged access so privilege remains intentional, time-bound, and continuously validated.

The chapter evaluated AD DS security and governance as a critical hybrid control plane, emphasizing authentication restrictions, credential hygiene, and lateral movement reduction. It addressed secure cloud tenant administration through identity-centric access, removal of public management exposure, portal-based access paths such as Azure Bastion, and JIT elevation.

The chapter also introduced CIEM as an evidence-based approach to reducing excess privilege, especially for non-human identities and automation. Finally, it positioned PAWs as the enforcement point that protects privileged credentials at the moment they are used, completing the privileged access architecture.

The next chapter focuses on regulatory compliance and data governance, examining how organizations translate obligations and internal policy into enforceable, auditable controls.

Questions

Success on any assessment depends on understanding the underlying technologies, concepts, and principles rather than memorizing facts. The following questions help readers confirm that they can apply this chapter's ideas in realistic design scenarios, including privileged role design, identity governance, attack-path disruption, Zero Trust assumptions, and PAW enforcement.

1. **An organization wants to ensure that compromise of a workload administrator cannot escalate into tenant-wide or identity-level control. Which architectural approach best achieves this outcome?**
   a. Granting permanent global administrator access with enhanced monitoring
   b. Using network segmentation alone to isolate workloads
   c. Implementing tiered administration with separation of identities and access paths
   d. Applying conditional access policies to all administrators
2. **Why is the enterprise access model most effective when treated as an architectural design framework rather than a role assignment checklist?**
   a. It reduces the number of administrators required
   b. It simplifies access reviews
   c. It defines blast radius, elevation paths, and trust boundaries by design
   d. It replaces the need for identity governance tools
3. **Which administrative roles belong in the highest security tier within the enterprise access model?**
   a. Application deployment operators
   b. Subscription owners managing workloads
   c. Identity and security control plane administrators
   d. Helpdesk operators resetting user passwords
4. **What is the primary risk of allowing standing privileged access across multiple administrative planes?**
   a. Increased operational overhead
   b. Reduced Secure Score
   c. Immediate multi-plane compromise if credentials are stolen
   d. Slower role activation
5. **Why does Microsoft Entra PIM reduce risk more effectively than permanent role assignment?**
   a. It removes the need for role separation
   b. It enforces identity synchronization
   c. It converts standing privilege into a time-bound, auditable elevation
   d. It automatically remediates all misconfigurations

6. **Which Microsoft Entra capability governs how access is granted, approved, grouped, and automatically removed over time?**
   a. Conditional access
   b. Identity protection
   c. Entitlement management
   d. PIM
7. **Why are access reviews considered a continuous governance control rather than a one-time validation exercise?**
   a. They reduce administrative effort
   b. They replace entitlement management
   c. They compensate for access drift caused by organizational change
   d. They eliminate the need for approvals
8. **Why must AD DS security still be evaluated in hybrid privileged access designs?**
   a. AD DS is automatically protected by Entra ID
   b. AD DS no longer participates in authentication
   c. AD DS remains a high-value control plane targeted for escalation
   d. AD DS prevents lateral movement by default
9. **Which control most directly enforces where privileged AD DS accounts are allowed to authenticate?**
   a. Network security groups
   b. Authentication policies and restricted admin usage
   c. VPN access controls
   d. Group Policy preferences
10. **Why are PAWs required for high-impact administrative roles?**
    a. They improve administrator productivity
    b. They replace identity governance controls
    c. They prevent privileged credentials from being exposed on user endpoints
    d. They eliminate the need for MFA

Answers

1. c: Implementing tiered administration with separation of identities and access paths.

   Tiered administration structurally limits blast radius by ensuring compromise of a lower-tier role cannot escalate into higher-impact control planes.

2. c: It defines blast radius, elevation paths, and trust boundaries by design.

   Treating the Enterprise access model as a design framework embeds security outcomes into architecture rather than relying on operational discipline.

3. c: Identity and security control plane administrators.

   These roles define authentication, authorization, and security enforcement and therefore require the strongest isolation and controls.

4. c: Immediate multi-plane compromise if credentials are stolen.

   Standing privilege across planes allows a single credential compromise to undermine identity, platform, and workload security simultaneously.

5. c: It converts standing privilege into time-bound, auditable elevation.

   PIM reduces exposure by ensuring privileges exist only when needed and that every elevation event is visible and reviewable.

6. c: Entitlement management.

   Entitlement management governs how access is requested, approved, grouped, expired, and removed across users, groups, and applications.

7. c: They compensate for access drift caused by organizational change.

   Access reviews continuously validate whether existing access remains appropriate as roles, projects, and responsibilities evolve.

8. c: AD DS remains a high-value control plane targeted for escalation.

   Even in modern environments, AD DS often underpins authentication and trust, making it a frequent target for privilege escalation attacks.

9. b: Authentication Policies and restricted admin usage.

   These controls explicitly define where privileged accounts are allowed to authenticate, enforcing tier boundaries structurally.

10. c: They prevent privileged credentials from being exposed on user endpoints.

    PAWs isolate administrative activity to hardened devices, reducing credential theft, lateral movement, and attack-path viability.

CHAPTER 7
Design Regulatory Compliance and Data Governance Solutions

Introduction

This chapter examines how to design regulatory compliance and data governance solutions using Microsoft security and governance platforms. It explains how legal, regulatory, and privacy requirements are translated into enforceable technical controls that can be evaluated, governed, and sustained across Azure, Microsoft 365, and hybrid environments.

The chapter explores how Microsoft Purview, Microsoft Priva, Azure Policy, and Microsoft Defender for Cloud work together to support compliance management, privacy obligations, configuration enforcement, and regulatory validation. It shows how architects can design layered compliance architectures that balance governance oversight, preventive controls, and continuous assessment. By applying these capabilities in a coordinated way, organizations can reduce audit complexity, improve visibility into compliance posture, and maintain regulatory alignment as cloud environments evolve.

Structure

This chapter covers the following topics:

- Translating compliance requirements into controls
- Compliance solutions using Microsoft Purview
- Privacy requirements with Microsoft Priva
- Azure Policy for security and compliance
- Regulatory alignment with Defender for Cloud

Objectives

This chapter covers the skills required to translate compliance requirements into enforceable security controls, ensuring that regulatory obligations are reflected in technical design decisions rather than treated as after-the-fact checks. It examines how to design solutions that address compliance requirements using Microsoft Purview, enabling organizations to classify, govern, and monitor data in line with regulatory expectations.

The chapter also explores how to design solutions that address privacy requirements, including the use of Microsoft Priva, to manage personal data responsibly and support Privacy Risk Management. It examines how to design Azure Policy solutions that enforce security and compliance requirements consistently across cloud resources through automated evaluation and remediation.

Finally, the chapter evaluates how to validate alignment with regulatory standards and benchmarks using Microsoft Defender for Cloud, ensuring that compliance posture can be continuously assessed, measured, and improved across cloud and hybrid environments. These skills fall under the exam domain: *Design security operations, identity, and compliance capabilities,* which represent approximately 25-30 % of the overall SC-100 skills[1] measured.

Translating compliance requirements into controls

Regulatory compliance in cloud environments begins long before any technical configuration is applied. Frameworks such as **General Data Protection Regulation** (GDPR), **International Organization for Standardization** (ISO) 27001, **Health Insurance Portability and Accountability Act** (HIPAA), or **National Institute of Standards and Technology** (NIST) 800-53 define required outcomes but deliberately avoid prescribing implementation details. In Microsoft-based environments, the architect's role is to translate those abstract obligations into concrete, measurable, and enforceable controls that can be applied consistently across Azure, Microsoft 365, and hybrid estates.

A recurring design failure is selecting tools first and attempting to justify them against regulatory language afterward. Effective compliance architecture reverses this sequence by starting with control intent, mapping that intent to technical capabilities, and only then selecting the appropriate Microsoft control plane that can evaluate, enforce, or report on the requirement. This section maps to the following SC-100 skills measured: *Translate compliance requirements into security controls.*

Mapping regulatory obligations to technical controls

The purpose of this stage is to convert regulatory language into actionable control objectives that can be measured and validated. Instead of thinking in terms of products, architects must first decide what the organization needs to prove, such as configuration conformance, access restriction, data residency, or auditability, and then determine how those outcomes translate into technical controls across different environments and workloads.

1 **https://learn.microsoft.com/en-us/credentials/certifications/resources/study-guides/sc-100**

Once regulatory objectives are expressed as measurable controls and correctly scoped, the next step is to refine those objectives by separating tool selection from scope, so the right control plane can be chosen later. That decision shapes how compliance is implemented, monitored, and sustained over time.

Control objectives vs. tooling selection

Regulatory requirements describe what must be achieved, not which product must be used. Control objectives such as restricting access to sensitive data, enforcing secure configurations, or maintaining audit visibility must be articulated independently of tooling. This prevents overfitting compliance requirements to a single service and helps avoid a common trap: implementing a reporting capability when enforcement is required, or implementing a blocking control where monitoring was the real need.

A reliable approach is to express each requirement as a testable statement. For example, only approved regions may be used, storage services must not permit public access, or administrative changes must be attributable to named identities. Once requirements are stated as measurable outcomes, the architect can confidently map them to evaluation mechanisms, enforcement mechanisms, or both.

Scope definitions

Compliance requirements rarely apply uniformly across platforms. Some obligations apply to Azure resource configuration, others apply to information stored in Microsoft 365 services, and many apply across hybrid estates that include on-premises systems. Correct scope definition ensures the right control plane is used, the right signals are collected, and the right remediation path exists.

This scope decision also shapes how controls are operationalized. Infrastructure configuration requirements typically depend on Azure governance and posture tooling. Information handling obligations often depend on classification, retention, and activity visibility. Hybrid requirements frequently require consistent evaluation across multiple subscriptions, tenants, or regions, which introduces additional design considerations such as hierarchy, delegation, and reporting rollups.

Selecting the correct Microsoft control plane

Once control objectives and scope are clear, the next design decision is selecting the Microsoft control plane that is responsible for delivering the capability. In practice, compliance architecture usually requires a combination of services, but each service has a primary responsibility. Selecting the correct control plane reduces operational friction, avoids duplicated controls, and ensures that evidence and reporting remain credible during audits.

Defender for Cloud vs. Compliance Manager

Microsoft Defender for Cloud is the primary platform for evaluating the compliance of Azure resources against security benchmarks and regulatory standards; it assesses configuration state, highlights gaps, and provides a consolidated view of alignment across subscriptions. This makes it the natural choice when the question: Are our Azure resources configured in a way that aligns with a regulatory standard or benchmark?

Microsoft Purview Compliance Manager focuses on compliance program management rather than infrastructure configuration; it helps organizations track requirements, manage assessments, document improvement actions, and maintain evidence over time. This makes it appropriate when the requirement centers on how we manage and demonstrate compliance progress across controls and obligations, rather than whether this specific Azure resource configuration is compliant.

Understanding this boundary prevents two common misdesigns: trying to use Compliance Manager as an Azure configuration enforcement platform, or relying on Defender for Cloud alone to satisfy broader compliance program governance, such as evidence workflows and compliance ownership. This distinction becomes clearer when infrastructure compliance and information compliance are treated as separate but complementary domains.

Azure resource compliance vs. information compliance boundaries

Azure resource compliance concerns the configuration and security posture of resources such as compute, network, storage, and platform services. Information compliance concerns how data is classified, retained, shared, and protected across collaboration and productivity services. These domains overlap in business impact, but they are implemented differently and measured using different signals.

A strong compliance design explicitly separates these domains while ensuring they support the same governance objectives. For example, a regulatory requirement might demand that sensitive data is protected and that systems are configured securely. That may require both infrastructure posture validation and information governance controls, but each must be implemented in the correct plane so that evaluation, enforcement, and reporting remain accurate.

Onboarding regulatory standards

Even when an organization has chosen the correct platforms, compliance assessment cannot occur until the relevant standards are enabled and scoped appropriately. Onboarding is not a formality; it establishes the baseline against which posture is evaluated and determines which control mappings and compliance views will be available for ongoing monitoring and audit preparation.

Enabling regulatory standards in Defender for Cloud

Regulatory standards such as NIST 800-53, ISO 27001, or industry-specific frameworks must be explicitly enabled in Defender for Cloud to generate compliance reporting. Enabling a standard activates the control set and maps applicable Azure signals to those controls. Without this step, teams can mistakenly assume the environment is being assessed when, in reality, no regulatory compliance view is active.

This onboarding decision should also reflect how the organization structures governance. Standards may need to be applied across multiple subscriptions, management groups, or environments, and the architect must ensure that the chosen scope aligns with how the organization intends to report compliance and assign remediation ownership.

Interpreting initial compliance posture and gaps

Onboarding a standard provides visibility; it does not remediate anything automatically. The initial posture typically reveals a mix of passing controls, failing controls, and controls that are not applicable. Architects must ensure that stakeholders interpret this correctly and understand which gaps require enforcement mechanisms, operational remediation, or architectural change.

This is also where evaluation vs. enforcement becomes operational. Defender for Cloud identifies and tracks gaps, but enforcement and drift prevention commonly require governance mechanisms such as Azure Policy. A well-designed compliance architecture treats onboarding as the starting point for continuous improvement, not as proof of compliance by itself.

Closing these gaps typically requires enforcement mechanisms rather than additional assessment, which is where governance controls such as Azure Policy become essential.

Compliance solutions using Microsoft Purview

Compliance programs require more than technical enforcement; they require structured oversight, evidence management, and the ability to demonstrate progress against regulatory obligations over time. Microsoft Purview provides the governance layer that connects regulatory requirements to organizational accountability, enabling compliance teams to manage assessments, track remediation activities, and maintain defensible evidence across Microsoft 365 and Azure-integrated environments.

Rather than enforcing infrastructure configuration, Purview focuses on managing compliance intent and assurance. It allows organizations to understand how regulatory frameworks apply to their environment, how controls are implemented across services, and where gaps remain. For security architects, the challenge is designing Purview as part of a broader compliance architecture without misusing it as a replacement for enforcement or posture management tools. This section maps to the following SC-100 skills measured: *Design a solution to address compliance requirements by using Microsoft Purview.*

Compliance Manager architecture and assessments

Compliance Manager acts as the central workspace for managing regulatory obligations and measuring organizational progress toward compliance goals. It translates complex regulatory frameworks into structured assessments that can be evaluated, tracked, and improved over time, providing a shared view for security, compliance, and risk stakeholders.

This centralized view is presented through the Compliance Manager dashboard, which summarizes compliance posture and progress across regulatory requirements:

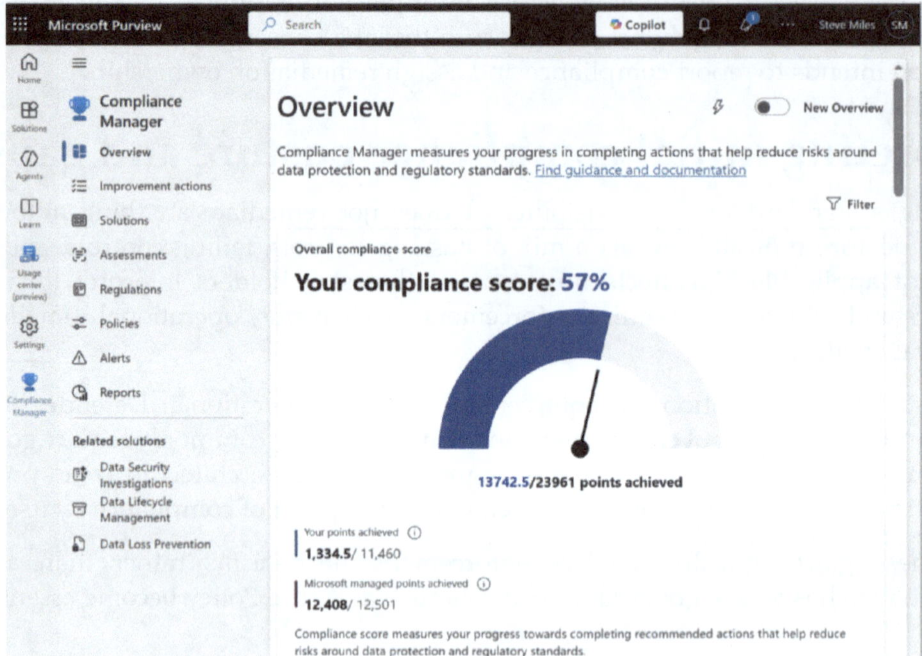

Figure 7.1: Microsoft Purview Compliance Manager overview

This dashboard provides a visual representation of compliance progress, enabling organizations to understand their current posture, identify gaps, and prioritize remediation activities aligned to regulatory requirements.

Assessment templates and framework alignment

Compliance Manager uses assessment templates that align Microsoft Services and controls to regulatory frameworks such as GDPR, ISO 27001, and NIST-based standards. These templates break high-level regulations into individual control requirements and map them to technical and organizational actions that can be performed within Microsoft environments.

For architects, this alignment is critical. It ensures that compliance efforts are not ad hoc or interpretation-driven, but instead grounded in a consistent mapping between regulatory language and platform capabilities. Selecting the correct assessment templates establishes clarity around which obligations apply, which Microsoft controls contribute to compliance, and where responsibility lies for each requirement.

Improvement actions and evidence tracking

Beyond assessment scoring, Compliance Manager provides improvement actions that describe how specific controls can be implemented or strengthened. These actions often reference technical configurations, policy decisions, or operational processes that must be completed to satisfy a regulatory requirement.

Evidence tracking is equally important. Compliance Manager allows organizations to associate documentation, configuration proof, and operational artifacts with each control. This capability supports audit readiness by ensuring that evidence is centrally managed and consistently updated, reducing reliance on manual data collection during compliance reviews.

Data discovery and classification for Compliance

Regulatory compliance is tightly coupled to understanding what data exists, where it resides, and how sensitive it is. Without reliable data discovery and classification, compliance assessments become speculative, and enforcement controls are applied inconsistently. Microsoft Purview addresses this challenge by providing mechanisms to identify and categorize sensitive information across Microsoft 365 services. Without accurate discovery and classification, downstream compliance controls, such as retention, protection, and monitoring, cannot be applied reliably or demonstrated during audits. This discovery process begins with identifying sensitive information across Microsoft 365 services.

Identifying sensitive data across Microsoft 365 services

Purview's data discovery capabilities inspect content stored in services such as SharePoint Online, Exchange Online, OneDrive, and Microsoft Teams. Through built-in and custom classifiers, Purview can identify data types such as personal data, financial information, or regulated identifiers without requiring manual tagging.

This automated visibility enables architects to design compliance solutions that are based on actual data presence rather than assumptions. It also allows organizations to understand the scale and distribution of regulated data, which directly informs risk assessments, retention strategies, and protection controls.

This discovery and classification capability provides visibility into sensitive data locations but does not, by itself, enforce protection or restrict access.

Role of inspection and classification in compliance reporting

Classification is not an end in itself; it feeds compliance reporting and governance decisions. By classifying data consistently, Purview enables compliance teams to report on how regulated information is handled, where it is stored, and which controls apply to it.

From a design perspective, this linkage ensures that compliance assessments are grounded in observable data usage patterns. It also enables downstream controls, such as data protection, retention, or monitoring, to be applied with precision, supporting both regulatory obligations and operational efficiency.

Purview scope and integration boundaries

While Purview is a central component of compliance architecture, it does not operate in isolation. Understanding what Purview governs, what it integrates with, and what it deliberately does not enforce is essential to avoiding gaps or duplicated controls in compliance designs.

Purview evaluation vs. enforcement

Purview evaluates compliance status by aggregating signals from Microsoft Services and mapping them to regulatory requirements. It provides visibility, assessment scoring, and governance workflows, but it does not directly enforce infrastructure configuration or block noncompliant deployments.

This distinction matters in architectural design. Purview answers questions such as:

- Are we meeting this requirement?
- What evidence do we have?

Enforcement questions, such as preventing noncompliant resources from being created, must be handled by other services. Treating Purview as an enforcement engine leads to false confidence and incomplete compliance controls. For enforcement and posture validation, Purview relies on signals and controls provided by other Microsoft security services.

Dependency on Azure Policy and Defender for Cloud

Effective compliance solutions use Purview in conjunction with Azure Policy and Defender for Cloud. Azure Policy enforces configuration standards, while Defender for Cloud evaluates resource posture and regulatory alignment. Purview then consumes and contextualizes these signals within a broader compliance management framework.

Architects must design these dependencies intentionally. Purview provides the governance narrative and evidence trail, while Azure Policy and Defender for Cloud provide the technical enforcement and evaluation signals. Together, they form a layered compliance architecture that supports both operational control and regulatory accountability.

Privacy requirements with Microsoft Priva

Privacy requirements introduce a distinct governance challenge that differs from general regulatory compliance. While compliance frameworks focus on organizational controls and audit readiness, privacy regulations emphasize individual rights, transparency, and responsible handling of personal data. In Microsoft environments, these obligations require solutions that support both operational automation and user-aware guidance without placing excessive burden on security or compliance teams.

Microsoft Priva is designed to address this privacy-specific dimension. It enables organizations to operationalize privacy obligations by automating subject rights processes and proactively identifying privacy risks in day-to-day collaboration. For architects, the goal is to integrate Priva into the broader governance architecture while clearly separating privacy management from infrastructure compliance and security posture evaluation.

While privacy governance focuses on protecting individual rights and guiding user behavior, regulatory compliance also requires consistent enforcement of technical controls across cloud resources. This enforcement layer is provided through Azure Policy, which translates compliance intent into preventative and corrective guardrails. This section maps to the following SC-100 skills measured: *Design a solution to address privacy requirements, including Microsoft Priva.*

DSAR design

Data subject access requests (**DSARs**) are a core requirement of privacy regulations such as GDPR, granting individuals specific rights over their personal data, including the right to access, correct, or delete information. Designing for DSAR fulfillment requires structured, repeatable workflows that can locate relevant data, coordinate responses across multiple systems, and maintain auditable records of how each request is handled. Manual or fragmented approaches do not scale and significantly increase operational and compliance risk.

Automating request intake and processing

Microsoft Priva Subject Rights Requests provides a centralized workflow for receiving, tracking, and processing privacy requests across Microsoft 365 services. It enables organizations to standardize how requests are submitted, validated, and assigned, ensuring consistency regardless of where the data resides.

From a design perspective, automation is critical. Priva reduces reliance on ad hoc processes and ensures that privacy requests are handled within required timeframes by integrating discovery, task assignment, and approval workflows. This also enables organizations to demonstrate accountability by maintaining a clear record of request-handling activities.

Reducing manual effort and operational risk

Privacy requests often involve coordination across legal, compliance, IT, and business teams. This coordination becomes fragmented and error-prone without automation. Priva minimizes manual effort by guiding stakeholders through predefined steps and consolidating activities into a single workflow.

Reducing operational risk is as important as efficiency. Automated workflows help ensure that responses are complete, consistent, and defensible, reducing the likelihood of missed data, inconsistent responses, or noncompliance with regulatory timelines. For architects, this capability supports privacy by design principles without introducing unnecessary complexity. This automation supports privacy-specific operational workflows and does not replace broader compliance enforcement or security posture controls.

Microsoft Priva Privacy Risk Management

Beyond responding to formal requests, privacy governance increasingly requires organizations to identify and mitigate privacy risks before violations occur. Privacy Risk Management in Microsoft Privacy focuses on proactive detection of risky personal data usage and on influencing user behavior at the point where risk arises.

Unlike enforcement-focused controls, Privacy Risk Management is designed to influence behavior and reduce privacy risk proactively rather than block activity or assess infrastructure compliance.

Detecting risky personal data usage

Privacy Risk Management analyzes activity signals across Microsoft 365 services to identify patterns that may indicate inappropriate handling of personal data. This includes scenarios such as oversharing sensitive information, retaining personal data longer than necessary, or accessing data outside expected usage patterns.

For architects, this capability enables a shift from reactive compliance to proactive risk reduction. Instead of relying solely on audits or incident response, organizations gain visibility into emerging privacy risks as they occur, allowing for earlier intervention.

User notifications and behavioural guidance

A defining characteristic of Privacy Risk Management is its emphasis on user guidance rather than enforcement alone. Priva can notify users when they are about to take actions that may increase privacy risk, such as sharing personal data broadly, and provide recommendations for safer alternatives.

This approach supports a culture of shared responsibility for privacy. Rather than treating privacy as a purely technical or compliance-driven function, Priva integrates privacy awareness into everyday workflows. For architects, this reinforces privacy controls without undermining productivity or requiring heavy-handed restrictions. These notifications guide users toward safer behavior without enforcing hard technical blocks or preventing the action outright.

Azure Policy for security and compliance

Enforcing compliance at scale requires more than visibility into configuration drift; it requires mechanisms that can prevent noncompliant resources from being deployed and correct deviations when they occur. Azure Policy is the primary service for expressing and enforcing governance intent across Azure environments, ensuring that regulatory and organizational requirements are applied consistently regardless of who deploys resources or where those resources reside.

From a compliance architecture perspective, Azure Policy translates governance rules into enforceable guardrails. It allows organizations to move from advisory posture management to active prevention and correction, reducing reliance on manual reviews and reactive remediation. For security architects, the challenge lies in designing policy structures that scale across complex environments without creating operational friction or governance blind spots. This section maps to the following SC-100 skills measured: *Design Azure Policy solutions to address security and compliance requirements*.

Policy definitions and assignments

Azure Policy operates by evaluating resources against defined rules and taking action based on the evaluation outcome. These rules are expressed as policy definitions and applied to environments through policy assignments. Understanding how definitions and assignments interact is fundamental to building effective compliance controls.

Built-in vs. custom policy definitions

Azure provides a large catalog of built-in policy definitions that address common security, compliance, and governance requirements. These include restrictions on resource locations, requirements for encryption, network exposure controls, and alignment with regulatory benchmarks. Built-in policies are maintained by Microsoft and evolve as platform capabilities change, making them suitable for most compliance scenarios.

Custom policy definitions are used when organizational requirements are more specific than what built-in policies provide. This may include enforcing naming conventions, tagging standards, or bespoke configuration requirements. Architects must balance flexibility with maintainability, as custom policies introduce long-term ownership and testing responsibilities.

Assignment scopes and inheritance

Policy assignments determine where and how policy definitions are enforced. Assignments can be applied at the resource group, subscription, or management group level, with inheritance ensuring that child scopes automatically receive applicable policies.

Designing the assignment scope is a strategic decision. Assigning policies at higher scopes promotes consistency and reduces administrative effort, but it also requires careful planning to avoid unintended impact. Architects must consider organizational structure, separation of duties, and exception handling when determining where policies should be applied.

Initiative-based governance

As compliance requirements grow in number and complexity, managing individual policy assignments becomes impractical. Azure Policy initiatives address this challenge by grouping multiple related policies into a single, reusable construct that represents a broader governance objective.

Grouping policies for regulatory enforcement

Initiatives allow architects to express regulatory requirements as a collection of related controls rather than isolated rules. For example, a regulatory standard may require encryption, access restriction, and logging across multiple resource types. Grouping these policies into an initiative ensures consistent enforcement and simplifies reporting.

This approach also improves clarity for stakeholders. Instead of reasoning about dozens of individual policies, teams can understand compliance in terms of initiatives that map directly to regulatory or organizational requirements.

Management group level assignment strategies

Assigning initiatives at the management group level enables governance to scale across large Azure estates. This ensures that new subscriptions automatically inherit compliance requirements without manual intervention, reducing the risk of gaps as environments grow.

Architects must design management group hierarchies deliberately, aligning them with organizational boundaries, regulatory scope, and operational responsibility. Well-designed hierarchies enable centralized governance while still allowing controlled flexibility where exceptions are required.

Policy-driven remediation

Enforcement alone does not address existing noncompliant resources. Azure Policy includes remediation capabilities that allow organizations to correct drift and bring resources back into compliance without manual intervention.

These remediation actions are often driven by posture and compliance findings surfaced through Microsoft Defender for Cloud.

Remediating Defender for Cloud recommendations

Azure Policy integrates with Microsoft Defender for Cloud by enabling remediation of certain security and compliance recommendations. When configured, policy remediation tasks can automatically apply changes to resources that do not meet required standards, reducing time to compliance.

This integration bridges the gap between posture assessment and enforcement. Defender for Cloud identifies gaps, while Azure Policy provides the mechanism to correct them in a controlled and auditable manner.

Continuous enforcement and drift correction

Compliance is not a one-time achievement. Resources change, configurations drift, and new services are introduced over time. Azure Policy supports continuous evaluation, ensuring that noncompliant changes are detected and addressed as they occur.

By combining preventive controls, remediation tasks, and ongoing evaluation, architects can design governance solutions that sustain compliance over time. This reduces reliance on periodic audits and manual reviews, creating a more resilient and trustworthy compliance posture.

Regulatory alignment with Defender for Cloud

Validating regulatory compliance requires continuous visibility into how cloud resources align with defined standards over time. Microsoft Defender for Cloud provides the primary platform for assessing Azure resource configurations against regulatory frameworks and security benchmarks, enabling organizations to understand their compliance posture and prioritize remediation efforts.

For security architects, the challenge is not simply enabling Defender for Cloud, but designing it as part of a broader compliance lifecycle. This includes selecting relevant standards, interpreting assessment results correctly, and ensuring that compliance evaluation remains accurate as environments evolve. This section maps to the following SC-100 skills measured: *Evaluate and validate alignment with regulatory standards and benchmarks by using Microsoft Defender for Cloud.*

Regulatory compliance dashboards

Defender for Cloud includes dedicated dashboards that map Azure resource configurations to regulatory standards and benchmarks. These dashboards provide a structured view of compliance status, allowing architects and compliance teams to assess alignment at scale.

Defender for Cloud surfaces compliance posture through a centralized regulatory dashboard, providing visibility into alignment across standards and highlighting areas of noncompliance. The dashboard overview is provided as follows:

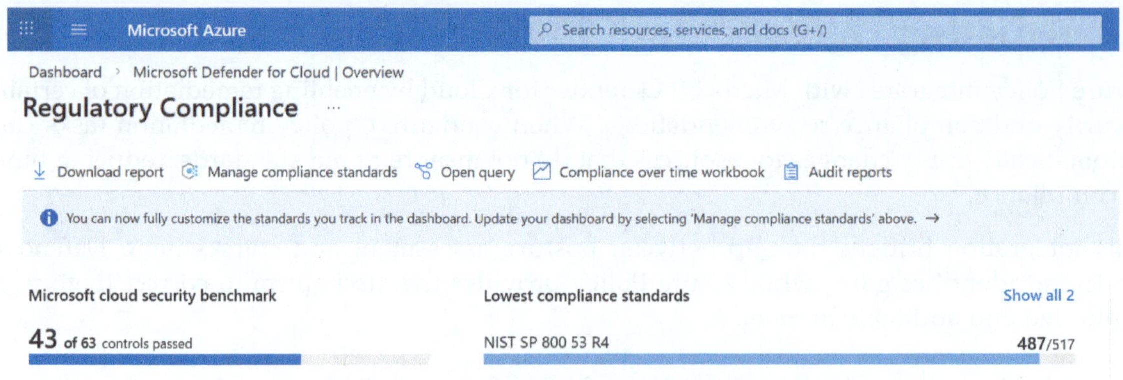

***Figure 7.2**: Regulatory compliance dashboard in Microsoft Defender for Cloud*

This dashboard provides a control-level view of compliance across enabled standards, enabling architects to identify gaps, understand their impact, and prioritize remediation based on regulatory requirements.

Supported standards and benchmarks

Defender for Cloud supports a range of regulatory standards and security benchmarks, including industry-recognized frameworks and regional compliance requirements. Each standard is represented as a collection of controls that map to Azure configuration signals, providing a consistent method for evaluating alignment.

Architects must ensure that the selected standards reflect the organization's regulatory obligations and operational context. Enabling unnecessary standards can introduce noise, while omitting required standards can create blind spots in compliance reporting.

Interpreting compliance control status

Compliance dashboards present controls in states such as compliant, noncompliant, or not applicable. Correct interpretation of these states is essential. A noncompliant control indicates a gap that must be addressed, while a not applicable control reflects a requirement that does not apply to the current environment.

Understanding these distinctions prevents misreporting and ensures that remediation efforts are focused on meaningful gaps rather than on controls that are irrelevant to the deployed architecture.

Secure Score vs. regulatory compliance

Defender for Cloud provides multiple views of security posture, each serving a different purpose. One of the most common sources of confusion is the relationship between Secure Score and regulatory compliance assessments.

Posture prioritization vs. audit readiness

Secure Score measures how well an environment aligns with Microsoft-recommended security best practices. It helps prioritize actions that reduce risk, but it is not designed to demonstrate compliance with specific regulatory standards.

Regulatory compliance dashboards, by contrast, assess alignment against defined frameworks and provide a control-based view suitable for audit preparation. Architects must ensure that stakeholders understand this distinction and avoid using Secure Score as a proxy for regulatory compliance. This distinction explains why Secure Score is frequently misunderstood in governance and compliance scenarios.

Common misinterpretations in governance scenarios

A frequent misinterpretation is assuming that improving Secure Score automatically improves regulatory compliance. While there is overlap, the two are not interchangeable. Some regulatory controls may not affect Secure Score, and some Secure Score recommendations may not map directly to regulatory requirements.

Clarifying this distinction in governance design prevents misplaced remediation efforts and ensures that compliance reporting remains credible and defensible.

Validating compliance over time

Regulatory compliance is a continuous process. As environments change, new resources are deployed, and configurations evolve, compliance posture must be reassessed and maintained. This involves embedding compliance validation into day-to-day operations rather than treating it as a periodic or audit-driven task. By aligning compliance checks with operational workflows, organizations can detect deviations early, respond proactively, and maintain a consistent security and governance posture.

Maintaining visibility across all resources and services is critical. As cloud environments scale and diversify, automated tools and clearly defined ownership models help ensure that accountability is established and compliance gaps are addressed without delay.

Ongoing assessment and evidence refresh

Defender for Cloud continuously evaluates resource configurations and updates compliance dashboards accordingly. This ongoing assessment ensures that compliance data reflects the current state of the environment rather than a point-in-time snapshot.

Architects must design processes to review these assessments regularly and ensure that compliance evidence remains current. This supports audit readiness and reduces the risk of discovering gaps late in the compliance cycle.

Trigger points for reassessment and remediation

Certain events should trigger a focused compliance review, such as onboarding new subscriptions, enabling new services, or expanding into new regions. These changes can introduce new regulatory considerations or alter the applicability of existing controls.

By defining clear trigger points and remediation workflows, architects can ensure that compliance validation remains aligned with architectural change, sustaining regulatory alignment as the environment grows and evolves. By implementing these validation cycles into operational processes, organizations ensure that compliance remains aligned with architectural change rather than lagging behind it.

Conclusion

Designing regulatory compliance and data governance solutions in Microsoft environments requires more than enabling individual security features. It demands a deliberate architectural approach that translates regulatory obligations into measurable control objectives, assigns those objectives to the correct control planes, and sustains compliance through continuous evaluation and governance.

This chapter demonstrated how compliance design begins by separating intent from implementation. Regulatory requirements must first be mapped to technical outcomes, such as configuration enforcement, data visibility, access control, or auditability, before selecting Microsoft Services to deliver those outcomes. By distinguishing between evaluation, enforcement, and governance responsibilities, architects can avoid common misalignments that weaken compliance posture.

Microsoft Purview was positioned as the governance backbone for managing compliance programs, assessments, evidence, and data discovery, while Microsoft Priva addressed the privacy-specific obligations that center on individual rights and responsible data usage. Azure Policy provided the enforcement layer required to prevent configuration drift and maintain consistent compliance at scale, and Microsoft Defender for Cloud delivered the continuous assessment and regulatory alignment validation needed to understand posture over time.

Together, these services form a layered compliance architecture in which governance, enforcement, and evaluation reinforce one another rather than operating in isolation. By applying these principles, security architects can design compliance solutions that are scalable, auditable, and resilient, supporting regulatory obligations while maintaining operational agility in cloud, hybrid, and multi-cloud environments.

The next chapter shifts from governance and regulatory alignment into the technical enforcement of security controls across cloud and hybrid environments. It examines how security posture management, workload protection, and hybrid integration extend governance intent into operational security controls that protect resources regardless of where they run.

Questions

Success on any assessment depends on understanding the underlying technologies, concepts, and principles rather than memorizing facts. The following questions help readers confirm that they can apply this chapter's ideas in realistic design scenarios, including regulatory compliance translation, governance boundaries, privacy operations, policy enforcement, and continuous compliance validation.

1. **An organization wants to evaluate whether Azure workloads align with a standardized baseline covering identity, network, data, and monitoring controls. Which architectural approach best achieves this outcome?**

   a. Enabling Microsoft Secure Score

   b. Reviewing individual security alerts

   c. Evaluating workloads using Microsoft Defender for Cloud and the Microsoft cloud security benchmark

   d. Applying Azure Policy remediation tasks manually

2. **Which Microsoft service is primarily responsible for managing compliance assessments, tracking remediation actions, and maintaining audit evidence over time?**

   a. Microsoft Defender for Cloud

   b. Azure Policy

   c. Microsoft Purview Compliance Manager

   d. Microsoft Priva

3. **An architect must evaluate whether Azure resource configurations align with NIST 800-53 across multiple subscriptions. Which service provides this capability?**

   a. Microsoft Purview

   b. Microsoft Defender for Cloud

   c. Azure Monitor

   d. Microsoft Priva

4. **Why must regulatory standards be explicitly enabled in Microsoft Defender for Cloud before compliance posture can be evaluated?**

   a. Defender for Cloud does not assess resources by default

   b. Standards activate control mappings and compliance views

   c. Azure Policy requires Defender for Cloud integration
   d. Secure Score depends on enabled standards

5. **Which capability allows an organization to identify where sensitive personal data exists across Microsoft 365 to support compliance reporting?**
   a. Azure Policy initiatives
   b. Microsoft Defender for Cloud dashboards
   c. Microsoft Purview data discovery and classification
   d. Microsoft Priva Subject Rights Requests

6. **Which scenario most clearly requires Microsoft Priva Subject Rights Requests rather than Microsoft Purview Compliance Manager?**
   a. Tracking progress against regulatory controls
   b. Responding to individual requests to access or delete personal data
   c. Maintaining audit evidence for ISO certification
   d. Evaluating configuration drift across Azure subscriptions

7. **Why is Microsoft Purview not suitable for enforcing Azure resource configuration compliance on its own?**
   a. It does not integrate with Azure Policy
   b. It focuses on governance and assurance rather than enforcement
   c. It cannot assess regulatory standards
   d. It only applies to Microsoft 365 workloads

8. **Which Azure Policy design choice ensures that compliance requirements are inherited automatically by new subscriptions?**
   a. Assigning policies at the resource group level
   b. Using only custom policy definitions
   c. Assigning policy initiatives at the management group level
   d. Tracking compliance through Compliance Manager

9. **Why should Secure Score not be used as primary audit evidence for regulatory compliance?**
   a. It applies only to Microsoft 365
   b. It measures security posture improvement, not regulatory alignment

c. It does not integrate with Azure Policy

d. It cannot be monitored over time

10. **Which event should trigger a focused reassessment of regulatory compliance posture?**

a. An increase in Secure Score

b. Deployment of resources in a new Azure region

c. Completion of a penetration test

d. Renewal of licensing agreements

Answers

1. c: Defining control objectives independently of tooling.

   Defender for Cloud evaluates Azure workloads against standardized baselines such as the Microsoft cloud security benchmark, providing consistent posture assessment across identity, network, data, and monitoring controls.

2. c: Microsoft Purview Compliance Manager.

   Compliance Manager is designed to manage regulatory obligations, track improvement actions, and store audit evidence over time, supporting ongoing compliance programs rather than infrastructure enforcement.

3. b: Microsoft Defender for Cloud.

   Defender for Cloud evaluates Azure resource configurations against regulatory standards and security benchmarks, providing visibility into alignment across subscriptions.

4. b: Standards activate control mappings and compliance views.

   Enabling a regulatory standard in Defender for Cloud establishes the baseline and control mappings required to generate compliance assessments and dashboards.

5. c: Microsoft Purview data discovery and classification.

   Purview identifies and classifies sensitive data across Microsoft 365 services, providing the visibility required for accurate compliance reporting and governance decisions.

6. b: Responding to individual requests to access or delete personal data.

   Microsoft Priva Subject Rights Requests is designed to automate and manage privacy rights workflows, such as data access or deletion requests, rather than compliance assessments.

7. b: It focuses on governance and assurance rather than enforcement.

   Microsoft Purview evaluates compliance status and manages evidence, but does not enforce Azure resource configurations or block noncompliant deployments.

8. c: Assigning policy initiatives at the management group level.

   Management group–level assignment ensures that all new subscriptions inherit compliance requirements automatically, reducing configuration drift.

9. b: It measures security posture improvement, not regulatory alignment.

   Secure Score prioritizes risk reduction actions but is not designed to demonstrate compliance with specific regulatory frameworks.

10. b: Deployment of resources in a new Azure region.

    Expanding into new regions can introduce new regulatory obligations and change control applicability, requiring reassessment of compliance posture.

Join our Discord space

Join our Discord workspace for latest updates, offers, tech happenings around the world, new releases, and sessions with the authors:

https://discord.bpbonline.com

Chapter 8
Design Cloud and Hybrid Security Solutions

Introduction

This chapter examines how to design cloud and hybrid security solutions by using posture management as a continuous, integrated security discipline. As organizations expand across Azure, Microsoft 365, on-premises infrastructure, and multi-cloud platforms, maintaining consistent security standards becomes increasingly complex. This chapter focuses on how security architects can evaluate, prioritize, and improve security posture across these environments using Microsoft's cloud security platforms.

The chapter explores how Microsoft Defender for Cloud, Microsoft Secure Score, Azure Arc, Defender **External Attack Surface Management** (**EASM**), and Microsoft Security Exposure Management work together to provide unified visibility, risk prioritization, and control. It explains how posture management extends beyond configuration assessment to include workload protection, external exposure awareness, and attack-path-driven prioritization. By applying these capabilities in a coordinated way, architects can design security solutions that reduce exposure, sustain alignment as environments evolve, and focus remediation efforts on the risks that matter most.

Structure

This chapter covers the following topics:

- Security posture with Defender for Cloud
- Security posture assessment with Secure Score
- Integrated security posture management across hybrid and multi-cloud
- Cloud workload protection using Defender
- Hybrid and multi-cloud integration with Azure Arc
- EASM with Defender
- Posture management using Security Exposure Management

Objectives

This chapter covers the skills required to evaluate security posture using Microsoft Defender for Cloud, including alignment with the **Microsoft cloud security benchmark** (**MCSB**), and to assess security posture using Microsoft Secure Score. It examines how these posture management tools provide measurable insight into configuration gaps, exposure, and risk across cloud environments.

The chapter also explores how to design integrated security posture management solutions that incorporate Microsoft Defender for Cloud across hybrid and multi-cloud environments, ensuring consistent visibility and control regardless of where workloads are deployed. It addresses how to select appropriate cloud workload protection solutions within Microsoft Defender for Cloud based on workload type, risk profile, and operational requirements.

In addition, the chapter examines how to design solutions that integrate hybrid and multi-cloud environments using Azure Arc, enabling centralized governance and security management beyond native Azure resources. It also covers how to design a solution for Microsoft Defender EASM to identify and monitor externally exposed assets.

Finally, the chapter addresses how to specify requirements and priorities for a posture management process that uses Microsoft Security Exposure Management capabilities, including attack paths, attack surface reduction, security insights, and initiatives, ensuring that remediation efforts are risk-driven, measurable, and aligned with organizational priorities. These skills fall under the exam domain: *Design security solutions for infrastructure,* which represents approximately 25-30 % of the overall SC-100 skills[1] measured.

Security posture with Defender for Cloud

Security posture is not a static state or a collection of hardened settings; it is a continuously evaluated measure of how closely an environment aligns with defined security expectations. Microsoft Defender for Cloud positions posture management as a foundational security discipline, allowing architects to assess whether essential controls are present, correctly configured, and consistently applied across Azure and hybrid environments. This posture-first framing deliberately shifts security design away from reactive fixes and toward sustained reduction of systemic risk.

At the center of this evaluation model is the MCSB. The benchmark defines a comprehensive, opinionated set of security controls spanning identity, network protection, data security, asset management, and monitoring. Rather than offering optional guidance, MCSB establishes a standardized baseline that reflects Microsoft's view of minimum acceptable security hygiene for cloud workloads. Defender for Cloud continuously evaluates resources against these controls, translating abstract security principles into concrete, testable requirements. This section maps

1 **https://learn.microsoft.com/en-us/credentials/certifications/resources/study-guides/sc-100**

to the following SC-100 skills measured: *Evaluate security posture by using Microsoft Defender for Cloud, including the MCSB.*

MCSB and posture evaluation

The value of the benchmark lies in its ability to normalize posture evaluation across diverse services and architectures. Cloud environments evolve rapidly, and without a shared baseline, security decisions quickly become inconsistent. By anchoring posture assessment to MCSB, Defender for Cloud allows architects to reason about security health using a common language, regardless of workload type or deployment model.

Within Defender for Cloud, MCSB compliance results are grouped into control families such as endpoint security, network security, and data protection. Checks that validate whether server protection is enabled, such as confirming that Defender for Servers is installed on Windows **virtual machines** (**VMs**), are surfaced under the endpoint security control family. Architects must understand this mapping when interpreting benchmark compliance reports and remediation requirements.

Purpose and scope of MCSB

MCSB exists to standardize security intent across heterogeneous environments. It abstracts security goals into control domains that apply equally to compute, platform services, and data workloads. This abstraction is particularly critical in hybrid environments, where architectural variation would otherwise lead to fragmented standards and uneven exposure. By defining what secure enough means at a control level, the benchmark enables consistent evaluation even when implementation details differ.

Mapping to Defender for Cloud recommendations

Defender for Cloud operationalizes the benchmark through recommendations. Each recommendation represents a specific deviation from expected control alignment, such as missing encryption, insufficient network segmentation, or inadequate logging configuration. These recommendations are not advisory in nature; they are the primary signal architects use to identify where posture has drifted from the benchmark. Importantly, recommendations translate high-level security intent into actionable remediation targets.

Defender for Cloud recommendations and Secure Score

Effective posture management depends on correctly interpreting what Defender for Cloud surfaces. Recommendations are preventative signals, designed to highlight latent weaknesses before they contribute to an incident. They form the basis of posture improvement strategies, guiding architects toward areas where control gaps meaningfully increase exposure.

The recommendations view in Defender for Cloud illustrates how posture insights are surfaced, prioritized, and tied directly to specific resources and risk conditions:

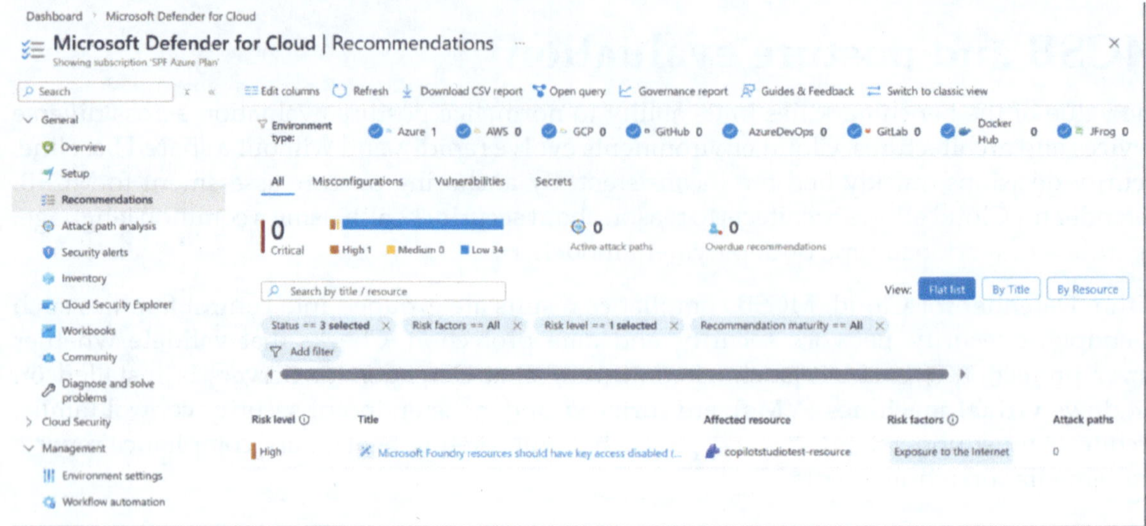

Figure 8.1: Microsoft Defender for Cloud recommendations

As shown in *Figure 8.1*, recommendations are not abstract findings, they are contextualized signals that link misconfigurations to affected resources, risk levels, and potential exposure paths. This allows architects to move beyond generic guidance and instead focus on actionable remediation, where each recommendation reflects a measurable contribution to Secure Score. By interpreting these signals within the recommendations blade, architects can validate whether coverage is complete, confirm that protection plans are active, and ensure that posture data accurately represents the organization's true risk surface.

For posture recommendations to be generated consistently, two foundational mechanisms must be in place: auto provisioning and the appropriate Defender for Cloud protection plans. Auto provisioning ensures that required agents and extensions are deployed automatically so resources can be assessed. Protection plans determine which resource types are evaluated and protected. If either is missing, workloads such as Kubernetes clusters or VMs may be excluded from posture evaluation, resulting in incomplete Secure Score coverage. Architects must therefore enable both auto provisioning and the relevant Defender plans to ensure that all supported resources contribute posture signals.

Posture signals are only reliable when coverage is complete. If protection plans or auto provisioning are misconfigured or scoped incorrectly, Secure Score and recommendations may underrepresent real exposure, leading architects to prioritize remediation based on incomplete posture data.

Interpreting posture recommendations vs. alerts

A critical distinction within Defender for Cloud is the separation of posture recommendations from security alerts. Recommendations indicate misalignment with security controls; they do not signal active exploitation or malicious behavior. Alerts, by contrast, represent detected threats that require investigation and response. Confusing these signals leads to flawed designs, either overreacting to configuration findings or underinvesting in preventative controls. Architects must treat recommendations as the primary input for reducing the attack surface over time.

Understanding Secure Score as posture improvement potential

Secure Score aggregates recommendation coverage into a measurable indicator of improvement potential. It does not represent absolute security, maturity, or compliance. Instead, it quantifies how much posture can be strengthened by implementing available recommendations. Secure Score allows architects to prioritize remediation based on impact, enabling structured improvement rather than reactive, piecemeal changes. Used correctly, it is a planning instrument that supports sustained posture evolution.

Taken together, the benchmark defines the standard, recommendations reveal deviation, and the Secure Score provides a measurable path to improvement. This model allows security architects to evaluate posture systematically, prioritize remediation deliberately, and maintain alignment as cloud and hybrid environments continue to change.

Security posture assessment with Secure Score

While Microsoft Defender for Cloud evaluates the security posture of infrastructure and platform resources, Microsoft Secure Score evaluates how securely an organization is using Microsoft 365. This distinction matters architecturally. Secure Score does not measure the presence of security tools or licenses; it measures whether security capabilities that protect identities, devices, data, and applications are actually being applied. Together with Defender for Cloud, Secure Score completes the posture picture by extending evaluation beyond infrastructure into the productivity and collaboration layer of the organization.

Secure Score exists to surface a specific category of risk: exposure created by incomplete or inconsistent adoption of available Microsoft 365 security controls. Many Microsoft 365 security incidents occur not because protections are unavailable, but because they are selectively applied, misconfigured, or deprioritized in favor of usability. Secure Score exposes these gaps by assessing control adoption at the tenant level and translating them into a measurable posture signal.

Secure Score evaluates security posture within the Microsoft 365 tenant only. Infrastructure and platform posture is evaluated through Defender for Cloud, while device-level posture may surface through endpoint and device management solutions, depending on the scenario. This section maps to the following SC-100 skills measured: *Evaluate security posture by using Microsoft Secure Score.*

Secure Score as a Microsoft 365 posture metric

Microsoft Secure Score evaluates tenant posture across identity protection, device security, data protection, and application governance. Each score reflects the degree to which recommended security actions have been implemented, such as enforcing multi-factor authentication, protecting privileged accounts, or applying data protection policies. The score, therefore, represents control adoption, not technical configuration depth.

Secure Score is intentionally comparative rather than absolute. It is designed to show improvement potential over time, allowing architects to track whether security posture is strengthening or stagnating as the organization evolves. This framing reinforces the idea that posture management is continuous. A higher score indicates that more recommended controls are in place, but it does not imply that risk has been eliminated or that compliance requirements have been met.

Prioritizing Secure Score improvement actions

Secure Score provides more than a numeric indicator; it includes improvement actions that describe specific changes capable of reducing risk. These actions are ranked based on estimated risk reduction, scope of impact, and implementation complexity. This prioritization is essential in large tenants, where attempting to implement all actions simultaneously would create operational disruption without proportional benefit.

Architects must interpret improvement actions as sequencing guidance, not a mandatory checklist. Some actions deliver broad risk reduction across the tenant, such as strengthening identity controls, while others address narrower exposure related to specific workloads or user populations. Effective posture design involves selecting improvement actions that align with organizational risk tolerance, technical readiness, and business constraints.

Secure Score also reinforces the distinction between posture improvement and incident response. Improvement actions are preventative by nature, aimed at reducing the likelihood and impact of future compromise. They are not a substitute for detection or response capabilities. When used correctly, Secure Score enables architects to design phased, sustainable security improvements that measurably strengthen Microsoft 365 posture over time.

By evaluating control adoption, prioritizing remediation actions, and tracking improvement, Secure Score provides a disciplined approach to managing Microsoft 365 security posture. It allows architects to move beyond subjective assessments and toward measurable, defensible security decisions.

Integrated security posture management across hybrid and multi-cloud

Hybrid and multi-cloud environments are no longer transitional states; they are the steady operating condition for most organizations. Security posture, therefore, fails when it is designed per platform rather than as a unified discipline. Integrated posture management answers a foundational architectural question: can security be evaluated, compared, and improved consistently across Azure, other cloud providers, and on-premises environments without fragmenting standards or decision-making? Microsoft Defender for Cloud provides the control plane that enables this integration by aggregating posture signals into a single evaluative model.

Integrated posture management is not about enforcing Azure-native configurations everywhere. It is about maintaining consistent security expectations and visibility even when implementation details differ. Without this integration, posture decisions become localized, remediation priorities diverge, and enterprise risk becomes difficult to reason about holistically. This section maps to the following SC-100 skills measured: *Design integrated security posture management solutions that include Microsoft Defender for Cloud in hybrid and multi-cloud environments*.

Unified posture visibility across cloud environments

Effective posture management begins with unified visibility. Defender for Cloud centralizes posture assessment for Azure resources and extends that assessment to supported multi-cloud and hybrid environments. This centralization allows architects to reason about security health using a common set of signals rather than stitching together findings from multiple, disconnected tools.

Aggregating posture signals

Defender for Cloud ingests posture data from Azure subscriptions and integrates posture assessments from supported **Amazon Web Services** (AWS) and **Google Cloud Platform** (GCP) accounts, as well as from connected on-premises resources. These findings are normalized into a consistent recommendation and scoring framework, enabling cross-environment comparison. The purpose of aggregation is not uniform enforcement, but uniform evaluation, ensuring that posture deviations are visible and comparable regardless of where workloads run.

This aggregation is especially important for prioritization. When posture signals are unified, architects can identify systemic weaknesses that span environments rather than treating each platform in isolation. This prevents remediation efforts from being skewed toward the most visible platform rather than the areas of greatest risk.

In practice, integrated posture management combines multiple onboarding paths. Azure subscriptions are assessed natively by Defender for Cloud. AWS and GCP environments are connected using Defender for Cloud multi-cloud connectors to surface posture recommendations for services such as Amazon **Elastic Compute Cloud** (**EC2**). On-premises and edge resources are onboarded using Azure Arc. This combination allows architects to evaluate posture across cloud, hybrid, and multi-cloud environments through a single control plane.

In design terms, multi-cloud connectors are used to assess native AWS and GCP services, while Azure Arc is used to project non-Azure servers and Kubernetes clusters into Azure Resource Manager. Choosing the correct onboarding method is essential, as it determines which resources can be evaluated and governed centrally.

Once assets are connected and posture signals are centralized, the next architectural challenge is interpreting security posture consistently when equivalent controls are implemented differently across platforms.

Design considerations for hybrid and multi-cloud posture

While unified visibility is essential, integrated posture management must account for real-world platform differences. Cloud providers expose different control models, configuration mechanisms, and security primitives. A successful posture design acknowledges these differences while still enforcing consistent security intent.

Consistency, visibility, and limitations across platforms

Defender for Cloud provides consistent insight into posture, but not all controls can be applied identically across environments. Architects must therefore design posture strategies that focus on equivalent security outcomes, not identical technical implementations. The goal is to reduce risk to a comparable level across platforms, even when the underlying controls differ.

Visibility is the non-negotiable requirement. As long as posture deviations are surfaced centrally and prioritized consistently, remediation can be planned intelligently. Integrated posture management succeeds when standards are shared, visibility is centralized, and risk decisions are made at the enterprise-level rather than within individual platforms.

By using Defender for Cloud as the aggregation and evaluation layer, architects can design posture management solutions that scale across hybrid and multi-cloud environments without sacrificing clarity or control. This integration enables consistent risk assessment, informed prioritization, and sustained security improvement as environments continue to diversify.

Cloud workload protection using Defender

Security posture management establishes whether environments are configured according to defined security expectations, but posture alone cannot detect or stop active exploitation. Even well-hardened workloads remain exposed to runtime threats such as malware execution, credential abuse, privilege escalation, and data exfiltration. Cloud workload protection exists to address this residual risk by monitoring workload behavior continuously and identifying malicious activity as it occurs. In Microsoft Defender for Cloud, workload protection is delivered through targeted protection plans that complement posture management rather than replacing it.

Architects must design workload protection deliberately. Treating runtime protection as an afterthought or enabling it indiscriminately undermines its effectiveness and increases operational noise. Defender for Cloud separates posture evaluation from workload protection to ensure that each layer serves a distinct purpose within a layered security architecture. This section maps to the following SC-100 skills measured: *Select cloud workload protection solutions in Microsoft Defender for Cloud*.

Defender for Cloud workload protection plans

Defender for Cloud provides workload protection plans aligned to specific resource categories, including servers, containers, databases, and storage services. Each plan activates detection and assessment capabilities tailored to the behaviors, attack patterns, and risk profiles associated with that workload type. Selecting the appropriate protection plan is therefore a deliberate architectural decision that must reflect the workloads actually deployed within the environment rather than a blanket enablement approach.

In design scenarios, protection plan selection follows workload type rather than location: server-based workloads require Defender for Servers, orchestrated environments require Defender for Containers, data platforms require database protection plans, and object storage requires Defender for Storage. Selecting the wrong plan leaves runtime threats undetected even when posture appears compliant.

For VMs, workload protection is delivered through Microsoft Defender for Servers, which combines runtime threat detection with vulnerability assessment. Vulnerability assessment for VMs is provided through the *Qualys* scanning engine, which is enabled as part of Defender for Servers. When scenarios specify the use of the Qualys engine or require VMs to be assessed for missing patches and known vulnerabilities, architects must select Defender for Servers to satisfy that requirement. In hybrid or mixed environments, this capability is commonly paired with endpoint protection onboarding to ensure both vulnerability data and runtime behavioral signals are available.

Container workload protection focuses on risks unique to orchestrated environments, including vulnerable container images, compromised clusters, and anomalous runtime behavior. Database workload protection targets threats such as suspicious query execution, privilege misuse, and abnormal access patterns, while storage workload protection monitors for unusual access behavior that may indicate data exfiltration or misuse. Each protection plan is scoped to a specific workload category and must be enabled explicitly to ensure relevant signals are generated.

Architects must understand that workload protection plans are distinct from posture recommendations. While posture management identifies configuration gaps and baseline misalignment, workload protection plans provide continuous monitoring for active threats. Enabling the wrong plan, or assuming one plan applies universally across workloads, creates false assurance and leaves detection gaps that posture controls alone cannot address.

Protection plans for servers, containers, databases, and storage

Server protection focuses on threats such as malware execution, suspicious process behavior, and lateral movement attempts. Container protection addresses risks unique to orchestrated environments, including vulnerable images, compromised clusters, and anomalous runtime behavior. Database protection concentrates on suspicious query patterns, privilege misuse, and abnormal access, while storage protection monitors for unusual access patterns that may indicate data exfiltration or abuse.

Each protection plan applies detection logic appropriate to the workload it protects. Architects must understand these distinctions to ensure that runtime protection aligns with how different workloads are realistically attacked. Enabling the wrong plan, or assuming one plan covers all workloads, creates false assurance and leaves gaps in detection.

With workload protection plans selected, the remaining architectural risk is assuming that coverage alone equates to security.

Distinguishing posture management from workload protection

A common architectural failure is conflating posture assessment with workload protection. Although both are delivered through Defender for Cloud, they address different phases of risk.

Posture management reduces exposure by correcting misconfigurations and enforcing baseline controls. Workload protection assumes that some risk remains even after posture improvements and focuses on detecting malicious behavior in real-time. Architects must design both layers together: posture controls to minimize attack surface and workload protection to detect and respond to threats that bypass preventative measures.

Confusing these roles leads either to overreliance on configuration hygiene or to excessive alerting without adequate preventative controls. Effective security architecture depends on recognizing the complementary relationship between posture management and workload protection and applying each where it delivers the greatest value.

By selecting appropriate workload protection plans and integrating them with posture management, Defender for Cloud enables layered defenses that address both preventative and detective security needs across cloud environments.

Hybrid and multi-cloud integration with Azure Arc

Hybrid and multi-cloud environments introduce a structural security challenge: most security services are designed to operate natively within a single cloud boundary. When workloads extend beyond Azure, posture assessment, policy enforcement, and protection capabilities often fragment across tools and teams. Azure Arc exists to address this fragmentation by extending Azure's management and security control planes to non-Azure resources, allowing architects to design security solutions that span environments without abandoning centralized governance.

Azure Arc does not replace native cloud tooling or impose Azure infrastructure requirements. Instead, it provides a unifying representation layer that allows non-Azure resources to participate in Azure-based security services. This distinction is essential for designing realistic hybrid architectures that preserve platform flexibility while maintaining consistent security oversight. This section maps to the following SC-100 skills measured: *Design a solution for integrating hybrid and multi-cloud environments by using Azure Arc.*

Extending Azure security management with Arc

Azure Arc enables non-Azure resources to be onboarded and managed as first-class Azure resources. Once connected, these resources can be evaluated, governed, and secured using Azure-native services, reducing the operational gap between Azure and non-Azure environments.

Arc-enabled servers and Kubernetes clusters

Arc-enabled servers allow on-premises and multi-cloud VMs to be represented within Azure Resource Manager. This representation enables centralized inventory, monitoring, and security assessment using Azure services such as Microsoft Defender for Cloud. Arc-enabled Kubernetes provides similar integration for container orchestration platforms, allowing clusters running outside Azure to be assessed consistently alongside Azure Kubernetes Service.

These capabilities are foundational for extending posture evaluation and security visibility beyond Azure. Without Arc, non-Azure workloads remain outside the scope of Azure security services, creating blind spots that undermine integrated posture management.

Using Azure Arc with Defender for Cloud

Azure Arc is a prerequisite for applying Defender for Cloud posture assessment and protection capabilities to hybrid and multi-cloud resources. The integration between Arc and Defender for Cloud allows architects to extend security evaluation without redesigning controls for each environment.

Enforcing configuration standards

While Azure Arc enables hybrid and multi-cloud resources to be assessed centrally, Azure Policy guest configuration provides the mechanism for auditing and enforcing operating system–level standards on those resources. Guest configuration allows architects to evaluate settings such as security baselines, password policies, and service configurations inside Arc-enabled servers, regardless of where they run. This capability is essential when posture requirements specify consistent configuration enforcement across on-premises and multi-cloud environments.

Enabling posture and security management beyond Azure

By onboarding Arc-enabled resources into Defender for Cloud, architects can assess security posture against the same benchmarks and recommendation models used for Azure-native workloads. This enables consistent visibility into configuration gaps, control alignment, and improvement opportunities across environments. Where appropriate, workload protection plans can also be applied, extending runtime detection capabilities to hybrid assets.

Azure Arc does not enforce identical configurations across platforms. Instead, it enables consistent evaluation and prioritization, allowing architects to design security strategies that focus on equivalent risk reduction outcomes rather than uniform technical implementation.

By acting as the bridge between Azure security services and non-Azure resources, Azure Arc enables coherent security architectures that scale across hybrid and multi-cloud environments without sacrificing visibility, control, or architectural flexibility.

EASM with Defender

Traditional security posture management evaluates environments from the inside outward, focusing on resources that are known, managed, and intentionally deployed. Attackers, however, operate from the outside inward. They discover exposed assets through public scanning, DNS enumeration, and service fingerprinting, often identifying weaknesses that internal inventories fail to capture. ESAM addresses this asymmetry by shifting posture evaluation to the attacker's perspective.

Microsoft Defender EASM is designed to give architects continuous visibility into the organization's publicly reachable assets, including those that fall outside formal governance processes. This capability is critical in environments shaped by rapid cloud adoption, decentralization, and shadow IT, where exposure can accumulate faster than internal controls can account for it. This section maps to the following SC-100 skills measured: *Design a solution for Microsoft Defender EASM.*

Discovering and classifying external assets

The first function of Defender EASM is discovery. Organizations rarely have complete awareness of their internet-facing footprint, particularly when assets are created by distributed teams or legacy projects. Defender EASM continuously scans and correlates public-facing signals to identify domains, IP addresses, services, and infrastructure that can be attributed to the organization.

Defender EASM produces an attributed inventory of internet-facing assets along with exposure findings such as open services, misconfigurations, and takeover risks. Effective use follows a clear workflow: discover assets, validate ownership, classify exposure, and prioritize remediation based on attacker visibility.

Identifying unknown and unmanaged internet-facing resources

Defender ESM surfaces assets that are unmanaged, forgotten, or incorrectly classified, including legacy services, temporary deployments, and cloud resources created outside centralized IT workflows. These assets often lack appropriate security controls and monitoring, making them attractive entry points for attackers. By identifying them, architects gain visibility into exposure that internal posture tools are unable to detect.

Understanding external exposure risk

Discovery alone does not equate to risk reduction. Once external assets are identified, posture management must assess how those assets contribute to the organization's exposure and how they might be targeted by adversaries.

Defender EASM does not assess internal configuration hygiene or enforce security controls. Its role is to illuminate what is visible and reachable from the public internet. This distinction is essential for correct design. External exposure data must be interpreted alongside internal posture signals from tools such as Defender for Cloud and Secure Score, not confused with them. Architects use EASM insights to prioritize remediation of externally exposed assets that present the greatest risk, rather than treating all exposure as equal.

By incorporating Defender EASM into posture management strategies, architects extend security evaluation beyond managed environments and gain a realistic view of organizational exposure. This external-in perspective ensures that risks introduced through growth, decentralization, or oversight are identified and addressed before they can be exploited.

Posture management with Security Exposure Management

As environments grow more complex, the challenges of posture management evolve from simply achieving visibility to effectively setting priorities. Organizations may identify thousands of issues spanning infrastructure, user identities, workloads, and external exposures, yet still find it difficult to mitigate genuine risks. The problem is not a shortage of information; rather, it is the lack of a decision-making framework to determine which vulnerabilities are most critical and why. Microsoft Security Exposure Management tackles this issue by shifting posture management focus toward exposure-driven risk, instead of viewing each control failure in isolation.

Exposure management assumes that attackers exploit chains of weakness, not individual misconfigurations. A low-severity issue can become critical when combined with excessive permissions, external exposure, or lateral movement opportunities. Designing an effective posture management process, therefore, requires understanding how risks compound across the environment and prioritizing remediation accordingly.

Attack paths matter because they reveal where a single control change can break an entire chain of exploitation. Architects use these insights to prioritize remediation at the highest-leverage choke point, often identity privilege, external exposure, or lateral movement, rather than addressing isolated findings in volume. This section maps to the following SC-100 skills measured: *Specify requirements and priorities for a posture management process that uses Microsoft Security Exposure Management attack paths, attack surface reduction, security insights, and initiatives.*

Exposure-driven risk prioritization

Security Exposure Management evaluates posture through the lens of attack paths—logical sequences that connect exposed assets, misconfigurations, and privileges to high-value targets. This approach allows architects to move beyond volume-based remediation and focus on reducing the likelihood of successful compromise.

Attack paths and correlated exposure insights

Attack paths reveal how individual posture findings interact to create material risk. A misconfigured workload may appear insignificant in isolation, but when paired with weak identity controls or external accessibility, it can enable a full attack chain. Security Exposure Management correlates posture data across domains to surface these relationships, allowing architects to identify which combinations of weaknesses are most likely to be exploited.

This correlation is critical for prioritization. Rather than addressing findings based solely on severity labels or compliance status, architects can target remediation efforts where they will break attack paths and meaningfully reduce exposure.

Continuous posture improvement through initiatives

Effective posture management is not a one-time hardening effort. As environments change, new attack paths emerge, and previously addressed risks can reappear. Security Exposure Management supports continuous improvement through initiatives that group related remediation actions into outcome-focused efforts.

From static compliance to dynamic risk reduction

Initiatives allow architects to define posture goals that evolve with threat conditions and organizational change. Instead of measuring success by control completion alone, initiatives emphasize sustained exposure reduction. This shift moves posture management away from static compliance and toward dynamic risk management, ensuring that security investments remain aligned to the most relevant threats over time.

By combining attack path analysis, correlated exposure insights, and initiative-driven remediation, Security Exposure Management provides the decision framework that modern posture management requires. It enables architects to prioritize effectively, reduce real-world risk, and sustain security improvement as environments grow in scale and complexity.

Conclusion

This chapter examined how to design effective cloud and hybrid security solutions by treating security posture management as a continuous, integrated discipline rather than a collection of isolated tools. It showed how Microsoft Defender for Cloud establishes a standardized posture baseline through the MCSB, translating security intent into measurable recommendations and actionable improvement paths. By distinguishing posture evaluation from threat detection, the chapter clarified how architects reduce risk proactively rather than reacting to incidents after the fact.

The chapter expanded posture management beyond Azure by addressing hybrid and multi-cloud environments, demonstrating how unified visibility is achieved through Defender for Cloud integration and Azure Arc. It reinforced the importance of selecting workload protection plans deliberately, ensuring runtime threats are detected while configuration hygiene is maintained through posture controls. The external perspective introduced by Defender EASM highlighted how unmanaged and internet-facing assets contribute to real-world exposure that internal assessments alone cannot capture.

Finally, the chapter brought posture management to its decision point through Microsoft Security Exposure Management, emphasizing attack paths, correlated insights, and initiatives as the mechanisms that transform visibility into prioritization. Together, these capabilities enable architects to design security strategies that consistently reduce exposure, sustain alignment as environments evolve, and focus remediation efforts on the risks that matter most.

The next chapter moves from securing cloud and hybrid platforms to protecting the endpoints and devices that access them. It examines how servers, clients, mobile devices, and specialized systems must be secured, monitored, and governed to prevent endpoints from becoming the primary entry point for compromise.

Questions

Success on any assessment depends on understanding the underlying technologies, concepts, and principles rather than memorizing facts. The following questions help readers confirm that they can apply this chapter's ideas in realistic design scenarios, including security posture evaluation, benchmark alignment, hybrid visibility, workload protection selection, external attack surface awareness, and exposure-driven risk prioritization.

1. **An organization wants to evaluate whether Azure workloads align with a standardized baseline covering identity, network, data, and monitoring controls. Which architectural approach best achieves this outcome?**
   a. Enabling Microsoft Secure Score
   b. Reviewing individual security alerts
   c. Evaluating workloads using Microsoft Defender for Cloud and the MCSB
   d. Applying Azure Policy remediation tasks manually
2. **Why is the MCSB most effective when used as a posture baseline rather than a compliance checklist?**
   a. It replaces the need for threat detection
   b. It enforces identical configurations across all cloud platforms
   c. It defines a consistent security intent that can be evaluated across diverse workloads
   d. It guarantees regulatory compliance
3. **Which signal most strongly indicates a systemic posture design issue rather than an isolated configuration error?**
   a. A single failed recommendation on one resource
   b. A recurring posture recommendation across multiple workloads
   c. A temporary Secure Score fluctuation
   d. An individual security alert
4. **What does Microsoft Secure Score primarily represent?**
   a. Real-time detection of active attacks
   b. Compliance status against regulatory frameworks
   c. Improvement potential based on the adoption of Microsoft 365 security controls
   d. Infrastructure misconfiguration severity

5. **An architect needs unified posture visibility across Azure, AWS, and on-premises servers. Which design best supports this requirement?**
   a. Native security tools on each platform
   b. Microsoft Secure Score alone
   c. Microsoft Defender for Cloud with multi-cloud connectors and Azure Arc
   d. Microsoft Sentinel analytics rules
6. **A scenario requires VMs to be assessed for missing patches and known vulnerabilities using the Qualys scanning engine. Which Defender for Cloud plan must be selected?**
   a. Defender for Containers
   b. Defender for servers
   c. Defender for databases
   d. Defender for storage
7. **Why does Azure Arc play a critical role in hybrid and multi-cloud posture management?**
   a. It enforces identical configurations across platforms
   b. It replaces native cloud security services
   c. It projects non-Azure resources into Azure security and management control planes
   d. It performs external vulnerability scanning
8. **Which capability is specifically designed to identify unknown or unmanaged internet-facing assets from an attacker's perspective?**
   a. Microsoft Secure Score
   b. Defender for Cloud recommendations
   c. Microsoft Defender EASM
   d. Azure Policy guest configuration
9. **Why is it architecturally incorrect to assume that enabling workload protection plans alone ensures adequate security?**
   a. Workload protection increases alert volume
   b. Protection plans are limited to Azure resources
   c. Coverage does not address configuration hygiene or systemic exposure
   d. Protection plans replace posture management
10. **What is the primary purpose of attack paths in Microsoft Security Exposure Management?**
   a. To list all vulnerabilities by severity
   b. To automate remediation across all findings

c. To reveal how combined weaknesses enable end-to-end compromise

d. To replace Secure Score and posture recommendations

Answers

1. c: Evaluating workloads using Microsoft Defender for Cloud and the MCSB.

   Defender for Cloud continuously evaluates Azure workload configurations against the MCSB across identity, network, data, and monitoring control families, providing a standardized posture baseline and highlighting alignment gaps through posture recommendations.

2. c: It defines consistent security intent that can be evaluated across diverse workloads.

   Using MCSB as a baseline embeds security expectations into posture evaluation rather than treating controls as optional or one-time checks.

3. b: A recurring posture recommendation across multiple workloads.

   Repeated findings indicate a systemic design gap in standards, templates, or inherited controls rather than an isolated misconfiguration.

4. c: Improvement potential based on adoption of Microsoft 365 security controls.

   Secure Score measures how much posture can be strengthened by implementing recommended controls, not absolute security or compliance.

5. c: Microsoft Defender for Cloud with multi-cloud connectors and Azure Arc.

   This design centralizes posture signals across Azure, other clouds, and on-premises environments into a single evaluative model.

6. b: Defender for Servers.

   Defender for Servers enables the Qualys vulnerability assessment engine and provides patch and vulnerability visibility for VMs.

7. c: It projects non-Azure resources into Azure security and management control planes.

   Azure Arc allows hybrid and multi-cloud assets to be evaluated and governed using Azure-native security services.

8. c: Microsoft Defender EASM.

   Defender EASM discovers and classifies publicly exposed assets that may fall outside internal inventories and governance processes.

9. c: Coverage does not address configuration hygiene or systemic exposure.

   Workload protection detects runtime threats, but posture management is required to reduce the attack surface and prevent recurrence.

10. c: To reveal how combined weaknesses enable end-to-end compromise.

    Attack paths correlate posture findings across domains, allowing architects to prioritize remediation that breaks real-world exploitation chains.

Chapter 9
Design Endpoint and Device Security Solutions

Introduction

This chapter examines how to design endpoint and device security solutions that protect servers, user endpoints, and specialized systems across cloud, on-premises, and hybrid environments. Endpoints represent the most common entry point for modern attacks and are critical enforcement points for Zero Trust decisions, making deliberate endpoint security design essential to reducing organizational risk.

The chapter explores how Microsoft Defender for Endpoint, Microsoft Defender for Servers, Microsoft Intune, and **Windows Local Administrator Password Solution** (**Windows LAPS**) work together to enforce execution control, device compliance, vulnerability management, and credential isolation. It also addresses how endpoint security requirements differ for **Internet of Things** (**IoT**), embedded systems, and **operational technology** (**OT**) environments, where availability and operational stability must be balanced with security visibility and control.

By applying these capabilities in a coordinated way, security architects can design endpoint protection architectures that limit attack surface, constrain lateral movement, and maintain a consistent security posture across diverse device types.

Structure

This chapter covers the following topics:

- Server security requirements across platforms
- Mobile and client endpoint security requirements
- IoT and embedded device security requirements
- Securing OT and ICS
- Security baselines for server and client endpoints
- Evaluating Windows LAPS security solutions

Objectives

This chapter covers the skills required to specify security requirements for servers across multiple platforms and operating systems, ensuring consistent protection regardless of underlying infrastructure. It also examines how to define security requirements for mobile devices and client endpoints, including endpoint protection, system hardening, and configuration standards.

The chapter explores how to specify security requirements for IoT devices and embedded systems, addressing the unique constraints and risk profiles associated with these technologies. It evaluates solutions for securing OT and **industrial control systems** (**ICSs**) using Microsoft Defender for IoT, with a focus on visibility, threat detection, and operational safety.

In addition, the chapter examines how to specify and apply security baselines for server and client endpoints to ensure consistent configuration and reduced attack surface. Finally, it covers how to evaluate Windows LAPS solutions to reduce the risk associated with local administrative credentials and improve credential hygiene across the environment. These skills fall under the exam domain: *Design security solutions for infrastructure*, which represents approximately 25-30 % of the overall SC-100 skills measured[1].

Server security requirements across platforms

Servers represent a distinct security problem space because they combine persistent availability, elevated privileges, and access to sensitive workloads. As organizations distribute servers across Azure, on-premises datacenters, and hybrid environments, traditional assumptions about perimeter protection and implicit trust no longer apply. Server security must be designed deliberately, treating servers as high-value endpoints whose behavior and configuration are continuously constrained rather than implicitly trusted.

Defining server security requirements begins by addressing two core risks that consistently appear in modern attack paths. The first is unauthorized code execution, where attackers deploy tools or payloads once access is obtained. The second is unmanaged vulnerability exposure, where missing patches or insecure configurations provide the initial foothold. An effective server security architecture mitigates both risks across Windows and Linux platforms without relying on manual enforcement. This section maps to the following SC-100 skills measured: *Specify security requirements for servers, including multiple platforms and operating systems.*

Controlling application execution on server workloads

Many server compromises succeed not because attackers exploit unknown vulnerabilities, but because they are able to execute unauthorized software once access is gained. Scripts, lateral movement tools, crypto miners, and ransomware all depend on execution capability. If execution is constrained, these attacks are either blocked entirely or significantly limited in impact.

1 **https://learn.microsoft.com/en-us/credentials/certifications/resources/study-guides/sc-100**

Modern server security, therefore, prioritizes preventive execution control over reactive detection. Instead of attempting to identify malicious behavior after it begins, security controls define which applications are permitted to run and block everything else by default. This model is especially effective for server workloads, where application behavior is typically stable and predictable once systems are deployed.

Adaptive application controls for authorized software enforcement

Microsoft Defender for Cloud implements execution control through adaptive application controls, which observe application behavior on servers over time and establish allowlists based on known, trusted execution patterns. These allowlists reflect how servers actually operate, rather than relying on static assumptions made during deployment.

From a design perspective, adaptive application controls allow organizations to enforce least privilege at the execution layer without introducing operational friction. When enforcement is enabled, any attempt to run software outside the approved set is blocked automatically until explicitly authorized. This prevents attackers from deploying unauthorized tooling even if they succeed in authenticating to the server.

Adaptive application controls are most effective when specified for workloads with consistent execution profiles, such as application servers, database hosts, and infrastructure components. Including this requirement directly reduces the attack surface and limits the potential impact of credential compromise or misconfiguration.

Vulnerability management for Windows and Linux servers

Execution controls alone are insufficient if underlying vulnerabilities remain unaddressed. Servers must also be continuously evaluated for missing updates and insecure configurations that attackers could exploit to gain initial access or escalate privileges. This requirement applies equally to Windows and Linux systems, particularly in hybrid environments where inconsistent tooling often creates blind spots.

Vulnerability management must be designed as a continuous process rather than a periodic assessment. Without ongoing visibility, security teams are unable to distinguish between low-risk issues and weaknesses that materially increase exposure across the server estate.

Cross-platform vulnerability assessment with Defender for servers

Microsoft Defender for Servers provides built-in vulnerability assessment capabilities for both Windows and Linux workloads. It identifies missing patches and insecure configurations using an integrated assessment engine, enabling consistent visibility across heterogeneous environments.

Microsoft Defender for Servers supports continuous vulnerability assessment by integrating with Microsoft Defender Vulnerability Management through Microsoft Defender for Endpoint. This capability provides unified visibility into missing patches, known vulnerabilities, and exposure across both Windows and Linux servers.

Microsoft Defender Vulnerability Management surfaces exposure across server workloads using risk-based scoring to prioritize remediation, as displayed in the following figure:

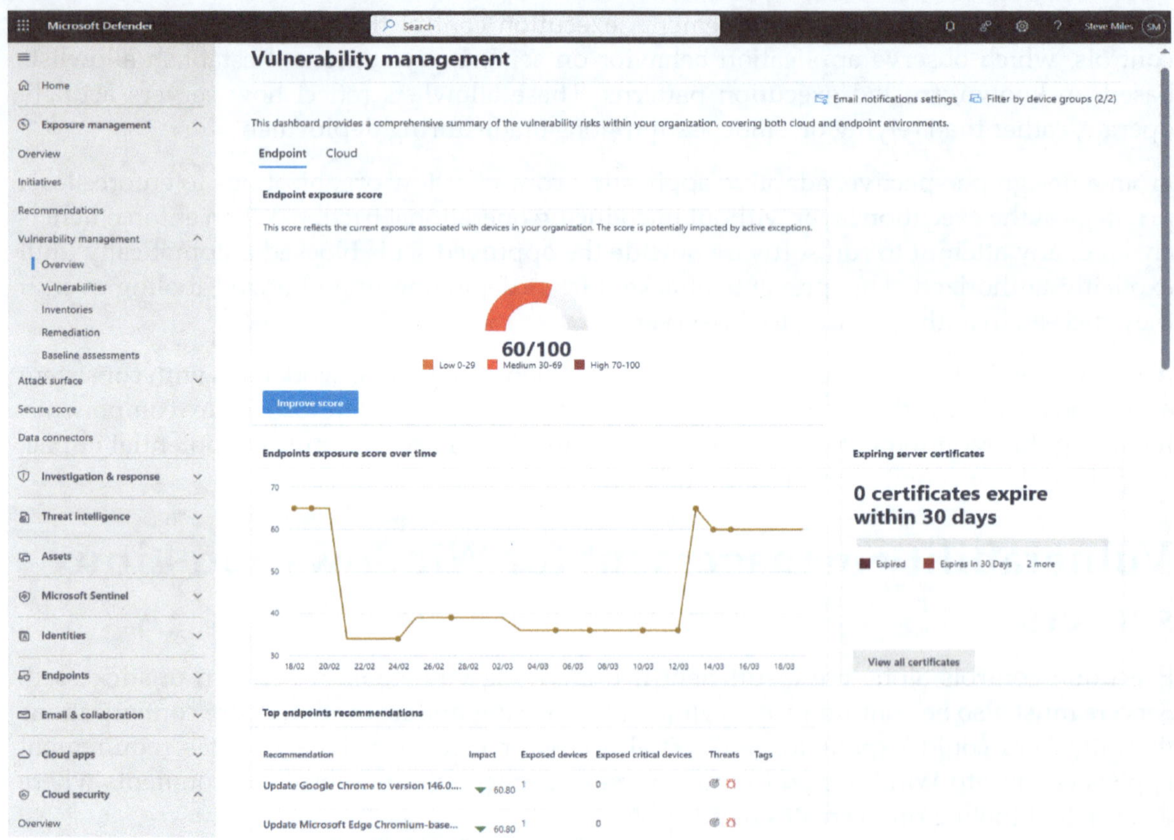

Figure 9.1: Microsoft Defender Vulnerability Management

From an architectural perspective, Defender for Servers is selected when the requirement is centralized, continuous vulnerability assessment, and risk-based prioritization for server workloads without relying on standalone scanning tools.

Architecturally, this capability embeds vulnerability assessment directly into server protection workflows instead of treating it as a separate scanning tool. Findings are surfaced in a way that supports prioritization, which allows remediation efforts to focus on issues that meaningfully impact risk rather than attempting to address every detected weakness.

When specifying server security requirements, architects should mandate continuous vulnerability assessment across all server platforms, integrated with centralized security tooling. This ensures consistent risk visibility, supports informed remediation decisions, and reduces configuration drift as environments scale.

Mobile and client endpoint security requirements

Client endpoints represent the most common entry point into modern environments; unlike servers, user devices are mobile, heterogeneous, and continuously exposed to untrusted networks, applications, and content. These endpoints also act as enforcement points for Zero Trust decisions, providing critical signals about device health, configuration, and risk. Designing security requirements for mobile and client endpoints, therefore, requires combining configuration enforcement, access control, Privilege Management, and post-compromise recovery into a coherent system.

Effective endpoint security design assumes that devices will eventually encounter threats. The goal is not to prevent all exposure, but to ensure that access is conditional, privileges are constrained, behavior is hardened, and compromised devices are isolated until they are demonstrably trustworthy again. This section maps to the following SC-100 skills measured: *Specify security requirements for mobile devices and clients, including endpoint protection, hardening, and configuration.*

Device compliance and Conditional Access enforcement

At the center of modern endpoint security is the ability to make access decisions based on device state rather than user identity alone. Devices that are outdated, misconfigured, or otherwise noncompliant represent a higher-risk and must not be treated as equivalent to healthy endpoints. Security requirements must therefore define how device compliance is evaluated and how that signal is enforced consistently across applications and services.

Compliance evaluation provides a binary outcome in the form of compliant or noncompliant, but its real value lies in how it is used. When integrated with access enforcement, compliance becomes a dynamic control that continuously adapts to device posture rather than a static configuration check.

Using Intune compliance signals for access decisions

Microsoft Intune is used to evaluate whether devices meet defined compliance requirements across Windows, macOS, iOS, and Android platforms. These requirements can include operating system version, encryption status, security configuration, and the presence of required protections. Once evaluated, Intune reports the compliance state of each device to the identity plane.

Conditional Access consumes this compliance signal to enforce policy. Access to Microsoft 365 and other protected resources can be allowed only from compliant devices, blocked entirely for noncompliant devices, or conditioned on additional controls. From a design standpoint, this integration ensures that device health directly influences access decisions, preventing outdated or insecure devices from silently expanding the attack surface.

Privilege Management on client devices

Even when devices are compliant, excessive local privileges can undermine security controls. Granting users permanent administrative rights increases the likelihood of accidental misconfiguration, malware persistence, and lateral movement. Endpoint security requirements must therefore include mechanisms that allow users to perform necessary administrative tasks without maintaining standing privilege.

This balance is particularly important on client devices, where users frequently need to install or update applications but should not retain unrestricted administrative access.

Endpoint Privilege Management for just-in-time elevation

Endpoint Privilege Management enables users to perform approved administrative actions on client devices without being permanent local administrators. Privilege elevation is granted only when required, scoped to specific tasks, and subject to policy enforcement.

From a design perspective, this control supports Zero Trust principles by eliminating standing privilege while preserving productivity. It ensures that administrative access is deliberate, auditable, and temporary. When specifying client security requirements, architects should favor just-in-time privilege elevation over static admin group membership, especially in environments with large user populations.

Endpoint hardening and threat protection

Client devices must be hardened to reduce exposure to common threats such as malicious websites, untrusted applications, and opportunistic attacks. Hardening does not rely on a single control but on layered enforcement that limits what users and applications can do, even when devices are connected to untrusted networks.

Endpoint protection requirements should account for specialized device types, such as kiosks and shared devices, as well as general-purpose user endpoints. In both cases, security controls must operate directly at the endpoint rather than relying solely on network-based defenses.

Securing kiosk and shared devices

Kiosks and shared devices present unique risks because they are often accessible to many users and perform a narrow set of functions. Security requirements for these devices must ensure that only authorized applications can run and that the devices remain hardened over time.

Enrolling kiosks into Intune and onboarding them to Microsoft Defender for Endpoint enables centralized configuration, threat visibility, and vulnerability management. This combination ensures that kiosks remain locked down while still receiving security updates and protection against emerging threats.

Web content filtering at the endpoint

Users frequently encounter threats through web access, particularly when devices operate outside corporate networks. Endpoint-based web content filtering allows organizations to block access to inappropriate or risky websites regardless of location.

Microsoft Defender for Endpoint enforces web protection directly on the device, ensuring consistent policy application whether users are on-premises, remote, or mobile. When designing endpoint security requirements, architects should specify endpoint-level web filtering rather than relying exclusively on network perimeter controls.

Post-incident access restoration for client devices

Endpoint security design must also account for what happens after a device is compromised. Malware removal alone does not automatically restore trust. Devices that were previously blocked must demonstrate that they meet security requirements before access is reinstated.

This phase is critical to preventing repeated compromise and ensuring that remediation actions are actually enforced across the environment.

Conditional Access re-evaluation after malware remediation

When a device is identified as compromised, Conditional Access can be used to suspend access based on risk or compliance state. After remediation, access is not restored until policy conditions are re-evaluated and authentication tokens are refreshed.

This design ensures that security decisions are recalculated based on current device health rather than previous access grants. It prevents stale sessions from bypassing enforcement and reinforces the principle that access is continuously verified, not permanently granted.

IoT and embedded device security requirements

IoT and embedded devices introduce security challenges that differ fundamentally from traditional servers and user endpoints; these systems are often purpose-built, resource-constrained, and tightly coupled to physical processes.

These solutions may run legacy operating systems, support limited patching, or operate continuously in environments where downtime directly impacts safety or business operations. Designing security requirements for these devices, therefore, requires a different balance between protection and operational stability.

Unlike general-purpose endpoints, IoT and embedded systems cannot always tolerate aggressive scanning, frequent configuration changes, or intrusive security agents. Security design must account for these constraints while still reducing exposure and improving visibility into device behavior. The goal is not maximum control, but appropriate control that aligns with device capabilities and risk. This section maps to the following SC-100 skills measured: *Specify security requirements for IoT devices and embedded systems.*

IoT and embedded Zero Trust principles

Zero Trust does not assume that devices are trustworthy simply because they are internal, specialized, or historically stable. However, applying Zero Trust to IoT environments requires adapting its principles to avoid disrupting critical operations. Security requirements must therefore emphasize visibility, monitoring, and controlled change rather than heavy-handed enforcement.

For IoT and embedded systems, Zero Trust focuses on understanding normal behavior, detecting deviation, and applying protection mechanisms that respect operational boundaries. This approach reduces blind spots without introducing instability.

Zero disruption threat monitoring and patch management

Effective IoT security design prioritizes threat monitoring over active interrogation. Passive monitoring techniques allow organizations to observe network traffic and device behavior without directly interacting with the device, reducing the risk of interference. This visibility enables detection of anomalous activity that could indicate compromise, misconfiguration, or unauthorized communication.

Patch management must also be approached cautiously. While keeping devices updated is essential, indiscriminate or frequent patching can disrupt operations or violate vendor support constraints. Security requirements should therefore specify controlled patching strategies that balance risk reduction with operational continuity, applying updates based on risk, criticality, and maintenance windows.

By combining passive threat monitoring with deliberate, risk-based patching, architects can apply Zero Trust principles to IoT and embedded devices in a way that reduces exposure while preserving reliability.

Securing OT and ICS

OT and ICS environments differ fundamentally from IT systems; they control physical processes, prioritize availability and safety, and often rely on legacy protocols and devices that were never designed with modern security controls in mind.

Applying conventional endpoint security techniques indiscriminately can introduce unacceptable risk, including system instability or operational shutdowns. Designing OT and ICS security, therefore, requires treating these environments as a distinct risk domain rather than an extension of enterprise endpoint security.

Security requirements for OT must acknowledge that prevention, detection, and response look different when devices cannot be easily patched, scanned, or instrumented. Visibility, segmentation, and anomaly detection become primary design goals, with enforcement applied carefully and deliberately. This section maps to the following SC-100 skills measured: *Evaluate solutions for securing OT and ICS by using Microsoft Defender for IoT*.

Designing as a distinct risk domain

OT security architecture begins by recognizing that industrial environments operate under constraints that do not exist in traditional IT systems. Devices may have fixed firmware, long service lifecycles, and strict vendor support requirements. Network communication patterns are often deterministic, and even minor disruptions can have physical or safety consequences.

As a result, OT security requirements must prioritize understanding normal behavior before attempting to enforce control. Rather than assuming devices can be hardened in the same way as servers or clients, architects should design security around visibility into traffic flows, device roles, and communication patterns. This enables risk to be identified without introducing instability.

Segmentation is also critical in OT environments. Separating industrial networks from enterprise IT systems limits the blast radius of compromise and reduces the likelihood that threats originating from user endpoints or servers can directly impact operational systems. This separation supports Zero Trust principles by removing implicit trust between IT and OT domains.

Visibility-first security design for industrial environments

Visibility-first security design focuses on observing OT environments without interfering with them. Passive monitoring techniques allow security teams to detect unexpected communication, unauthorized devices, or deviations from established traffic patterns. These signals provide early indicators of compromise while preserving system stability.

By emphasizing visibility over intrusive control, architects can design OT security solutions that respect operational constraints while still reducing risk. This approach enables informed decision-making, supports incident investigation, and creates a foundation for gradual security improvement without forcing disruptive changes.

Security baselines for server and client endpoints

Security baselines define what *good* looks like for endpoints before incidents occur. Without a clear baseline, security teams cannot reliably distinguish between acceptable configuration, accidental drift, and meaningful risk. For servers and client devices, baselines provide the reference point that allows posture to be evaluated consistently across environments, operating systems, and device roles.

Designing endpoint security baselines is not about enforcing identical configurations everywhere. Servers and clients serve different purposes, operate under different constraints, and face different threats. Effective baseline design, therefore, establishes role-appropriate standards while ensuring that deviation from those standards is visible, measurable, and actionable. This section maps to the following SC-100 skills measured: *Specify security baselines for server and client endpoints.*

Defining and assessing endpoint security baselines

A security baseline represents a minimum acceptable configuration for an endpoint, incorporating operating system settings, security controls, and hardening requirements. Industry frameworks such as the **Center for Internet Security** (**CIS**) Benchmarks are commonly used as reference points because they provide tested, platform-specific guidance for reducing the attack surface.

However, defining a baseline is only the first step. Security requirements must also specify how compliance with that baseline is assessed over time. Without continuous assessment, endpoints can drift due to configuration changes, software updates, or administrative actions, eroding the original security posture without obvious signs of failure.

CIS Benchmark alignment and baseline drift detection

Microsoft Defender Vulnerability Management supports security baseline assessment by evaluating endpoint configurations against established standards such as CIS Benchmarks. This capability enables organizations to identify devices that were initially compliant but have since drifted due to configuration changes or environmental factors.

From a design perspective, baseline drift detection is critical because it shifts security posture management from a one-time validation to an ongoing discipline. Architects should require continuous assessment of baseline alignment so that deviations are detected early, prioritized appropriately, and addressed before they are exploited as part of an attack chain.

This approach applies equally to servers and client devices, ensuring that both infrastructure and user endpoints maintain their intended security posture as environments evolve.

Evaluating endpoint and server posture

Baseline assessment must be paired with broader posture evaluation to understand how endpoints contribute to overall security risk. While baselines define minimum standards, posture evaluation provides context by aggregating configuration state, exposure, and security signals across devices.

Posture evaluation allows security teams to answer higher-level questions, such as which endpoints represent the greatest risk and where remediation efforts should be focused. This perspective is essential in large environments where addressing every issue simultaneously is neither practical nor effective.

Defender-based posture insights for baseline validation

Microsoft Defender-based posture insights enable organizations to evaluate endpoint and server security state in a consolidated view. By surfacing baseline compliance information alongside other security signals, these tools help teams validate whether endpoints remain aligned with defined standards.

Posture evaluation must also be matched to the type of asset being assessed. Windows client device posture is evaluated using Microsoft Defender for Endpoint-based posture and exposure insights, reflecting device-level configuration and risk. Azure **virtual machines** (**VMs**) and Azure storage accounts, by contrast, are evaluated using Microsoft Defender for Cloud, which assesses cloud resource configuration against security benchmarks and recommendations. Correctly mapping each asset type to its posture evaluation surface is essential when designing baseline validation across mixed environments.

Architecturally, this capability supports risk-based decision-making. Instead of treating baseline deviations as isolated configuration issues, posture insights allow architects to understand how those deviations affect overall exposure. This ensures that baseline enforcement remains relevant, targeted, and aligned with real-world risk rather than becoming a purely compliance-driven exercise.

Evaluating Windows LAPS security solutions

Local administrator accounts remain a persistent source of risk on Windows endpoints. When the same local administrator credentials are reused across devices or left unmanaged, a single compromise can enable lateral movement, privilege escalation, and widespread ransomware propagation. Designing endpoint security, therefore, requires explicit controls for how local administrative access is granted, protected, and audited.

Windows LAPS addresses this risk by removing shared secrets and enforcing unique, rotated local administrator passwords per device. Evaluating LAPS as part of endpoint security design requires understanding both how it enforces least privilege and how it reduces the impact of credential compromise in real-world attack scenarios. This section maps to the following SC-100 skills measured: *Evaluate Windows LAPS solutions*.

Managing local administrator credentials on endpoints

Local administrator access is sometimes necessary for device maintenance, troubleshooting, or specialized tasks. However, permanently assigning users to local administrator groups undermines security controls and increases exposure. Endpoint security requirements must therefore specify how administrative access is provided without introducing standing privilege.

Effective local admin management focuses on credential protection rather than user convenience. By controlling how local administrator passwords are generated, stored, and rotated, organizations can significantly reduce the risk associated with administrative access.

Password rotation and least privilege local admin design

Windows LAPS automatically generates and rotates unique local administrator passwords for each device and stores them securely for authorized retrieval. This design ensures that compromising one device does not grant administrative access to others, enforcing least privilege at the credential level.

From an architectural standpoint, LAPS removes the need to distribute or manually manage local admin passwords. It allows administrators to access devices when required while ensuring that credentials are short-lived and not reused. This capability directly supports secure endpoint design by reducing the attack surface associated with local administrative access.

Windows LAPS also supports a legacy Microsoft LAPS emulation mode, which enables organizations to transition from older LAPS implementations without redesigning existing operational processes. In environments with privileged access devices or established local admin workflows, this mode allows continued use of familiar patterns while still benefiting from centralized password rotation and credential isolation. Selecting legacy emulation mode can therefore be an intentional least privilege design choice during phased modernization.

Reducing lateral movement through credential isolation

Credential reuse is a key enabler of lateral movement in ransomware and post-exploitation attacks. Attackers often harvest local administrator credentials from one compromised device and reuse them to access others. Preventing this reuse is therefore a critical security requirement for Windows endpoints.

Security controls that isolate credentials limit how far an attacker can move, even after initial compromise. This containment effect significantly reduces the scale and impact of attacks.

Using Windows LAPS to limit ransomware propagation

Windows LAPS mitigates lateral movement by ensuring that each device has a unique local administrator password. Even if an attacker obtains administrative access on one endpoint, those credentials cannot be reused elsewhere.

In ransomware scenarios, this containment prevents attackers from rapidly spreading across endpoints using shared local admin accounts. When designing endpoint security solutions, specifying Windows LAPS is a foundational requirement for limiting the blast radius of credential-based attacks and supporting resilient recovery.

Conclusion

Endpoint and device security design forms the foundation of modern security architectures because it governs how threats first encounter, interact with, and attempt to move through an environment. In this chapter, endpoint security was treated not as a collection of tools, but as a set of deliberate design decisions that constrain behavior, enforce trust conditions, and reduce blast radius across servers, client devices, and specialized systems.

Server security design emphasized preventive controls and continuous visibility, combining execution restriction with cross-platform vulnerability assessment to reduce exposure across Windows and Linux workloads. Client and mobile endpoint security extended these principles to user-operated devices, integrating compliance evaluation, Conditional Access enforcement, just-in-time privilege elevation, endpoint hardening, and post-incident access revalidation into a cohesive Zero Trust model.

The chapter also addressed environments that fall outside traditional endpoint assumptions. IoT, embedded, and OT systems were approached as constrained, availability-sensitive domains where visibility-first security, passive monitoring, and controlled change provide protection without operational disruption. Security baselines were positioned as the reference point that makes posture measurable and actionable, while Windows LAPS illustrated how credential isolation at the endpoint can materially limit lateral movement and ransomware spread.

Together, these design principles enable architects to specify endpoint security requirements that are consistent, scalable, and resilient, ensuring that devices across the organization actively participate in enforcing security rather than silently expanding the attack surface.

The next chapter shifts focus from securing individual endpoints to protecting the workloads and platforms those endpoints interact with. It examines how security baselines, runtime protections, and platform-specific controls are applied across cloud services, containers, and application platforms to reduce attack surface and defend critical workloads.

Questions

Success on any assessment depends on understanding the underlying technologies, concepts, and principles rather than memorizing facts. The following questions help readers confirm that they can apply this chapter's ideas in realistic design scenarios, including server and client endpoint protection, execution control, device compliance enforcement, vulnerability assessment, Zero Trust access validation, credential isolation, and protection of constrained and specialized systems.

1. **An organization wants to prevent attackers from running unauthorized tools and scripts on Windows and Linux servers after gaining access. Which architectural approach best achieves this outcome?**
   a. Enabling antivirus signature updates
   b. Applying adaptive application controls in Microsoft Defender for Cloud
   c. Restricting inbound traffic using network security groups
   d. Enforcing Conditional Access policies
2. **Why is execution allowlisting particularly effective for server workloads compared to user endpoints?**
   a. Server workloads are rarely targeted by attackers
   b. Server application behavior is typically stable and predictable
   c. Execution control eliminates the need for patching
   d. Servers do not require continuous monitoring
3. **A scenario requires continuous assessment of missing patches and insecure configurations across both Windows and Linux servers using the vulnerability scanning engine. Which Defender for Cloud plan must be selected?**
   a. Defender for Containers
   b. Defender for Servers
   c. Defender for Databases
   d. Defender for Storage
4. **An architect needs device health to directly influence access to Microsoft 365 and other protected resources. Which design best supports this requirement?**
   a. Role-based access control alone
   b. Network location-based policies
   c. Intune device compliance integrated with Conditional Access
   d. Endpoint firewall rules

5. **Why is granting users permanent local administrator rights on client devices considered a systemic security risk?**
   a. It increases authentication latency
   b. It complicates device enrollment
   c. It enables persistence and lateral movement after compromise
   d. It prevents security updates
6. **Which capability allows users to perform approved administrative tasks on client devices without maintaining standing local administrator privileges?**
   a. Windows LAPS
   b. Endpoint Privilege Management
   c. Microsoft Defender Antivirus
   d. Azure role-based access control
7. **An organization operates a kiosk and shared devices that must remain locked down while still receiving centralized protection and updates. Which design best meets this requirement?**
   a. Network isolation only
   b. Local administrator restrictions without management tooling
   c. Intune enrollment combined with Microsoft Defender for Endpoint
   d. Manual configuration and monitoring
8. **Why is endpoint-based web content filtering preferred over network-only filtering for mobile and remote users?**
   a. Network filtering provides stronger encryption
   b. Endpoint filtering applies policies regardless of network location
   c. Endpoint filtering replaces Conditional Access
   d. Network filtering is limited to Microsoft 365 traffic
9. **An organization uses IoT and embedded devices that cannot tolerate aggressive scanning or frequent configuration changes. Which Zero Trust-aligned approach best reduces risk without disrupting operations?**
   a. Active vulnerability scanning
   b. Frequent forced patch cycles
   c. Passive threat monitoring and controlled patching
   d. Endpoint privilege elevation
10. **What security risk does Windows LAPS primarily mitigate?**
   a. Phishing-based credential theft
   b. Unauthorized application execution

c. Lateral movement using shared local administrator credentials

d. Network-based denial-of-service attacks

Answers

1. b: Applying adaptive application controls in Microsoft Defender for Cloud.

   Adaptive application controls restrict execution to approved software, preventing attackers from running unauthorized tools even after initial access.

2. b: Server application behavior is typically stable and predictable.

   This stability allows allowlists to be enforced effectively with minimal operational impact.

3. b: Defender for Servers.

   Defender for Servers enables server threat protection and integrates with Microsoft Defender Vulnerability Management (via Defender for Endpoint) to provide continuous vulnerability assessment and exposure visibility for Windows and Linux server workloads.

4. c: Intune device compliance integrated with Conditional Access.

   This design ensures device health directly influences access decisions rather than relying on user identity alone.

5. c: It enables persistence and lateral movement after compromise.

   Standing administrative privileges increase the impact of endpoint compromise and undermine Zero Trust principles.

6. b: Endpoint Privilege Management.

   Endpoint Privilege Management enables just-in-time elevation without permanent local administrator membership.

7. c: Intune enrollment combined with Microsoft Defender for Endpoint.

   This combination provides centralized configuration, threat visibility, and vulnerability management for shared devices.

8. b: Endpoint filtering applies policies regardless of network location.

   Endpoint-based filtering enforces protection consistently for users on and off corporate networks.

9. c: Passive threat monitoring and controlled patching.

   This approach improves visibility and reduces risk without disrupting operationally sensitive systems.

10. c: Lateral movement using shared local administrator credentials.

    Windows LAPS enforces unique local administrator passwords per device, limiting credential reuse and ransomware spread.

Chapter 10
Design Workload and Platform Protection Solutions

Introduction

This chapter examines how to design workload and platform protection solutions across **software as a service** (**SaaS**), **platform as a service** (**PaaS**), and **infrastructure as a service** (**IaaS**) environments by defining consistent security requirements that remain enforceable as workloads scale and change. It focuses on how security architects translate shared responsibility models into practical baseline expectations that can be measured, validated, and sustained across cloud-native, hybrid, and multi-cloud platforms. Readers explore how Microsoft Defender for Cloud, Defender for Cloud Secure Score, Azure Policy, and related workload protection capabilities are used to establish security baselines, detect configuration drift, and identify exposure across different workload types.

The chapter also examines how specialized workloads, including IoT systems, internet-facing web applications, container platforms, container orchestration environments, and Azure AI services, introduce unique risk patterns that require targeted security requirements. By applying these principles, architects can design protection strategies that reduce attack surface, maintain visibility, and ensure workloads remain protected throughout their lifecycle.

Structure

This chapter covers the following topics:

- Security baselines for SaaS, PaaS, and IaaS
- Security requirements for IoT workloads
- Security requirements for web workloads
- Security requirements for container workloads
- Security requirements for container orchestration
- Azure AI services security evaluation

Objectives

This chapter covers the skills required to specify security baselines for SaaS, PaaS, and IaaS environments, ensuring that foundational security expectations are defined consistently across different cloud service models. It examines how these baselines establish minimum controls for identity, networking, data protection, and monitoring.

The chapter explores how to specify security requirements for IoT workloads, addressing device identity, communication security, and lifecycle management. It also examines how to define security requirements for web workloads, including protection against common application layer threats and secure configuration of internet-facing services.

In addition, the chapter covers how to specify security requirements for containerized workloads and container orchestration platforms, focusing on image security, runtime protection, and control plane hardening. Finally, the chapter evaluates solutions that include Azure AI services security, examining how security requirements must adapt to protect AI workloads, data pipelines, and model operations within cloud environments.

These skills fall under the exam domain: *Design security solutions for infrastructure,* which represents approximately 25-30 % of the overall SC-100 skills measured[1].

Security baselines for SaaS, PaaS, and IaaS

Security baselines are the point at which cloud security architecture either becomes coherent or collapses into exception handling. In environments that span SaaS, PaaS, and IaaS, responsibility is shared differently at each layer, but risk is not. Attackers exploit inconsistencies between service models far more effectively than weaknesses within a single one. If security expectations vary depending on how a workload is hosted, the organization no longer has a defensible posture—it has a collection of partial assumptions.

A baseline is therefore not a checklist of settings, nor a set of best practices tied to a specific service. It is a declaration of minimum acceptable conditions under which any workload is allowed to operate. That declaration must hold regardless of abstraction level, deployment speed, or hosting location. Without this consistency, security teams lose the ability to compare risk, auditors lose the ability to validate controls, and architects lose confidence that protections scale as environments evolve. This section maps to the following SC-100 skills measured: *Specify security baselines for SaaS, PaaS, and IaaS services.*

1 **https://learn.microsoft.com/en-us/credentials/certifications/resources/study-guides/sc-100**

Workload security baselines with Microsoft Defender for Cloud

One of the most common architectural mistakes in cloud security is defining security differently for each service type. **Virtual machines** (**VMs**) receive one set of controls, managed databases another, and SaaS platforms are often treated as implicitly secure because the infrastructure is abstracted away. Over time, this results in fragmented standards that cannot be measured or enforced consistently.

Microsoft Defender for Cloud addresses this problem by defining security expectations in terms of control intent rather than service implementation. Instead of asking how each service should be configured individually, architects define what outcomes must be achieved, such as vulnerability management, secure network exposure, identity integration, and monitoring, and evaluate all workloads against those outcomes. This shifts baseline design from service familiarity to architectural consistency.

Microsoft cloud security benchmark

The **Microsoft cloud security benchmark** (**MCSB**) provides the structural foundation for this approach. It abstracts security controls away from individual services and organizes them around universal security objectives. This allows workloads with very different operational characteristics to be evaluated against the same expectations without forcing identical configurations.

For example, a VM and a managed database service implement vulnerability management differently, but both are accountable to the same requirement: known vulnerabilities must be identified and addressed. By anchoring baselines to intent rather than mechanism, architects avoid redefining security every time a new service is introduced. This is what allows security standards to scale without constant redesign.

Secure Score measurement and prioritization mechanism

Defender for Cloud Secure Score reflects how closely deployed workloads align with the defined baseline and surfaces prioritized recommendations that help architects evaluate and improve that alignment.

Secure Score is not a static measurement; it is continuously recalculated as workloads are onboarded, configurations change, and new recommendations are introduced. This dynamic behavior allows architects to understand not only current alignment with the baseline, but also how changes in configuration and coverage directly impact overall risk. As a result, it becomes a practical tool for tracking posture improvement over time rather than a one-time assessment.

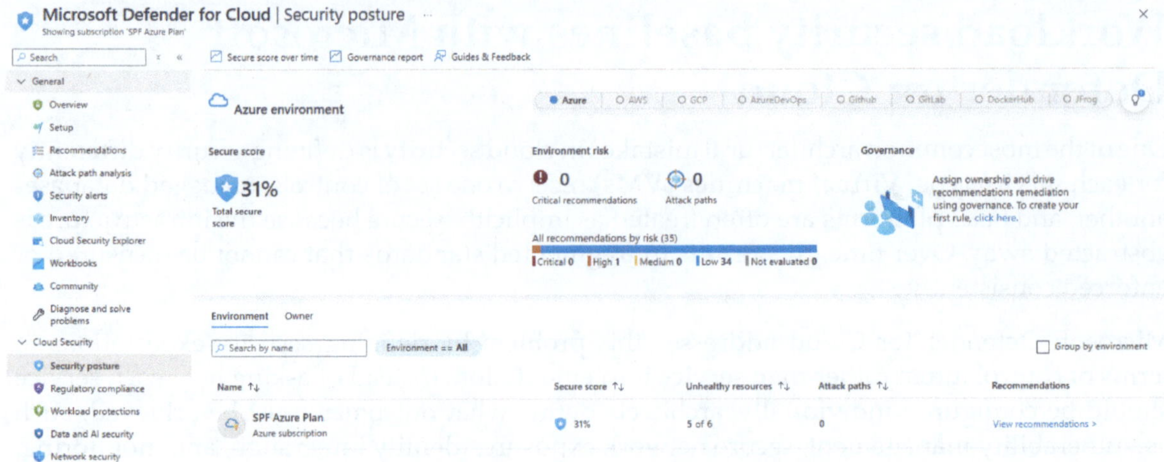

Figure 10.1: Microsoft Defender for Cloud Secure Score

However, the most important signal is not the numeric score, but whether workloads are being assessed at all. Recommendations are generated only when the appropriate Defender for Cloud protection plans are enabled, and workloads are successfully onboarded. When recommendations are missing, the most common cause is not compliance, but lack of coverage.

From an architectural standpoint, a Secure Score becomes a validation of both security posture and control activation. Architects must ensure that the relevant Defender for Cloud plans are enabled and that automatic onboarding is configured so workloads are continuously assessed. Without this, it presents an incomplete risk picture, and remediation decisions are based on partial data rather than actual exposure.

Enforcing baseline compliance with Azure Policy

Defining a baseline without enforcement guarantees erosion. As environments scale, teams change, and deployment velocity increases, manual adherence becomes impossible to sustain. Even well-documented standards degrade when enforcement relies on individual discipline or post-deployment review.

Azure Policy converts baseline intent into continuous control by evaluating resources throughout their lifecycle. It ensures that security requirements apply consistently, regardless of who deploys a workload, how it is deployed, or when it is created. This transforms baselines from guidance into enforceable architectural constraints.

Automatic detection of noncompliant resources

Continuous evaluation is essential because most security failures are not deliberate; they are incremental. A configuration change here, a temporary exception there, and posture drifts without triggering alarms. Automatic detection ensures that deviations from baseline are surfaced as soon as they occur, shortening the gap between misconfiguration and awareness.

From an architectural perspective, this protects against silent degradation. Instead of discovering issues during audits or incidents, teams are alerted while remediation is still simple, and the impact is low.

Policy-based enforcement for new and existing resources

Effective enforcement must apply both forward and backward. New resources must be prevented from introducing risk by default, but existing workloads must also be evaluated and corrected over time. Many environments contain a mix of modern deployments and legacy systems, and baselines that apply only to new workloads leave long-lived risk untouched.

Policy-based enforcement allows architects to design baselines that evolve without abandoning existing estates. This is critical for maintaining a single security standard across environments that modernize incrementally rather than all at once.

Regulatory compliance assessment for workloads

Regulatory failures are rarely caused by missing controls. They are caused by inconsistency: controls applied in some places but not others, or implemented without sufficient evidence. Translating regulatory requirements into technical enforcement manually is slow, subjective, and difficult to keep aligned as environments change.

Effective baseline design must therefore include a clear relationship between technical controls and regulatory expectations, without allowing compliance reporting to replace enforcement.

ISO 27001 and industry compliance mappings

Regulatory compliance mappings provide a structured way to assess how technical controls align with external standards. They remove ambiguity by showing which baseline controls support specific regulatory requirements, allowing architects to reason about compliance without redefining controls for each framework.

This approach also supports continuous compliance. Instead of treating audits as point-in-time exercises, organizations can assess regulatory alignment continuously, using the same baseline controls that protect workloads day-to-day.

Visibility vs. enforcement responsibilities

Assessment and enforcement serve different purposes and must not be conflated. Compliance dashboards provide visibility into alignment; they do not prevent noncompliant configurations from being deployed. Treating visibility as enforcement creates recurring audit findings because the underlying controls remain unchanged.

Architects must ensure that regulatory assessment informs baseline enforcement rather than replacing it. Compliance is sustained through control, not reporting.

Extending baselines to hybrid and multi-cloud workloads

A baseline that applies only to native cloud resources is not a baseline—it is a platform preference. In hybrid and multi-cloud environments, workloads move between locations, are replicated for resilience, or remain on-premises for operational reasons. If security expectations change based on location, risk assessment becomes inconsistent, and enforcement becomes fragmented.

Extending baselines beyond a single cloud is therefore not optional. It is required to preserve the integrity of the security model as environments evolve.

Azure Arc-enabled servers and guest configuration

Azure Arc enables non-Azure workloads to be evaluated against the same baseline logic as native resources by projecting them into a common control plane. This eliminates the artificial distinction between cloud and non-cloud security and allows architects to apply consistent expectations regardless of hosting location.

Guest configuration extends this capability to the operating system and configuration level, ensuring that baseline requirements can still be assessed even when native platform controls are unavailable. Together, these capabilities restore comparability across environments that would otherwise require separate standards.

Consistent baseline enforcement across environments

Consistency is the control that scales. When a single baseline applies everywhere, security posture can be compared meaningfully, remediation can be prioritized rationally, and workload movement does not silently introduce risk. Without this consistency, organizations accumulate parallel standards that increase complexity and guarantee blind spots.

A universal baseline allows security architecture to remain coherent even as deployment models diversify.

Security requirements for IoT workloads

IoT workloads expose the limits of traditional cloud security thinking; they combine constrained devices, long operational lifecycles, physical access, and continuous connectivity to cloud services. These characteristics make IoT environments difficult to patch, hard to monitor, and easy to underestimate. When IoT security fails, the impact is rarely confined to data loss; it can disrupt operations, undermine safety, and compromise trust in downstream cloud systems.

For architects, the core challenge is that IoT workloads behave unlike servers or applications, yet they are deeply integrated with identity systems, automation platforms, and data pipelines.

Security requirements must therefore focus on containment, visibility, and continuous assessment rather than assuming uniform control or rapid remediation. Treating IoT as *just another workload type* guarantees blind spots. This section maps to the following SC-100 skills measured: *Specify security requirements for IoT workloads.*

IoT and OT security in Zero Trust modernization

Zero Trust modernization is about prioritization as much as protection. Not all workloads pose equal risk when compromised, and IoT and operational technology systems often sit at points of disproportionate impact. These systems control physical processes, collect sensitive telemetry, or act as gateways between isolated networks and cloud services. A compromise here can propagate outward, affecting availability, safety, and regulatory posture.

Security requirements must therefore recognize IoT and OT environments as high-risk domains within Zero Trust architectures. Ignoring them or deferring their protection creates gaps that undermine controls elsewhere in the environment.

IoT and OT as prioritized modernization domains

IoT and OT systems frequently operate with weaker built-in security controls than traditional IT assets, yet they are increasingly connected to modern cloud platforms. This combination makes them attractive targets and effective pivot points. Elevating these environments within modernization efforts ensures that security investment aligns with business impact rather than deployment convenience.

From an architectural perspective, this prioritization shifts the focus from device hardening alone to systemic risk reduction. It acknowledges that some devices cannot be patched quickly or at all, and that compensating controls, such as isolation, monitoring, and posture assessment, must carry more weight. Treating IoT and OT as first-class domains prevents them from becoming unmonitored exceptions that attackers exploit to bypass stronger controls elsewhere.

Posture management for IoT workloads

IoT security strategies fail when they rely on assumptions inherited from server or application security. Many IoT devices cannot support full-featured agents, follow irregular patch cycles, or be centrally administered in the same way as traditional workloads. As a result, security requirements must emphasize centralized posture assessment and visibility rather than uniform configuration enforcement.

Posture management provides architects with a way to reason about risk even when direct control is limited. It answers a critical question: *given the constraints of IoT environments, how do we know whether our security expectations are being met?*

IoT Edge device security assessment

IoT Edge devices occupy a critical position between physical devices and cloud services. They aggregate data, execute local logic, and often maintain persistent connectivity to the cloud. They represent a high-value target and a natural enforcement point for security controls because of this role.

Assessing the security posture of IoT Edge devices allows architects to evaluate configuration state, vulnerability exposure, and behavioral risk in a consistent way, even when underlying devices vary widely. Treating these edge components as managed workloads brings IoT security into the same assessment model used for other cloud-connected systems, reducing fragmentation and improving visibility at a key junction point.

Since IoT Edge devices act as aggregation and control points, assessing them in isolation is not sufficient; without visibility into how they connect across environments, posture awareness collapses as soon as IoT workloads span multiple platforms.

Multi-cloud IoT and compute visibility

IoT solutions are rarely confined to a single environment. Devices may connect to on-premises gateways, edge systems, or workloads running in multiple cloud providers. Without unified visibility, security posture fragments along environmental boundaries, making it difficult to identify gaps or correlate risk.

Security requirements must therefore include centralized visibility across hybrid and multi-cloud IoT deployments. This allows architects to detect unmanaged devices, inconsistent controls, and exposure paths that would otherwise remain hidden. Unified posture assessment ensures that IoT environments do not become unmonitored entry points into broader cloud architectures as they scale and evolve.

Security requirements for web workloads

Web workloads are designed to be reachable, which makes them uniquely exposed; unlike internal services, they operate under a permanently hostile assumption. Discovery is inevitable, probing is constant, and exploitation attempts begin as soon as an endpoint becomes accessible; this exposure makes web workloads the most common initial access point in cloud environments and a frequent pivot into backend systems and data.

Effective security requirements for web workloads, therefore, cannot rely on a single control or layer. They must assume imperfect code, rapid change, and persistent attack pressure. The goal is not to prevent all attacks, but to constrain how far an attacker can get, how quickly exposure is detected, and how reliably backend systems are protected when the web layer is stressed or compromised. This section maps to the following SC-100 skills measured: *Specify security requirements for web workloads*.

Protecting internet-facing web applications

Internet-facing applications operate under a different threat model from internal services. They are continuously scanned for known weaknesses, misconfigurations, and unintended exposure paths. Security requirements at this layer must therefore prioritize resilience against common attack techniques while avoiding assumptions that exposure can be tightly controlled.

This creates a tension for architects: protections must be strong enough to absorb malicious traffic at scale, yet they cannot be treated as trust boundaries for the rest of the application stack. Understanding where edge protection ends and where explicit trust decisions must begin is critical.

Web application firewall in web workload protection

Web application firewalls (**WAFs**) provide application layer inspection that identifies and blocks common attack patterns such as injection attempts, cross-site scripting, and malformed requests. In practice, WAFs reduce noise by filtering opportunistic attacks and automated scanning before traffic reaches the application. This improves availability and reduces the likelihood that trivial exploits succeed.

However, WAFs operate by pattern recognition and rule evaluation. They do not understand application intent, identity context, or backend authorization. As a result, they are effective as a protective buffer but insufficient as a standalone security control. Architects use WAFs to raise the cost of attack and absorb volume, not to establish trust.

Limitations of WAF in Zero Trust architectures

Zero Trust architectures assume that no component is implicitly trusted based on location or placement. Treating a WAF as a trust boundary violates this assumption. While a WAF can block known attack patterns, it does not guarantee that traffic reaching backend services is legitimate or authorized.

Security requirements must therefore ensure that backend services enforce their own access controls and do not rely solely on the presence of a WAF upstream. Failure to do so creates bypass scenarios where attackers target backend endpoints directly or exploit assumptions about trusted ingress paths.

Securing application connectivity and exposure

Many web security failures occur not because the application itself is vulnerable, but because exposure paths are poorly controlled. Modern cloud platforms make it easy to expose services quickly, but they also make it easy to create unintended access routes that bypass intended entry points.

Security requirements must explicitly define how traffic is allowed to reach web workloads and how backend connectivity is restricted. Implicit assumptions about routing or platform defaults are a common source of exposure.

Application ingress and backend access control

Global entry points and regional gateways provide traffic management and protection, but they do not automatically enforce exclusivity. Without additional controls, backend services may still be reachable directly, bypassing front-end inspection and protection.

Architects must ensure that backend resources accept traffic only from approved entry points. This typically involves restricting network access paths and enforcing private connectivity between the web front-end and backend services. Doing so ensures that front-end protections cannot be bypassed and that all inbound traffic is subject to the same inspection and control logic.

Restricting access paths to web applications

Unintended exposure often results from default configurations, temporary testing changes, or automated deployments that bypass manual review. Once exposed, web applications are often discovered externally within minutes.

Security requirements must therefore account for exposure as a dynamic condition, not a static configuration. Controls that rely on periodic review are insufficient. Architects must design for continuous identification of exposed endpoints so that accidental exposure is detected and corrected before it becomes an entry point for attack.

Identifying vulnerabilities in web applications

Preventive controls cannot account for every weakness introduced during development and operation. Web applications evolve continuously, and vulnerabilities are often introduced through dependency updates, configuration changes, or new functionality. Security requirements must therefore include mechanisms to identify vulnerabilities in deployed applications, not just in code repositories.

This shifts vulnerability identification from a pre-deployment activity to an ongoing operational concern.

Dynamic application security testing for running apps

Dynamic application security testing evaluates applications while they are running and exposed, using techniques that mirror real attack behavior. By interacting with the live application, dynamic testing reveals vulnerabilities that only emerge when components interact under real conditions, such as injection flaws, insecure error handling, or authentication weaknesses.

For architects, the value of dynamic testing lies in its realism. It validates whether design assumptions still hold after deployment and change. This allows security decisions to be based on observed behavior rather than theoretical correctness, which is essential in environments where applications change frequently.

Detecting exposed and newly deployed web workloads

Deployment velocity has collapsed the window between configuration change and external discovery. New or modified web workloads are often detected by attackers within minutes, frequently before internal teams are aware they are exposed. In this environment, exposure risk is defined not by intent, but by reachability.

Security requirements must therefore include a posture-based detection capability that continuously identifies internet-exposed web applications and associated weaknesses. This allows architects to detect unintended exposure and vulnerable configurations across web workloads as they are deployed, rather than relying on periodic review or manual discovery. Without this capability, accidental exposure becomes an inevitable entry point regardless of application design quality.

Security requirements for container workloads

Containers change how applications are built and deployed, but they do not remove risk; they redistribute it. By abstracting dependencies and packaging applications into portable units, containers accelerate delivery and scale, yet they also make it easy to propagate mistakes at speed. A vulnerable image, once introduced, can be deployed hundreds of times in minutes. Traditional security assumptions that rely on long-lived servers and manual review no longer apply.

Security requirements for container workloads must therefore address the entire lifecycle of a containerized application. Protection must begin before deployment, continue while containers are running, and extend to the host environment that ultimately executes container processes. Ignoring any part of this lifecycle creates blind spots that scale as fast as the workloads themselves. This section maps to the following SC-100 skills measured: *Specify security requirements for containers*.

Securing container images

Container images are the starting point for every containerized workload. Any weakness embedded in an image, such as outdated libraries, misconfigurations, or known vulnerabilities, is replicated every time that image is deployed. In container environments, risk is not introduced gradually; it is cloned.

Security requirements must therefore focus on preventing vulnerable images from entering the environment in the first place. Relying on runtime detection alone is insufficient, as it allows known weaknesses to reach production before they are identified.

Image vulnerability scanning in Azure container registry

Image vulnerability scanning evaluates container images stored in the registry to identify known vulnerabilities in operating system packages and application dependencies before deployment occurs. This assessment allows security teams to identify risk while remediation is still straightforward, rather than after vulnerable images are already running at scale.

For architects, the key decision point is that registry-based scanning is enabled through the container protection capabilities in Defender for Cloud. This ensures that images are assessed centrally and that results feed into security posture measurement. Without enabling the appropriate protection plan, images may be stored and deployed without ever being evaluated, creating systemic risk that is replicated across every workload using that image.

Runtime protection for containerized workloads

Even with strong pre-deployment controls, containers remain exposed to runtime threats. Misconfigurations, zero-day vulnerabilities, and malicious behavior introduced after deployment cannot be detected through static analysis alone. Containers also operate in highly dynamic environments, where processes start and stop rapidly, and traditional monitoring assumptions break down.

Security requirements must therefore include runtime protection that observes container behavior as it executes and detects activity that deviates from expected patterns.

Runtime threat detection for containers

Runtime threat detection monitors container behavior to identify suspicious activity such as unexpected process execution, abnormal network connections, or attempts to access sensitive resources. Unlike image scanning, which addresses known issues, runtime detection focuses on identifying active threats and emerging exploitation attempts.

This capability is essential for containing attacks that bypass preventive controls. By detecting malicious behavior early, architects can limit dwell time and prevent attackers from using compromised containers as footholds for lateral movement within the environment.

Controlling execution on container hosts

Containers abstract application packaging, but they do not eliminate the fact that container processes ultimately execute on host operating systems. If execution on the host is not controlled, attackers who compromise a container can potentially run unauthorized software alongside legitimate workloads.

Security requirements must therefore address execution control at the host level, even in highly containerized environments.

Adaptive application controls for workload protection

Adaptive application controls establish an allow listing based on observed behavior, identifying which applications are expected to run on a workload and blocking execution that falls outside this profile. When applied to container hosts, these controls reduce the risk of unauthorized tools or malware executing alongside containerized applications.

For architects, adaptive controls provide a balance between security and operational flexibility. Rather than relying on static allowlists that are difficult to maintain, adaptive controls evolve as workloads change, enforcing execution boundaries without undermining agility.

Ensuring container workload security posture coverage

Visibility is a prerequisite for control. In container environments, it is easy for workloads to exist outside centralized security assessment if coverage is not explicitly configured. When this happens, security posture metrics present an incomplete picture, leading to false confidence.

Security requirements must ensure that container workloads are fully included in posture assessment from the moment they are created.

Defender for Containers enablement and auto provisioning

Container environments are only included in security posture measurement when the appropriate container protection plan is enabled, and automatic onboarding is configured. Without this activation step, clusters and workloads may exist outside centralized assessment, even though they are actively running production applications.

From an architectural perspective, enabling Defender for Containers and configuring auto provisioning ensures that new clusters and workloads are assessed as soon as they are created. This prevents visibility gaps from emerging as environments scale and ensures that Defender for Cloud's Secure Score reflects actual container risk rather than partial coverage.

Security requirements for container orchestration

Container orchestration platforms fundamentally change the blast radius of security decisions; while a misconfiguration in a single container affects one workload, a mistake at the orchestration layer can affect hundreds or thousands simultaneously. Orchestration introduces centralized scheduling, shared infrastructure, and automated lifecycle management, all of which amplify both efficiency and failure.

Security requirements at this layer must therefore address systemic risk rather than individual workload correctness. The goal is not only to secure containers, but to ensure that the platform responsible for deploying and operating them does not become a force multiplier for vulnerabilities, misconfigurations, or outdated components. This section maps to the following SC-100 skills measured: *Specify security requirements for container orchestration.*

Securing Kubernetes worker nodes

Worker nodes form the execution foundation of a container orchestration platform. Every container ultimately relies on the node's operating system kernel, networking stack, and runtime configuration. If worker nodes are insecure or outdated, vulnerabilities at the host level can be exploited to compromise multiple containers regardless of how well the applications themselves are designed.

In orchestrated environments, worker nodes represent a shared failure domain. A compromised node is not just a host level issue—it becomes a launch point for container escape, credential access, and lateral movement across the cluster. Since scheduling decisions are automated and opaque to application teams, node security failures propagate faster and further than in traditional infrastructure models. Treating node integrity as an operational concern rather than a platform protection requirement creates systemic risk. Security requirements must therefore treat worker node maintenance as a core orchestration concern, not an operational afterthought.

Node image lifecycle and kernel update strategy

In orchestrated environments, worker nodes are typically created and replaced automatically rather than maintained as long-lived servers. Attempting to patch nodes in place conflicts with this model and often results in an inconsistent security posture across the cluster.

Updating the node image itself aligns security with orchestration principles. By baking kernel updates and security patches into the node image, architects ensure that newly created or recycled nodes inherit a known-good security state automatically. This approach reduces administrative overhead while maintaining consistent protection at scale, preventing outdated nodes from silently persisting in the environment.

Governance and visibility for Kubernetes environments

As orchestration platforms scale, maintaining visibility into their security posture becomes increasingly difficult. Clusters may be created for development, testing, or temporary workloads and left running without consistent oversight. When orchestration environments fall outside centralized security assessment, they quickly become blind spots.

Security requirements must therefore ensure that container orchestration platforms are included in centralized posture measurement and governance from the moment they are deployed.

Defender for Cloud Secure Score inclusion for AKS clusters

Including Kubernetes clusters in centralized posture assessment requires explicit onboarding and coverage through Defender for Cloud. Defender for Cloud Secure Score recommendations for orchestration environments are generated only when clusters are properly connected and assessed under the relevant protection plan.

Architects must therefore ensure that **Azure Kubernetes Service** (**AKS**) clusters are onboarded and continuously evaluated, not merely deployed. Without this step, orchestration environments become invisible to posture management, creating blind spots at exactly the layer where misconfigurations have the largest blast radius.

Azure AI services security evaluation

AI services introduce a different category of workload risk because they concentrate data, privilege, and automation into a single execution plane. Training datasets, prompts, embeddings, intermediate computations, and outputs often contain highly sensitive or regulated information. At the same time, AI services operate at scale and frequently rely on opaque execution paths that are difficult to observe using traditional controls. This combination erodes many of the trust assumptions that underpin conventional cloud security design.

Security requirements for Azure AI services must therefore address more than storage protection or network isolation. They must explicitly consider how data is handled while it is actively being processed and how trust is established when administrators, operators, and platforms themselves should not have unrestricted visibility into that processing. Treating AI workloads as ordinary platform services leaves a critical gap at exactly the point where data is most exposed.

From a platform protection perspective, Azure AI services remain workloads governed by the same baseline logic introduced earlier in this chapter. What differentiates them is not abstraction, but trust collapse: data must be exposed to computation itself. This shifts protection requirements away from perimeter and configuration controls toward execution integrity and verifiable isolation. This section maps to the following SC-100 skills measured: *Evaluate solutions that include Azure AI services security*.

Protecting sensitive data processing in AI workloads

Most cloud security controls focus on protecting data at rest or in transit. AI workloads challenge this model because sensitive data is routinely decrypted in memory during processing. If protections stop at the storage or network boundary, data can still be exposed to privileged users, compromised platforms, or malicious insiders while computations are underway.

Security requirements for AI workloads must therefore extend protection into the execution phase itself. Architects must be able to reason about who, or what, can access data while models are running, and how that access is constrained and verified.

In practical design scenarios, this requirement maps to using Azure confidential computing so sensitive data is protected while in use. When the scenario emphasizes protecting data during processing (not just at rest or in transit), architects should place the processing components on hardware-backed trusted execution environments (for example, confidential VMs or confidential Kubernetes nodes) and use attestation to verify the trusted runtime before releasing sensitive data. This approach reduces the trust placed in platform administrators and underlying infrastructure by enforcing isolation in hardware rather than software policy alone.

Confidential computing and enclave-based isolation

Confidential computing introduces hardware-enforced trusted execution environments that isolate sensitive workloads from the rest of the system, including the operating system and hypervisor. By executing AI workloads inside secure enclaves, data remains protected while it is being processed, not just before and after execution.

For architects, enclave-based isolation changes the trust model. Instead of assuming that platform administrators or infrastructure components are fully trusted, confidential computing reduces the trust surface to the processor itself. This is particularly important for AI scenarios involving regulated data, proprietary models, or cross-organization collaboration, where assurance about data handling must extend beyond contractual controls.

Hardware-backed encryption and attestation requirements

Hardware-backed encryption ensures that sensitive data is protected using cryptographic keys enforced by the underlying processor, rather than by software alone. Attestation builds on this by providing cryptographic proof that a workload is running in a trusted environment with the expected security configuration.

Attestation allows architects to make trusted decisions based on a verified execution state. Before sensitive data is released to an AI workload, its execution environment can be validated to ensure that enclave protections are in place and have not been tampered with. This capability is essential in AI architectures where data owners and compute operators may not be the same entity, and where trust must be established technically rather than assumed.

Conclusion

Workload and platform protection depend on enforcing consistent security expectations across environments that differ in responsibility, abstraction, and scale. This chapter established security baselines as architectural contracts rather than configuration checklists, showing how Defender for Cloud, Defender for Cloud Secure Score, and Azure Policy work together to define, measure, and enforce those expectations across SaaS, PaaS, IaaS, hybrid, and multi-cloud workloads.

The chapter demonstrated how specialized workloads amplify risk when treated as exceptions. IoT environments require prioritization within Zero Trust architectures because of their physical impact, constrained control, and deep cloud integration. Web workloads demand continuous exposure management and explicit trust boundaries due to their permanent reachability and rapid change. Containerized and orchestrated workloads require lifecycle-aware protection that prevents vulnerabilities from scaling through images, runtime behavior, and platform misconfiguration.

Finally, the chapter addressed Azure AI services as a distinct trust challenge, where sensitive data must remain protected while in use. By examining confidential computing, hardware-backed encryption, and attestation, it showed how architects restore trust in environments where traditional boundaries collapse.

Together, these design principles enable security architects to specify, validate, and enforce workload protection requirements that scale with modern cloud architectures while remaining resilient, measurable, and exam-ready.

The next chapter builds on workload and platform protection by focusing on the network architectures that control how traffic flows between users, services, and resources. It examines how network design, access boundaries, and traffic inspection enforce security controls, reduce exposure, and support Zero Trust principles across cloud and hybrid environments.

Questions

Success on any assessment depends on understanding the underlying technologies, concepts, and principles rather than memorizing facts. The following questions help readers confirm that they can apply this chapter's ideas in realistic design scenarios, including baseline enforcement across SaaS, PaaS, and IaaS, posture measurement and coverage validation, hybrid and multi-cloud consistency, workload-specific protection requirements, container and orchestration risk scaling, and protecting sensitive data during AI processing.

1. **An organization wants every workload, such as SaaS, PaaS, and IaaS, to be evaluated against the same baseline intent rather than service-specific checklists. Which design best achieves this?**
   a. Enabling Azure Policy only after deployment
   b. Defining the baseline using MCSB and evaluating it through Microsoft Defender for Cloud
   c. Relying on threat alerts to indicate configuration gaps
   d. Using Microsoft Sentinel to enforce configuration standards

2. **Why is Defender for Cloud's Secure Score most useful to an architect when designing baselines?**
   a. It proves the environment is secure if the score is high
   b. It provides regulatory compliance certification
   c. It validates both posture alignment and whether assessment coverage is enabled
   d. It replaces the need for benchmark frameworks
3. **An architect notices some subscriptions have no posture recommendations or Defender for Cloud Secure Score impact, even though workloads exist. What is the most likely design issue?**
   a. The workloads are fully compliant and require no recommendations
   b. Defender for Cloud protection plans and onboarding coverage are not enabled for those workloads
   c. Azure Policy is generating too many exemptions
   d. The workloads are not generating security alerts
4. **Why is Azure Policy essential to baseline design rather than just governance documentation?**
   a. It generates threat intelligence for exposed workloads
   b. It provides continuous evaluation and enforcement of baseline intent across the resource lifecycle
   c. It replaces Defender for Cloud Secure Score measurement
   d. It eliminates the need for identity governance
5. **A web application must be protected from common application layer attacks while ensuring backend services cannot be reached directly. Which design best meets this requirement?**
   a. Deploy a WAF and allow backend endpoints to remain publicly reachable
   b. Use a WAF at the entry point and restrict backend access paths so only approved gateways can reach them
   c. Rely on DAST scans to prevent runtime attacks
   d. Enable Defender for Cloud Secure Score recommendations for the subscription
6. **Why is it architecturally incorrect to treat a WAF as a Zero Trust boundary?**
   a. WAFs increase latency and cost
   b. WAFs cannot scale globally
   c. WAFs filter attack patterns but do not provide identity-aware authorization guarantees for backend access
   d. WAFs replace logging and monitoring

7. **A team needs to reduce systemic risk caused by vulnerable container images being repeatedly deployed across environments. Which requirement best addresses this?**
   a. Increase runtime logging in the cluster
   b. Scan and evaluate container images in the registry before deployment and enforce promotion rules
   c. Disable container orchestration auto-scaling
   d. Apply manual patching to running containers
8. **A cluster is running production workloads, but it does not appear in Defender for Cloud posture recommendations or Defender for Cloud Secure Score. What is the best architectural explanation?**
   a. Kubernetes clusters are excluded from posture measurement by default
   b. Defender for Cloud Secure Score only supports IaaS workloads
   c. The relevant Defender for Cloud coverage and onboarding for containers/orchestration is not enabled
   d. The cluster is fully patched and therefore hidden
9. **In Kubernetes environments, why is worker node security treated as a platform protection requirement rather than an operations detail?**
   a. Node patching has no impact on container security
   b. A compromised node can become a shared failure domain that enables cluster-wide compromise paths
   c. Nodes are managed entirely by application developers
   d. Containers eliminate host level risk
10. **An AI workload must process highly sensitive data while reducing the trust placed in platform administrators and underlying infrastructure. Which design choice best addresses this requirement?**
    a. Encrypt data at rest only and rely on RBAC for access control
    b. Use confidential computing with hardware-backed isolation and attestation to protect data during processing
    c. Enable a WAF in front of the AI endpoint
    d. Increase log retention to detect misuse after the fact

Answers

1. b: Defining the baseline using MCSB and evaluating it through Microsoft Defender for Cloud.

MCSB establishes consistent security intent, and Defender for Cloud evaluates diverse workloads against that intent without requiring identical configurations.

2. c: It validates both posture alignment and whether assessment coverage is enabled.

   Defender for Cloud Secure Score is only meaningful when the right plans and onboarding are in place; missing signals often indicate coverage gaps, not compliance.

3. b: Defender for Cloud protection plans and onboarding coverage are not enabled for those workloads.

   If workloads do not appear in recommendations, the common cause is a lack of assessment activation rather than perfect compliance.

4. b: It provides continuous evaluation and enforcement of baseline intent across the resource lifecycle.

   Azure Policy converts baseline standards into enforceable constraints and continuously detects drift across new and existing resources.

5. b: Use a WAF at the entry point and restrict backend access paths so only approved gateways can reach them.

   This prevents bypass of edge controls and ensures backend services are not exposed directly to the internet.

6. c: WAFs filter attack patterns but do not provide identity-aware authorization guarantees for backend access.

   Zero Trust requires explicit authorization at the service boundary; WAFs reduce attack noise but cannot establish trust.

7. b: Scan and evaluate container images in the registry before deployment and enforce promotion rules.

   Registry scanning prevents vulnerable images from becoming a replicated risk across deployments and environments.

8. c: The relevant Defender for Cloud coverage and onboarding for containers/orchestration is not enabled.

   Clusters appear in posture only when assessed through the appropriate protection plan and onboarding path.

9. b: A compromised node can become a shared failure domain that enables cluster-wide compromise paths.

   Orchestration amplifies blast radius; node integrity failures propagate faster and further than in traditional infrastructure.

10. b: Use confidential computing with hardware-backed isolation and attestation to protect data during processing.

    Confidential computing protects data in use and reduces trust in administrators and infrastructure by enforcing isolation in trusted execution environments.

CHAPTER 11
Design Network Security Architecture Solutions

Introduction

This chapter examines how to evaluate and design network security architectures that remain effective as organizations operate across hybrid, multi-cloud, and **software as a service** (**SaaS**) first environments. As traditional perimeter models give way to identity-driven access and policy-based enforcement, network security decisions must assume compromise, limit implicit trust, and deliberately constrain connectivity. Rather than focusing on individual controls in isolation, this chapter frames network security as an architectural discipline where trust decisions, enforcement points, and failure containment are intentionally designed.

The chapter explores how security architects assess network designs to reduce attack surface, prevent lateral movement, and govern access across internet traffic, Microsoft Services, and private applications. It examines how Microsoft Entra Internet Access and Entra Private Access enable **security service edge** (**SSE**) and **Zero Trust Network Access** (**ZTNA**) patterns, and how scope definition, assignment, connector placement, and availability design determine whether enforcement works consistently in real-world environments. By applying these principles, architects can recommend network security architectures that balance protection, performance, and operational sustainability while aligning with Zero Trust objectives.

Structure

This chapter covers the following topics:

- Evaluating network designs against security requirements
- Entra Internet Access as a secure web gateway
- Entra Internet Access for Microsoft Services
- Evaluating solutions with Entra Private Access

Objectives

This chapter covers the skills required to evaluate network designs to ensure they align with security requirements and best practices, focusing on how network architecture enforces segmentation, traffic inspection, and access boundaries. It examines how design decisions influence exposure, resilience, and the ability to apply consistent security controls across environments.

The chapter explores solutions that use Microsoft Entra Internet Access as a secure web gateway, including how web traffic is protected, monitored, and governed. It also evaluates the use of Microsoft Entra Internet Access for Microsoft Services, including cross-tenant configurations, to ensure secure and controlled access to Microsoft-hosted resources.

Finally, the chapter examines solutions that use Microsoft Entra Private Access to securely connect users to private applications without relying on traditional network perimeter controls, aligning network access design with Zero Trust principles. These skills fall under the exam domain: *Design security solutions for infrastructure*, which represents approximately 25-30 % of the overall SC-100 skills measured.[1]

Evaluating network designs against security requirements

Network security architecture is judged by outcomes, not diagrams. A design is effective only if it consistently enforces least privilege connectivity, minimizes exposure to untrusted networks, and prevents a single compromised identity or workload from becoming a pathway to broader compromise. In hybrid and cloud environments, identities, devices, and network locations are fluid and frequently abused, which means designs can no longer rely on implicit trust based on where traffic originates. Instead, they must deliberately constrain how traffic flows, where trust decisions are enforced, and how access is governed over time.

Evaluating a network design, therefore, begins by identifying where trust is granted, how that trust is validated, and how quickly it can be withdrawn. Designs that depend on manual exceptions or scattered controls tend to degrade under operational pressure. Designs that centralize policy intent, reduce exposed entry points, and treat administrative access as a governed workflow are more resilient. This section examines these evaluation criteria in depth, grounding Zero Trust principles in concrete architectural decisions. This section maps to the following SC-100 skills measured: *Evaluate network designs to align with security requirements and best practices*.

Designing Zero Trust network architectures

Zero Trust network architecture starts from the premise that network location is not a reliable indicator of trust. Traditional designs implicitly grant broad reachability to anything considered inside, then attempt to mitigate risk with downstream controls. In cloud-centric environments, this model collapses because attackers exploit that reachability once any credential or endpoint is compromised.

1 **https://learn.microsoft.com/en-us/credentials/certifications/resources/study-guides/sc-100**

Eliminating implicit trust based on network location

A Zero Trust-aligned network design removes the assumption that being connected to a network segment implies legitimacy. Instead of granting users or systems access to entire address spaces, access is scoped to specific services, applications, or management planes. From an evaluation standpoint, a strong design is one where default connectivity is minimal, and every permitted flow can be justified in terms of business need.

To understand how Zero Trust changes network access, *Figure 11.1* contrasts a traditional network-trust model with a policy-driven approach based on identity and explicit access controls:

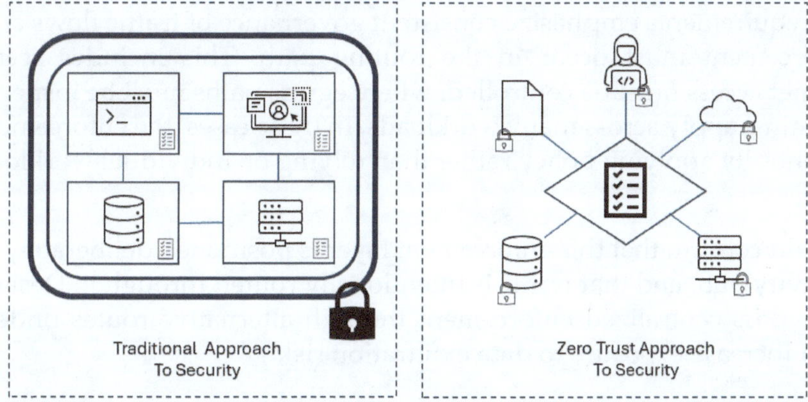

***Figure 11.1**: Transition from network-based trust to a policy-driven access model*

This approach materially reduces blast radius. If a credential is compromised, the attacker does not inherit broad network visibility; they inherit only the connectivity explicitly granted to that identity and session. When reviewing a design, the absence of large, flat network segments and unrestricted east-west traffic is a strong indicator of Zero Trust maturity.

Designing for containment under assumed breach

Zero Trust assumes failure. Credentials will be stolen, and endpoints will be compromised. The role of the network is therefore not to prevent every intrusion, but to contain the impact of inevitable ones. Evaluation should focus on what happens after initial access: which systems become reachable, how quickly controls activate, and whether lateral movement is meaningfully constrained.

Architectures that rely on post-compromise detection alone are fragile. Architectures that combine scoped connectivity, segmentation, and identity-aware enforcement create natural containment boundaries. A useful test during evaluation is to trace an attack path from a compromised endpoint and determine how many additional systems are reachable without triggering additional trust decisions.

Selecting the correct network enforcement layer

Effective network security architectures align enforcement layers with the decisions they are meant to enforce. A common design failure is using controls designed for application protection to solve network-wide governance problems, or expecting routing-based controls to provide application-level inspection. Evaluating a design requires confirming that each enforcement layer is used for its intended purpose.

Centralized traffic governance and routing-based enforcement

When security requirements emphasize consistent governance of traffic flows across multiple networks, enforcement must occur in the routing path. This includes scenarios where outbound internet access must be controlled, where egress paths must be inspected, or where uniform policy must apply across many workloads. In these cases, the enforcement layer must be capable of centrally applying policy rather than relying on individual workloads to behave correctly.

Evaluation should confirm that this enforcement layer is positioned deliberately, typically in a shared connectivity hub, and that traffic is intentionally routed through it. Designs that allow workloads to bypass centralized enforcement through alternative routes undermine policy consistency and increase exposure to data exfiltration risk.

Application ingress protection and request inspection

When the requirement is to protect applications from malicious or malformed requests, enforcement belongs at the application ingress. This layer focuses on inspecting protocol-level behavior and blocking common exploitation techniques. Evaluating a design involves ensuring that ingress protection is applied where applications terminate traffic, rather than being stretched to cover broader network governance requirements.

Strong architectures layer ingress protection with centralized traffic controls. This ensures that failure or bypass of one layer does not invalidate the other, and that network-wide governance and application-specific protection reinforce rather than replace each other.

Minimizing attack surface while maintaining connectivity

Attack surface reduction is a concrete architectural outcome. Every publicly exposed endpoint increases the likelihood of scanning and exploitation attempts. Evaluating a network design, therefore, involves identifying which services must remain publicly reachable and ensuring that everything else is shielded behind controlled access paths.

Restricting exposure for required public endpoints

Some workloads must remain accessible via a public endpoint due to protocol constraints, platform limitations, or business requirements. In these scenarios, the architectural goal is not to eliminate the public endpoint, but to strictly limit who can reach it. Restricting access to known source **Internet Protocol** (**IP**) addresses is the correct design choice when the service must stay public but should only be reachable from defined network locations.

This distinction matters because private endpoints and service endpoints change the exposure model entirely. Private endpoints remove public exposure by placing the service on a private IP address, while service endpoints extend virtual network identity to a platform service. When neither of those patterns is viable, and the endpoint must remain public, authorized IP ranges provide a deliberate, exam-relevant mechanism to reduce exposure without redesigning the service. Evaluation should confirm that IP restriction is used intentionally in these cases and not as a substitute for identity-aware access where private exposure is feasible.

Balancing exposure reduction with operational simplicity

Overly complex exposure models often fail in practice. Designs that rely on numerous bespoke exceptions become difficult to audit and maintain, leading to configuration drift. Effective architectures balance exposure reduction with clarity of ownership, ensuring that controls can be governed and adjusted without introducing fragility.

From an evaluation perspective, simplicity is a security property. Designs that are understandable and repeatable are more likely to remain secure over time than designs that depend on intricate, undocumented exceptions.

Securing administrative access paths

Administrative access paths represent a high-impact risk plane because they often provide direct control over infrastructure and workloads. Evaluating how a design handles administrative access is therefore central to assessing its overall security posture.

Removing public exposure of management interfaces

Exposing management ports directly to the internet, even with restrictions, creates persistent attack surfaces. A secure design avoids public exposure of administrative interfaces altogether, reducing scanning and brute-force risk and eliminating entire classes of attack.

Evaluation should confirm that management access is mediated through controlled paths rather than open network ports. Designs that require administrators to open ports temporarily or manage ad hoc exceptions tend to drift toward permanent exposure under operational pressure.

Planning Bastion deployment scope and topology impact

Azure Bastion is scoped at the virtual network level and requires a dedicated subnet within each virtual network where it is deployed. This architectural constraint directly affects how many Bastion instances are required in a given design. Bastion is not deployed per virtual machine, per workload subnet, or per region; it is deployed per virtual network boundary.

When evaluating a network design, it is therefore essential to count virtual networks, not subnets or servers, when determining Bastion requirements. Designs with multiple **virtual networks** (**VNets**) require multiple Bastion deployments if secure administrative access is needed in each VNet. Making this relationship explicit prevents under-designing administrative access paths and ensures that secure connectivity scales correctly as environments grow.

Enforcing identity-mediated administrative workflows

Administrative access should be granted through identity-based authorization and should exist only for the duration required to perform a task. Treating administrative connectivity as a governed workflow rather than a static configuration improves auditability and reduces the risk of privilege misuse.

Topology awareness reinforces this model. Since administrative access solutions align with network boundaries, they must be planned alongside segmentation decisions rather than bolted on later. Evaluating a design involves confirming that these access paths are deliberate, auditable, and capable of scaling without reintroducing public exposure.

Entra Internet Access as a secure web gateway

Internet access has become one of the most critical enforcement planes in modern security architecture; for many organizations, the majority of business activity now occurs over the internet and SaaS connections rather than within private networks. This shift fundamentally changes how network security must be designed and evaluated. The question is no longer whether users can reach the internet, but whether internet-bound access is governed, identity-aware, and continuously enforceable across users, devices, and locations.

Microsoft Entra Internet Access introduces a SSE model where outbound traffic is no longer treated as inherently trusted once it leaves the corporate network. Instead, access to the internet and SaaS destinations becomes conditional on identity, device posture, and policy context. Evaluating solutions in this space requires understanding where enforcement occurs, how policies are applied, and how scope is controlled so that security decisions are consistent rather than accidental. This section maps to the following SC-100 skills measured: *Evaluate solutions that use Microsoft Entra Internet Access as a secure web gateway.*

Identity-aware internet and SaaS access

Traditional secure web gateways focused primarily on filtering destinations and inspecting content. While those functions remain relevant, they are insufficient on their own in environments where identities and devices are the primary attack targets. Identity-aware internet access shifts the enforcement decision from where the traffic is going to who is accessing it and under what conditions.

Enforcing authentication before outbound connectivity

In an identity-aware model, outbound access to SaaS and internet services is not merely routed; it is mediated. Users authenticate using organizational identities before traffic is allowed to reach protected destinations. This ensures that access to business-critical SaaS applications is explicitly tied to an identity decision rather than implicitly granted by network location.

From an architectural evaluation standpoint, this changes how trust is applied. Access is no longer assumed because a device is on a corporate network or connected through a **virtual private network** (**VPN**). Instead, the secure web gateway becomes a control point where identity is validated, and policy is enforced before connectivity is established. Designs that achieve this reduce the risk of credential misuse from unmanaged or compromised environments.

Integrating device posture into access decisions

Identity alone is not sufficient to determine trust. Device posture, such as compliance with security baselines, provides critical context for whether access should be allowed. An effective secure web gateway design integrates device signals so that access can be conditioned on the security state of the endpoint.

When evaluating a solution, it is important to confirm that device compliance is not merely checked at sign-in, but actively influences network access decisions. This ensures that users on noncompliant devices cannot simply authenticate and gain unrestricted access to SaaS or internet resources. Architectures that integrate identity and device posture at the gateway level create a stronger alignment between endpoint security and network enforcement.

Policy enforcement with Conditional Access

Conditional Access is the policy engine through which many organizations express their access requirements. However, policies only become meaningful when there is a reliable enforcement point. In the context of internet access, the secure web gateway must be able to apply Conditional Access decisions directly to traffic flows.

Binding traffic profiles to Conditional Access policies

In Microsoft Entra Internet Access, traffic profiles provide the explicit binding between network traffic and identity policy enforcement. Traffic profiles define which categories of internet or

SaaS traffic are subject to inspection and control, and these profiles are then associated with Conditional Access policies that determine whether access is permitted.

This distinction is architecturally important. Conditional Access alone does not intercept or redirect traffic; it evaluates conditions and returns an allow or deny decision. Traffic profiles ensure that internet-bound traffic is actually brought into the enforcement plane, where Conditional Access decisions can be applied. Evaluating a design, therefore, requires confirming that the correct traffic profiles are enabled and linked to the intended Conditional Access policies, rather than assuming that identity policy automatically governs network behavior.

Enabling continuous enforcement during active sessions

Modern threats often emerge during an active session rather than at initial sign-in. Continuous enforcement ensures that changes in risk, device posture, or policy are reflected in real-time. Evaluating a secure web gateway solution involves confirming that it supports ongoing enforcement rather than one-time authorization.

This capability is especially important for SaaS-heavy environments where long-lived sessions are common. Architectures that support continuous enforcement reduce the window in which compromised sessions can be abused, aligning network behavior with evolving security signals rather than static assumptions.

Scope control and traffic assignment

Even well-designed policies fail if they are applied inconsistently. Scope control determines which devices, users, and networks are subject to secure web gateway enforcement. From an evaluation perspective, scope misalignment is one of the most common causes of security gaps.

Device-based assignment as an enforcement prerequisite

Secure web gateway enforcement applies only to devices that are explicitly assigned to the Entra Internet Access service. If a device is not within the assignment scope, its traffic will not be intercepted or governed, regardless of how strong the associated policies may be.

When evaluating a design, it is therefore essential to verify that device assignment aligns with the intended user population. Partial or inconsistent assignment explains scenarios where some users experience enforced access while others bypass controls entirely. This is not a policy failure but a scope definition failure, and recognizing that distinction is key to diagnosing enforcement gaps.

Remote network association and location-based coverage

In addition to device assignment, remote network association determines which physical or logical locations are covered by Internet Access enforcement. Traffic originating from networks that are not associated with the service will not be subject to inspection or Conditional Access enforcement.

Architectural evaluation should confirm that remote network definitions reflect actual connectivity patterns. If one site is associated and another is not, enforcement will differ by location even for identical users and policies. Understanding this cause-and-effect relationship allows architects to explain and correct inconsistent enforcement outcomes without redesigning policy intent.

Entra Internet Access for Microsoft Services

Microsoft Services traffic, particularly Microsoft 365, occupies a unique position in enterprise network security architecture; it is both business-critical and identity-centric, carrying authentication tokens, collaboration data, and sensitive organizational content across globally distributed endpoints. As a result, Microsoft Services traffic cannot be treated as generic internet traffic without introducing governance gaps. Evaluating network security solutions in this space requires understanding how access to Microsoft Services is constrained, monitored, and continuously enforced in alignment with organizational identity boundaries.

Microsoft Entra Internet Access extends secure web gateway principles specifically to Microsoft Services by allowing architects to apply identity-aware, tenant-scoped, and continuously enforced access controls to Microsoft 365 traffic. The evaluation focus shifts from basic reachability to boundary control: which tenants users are allowed to authenticate to, under what conditions sessions remain valid, and how network-level enforcement ensures identity policy intent is actually applied to service access. This section maps to the following SC-100 skills measured: *Evaluate solutions that use Microsoft Entra Internet Access for Microsoft Services, including cross-tenant configurations*.

Protecting Microsoft 365 traffic flows

Microsoft 365 traffic differs from general SaaS traffic because it represents the primary channel for collaboration, data sharing, and identity authentication. Treating this traffic as just another internet destination risks losing visibility and control over how organizational identities interact with Microsoft's service ecosystem.

Applying Microsoft service traffic profiles

Microsoft Entra Internet Access governs Microsoft Services traffic through dedicated Microsoft Services traffic profiles. These profiles explicitly identify Microsoft 365 endpoints and ensure that traffic is routed into the enforcement plane where identity and policy decisions can be applied.

This mechanism is critical from an architectural standpoint. Conditional Access evaluates identity and session conditions, but it does not, by itself, intercept network traffic. Microsoft

Services traffic profiles provide the binding that brings Microsoft 365 access under network-level enforcement, enabling Conditional Access and continuous access evaluation to apply consistently. Evaluating a solution, therefore, requires confirming that the correct Microsoft Services traffic profile is enabled, rather than assuming Microsoft 365 traffic is automatically governed by identity policy alone.

Enforcing consistent access regardless of user location

One of the challenges in hybrid environments is ensuring that Microsoft 365 access is governed consistently across corporate offices, remote users, and mobile devices. Location-based assumptions quickly break down as users move between networks.

An effective design ensures that Microsoft Services access is enforced based on identity and policy rather than physical location. Evaluating this aspect involves confirming that enforcement follows the user and device, providing the same access conditions whether the user is on a trusted network, a home connection, or a public hotspot. Designs that achieve this reduce the risk of policy bypass caused by location changes.

Tenant-scoped access control

Cross-tenant access introduces significant risk if left unmanaged. Users may be invited into external tenants, authenticate to unintended environments, or inadvertently share data across organizational boundaries. Evaluating network security for Microsoft Services, therefore, requires explicit consideration of tenant scope.

Restricting authentication to approved tenants

Tenant-scoped access control limits where organizational identities are allowed to authenticate. By constraining authentication to approved Microsoft Entra tenants, architects reduce the risk of data leakage, shadow collaboration, and identity misuse.

From an evaluation perspective, this control answers a fundamental boundary question: where do our identities belong? Designs that allow unrestricted cross-tenant authentication effectively dissolve organizational boundaries, making it harder to reason about data ownership and compliance. Evaluating a solution involves confirming that tenant restrictions are intentional, centrally governed, and aligned with business requirements rather than left to default behavior.

Reducing cross-tenant attack risk

Cross-tenant scenarios are frequently exploited through phishing, consent abuse, and malicious collaboration invitations. Tenant-scoped enforcement reduces these risks by preventing identities from being used in untrusted tenants, even if a user is socially engineered into attempting access.

Evaluating this capability involves understanding how network-level enforcement reinforces identity boundaries. When tenant restrictions are applied consistently at the access layer, they reduce reliance on user judgment and close off common attack paths that exploit trust between tenants.

Continuous access evaluation for Microsoft Services

Access to Microsoft Services is often long-lived, with sessions persisting for extended periods. This creates risk when the conditions under which access was granted change during an active session. This approach emphasizes the importance of integrating identity, device compliance, and network signals into a unified enforcement model. By doing so, organizations can respond in near real-time to changes that may impact the security of an active session, reducing exposure to risk and strengthening overall access governance.

Maintaining enforcement throughout the session lifecycle

Continuous access evaluation ensures that access to Microsoft Services remains aligned with current policy and risk signals. If a device becomes noncompliant or a risk condition is detected, the system can re-evaluate access without waiting for the user to sign out.

Evaluating a design in this area involves confirming that enforcement is not limited to initial authentication. Architectures that support ongoing evaluation reduce the window in which compromised sessions can be abused, aligning network behavior with real-time security context rather than static assumptions.

Scope and assignment for Microsoft Services enforcement

Microsoft Services enforcement through Entra Internet Access applies only where the scope is explicitly defined. Devices must be assigned to the Internet Access service and, where applicable, networks must be associated for Microsoft Services traffic to be intercepted and governed.

This cause-and-effect relationship explains common enforcement inconsistencies. If Microsoft 365 access is governed for some users or locations but not others, the issue is typically a misaligned assignment or a missing network association rather than a policy failure. Evaluating a solution, therefore, requires verifying that the assignment scope and network coverage match the intended enforcement footprint, ensuring Microsoft Services access is consistently governed wherever it is expected to apply.

Evaluating solutions with Entra Private Access

Private application access is where many network security architectures quietly fail. Legacy VPN-based designs grant broad network reachability to users who only need access to one or two applications, creating an unnecessary blast radius and making lateral movement trivial once a credential or device is compromised. Evaluating modern network security architectures, therefore, requires a clear understanding of how private applications are exposed, how access decisions are enforced, and how connectivity can be constrained without sacrificing usability.

Microsoft Entra Private Access introduces a ZTNA model that shifts private connectivity from network-level trust to identity-level authorization. Rather than connecting users to entire networks, access is granted to specific private applications based on identity, device posture, and policy context. The evaluation focus is not simply whether users can reach private resources, but whether access is scoped, auditable, resilient, and aligned with Zero Trust principles. This section maps to the following SC-100 skills measured: *Evaluate solutions that use Microsoft Entra Private Access.*

Identity-based access to private applications

Private applications include on-premises services, internal web apps, legacy systems, and cloud-hosted workloads that are not intended to be publicly exposed. Traditional designs often rely on VPNs to provide access to these resources, but VPNs fundamentally operate by extending network trust rather than enforcing application-specific authorization.

Replacing VPN trust with application access

Entra Private Access replaces the assumption that connected equals trusted with an explicit access model where identities are authorized to individual applications. Users do not gain broad network visibility simply by authenticating; they gain access only to the applications they are permitted to use.

From an evaluation standpoint, this distinction is critical. A ZTNA-based design dramatically reduces blast radius by preventing lateral movement across the private address space. If a user's credentials are compromised, the attacker inherits only the application-level access granted to that identity, not a tunnel into the internal network. Evaluating a solution, therefore, involves confirming that access is defined per application and that no implicit network reachability is introduced as a side effect.

Applying Conditional Access to private application connectivity

Private application access must be governed by the same identity policies that protect SaaS and cloud services. Entra Private Access integrates with Conditional Access so that requirements such as multi-factor authentication, device compliance, and risk evaluation apply before connectivity to private apps is established.

Evaluating this capability involves confirming that access to private applications is conditional, not static. If a device becomes noncompliant or a risk signal changes, access decisions should reflect that change. Designs that treat private connectivity as an exception to identity policy undermine Zero Trust consistency and create uneven enforcement across access types.

Connector placement and network optimization

The connector is the enforcement bridge between Entra Private Access and the private application. Rather than treating connectors as generic infrastructure components, they should be positioned and scaled based on how applications are accessed and where they reside. Where and how connectors are deployed has a direct impact on performance, resiliency, and operational complexity.

This approach ensures that traffic paths remain efficient, predictable, and secure, while also supporting a consistent user experience. By carefully considering placement, architects can reduce unnecessary hops, avoid bottlenecks, and create a foundation that supports both performance and high availability.

Placing connectors close to the application

Connectors should be deployed as close as possible to the application they publish, typically within the same network or a directly connected segment. This minimizes latency, reduces dependency on complex routing, and avoids unnecessary traffic backhauling.

This placement rule is explicit: connectors are positioned near the application, not near the user, and not arbitrarily centralized in a connectivity hub unless the applications themselves reside there. Designs that place connectors near users or in distant hubs introduce avoidable latency and additional failure points. Evaluating a solution, therefore, involves tracing the traffic path and confirming that the connector placement aligns with application proximity rather than user distribution.

Minimizing complexity while ensuring resiliency

Connector design must balance simplicity and availability. While multiple connectors improve resiliency, scattering connectors across many networks without a clear rationale increases operational overhead and complicates troubleshooting.

A strong architecture uses a deliberate number of well-placed connectors with sufficient redundancy to tolerate failures. Evaluation focuses on whether connector placement and quantity are justified by application location and availability requirements, rather than by convenience or habit.

Designing for availability and scale

Private application access must remain reliable as environments grow and change. Evaluating scalability involves understanding how the access model behaves under increased load, during failures, and as new applications are onboarded.

Achieving high availability through multiple connectors

High availability in Entra Private Access is achieved by deploying multiple connectors for the same application or application group. Availability is provided by connector redundancy, not by duplicating application definitions or creating parallel access paths.

This is a minimum design requirement, not an optimization. If only a single connector exists for an application, that connector represents a single point of failure. Evaluating a solution, therefore, requires confirming that at least two connectors are available for each critical application so that access can continue if one connector becomes unavailable.

Scaling private access without increasing administrative overhead

As more applications are onboarded, the access model should remain predictable and repeatable. Effective designs standardize how applications are published, how connectors are shared or assigned, and how policies are applied. This prevents configuration sprawl and ensures that scaling does not reintroduce broad network trust.

From an evaluation standpoint, scalability is demonstrated when additional applications can be added without redesigning the access model or increasing blast radius. Architectures that emphasize repeatable connectors and policy patterns are better positioned to support growth while maintaining Zero Trust guarantees.

Conclusion

This chapter demonstrated that modern network security architecture is no longer about perimeter placement or connectivity diagrams, but about where trust is evaluated, how access is enforced, and how failure is contained. As hybrid work, SaaS dependency, and cloud-native platforms dissolve traditional network boundaries, security architects must design networks that assume compromise and enforce policy through identity-aware control points rather than implicit location-based trust.

The chapter began by establishing how Zero Trust principles translate into concrete network design decisions, showing how centralized enforcement, deliberate segmentation, attack surface reduction, and governed administrative access combine to limit blast radius and prevent lateral movement. It then examined how Microsoft Entra Internet Access extends these principles to internet and SaaS traffic, ensuring outbound connectivity is authenticated, policy-driven, and consistently enforced across users, devices, and locations.

Building on this, the chapter explored how Microsoft Services traffic, particularly Microsoft 365, requires tenant-scoped, continuously evaluated access controls to prevent cross-tenant exposure and identity misuse. Finally, it showed how Entra Private Access replaces legacy VPN models with application-level authorization, emphasizing connector placement, availability design, and scalable patterns that preserve security without sacrificing usability.

Taken together, these architectures form a cohesive network security strategy where identity defines access, policy defines behavior, and the network enforces intent. By applying these design principles, security architects can evaluate and recommend network solutions that are resilient, governable, and aligned with both Zero Trust objectives and real-world operational demands.

The next chapter shifts from network-level enforcement to securing the productivity and collaboration services that users rely on every day. It examines how Microsoft 365 security controls protect identities, devices, data, and collaboration workflows, extending Zero Trust principles into email, files, and real-time collaboration services.

Questions

Success on any assessment depends on understanding the underlying technologies, concepts, and principles rather than memorizing facts. The following questions help readers confirm that they can apply this chapter's ideas in realistic design scenarios, including security posture evaluation, benchmark alignment, hybrid visibility, workload protection selection, external attack surface awareness, and exposure-driven risk prioritization.

1. **An organization wants to evaluate whether Azure workloads align with a standardized baseline covering identity, network, data, and monitoring controls. Which architectural approach best achieves this outcome?**
   a. Enabling Microsoft Secure Score
   b. Reviewing individual security alerts
   c. Evaluating workloads using Microsoft Defender for Cloud and the MCSB
   d. Applying Azure Policy remediation tasks manually
2. **Why is the MCSB most effective when used as a posture baseline rather than a compliance checklist?**
   a. It replaces the need for threat detection
   b. It enforces identical configurations across all cloud platforms
   c. It defines a consistent security intent that can be evaluated across diverse workloads
   d. It guarantees regulatory compliance
3. **Which signal most strongly indicates a systemic posture design issue rather than an isolated configuration error?**
   a. A single failed recommendation on one resource
   b. A recurring posture recommendation across multiple workloads
   c. A temporary Secure Score fluctuation
   d. An individual security alert

4. **What does Microsoft Secure Score primarily represent?**
   a. Real-time detection of active attacks
   b. Compliance status against regulatory frameworks
   c. Improvement potential based on the adoption of Microsoft 365 security controls
   d. Infrastructure misconfiguration severity
5. **An architect needs unified posture visibility across Azure, AWS, and on-premises servers. Which design best supports this requirement?**
   a. Native security tools on each platform
   b. Microsoft Secure Score alone
   c. Microsoft Defender for Cloud with multi-cloud connectors and Azure Arc
   d. Microsoft Sentinel analytics rules
6. **A scenario requires virtual machines to be assessed for missing patches and known vulnerabilities using the Qualys scanning engine. Which Defender for Cloud plan must be selected?**
   a. Defender for Containers
   b. Defender for Servers
   c. Defender for Databases
   d. Defender for Storage
7. **Why does Azure Arc play a critical role in hybrid and multi-cloud posture management?**
   a. It enforces identical configurations across platforms
   b. It replaces native cloud security services
   c. It projects non-Azure resources into Azure security and management control planes
   d. It performs external vulnerability scanning
8. **Which capability is specifically designed to identify unknown or unmanaged internet-facing assets from an attacker's perspective?**
   a. Microsoft Secure Score
   b. Defender for Cloud recommendations
   c. Microsoft Defender External Attack Surface Management
   d. Azure Policy guest configuration
9. **Why is it architecturally incorrect to assume that enabling workload protection plans alone ensures adequate security?**
   a. Workload protection increases alert volume

b. Protection plans are limited to Azure resources

c. Coverage does not address configuration hygiene or systemic exposure

d. Protection plans replace posture management

10. **What is the primary purpose of attack paths in Microsoft Security Exposure Management?**

    a. To list all vulnerabilities by severity

    b. To automate remediation across all findings

    c. To reveal how combined weaknesses enable end-to-end compromise

    d. To replace Secure Score and posture recommendations

Answers

1. c: Evaluating workloads using Microsoft Defender for Cloud and the MCSB.

   Defender for Cloud continuously evaluates resources against MCSB controls, translating baseline security intent into measurable posture signals across workloads.

2. c: It defines consistent security intent that can be evaluated across diverse workloads.

   Using MCSB as a baseline embeds security expectations into posture evaluation rather than treating controls as optional or one-time checks.

3. b: A recurring posture recommendation across multiple workloads.

   Repeated findings indicate a systemic design gap in standards, templates, or inherited controls rather than an isolated misconfiguration.

4. c: Improvement potential based on adoption of Microsoft 365 security controls.

   Secure Score measures how much posture can be strengthened by implementing recommended controls, not absolute security or compliance.

5. c: Microsoft Defender for Cloud with multi-cloud connectors and Azure Arc.

   This design centralizes posture signals across Azure, other clouds, and on-premises environments into a single evaluative model.

6. b: Defender for Servers.

   Defender for Servers enables the Qualys vulnerability assessment engine and provides patch and vulnerability visibility for virtual machines.

7. c: It projects non-Azure resources into Azure security and management control planes.

   Azure Arc allows hybrid and multi-cloud assets to be evaluated and governed using Azure-native security services.

8. c: Microsoft Defender External Attack Surface Management.

   Defender EASM discovers and classifies publicly exposed assets that may fall outside internal inventories and governance processes.

9. c: Coverage does not address configuration hygiene or systemic exposure.

   Workload protection detects runtime threats, but posture management is required to reduce the attack surface and prevent recurrence.

10. c: To reveal how combined weaknesses enable end-to-end compromise.

    Attack paths correlate posture findings across domains, allowing architects to prioritize remediation that breaks real-world exploitation chains.

Join our Discord space

Join our Discord workspace for latest updates, offers, tech happenings around the world, new releases, and sessions with the authors:

https://discord.bpbonline.com

Chapter 12
Design Microsoft 365 Security Solutions

Introduction

Microsoft 365 is the primary productivity platform for most organizations, making it one of the most critical and most frequently targeted security surfaces in the modern enterprise. Email, document collaboration, chat, and cloud-based file sharing concentrate identity, data, and user activity into a tightly integrated environment where small design weaknesses can rapidly translate into large-scale exposure.

This chapter examines how to design security solutions for Microsoft 365 that protect collaboration workloads without undermining productivity. It focuses on evaluating security posture, applying service-native threat protection, enforcing device trust, and governing data access across Exchange Online, SharePoint Online, OneDrive, Teams, and connected SaaS applications. Rather than treating these services in isolation, the chapter approaches Microsoft 365 as a unified security boundary where controls must work together to reduce risk.

The chapter also addresses how emerging AI-powered experiences, such as Microsoft Copilot, inherit and amplify existing security decisions. By understanding how identity, access, device compliance, and data protection controls intersect, security architects can design Microsoft 365 environments that are resilient, measurable, and aligned with organizational security and compliance objectives.

Structure

This chapter covers the following topics:

- Security posture for productivity and collaboration
- Defender for Office 365 and Cloud Apps
- Evaluating device management with Microsoft Intune
- Securing Microsoft 365 data with Purview
- Data security and compliance in Microsoft Copilot

Objectives

This chapter covers the skills required to evaluate the security posture of productivity and collaboration workloads using measurable indicators, including Microsoft Secure Score. It examines how these metrics provide visibility into configuration gaps and risk across Microsoft 365 services.

The chapter explores solutions that include Microsoft Defender for Office 365 and Microsoft Defender for Cloud Apps, focusing on how threat protection and activity monitoring are applied across email, collaboration, and connected SaaS applications. It also evaluates device management solutions that include Microsoft Intune, examining how device compliance, configuration enforcement, and endpoint governance contribute to overall security posture.

In addition, the chapter examines solutions for securing data in Microsoft 365 using Microsoft Purview, including information protection, **data loss prevention** (**DLP**), and auditing capabilities. Finally, it evaluates data security and compliance controls in Microsoft Copilot for Microsoft 365 services, focusing on governance, access controls, and data protection. These skills fall under the exam domain: *Design security solutions for applications and data,* which represents approximately 20-25 % of the overall SC-100 skills measured[1].

Security posture for productivity and collaboration

Productivity and collaboration workloads introduce a unique security challenge because they collapse identity, devices, data, and user behavior into a single, continuous interaction surface. Email messages, shared documents, and real-time collaboration sessions move rapidly across Exchange Online, SharePoint Online, OneDrive, and Teams, often without clear boundaries between access, execution, and data movement. As a result, security posture for Microsoft 365 cannot be evaluated by inspecting individual services or reviewing isolated configuration settings.

Posture in this context is defined by how consistently security controls work together to reduce exposure across common collaboration attack paths. These paths frequently begin with deception through email, continue with access from unmanaged or weakly governed devices, and culminate in the rapid sharing or downloading of sensitive information. A failure at any point in this chain can undermine protections elsewhere, which is why posture must be assessed holistically rather than service by service. This section maps to the following SC-100 skills measured: *Evaluate security posture for productivity and collaboration workloads by using metrics, including Microsoft Secure Score.*

1 **https://learn.microsoft.com/en-us/credentials/certifications/resources/study-guides/sc-100**

Effective posture evaluation, therefore, focuses on outcomes, not features. The question is not whether a specific control exists, but whether identity enforcement, device trust, data protection, and threat defenses combine to meaningfully reduce risk across the tenant. Security architects must be able to determine whether protections are applied consistently, whether gaps exist between control layers, and where remediation will produce the greatest reduction in exposure.

Microsoft 365 provides a purpose-built mechanism to support this type of evaluation. Rather than aggregating alerts or presenting configuration inventories, it expresses security readiness as a measurable state aligned to Microsoft's recommended baseline for productivity and collaboration workloads. This enables architects to establish a baseline view of posture, identify systemic weaknesses, and track improvement over time as controls are strengthened.

Evaluate Microsoft 365 security posture using Microsoft Secure Score

Microsoft Secure Score is the tenant-level metric used to evaluate security posture across Microsoft 365 productivity and collaboration services. It aggregates prioritized improvement actions and control signals across identity protection, device management, data protection, and threat defense into a single score that reflects how closely the environment aligns with Microsoft's security guidance.

Secure Score is valuable because it evaluates posture as a system rather than as a collection of independent settings. Collaboration risk is cumulative: strong email protection can be undermined by permissive device access, and durable data classification can be weakened by inconsistent sharing controls. Secure Score highlights these combined gaps by showing where missing or under-enforced controls increase exposure across multiple services simultaneously.

The Secure Score dashboard provides a consolidated view of these signals, allowing architects to correlate improvement actions with specific control gaps across Microsoft 365 services. The following is an overview of the Microsoft Secure Score dashboard:

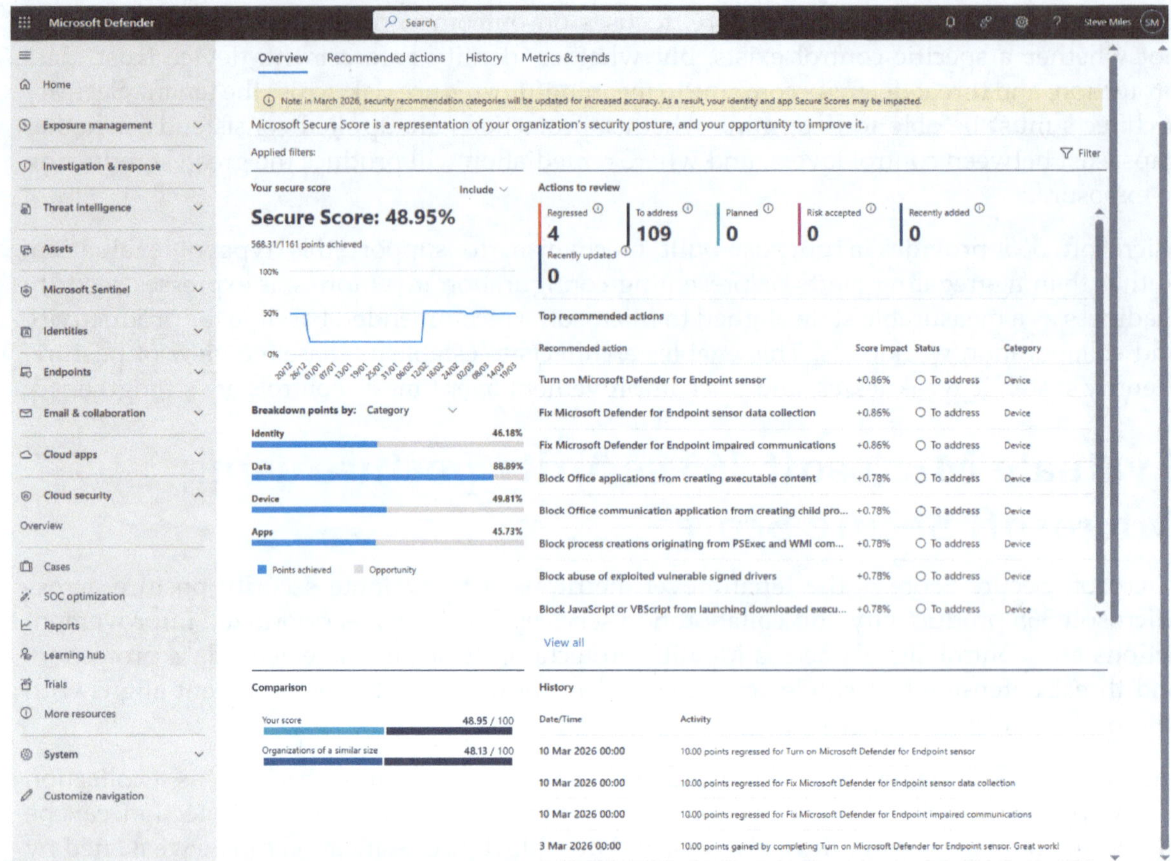

Figure 12.1: Microsoft Secure Score dashboard

Used correctly, Secure Score functions as a posture evaluation and prioritization tool. It allows security architects to identify which control areas require attention first and to assess whether changes to identity, device access, threat protection, or data security are improving overall resilience. For productivity and collaboration workloads, it provides the authoritative view of whether Microsoft 365 protections are aligned, complete, and effective at the tenant level.

Defender for Office 365 and Cloud Apps

Productivity and collaboration threats in Microsoft 365 increasingly exploit legitimate user activity rather than technical vulnerabilities. Attackers impersonate trusted senders, leverage valid credentials, and move data through approved cloud services at speed. In these scenarios, traditional perimeter controls and post-event detection provide limited protection because the activity appears normal until damage is already done.

Effective security design for Microsoft 365 must therefore apply controls at the service boundary and during user interaction, not after content has been delivered or accessed. Email threats must be intercepted within Exchange Online itself, and risky behavior in SharePoint or SaaS applications must be governed while sessions are active. This section examines how Microsoft Defender for Office 365 and Microsoft Defender for Cloud Apps provide those controls and how they are used together to reduce collaboration risk.

The argument in this section is deliberate. Defender for Office 365 addresses deception at the point of email delivery, while Defender for Cloud Apps governs how authenticated users interact with data inside cloud services. Together, they protect collaboration workflows where identity is valid, but behavior is risky. This section maps to the following SC-100 skills measured: *Evaluate solutions that include Microsoft Defender for Office 365 and Microsoft Defender for Cloud Apps*.

Email protection with Defender for Office 365

Email remains the most common entry point for collaboration-driven attacks because it provides direct access to users and exploits established trust relationships. Messages that appear to originate from colleagues, executives, or internal departments can prompt actions with significant impact even when no malware is involved.

Microsoft Defender for Office 365 applies advanced threat protection directly within Exchange Online to address this risk. A critical capability in this design is protection against impersonation, including spoofing of internal sender identities. These attacks rely on social engineering rather than malicious payloads, making them difficult to detect using traditional filtering techniques.

Defender for Office 365 analyzes sender identity, message characteristics, and communication patterns across the tenant to identify impersonation attempts before messages reach users. This enforcement occurs entirely at the service layer, ensuring consistent protection regardless of device type, location, or client application. By stopping deceptive email at delivery, Defender for Office 365 prevents attackers from gaining the initial foothold that enables downstream collaboration abuse.

Real-time controls with Defender for Cloud Apps

Once users are authenticated and working inside collaboration platforms, risk shifts from identity compromise to data misuse. Many security incidents occur during legitimate sessions, when users download, copy, or move sensitive information through SharePoint Online or other SaaS applications. In these cases, controls must operate during the interaction, not after data has already left organizational control.

Microsoft Defender for Cloud Apps provides real-time, session-based enforcement for cloud services. It evaluates user actions as they occur and applies controls inline, allowing security decisions to be made at the moment risk increases. This capability is essential for governing collaboration activity without blocking productivity outright. In practice, this real-time enforcement typically takes one of two forms, depending on whether the risk requires stronger identity assurance or immediate data classification.

Step-up authentication for SharePoint downloads

Some collaboration scenarios require stronger identity assurance only when risk is elevated. For example, a user may be permitted to browse SharePoint content normally but must provide additional authentication when attempting to download files that contain sensitive information. This is an adaptive requirement that cannot be met by static access rules alone.

Defender for Cloud Apps session policies can trigger step-up authentication during high-risk actions, such as downloading sensitive documents from SharePoint Online. Enforcement occurs inline, within the active session, and targets only the risky action rather than the entire workload. This approach strengthens security without unnecessarily disrupting normal collaboration.

Apply real-time sensitivity labels during file access

In other scenarios, the objective is not to block access or require reauthentication, but to ensure that sensitive content is classified correctly at the moment it is accessed. Applying classification after download does not meet this requirement, because data may already have been copied, shared, or stored elsewhere.

Defender for Cloud Apps can inspect file contents during access and apply sensitivity labels in real-time as users download documents from SharePoint Online. This inline labeling capability ensures that protection follows the data immediately, enabling downstream controls to act consistently based on classification.

Restrict SaaS access by device compliance

Collaboration environments frequently extend beyond Microsoft-native services to include third-party SaaS applications. Without consistent enforcement, these applications can become an unmanaged path for data exposure, even when Microsoft 365 controls are strong.

Microsoft Defender for Cloud Apps integrates with Microsoft Entra Conditional Access to enforce access conditions for SaaS applications based on contextual signals such as device compliance. In this model, Conditional Access determines whether a user can sign in, while Defender for Cloud Apps governs the session to ensure that access is limited to compliant devices.

By applying device-based restrictions consistently across Microsoft and non-Microsoft Services, this approach ensures that collaboration security does not fragment as users move between platforms. It reinforces the principle that access decisions are continuous and context-aware, not static or application-specific.

Evaluating device management with Microsoft Intune

Productivity and collaboration security in Microsoft 365 depend on whether access decisions account for the state of the device, not just the identity of the user. Email, SharePoint, OneDrive, and Teams are accessible from virtually anywhere, and without device-based enforcement, strong identity controls can be bypassed by unmanaged or poorly secured endpoints. The architectural challenge addressed in this section is how device trust is evaluated and enforced consistently across Microsoft 365 workloads.

Microsoft's design model deliberately separates device evaluation from access enforcement. Devices are assessed against defined security requirements independently, and the outcome of that assessment is then used to govern access to services. This separation allows device posture to be evaluated continuously while access decisions are enforced centrally and consistently at the service boundary.

This section focuses on Microsoft Intune as the authoritative source of device compliance and explains how that compliance state is used to control access to Microsoft 365 services. The goal is to ensure that collaboration workloads are accessed only from devices that meet organizational security standards, regardless of user location or application. This section maps to the following SC-100 skills measured: *Evaluate device management solutions that include Microsoft Intune.*

Enforce Microsoft 365 access with Intune

Microsoft Intune evaluates whether devices meet defined security requirements such as disk encryption, operating system version, and baseline configuration standards. These requirements are expressed through Intune compliance policies, which continuously assess device posture and produce a compliant or noncompliant state.

Device compliance on its own does not grant or deny access to Microsoft 365. Instead, the compliance state generated by Intune is consumed by Microsoft Entra Conditional Access. Conditional Access uses that signal to determine whether a user is allowed to access Exchange Online, SharePoint Online, Teams, and other Microsoft 365 services. This two-step model ensures that access enforcement is based on both identity and device trust.

By separating evaluation from enforcement, this approach allows device requirements to be updated without redesigning access policies and ensures consistent enforcement across all productivity workloads. Access decisions remain centralized, predictable, and aligned to Zero Trust principles.

Block Microsoft 365 access from noncompliant devices

Once device compliance is established as an access signal, a common security requirement is preventing access from devices that do not meet baseline security standards, such as devices without disk encryption or with outdated operating systems. In this scenario, Intune evaluates the device against the defined compliance policy and marks it as noncompliant when requirements are not met.

Conditional Access then uses the noncompliant status to block access to Microsoft 365 services until the device is remediated. This ensures that access enforcement is applied consistently across email, file sharing, and collaboration tools and does not depend on the application being used or the user's network location.

By enforcing access decisions based on device compliance, organizations ensure that productivity and collaboration workloads are accessed only from devices that meet minimum security requirements. This reinforces the principle that device trust is a prerequisite for service access, not an optional enhancement layered on afterwards.

Securing Microsoft 365 data with Purview

Protecting productivity and collaboration data in Microsoft 365 requires controls that understand what the data is, not just where it resides or who is accessing it. Documents, messages, and files move continuously across Exchange Online, Teams, SharePoint Online, and OneDrive, often crossing organizational and geographic boundaries in the course of normal work. Without data-aware controls, sensitive information can be exposed even when identity and device protections are correctly enforced.

Microsoft Purview provides the data security layer for Microsoft 365 by enabling classification-driven and content-aware protection. Rather than relying on application-specific rules or user discretion, Purview applies consistent data protection logic across collaboration workloads based on the sensitivity of the information itself. The architectural premise of this section is that sustainable data protection at scale depends on centralized classification and policy enforcement.

This section focuses on how Purview is used to prevent sensitive data from being shared inappropriately and to apply durable protection through classification. Together, these capabilities ensure that sensitive information is governed consistently as it moves through Microsoft 365 collaboration services. This section maps to the following SC-100 skills measured: *Evaluate solutions for securing data in Microsoft 365 by using Microsoft Purview*. These controls ensure that data protection decisions remain consistent regardless of how users collaborate or which Microsoft 365 service they use.

Prevent data sharing with Purview DLP

Microsoft Purview DLP is used to prevent sensitive information from being shared outside approved boundaries across Microsoft 365 workloads. DLP policies evaluate content in context and can block, restrict, or audit actions that would expose regulated or confidential data through email, chat, document sharing, or file downloads.

The key design objective of DLP is prevention. DLP is applied when the requirement is to stop sensitive data from leaving the organization or being shared inappropriately, rather than simply identifying or labeling that data. Since DLP policies operate across Exchange Online, Teams, SharePoint Online, and OneDrive, they provide consistent enforcement regardless of how users collaborate.

By grounding enforcement decisions in content inspection and contextual signals, Purview DLP ensures that protection follows the data rather than the application. This makes it suitable for collaboration environments where users move fluidly between services and share information in multiple ways.

Classify data with sensitivity labels

While DLP focuses on controlling actions, long-term data protection requires durable classification that persists with the content itself. Sensitivity labels provide this capability by assigning classifications that inform how data is protected, shared, and accessed over time.

Sensitivity labels are particularly important in large Microsoft 365 environments where vast amounts of data are created and stored in SharePoint Online and OneDrive. Labels enable organizations to apply consistent protection behaviors centrally, reducing reliance on manual user decisions and application-specific controls. Once applied, labels can enforce protection such as encryption or access restrictions wherever the data is accessed.

By separating classification from enforcement, sensitivity labels establish the foundation for scalable data governance. Other controls, including DLP and access restrictions, can then act based on that classification to ensure sensitive information is protected consistently across collaboration workflows.

Data security and compliance in Microsoft Copilot

Microsoft Copilot for Microsoft 365 does not introduce a new data plane or a separate security boundary; it operates entirely within the permissions, policies, and protections that already govern Microsoft 365 workloads. As a result, Copilot amplifies existing security design decisions rather than replacing or bypassing them. Where controls are strong, Copilot operates safely. Where controls are weak, Copilot accelerates exposure.

The primary security consideration with Copilot is therefore not how to secure the service itself, but how to ensure that identity, access, and data controls across Microsoft 365 are correctly designed and enforced. Copilot can only reference information that users are authorized to access through services such as SharePoint, Teams, OneDrive, and Exchange. Any over-permissive access, insufficient classification, or weak enforcement in those services directly affects what Copilot can surface.

This section examines how data security and compliance for Copilot are achieved by strengthening the Microsoft 365 control framework that Copilot inherits. The objective is to ensure that conversational access to information operates within clearly defined and consistently enforced boundaries. This section maps to the following SC-100 skills measured: *Evaluate data security and compliance controls in Microsoft Copilot for Microsoft 365 services.*

Secure Copilot interactions using existing Microsoft 365 controls

Copilot relies on the same authorization and access framework used by Microsoft 365 services. Identity permissions, Conditional Access policies, device compliance requirements, and content protection rules apply equally whether users access data directly or through Copilot. There is no Copilot-specific permission model that overrides these controls.

This means Copilot can only retrieve and summarize content that the user is already permitted to access. If a document is restricted by identity scope, blocked due to device noncompliance, or protected by sensitivity-based access controls, Copilot cannot access or reference that content. The security boundary remains the Microsoft 365 authorization layer, not the conversational interface.

Effective Copilot security, therefore, depends on validating that permissions are least-privileged, access conditions are enforced consistently, and data protection controls are correctly applied. Any gaps in these areas increase the risk that Copilot will surface information more broadly than intended.

Control Copilot data exposure with Purview

Copilot surfaces data from across collaboration workloads, and thus, data classification and prevention controls play a central role in limiting unintended exposure. Microsoft Purview sensitivity labels define how content is protected and shared, and those protections persist regardless of whether content is accessed directly or referenced by Copilot.

Purview DLP policies further restrict actions that could expose sensitive information outside approved boundaries. These policies ensure that even when Copilot references data internally, it cannot be used to facilitate prohibited sharing or disclosure. Protection is enforced based on content sensitivity and context, not on how the data is accessed.

Where additional adaptive enforcement is required, session controls can provide further safeguards by governing how data is accessed during active sessions. Together, these controls ensure that Copilot operates within the same security and compliance framework that governs Microsoft 365 collaboration services, reinforcing existing protections rather than introducing new risk. By reinforcing these inherited controls, organizations ensure that AI-driven collaboration accelerates productivity without expanding the attack surface.

Conclusion

This chapter examined how to design comprehensive security solutions for Microsoft 365 by treating productivity and collaboration as an integrated security surface rather than a collection of individual services. It showed that effective protection depends on how identity, devices, data, and threat controls work together across Exchange Online, SharePoint Online, OneDrive, Teams, and connected SaaS applications.

The chapter began by establishing security posture as a tenant-level condition that must be evaluated holistically. Microsoft Secure Score was positioned as the mechanism for measuring whether recommended protections are consistently applied and whether gaps exist across identity, device access, data protection, and threat defense. This posture-driven view provides the baseline for all subsequent design decisions.

It then explored how collaboration threats are addressed at the points where risk materializes. Microsoft Defender for Office 365 was presented as the control that intercepts deception and impersonation within email delivery, while Microsoft Defender for Cloud Apps governs risky behavior during active sessions in SharePoint and SaaS applications. Together, these services protect collaboration workflows where identity may be valid, but behavior introduces risk.

The chapter also demonstrated how device trust is enforced using Microsoft Intune and Conditional Access, ensuring that Microsoft 365 workloads are accessed only from compliant devices. It showed how Microsoft Purview extends protection into the data layer by preventing sensitive information from being shared inappropriately and by applying durable classification through sensitivity labels.

Finally, the chapter addressed Microsoft Copilot, emphasizing that Copilot does not introduce a new security model but instead inherits the controls already governing Microsoft 365. By designing strong identity, access, and data protections, organizations ensure that Copilot operates safely within established security and compliance boundaries.

Together, these design principles provide a cohesive framework for securing Microsoft 365 collaboration environments—measuring posture, enforcing protection where risk occurs, governing device and data access, and ensuring that emerging AI-driven experiences reinforce rather than weaken the organization's security stance.

The next chapter moves from securing productivity and collaboration services to protecting the applications and APIs that underpin modern digital services. It examines how application security, workload identity, and API protection controls reduce exposure, manage trust boundaries, and defend business-critical applications across cloud environments.

Questions

Success on any assessment depends on understanding the underlying technologies, concepts, and principles rather than memorizing facts. The following questions help readers confirm that they can apply this chapter's ideas in realistic Microsoft 365 security design scenarios, including Secure Score posture evaluation, collaboration threat protection, device trust enforcement, and Purview-based data governance and Copilot controls.

1. **An organization wants to evaluate whether Microsoft 365 collaboration workloads are aligned with Microsoft's recommended security baseline across identity, device access, data protection, and threat defense. Which architectural approach best achieves this outcome?**
   a. Reviewing individual security alerts
   b. Enabling Microsoft Sentinel analytics rules
   c. Evaluating tenant posture using Microsoft Secure Score
   d. Manually auditing Exchange, SharePoint, and Teams settings
2. **Why is Microsoft Secure Score most effective when used as a posture evaluation tool rather than a detection mechanism?**
   a. It replaces the need for threat protection services
   b. It measures the adoption of recommended controls and highlights prioritized improvement actions
   c. It enforces security controls automatically
   d. It provides real-time attack detection
3. **Which signal most strongly indicates a systemic Microsoft 365 security design issue rather than an isolated configuration error?**
   a. A single Secure Score recommendation on one service
   b. A recurring Secure Score improvement action affecting multiple services
   c. A temporary Secure Score fluctuation
   d. An individual Defender alert
4. **What does Microsoft Secure Score primarily represent for Microsoft 365 environments?**
   a. Real-time detection of active attacks
   b. Compliance status against regulatory frameworks
   c. Improvement potential based on the adoption of Microsoft 365 security controls
   d. Endpoint vulnerability severity
5. **An organization wants to stop impersonation-based email attacks that rely on social engineering rather than malware. Which solution directly addresses this risk at message delivery?**
   a. Microsoft Defender for Cloud Apps
   b. Microsoft Purview DLP

c. Microsoft Defender for Office 365

d. Microsoft Sentinel

6. **Why is Microsoft Defender for Cloud Apps required in addition to Microsoft Defender for Office 365 for collaboration security?**

a. Defender for Office 365 does not support Exchange Online

b. Defender for Cloud Apps governs user behavior and data access during active sessions

c. Defender for Office 365 only detects malware

d. Defender for Cloud Apps replaces Conditional Access

7. **An architect needs to require additional authentication only when users attempt to download sensitive documents from SharePoint Online. Which capability best supports this requirement?**

a. Static Conditional Access policies

b. Exchange transport rules

c. Defender for Cloud Apps session policies with step-up authentication

d. SharePoint permission inheritance

8. **Why does Microsoft Intune integrate with Conditional Access instead of enforcing access decisions directly?**

a. Intune cannot evaluate device posture

b. Device trust must be evaluated independently and enforced centrally

c. Conditional Access applies only to identity

d. Intune compliance policies replace Conditional Access

9. **Which Microsoft Purview capability is specifically designed to prevent sensitive data from being shared inappropriately across Microsoft 365 services?**

a. Sensitivity labels

b. Audit logging

c. DLP

d. eDiscovery

10. **Why does Microsoft Copilot increase risk when Microsoft 365 permissions and data controls are poorly designed?**

a. Copilot bypasses access controls

b. Copilot creates a new data plane

c. Copilot surfaces data based on existing permissions and protections

d. Copilot disables DLP enforcement

Answers

1. c: Evaluating tenant posture using Microsoft Secure Score.

   Secure Score aggregates identity, device, data, and threat controls across Microsoft 365 into a single posture view aligned with Microsoft guidance.

2. b: It measures adoption of recommended controls and highlights prioritized improvement actions.

   Secure Score evaluates security readiness and improvement potential rather than detecting active attacks.

3. b: A recurring Secure Score improvement action affecting multiple services.

   Repeated findings indicate systemic design gaps rather than isolated misconfigurations.

4. c: Improvement potential based on adoption of Microsoft 365 security controls.

   Secure Score reflects how much posture can be strengthened by implementing recommended protections.

5. c: Microsoft Defender for Office 365.

   Defender for Office 365 intercepts impersonation and social engineering attacks at email delivery.

6. b: Defender for Cloud Apps governs user behavior and data access during active sessions.

   It enforces real-time controls when identity is valid, but behavior introduces risk.

7. c: Defender for Cloud Apps session policies with step-up authentication.

   Session policies apply adaptive enforcement only during high-risk actions.

8. b: Device trust must be evaluated independently and enforced centrally.

   Intune evaluates device compliance, while Conditional Access enforces access decisions.

9. c: DLP.

   DLP prevents sensitive data from being shared based on content and context.

10. c: Copilot surfaces data based on existing permissions and protections.

    Copilot inherits Microsoft 365 access, device, and data controls rather than replacing them.

CHAPTER 13
Design Application and API Security Solutions

Introduction

This chapter examines how to design application and **application programming interface** (**API**) security solutions that protect modern cloud-native and hybrid workloads. Applications and APIs represent one of the most exposed and fast-changing security surfaces in the enterprise, concentrating identity, data access, and external connectivity into components that are frequently updated and widely consumed; as a result, weaknesses in application design or governance can rapidly undermine otherwise strong infrastructure and identity controls.

The chapter focuses on how security architects evaluate application security posture, apply threat modeling, and embed security across the full application lifecycle. It explores how secure development practices, workload identities, API management, and **web application firewall** (**WAF**) protections work together to reduce attack surface and enforce least privilege. By treating applications as first-class security entities rather than as byproducts of infrastructure, architects can design resilient application architectures that align with Zero Trust principles and remain enforceable as environments evolve.

Structure

This chapter covers the following topics:

- Security posture of existing application portfolios
- Threat modeling for business-critical applications
- Full lifecycle strategy for application security
- Standards and practices for secure development
- Mapping technologies to application security requirements
- Workload identities for Azure resource access
- API management and security solutions
- Securing applications with Azure WAF

Objectives

This chapter covers the skills required to evaluate the security posture of existing application portfolios, focusing on how application design, dependencies, and exposure influence organizational risk. It examines how to evaluate threats to business-critical applications using threat modeling to identify attack paths, trust boundaries, and potential impact.

The chapter explores how to design and implement a full lifecycle strategy for application security, ensuring that security considerations are integrated from design and development through deployment and ongoing operation. It also examines how to design and implement standards and practices for securing the application development process, establishing consistent expectations for secure coding, testing, and validation.

In addition, the chapter addresses how to map technologies to application security requirements, ensuring that controls are selected based on workload characteristics and threat models. It covers how to design workload identity solutions to authenticate and access Azure cloud resources securely, reducing reliance on secrets and long-lived credentials.

Finally, the chapter examines how to design solutions for API management and security, as well as how to secure applications using Azure WAF, ensuring that application traffic is inspected, protected, and governed against common and emerging threats. These skills fall under the exam domain: *Design security solutions for applications and data,* which represents approximately 20-25% of the overall SC-100 skills measured[1].

Security posture of existing application portfolios

Application portfolios represent a distinct security challenge because they concentrate identity, data access, and external exposure into components that evolve far more rapidly than the infrastructure that hosts them. Most organizations operate a heterogeneous mix of legacy applications, platform services, containerized workloads, APIs, and third-party integrations. This diversity increases business agility, but it also makes security posture difficult to assess unless applications are treated as first-class security entities rather than as incidental workloads.

Traditional infrastructure controls provide only partial insight into application risk. An application can be hosted on a compliant infrastructure while still exposing insecure endpoints, over-privileged identities, or vulnerable dependencies. As a result, evaluating application security posture must begin with explicit visibility into which applications exist, how they are deployed, and whether they are included in posture management tooling. This section maps to the following SC-100 skills measured: *Evaluate the security posture of existing application portfolios.*

1 **https://learn.microsoft.com/en-us/credentials/certifications/resources/study-guides/sc-100**

Evaluating Microsoft Defender for Cloud workload coverage

Effective posture evaluation starts by confirming that application workloads are actually covered by security assessment services. In Microsoft Defender for Cloud, application visibility depends on enabling the appropriate Defender plans for the technologies in use, such as App Service, container platforms, or Kubernetes. If these plans are not enabled, applications may operate normally while remaining invisible to posture insights and risk prioritization.

Security architects must therefore validate coverage deliberately rather than assuming it exists. This includes confirming that application workloads are onboarded, that automatic provisioning is configured where appropriate, and that posture assessments reflect the full scope of the application estate. Without this validation, security posture data can present an incomplete or misleading view of risk.

Secure Score visibility gaps for application workloads

Even when Defender for Cloud is enabled, the Secure Score does not automatically reflect all application risks. Workloads that fall outside assessment scope, such as newly introduced platform services or misconfigured environments, can create visibility gaps that inflate posture metrics while leaving real exposure unaddressed. These gaps are particularly common in environments that evolve faster than their original security baselines.

Secure Score should therefore be interpreted as a directional indicator rather than a definitive measure of application security. Architects must understand which resource types contribute to scoring and which do not, and adjust their evaluation accordingly. Where application workloads are excluded, additional onboarding or compensating visibility controls may be required.

By identifying and correcting Secure Score blind spots early, organizations ensure that posture management focuses on reducing real application risk rather than optimizing metrics. This establishes a reliable foundation for subsequent threat modeling, lifecycle security controls, and runtime protections.

Threat modeling for business-critical applications

Threat modeling provides the structured lens through which application risk becomes explicit before it becomes operationally expensive to fix. Business-critical applications often handle sensitive data, enforce complex authorization rules, or expose externally reachable interfaces, making them attractive targets for attackers. Without a formal threat modeling process, security decisions tend to be reactive, addressing symptoms after deployment rather than preventing architectural weaknesses during design.

Unlike vulnerability scanning or penetration testing, threat modeling is not focused on identifying known flaws in existing code. Instead, it examines how an application is intended to work, how data flows through it, and how those flows could be abused if trust assumptions fail. This allows architects to reason about risk in advance, before implementation choices harden into production dependencies.

Once threats are identified at design time, they must be addressed consistently throughout development and deployment rather than treated as isolated findings. This requires security controls to be deliberately embedded across the application lifecycle so that identified risks are continuously mitigated as applications evolve. This section maps to the following SC-100 skills measured: *Evaluate threats to business-critical applications by using threat modeling*.

Applying threat modeling during the application design

Threat modeling is most effective when applied early in the application lifecycle, while design decisions are still flexible. During the design phase, architects can identify trust boundaries, privileged components, and external dependencies that shape the application's attack surface. Addressing these risks at design time typically requires fewer compromises than attempting to retrofit controls once an application is deployed.

By modeling threats before development begins, teams can establish clear security requirements that guide subsequent implementation choices. This includes defining authentication expectations, data protection requirements, and assumptions about upstream and downstream services. Threat modeling at this stage also helps prioritize which risks must be mitigated architecturally versus those that can be monitored or constrained at runtime.

Aligning threat modeling with Microsoft SDL

Threat modeling is a foundational activity within the Microsoft **Security Development Lifecycle** (**SDL**), providing continuity between design intent and security enforcement throughout development and deployment. When integrated into a lifecycle framework, threat modeling informs secure coding standards, testing strategies, and deployment controls rather than existing as a one-time exercise.

Aligning threat modeling with a structured lifecycle ensures that identified risks are tracked and revisited as the application evolves. Changes in functionality, dependencies, or exposure can invalidate earlier assumptions, requiring the threat model to be updated accordingly. This lifecycle alignment ensures that threat modeling remains a living artifact that evolves alongside the application, supporting consistent risk reduction rather than isolated analysis.

Full lifecycle strategy for application security

Application security cannot simply be achieved through isolated controls applied at deployment time; modern applications are built, updated, and redeployed continuously, often through automated pipelines that move changes into production far faster than traditional security review processes can keep pace with. As a result, security architecture must span the entire application lifecycle, from initial design through development, testing, deployment, and ongoing operation.

A full lifecycle strategy ensures that security decisions made early in the process are reinforced rather than undermined as the application evolves. It also allows risks to be detected as close to their point of introduction as possible, reducing remediation cost and preventing vulnerable code or configurations from reaching production environments. This section maps to the following SC-100 skills measured: *Design and implement a full lifecycle strategy for application security*.

Integrating security controls across CI/CD pipelines

Continuous integration and continuous deployment (**CI/CD**) pipelines represent a critical enforcement point for application security. These pipelines determine how code is built, validated, and released, making them an ideal place to embed automated security controls. Integrating security into CI/CD pipelines ensures that vulnerabilities are detected consistently, regardless of how frequently applications change.

Security controls in pipelines should be automated wherever possible to avoid becoming bottlenecks. This includes scanning source code, validating configurations, and enforcing approval gates before deployment. When security checks are treated as a standard part of the pipeline rather than as an exception, teams are more likely to address issues promptly and maintain development velocity without bypassing controls.

Dependency testing

Modern applications rely heavily on third-party libraries and open-source components, which can introduce significant supply-chain risk. Vulnerabilities in dependencies often propagate across multiple applications simultaneously, creating widespread exposure from a single flaw. Dependency testing addresses this risk by identifying known vulnerabilities in libraries before they are deployed into production.

Incorporating dependency testing into the application lifecycle allows organizations to detect risky components early and take corrective action, such as upgrading libraries or applying mitigations. Dependency vulnerabilities frequently emerge after initial deployment; thus, ongoing scanning is essential to ensure that applications remain protected as new threats are disclosed.

Assigning security activities to DevSecOps pipeline stages

A lifecycle-based approach requires security activities to be applied at the stages where they are most effective. Not all security controls belong at deployment time, and attempting to enforce them too late in the process often results in incomplete coverage or operational friction. Instead, threat modeling, scanning, validation, and approval activities should be mapped deliberately to specific pipeline stages.

For example, design time activities establish security expectations, build-time checks validate code and dependencies, and release-time controls enforce deployment standards. By aligning security tasks with the appropriate lifecycle stages, organizations reduce duplication, improve signal quality, and ensure that security remains proportional to risk rather than reactive to incidents.

Standards and practices for secure development

Secure application development depends on more than individual tools or point-in-time testing; it requires agreed standards and repeatable practices that guide how applications are built, validated, and maintained over time. Without shared expectations, security controls are applied inconsistently, leaving gaps that vary by team, technology stack, or release cadence.

Establishing secure development standards ensures that security is treated as a normal quality attribute rather than as a specialized activity reserved for late-stage reviews. These standards define what secure by default means for the organization and provide a common baseline against which applications can be assessed, regardless of who builds them or where they are deployed. This section maps to the following SC-100 skills measured: *Design and implement standards and practices for securing the application development process*.

Dynamic application security testing for runtime vulnerabilities

Dynamic application security testing (**DAST**) focuses on identifying vulnerabilities that only become visible when an application is running. These include issues such as insecure server configurations, injection flaws, and cross-site scripting vulnerabilities that cannot be reliably detected through static analysis alone. Since DAST evaluates applications from an external perspective, it mirrors how attackers probe live systems for weaknesses.

Incorporating dynamic testing into development and validation processes allows organizations to identify exploitable conditions before applications are exposed broadly. When used consistently, DAST complements other testing methods by validating how applications behave in realistic execution scenarios, rather than relying solely on code inspection.

Automating vulnerability detection and remediation

Automation plays a critical role in making secure development practices sustainable at scale. As application portfolios grow, manual review and remediation become impractical, especially when vulnerabilities are introduced frequently through code changes or dependency updates. Automating detection and remediation with Defender for DevOps helps ensure that issues are addressed promptly without relying on individual vigilance.

Organizations can surface vulnerabilities where developers already work and streamline remediation through automated fixes or guided pull requests by integrating security tooling directly into development workflows. This reduces the friction between security and development teams and helps maintain a consistent security baseline without slowing delivery.

These practices define how applications should be built and validated, but they do not enforce themselves. Translating secure development intent into enforceable outcomes requires selecting the right platform controls to implement those requirements consistently.

Mapping technologies to application security requirements

Application security design is ultimately expressed through technology choices. Even when risks are well understood and security standards are clearly defined, selecting the wrong control for a given requirement can undermine the intended security outcome. Effective application security architecture, therefore, depends on mapping specific security requirements to technologies that enforce them accurately and consistently.

This mapping process requires architects to reason about what problem is being solved, not simply which security service is available. Requirements such as restricting exposure paths, enforcing trusted ingress points, or validating upstream services demand different controls than those used for runtime inspection or identity enforcement. Applying technologies without this alignment often results in overlapping controls in some areas and critical gaps in others. This section maps to the following SC-100 skills measured: *Map technologies to application security requirements*.

Enforcing controlled application access paths

Many application security risks arise not from vulnerabilities in code, but from unintended exposure. Applications that are designed to be accessed through a specific gateway or edge service can become vulnerable when alternative access paths are left open. Enforcing controlled access paths ensures that traffic reaches the application only through approved services where inspection, authentication, and policy enforcement can occur.

From a design perspective, this means explicitly restricting direct access to application endpoints and validating that requests originate from trusted upstream components. This approach reduces the attack surface by eliminating bypass routes that attackers commonly exploit to avoid centralized security controls.

Restricting application exposure using Azure Front Door

Edge services such as Azure Front Door play a critical role in modern application architectures by providing global entry points, traffic optimization, and integrated security capabilities. When applications are designed to be accessed exclusively through such services, the backend must enforce this assumption rather than rely on convention.

Access validation mechanisms allow applications to verify that incoming requests have passed through the expected edge service. By enforcing these checks, architects ensure that backend applications are not inadvertently exposed to the internet or to untrusted sources. A WAF alone does not enforce exclusive ingress paths; it inspects traffic but does not prove that requests originated from an approved entry point. Backend validation is therefore required to prevent direct access paths that bypass edge controls, reinforcing Zero Trust principles by requiring every request to demonstrate its legitimacy.

Workload identities for Azure resource access

Applications require identities just as users do, but the risks associated with application identities are often greater because they operate continuously and frequently hold broad access. When applications authenticate using shared secrets, long-lived credentials, or hard-coded keys, those credentials become high-value targets that are difficult to rotate and easy to misuse if compromised. Designing secure workload identity is therefore a foundational requirement for protecting application-to-resource access.

A strong workload identity strategy treats applications as first-class security principals with clearly defined permissions, lifetimes, and trust boundaries. Rather than focusing solely on how applications authenticate, architects must also consider how identity choices affect privilege scope, operational overhead, and the ability to audit and govern access over time. This section maps to the following SC-100 skills measured: *Design a solution for workload identity to authenticate and access Azure cloud resources*.

Using managed identities for application authentication

Managed identities provide a secure and operationally simple way for applications to authenticate to Azure resources without managing secrets. By binding identity lifecycle to the application or resource itself, managed identities eliminate the need to store credentials in code, configuration files, or external vaults solely for authentication purposes.

From a design perspective, managed identities support least privilege by allowing permissions to be granted directly to the application identity through role assignments. This approach reduces blast radius by ensuring that access is scoped precisely to what the application requires, while also simplifying credential rotation and reducing the likelihood of accidental exposure.

Applying workload identity federation in CI/CD pipelines

CD pipelines also require access to Azure resources, but their identity requirements differ from those of running workloads. Workload identity federation allows pipelines to authenticate using short-lived, federated credentials rather than persistent secrets. This reduces the risk associated with compromised pipeline credentials and aligns with modern Zero Trust principles.

By federating identities from the pipeline platform to Azure, architects can enforce least privilege access while maintaining strong separation between development tooling and production resources. This approach also simplifies governance by making pipeline access explicit, auditable, and easier to revoke when workflows change.

Supporting cross-tenant application access

In multi-tenant and partner scenarios, applications often need to authenticate users or services from external Microsoft Entra tenants. In these cases, service principals act as the local representation of an application within the consuming tenant, enabling access to be governed without duplicating application definitions.

Designing cross-tenant access using service principals allows organizations to apply their own access controls, monitoring, and governance policies while still supporting external collaboration. This ensures that application access remains deliberate and auditable, even when trust boundaries extend beyond a single tenant.

API management and security solutions

APIs have become the connective tissue of modern applications, enabling integration between internal services, partner systems, and third-party platforms. While this flexibility accelerates development and business innovation, it also expands the attack surface by exposing functionality and data in a form that is designed to be consumed programmatically. Securing APIs, therefore, requires deliberate architectural controls that differ from those used to protect user-facing applications.

Effective API security design separates concerns such as administration, access control, and consumption enforcement. Rather than embedding security logic into every API implementation, centralized API management allows organizations to apply consistent controls across services while maintaining visibility into how APIs are used. This approach reduces duplication, simplifies governance, and makes it easier to evolve security requirements as APIs and consumers change. This section maps to the following SC-100 skills measured: *Design a solution for API management and security*.

Separating API administration from API consumption

API platforms support different classes of access that must be governed independently. Administrative access determines who can publish, configure, and manage APIs, while consumption access governs who can call APIs and under what conditions. Conflating these two concerns increases the risk of over-privilege, allowing users or services to manage APIs when they should only be able to consume them.

By explicitly separating administrative roles from consumption mechanisms, architects can enforce least privilege across both dimensions. Administrative access can be tightly controlled and audited, while consumption access can be scoped, monitored, and throttled based on usage patterns. This separation ensures that operational control of APIs remains restricted even as the number of API consumers grows.

Applying RBAC and keys in API management

Role-based access control (**RBAC**) provides a structured way to manage who can administer APIs and apply configuration changes within an API management platform. This allows organizations to delegate operational responsibilities without exposing sensitive management capabilities broadly. RBAC also integrates naturally with identity governance processes, enabling access to be reviewed and adjusted over time.

Subscription keys and similar mechanisms control how APIs are consumed by applications and partners. By issuing and managing keys at the consumption layer, architects can enforce usage limits, track API activity, and revoke access without impacting API definitions themselves. Combined with RBAC, this layered approach ensures that both management and consumption of APIs are governed consistently and securely.

Securing applications with Azure WAF

Web applications are continuously exposed to automated scanning, opportunistic attacks, and targeted exploitation attempts; even well-designed applications can be compromised if common web attack techniques are not mitigated consistently at the edge.

Azure WAF provides a critical protection layer by inspecting inbound traffic before it reaches application workloads, helping to detect and block malicious behavior at scale.

WAF should be understood as a compensating and protective control rather than a substitute for secure application design. Its role is to reduce exposure to known attack patterns and provide early detection of suspicious activity, particularly for internet-facing applications that must remain accessible while development teams address underlying risks. This section maps to the following SC-100 skills measured: *Design solutions that secure applications by using Azure WAF*.

Detecting vulnerability scans and exposed applications with WAF

One of the primary strengths of a WAF is its ability to identify automated reconnaissance and vulnerability scanning activity. These scans are often the first step in an attack chain, probing applications for misconfigurations, outdated components, or exploitable endpoints. By detecting and responding to this activity, WAF reduces the likelihood that attackers can enumerate weaknesses unnoticed.

WAF also provides visibility into newly deployed applications that may not yet be fully hardened. In fast-moving environments, applications can be exposed before security reviews are complete, creating temporary windows of risk. WAF helps mitigate this exposure by applying baseline protections immediately, buying time for teams to remediate configuration or code-level issues.

Understanding WAF limits in Zero Trust architectures

While WAF is effective at protecting against common web-based attacks, it does not address all application security requirements. In particular, WAF does not establish trust between internal components or enforce authorization decisions beyond **Hypertext Transfer Protocol** (**HTTP**) request inspection. Relying on WAF alone to secure backend service-to-service communication can create a false sense of security.

In Zero Trust architectures, every access decision must be explicitly validated, regardless of network location. This requires strong identity-based authentication, authorization, and segmentation controls in addition to edge protection. WAF should therefore be positioned as one layer in a broader security design, complementing identity, access, and application-level controls rather than replacing them.

Concusion

This chapter examines how to design application and API security solutions that protect modern workloads across their full lifecycle. It established application portfolios as a distinct security surface, requiring explicit posture visibility rather than inherited infrastructure controls. By grounding application security in posture assessment, architects gain the baseline needed to reason about exposure before applying mitigations.

The chapter showed how threat modeling anchors application security decisions early in the design process, ensuring risks are identified before they become costly to remediate. It then extended this reasoning across the application lifecycle, demonstrating how DevSecOps practices embed security into development, testing, and deployment without slowing delivery. Secure development standards and automated testing were positioned as enablers of scale and consistency rather than isolated security checks.

Finally, the chapter mapped security requirements to concrete architectural controls, covering workload identities, API governance, and edge protection. By separating identity, access, and inspection concerns. By understanding the limits of individual controls, such as WAF, architects can design resilient application architectures that reduce attack surface, enforce least privilege, and align with Zero Trust principles across cloud-native and hybrid environments.

The next chapter shifts focus from securing applications and interfaces to protecting the data that those applications create, process, and store. It examines how data classification, encryption, access controls, and threat detection ensure sensitive information remains protected across cloud platforms and data services.

Questions

Success on any assessment depends on understanding the underlying technologies, concepts, and principles rather than memorizing facts. The following questions help readers confirm that they can apply this chapter's ideas in realistic design scenarios, including application security posture evaluation, threat modeling, DevSecOps lifecycle integration, workload identity design, API security governance, and web application protection.

1. **An organization wants to evaluate whether application workloads align with a standardized security baseline covering identity, access, exposure, and development lifecycle controls. Which architectural approach best achieves this outcome?**

    a. Enabling Microsoft Secure Score

    b. Reviewing individual application security alerts

    c. Evaluating application workloads using Microsoft Defender for Cloud and secure development standards

    d. Applying WAF rules manually

2. **Why is threat modeling most effective when used as a design input rather than a post-deployment activity?**
   a. It replaces the need for vulnerability scanning
   b. It enforces identical security controls across all applications
   c. It defines architectural security intent before implementation decisions are fixed
   d. It guarantees regulatory compliance
3. **Which signal most strongly indicates a systemic application security design issue rather than an isolated defect?**
   a. A single failed vulnerability scan on one application
   b. A recurring security weakness across multiple applications
   c. A temporary deployment failure
   d. An individual security alert
4. **What does application security posture primarily represent?**
   a. Real-time detection of active application attacks
   b. Compliance status against regulatory frameworks
   c. Exposure and improvement potential based on security design and configuration
   d. Infrastructure misconfiguration severity
5. **An architect needs unified security visibility across Azure App Service, containerized workloads, and hybrid application environments. Which design best supports this requirement?**
   a. Native security tools for each application platform
   b. Microsoft Secure Score alone
   c. Microsoft Defender for Cloud with application workload coverage enabled
   d. Microsoft Sentinel analytics rules
6. **A scenario requires applications to access Azure resources without storing secrets in code or configuration files. Which identity design must be selected?**
   a. Service principals with client secrets
   b. Managed identities
   c. API subscription keys
   d. Shared access signatures

7. **Why is it architecturally incorrect to assume that secure development practices alone ensure application security?**

   a. Secure development increases operational overhead

   b. Development standards apply only to code

   c. Practices do not enforce runtime access, identity, or exposure controls

   d. Secure development replaces workload protection

8. **Which capability is specifically designed to protect internet-facing applications from common web attacks and automated scanning?**

   a. Microsoft Secure Score

   b. Defender for Cloud recommendations

   c. Azure WAF

   d. Azure Policy guest configuration

9. **Why is workload identity design a critical part of application security architecture?**

   a. It simplifies application deployment

   b. It replaces network security controls

   c. It enforces least privilege and eliminates secret-based authentication

   d. It guarantees application availability

10. **What is the primary purpose of separating API administration from API consumption?**

    a. To simplify API deployment

    b. To reduce API latency

    c. To enforce least privilege and governance boundaries

    d. To replace identity-based access controls

Answers

1. c: Evaluating application workloads using Microsoft Defender for Cloud and secure development standards.

   Defender for Cloud evaluates application workloads against security controls and configuration expectations, translating security intent into measurable posture signals.

2. c: It defines architectural security intent before implementation decisions are fixed.

Threat modeling identifies design-level risks early, allowing architects to address weaknesses before they become embedded in deployed applications.

3. b: A recurring security weakness across multiple applications.

   Repeated findings indicate a systemic design, or standards issue rather than an isolated implementation error.

4. c: Exposure and improvement potential based on security design and configuration.

   Application security posture reflects how security can be strengthened through improved design and configuration, not real-time attack detection.

5. c: Microsoft Defender for Cloud with application workload coverage enabled.

   This design centralizes application posture signals across platforms into a single evaluation model.

6. b: Managed identities.

   Managed identities eliminate the need to store secrets while enabling least-privilege access to Azure resources.

7. c: Practices do not enforce runtime access, identity, or exposure controls.

   Secure development must be complemented by identity, access, and runtime protections to reduce real-world risk.

8. c: Azure WAF.

   WAF protects applications by detecting and blocking common web attacks and automated reconnaissance activity.

9. c: It enforces least privilege and eliminates secret-based authentication.

   Workload identities reduce credential exposure and improve governance for application-to-resource access.

10. c: To enforce least privilege and governance boundaries.

    Separating API administration from consumption ensures operational control is restricted while enabling controlled API usage.

Chapter 14
Design Data Protection and Governance Solutions

Introduction

Data is the asset most attackers ultimately seek, yet it is also the hardest part of the environment to govern consistently. As organizations expand across cloud services, analytics platforms, collaboration tools, and globally distributed storage, sensitive information is created, copied, and transformed continuously. Traditional perimeter-based assumptions no longer hold, and security design must account for the reality that data often outlives the systems, identities, and controls that were originally intended to protect it.

Designing effective data protection solutions, therefore, requires more than enabling encryption or restricting access. Architects must decide which risks matter most, how trust boundaries are enforced, and how data remains recoverable and observable when preventive controls fail. Recovery, encryption, access governance, and threat detection must work together as a cohesive system rather than as independent features applied in isolation.

This chapter examines how to design data protection and governance solutions that remain resilient under real-world conditions. It explores how threat prioritization shapes data security decisions, how encryption models define control and trust, how workload characteristics influence protection strategies, and how detection capabilities provide visibility into misuse and attack behavior. By treating data protection as a deliberate architectural discipline, this chapter equips security architects to safeguard sensitive information across modern cloud and hybrid environments while maintaining operational resilience and regulatory alignment.

Structure

This chapter covers the following topics:

- Data discovery and classification solutions
- Priorities for mitigating data threats
- Data encryption at rest and in transit
- Securing data in Azure SQL, Synapse, and Cosmos DB

- Securing data stored in Azure Storage
- Defender for Storage and Databases solutions

Objectives

This chapter covers the skills required to specify priorities for mitigating threats to data, focusing on how data sensitivity, exposure, and business impact influence protection decisions. It examines how to evaluate solutions for encrypting data at rest and in transit, including the use of Azure Key Vault and infrastructure encryption to protect cryptographic keys and enforce confidentiality.

The chapter explores how to design security solutions for data in Azure workloads, including Azure SQL, Azure Synapse Analytics, and Azure Cosmos DB, ensuring that access controls, encryption, and monitoring are applied consistently across data platforms. It also examines how to design security solutions for data stored in Azure Storage, addressing protection requirements for structured and unstructured data.

Finally, the chapter covers how to design security solutions that include Microsoft Defender for Storage and Microsoft Defender for Databases, focusing on threat detection, alerting, and response capabilities that help identify and mitigate data-related attacks. These skills fall under the exam domain: *Design security solutions for applications and data,* which represents approximately 20-25 % of the overall SC-100 skills measured[1].

Data discovery and classification solutions

Data protection is fundamentally a visibility and decision problem. Organizations cannot meaningfully protect sensitive information until they understand where that information exists, what type of data it is, and how it is being used. In modern environments, sensitive data is no longer confined to a single system. It flows through email, collaboration platforms, cloud storage, and automated processes, often without deliberate user intent.

Data discovery and classification establish the foundation that makes data protection enforceable. By identifying sensitive information consistently and assigning it a clear meaning, organizations enable downstream security controls to behave predictably. Classification does not protect data by itself. Instead, it provides the signal that other controls rely on to decide when to restrict access, prevent sharing, or monitor activity. Without this foundation, encryption, **data loss prevention** (**DLP**), and monitoring controls operate inconsistently and leave gaps that attackers and mistakes can exploit.

Data discovery and classification solutions create a common understanding of sensitive data across the organization. Their role is not simply to scan content, but to define what constitutes sensitive information and apply that definition consistently across collaboration workloads.

---

1 **https://learn.microsoft.com/en-us/credentials/certifications/resources/study-guides/sc-100**

When classification is accurate and uniformly applied, security controls can enforce policy automatically rather than depending on users to make correct decisions in every situation.

Effective design treats discovery and classification as continuous processes. As data is created, modified, and shared, classification must be re-evaluated so that governance decisions remain aligned with actual data usage. This ensures that sensitive information remains visible and governable even as collaboration patterns, storage locations, and workflows change. This section maps to the following SC-100 skills measured: *Evaluate solutions for data discovery and classification*.

Discovering and classifying sensitive data across Microsoft 365

Discovery begins by inspecting content where work actually happens, including Exchange, SharePoint, OneDrive, and Teams. By analyzing content across these services, organizations can identify where sensitive information resides and how widely it is distributed. This visibility is essential for understanding exposure patterns that are otherwise hidden by the scale and speed of collaboration.

Classification builds on discovery by attaching meaning to identified data. Sensitivity labels and classification definitions provide a shared language for describing information risk, ensuring that the same type of data is treated consistently across workloads and file formats. Classification alone does not encrypt data, restrict access, or mask values. Instead, it defines the sensitivity of the data so that other controls can make correct enforcement decisions when the data is accessed, shared, or moved.

Using DLP to identify and act on sensitive content

While classification defines what data is sensitive, DLP is responsible for acting on that knowledge. DLP continuously inspects content and evaluates it in context, such as where the data is being shared, who is accessing it, and whether the destination is trusted. When sensitive information is detected in risky scenarios, DLP enforces policy by blocking, restricting, or auditing the activity.

The Microsoft Purview DLP interface provides a centralized view of policies, alerts, and recommendations used to monitor and enforce data protection across Microsoft 365 services.

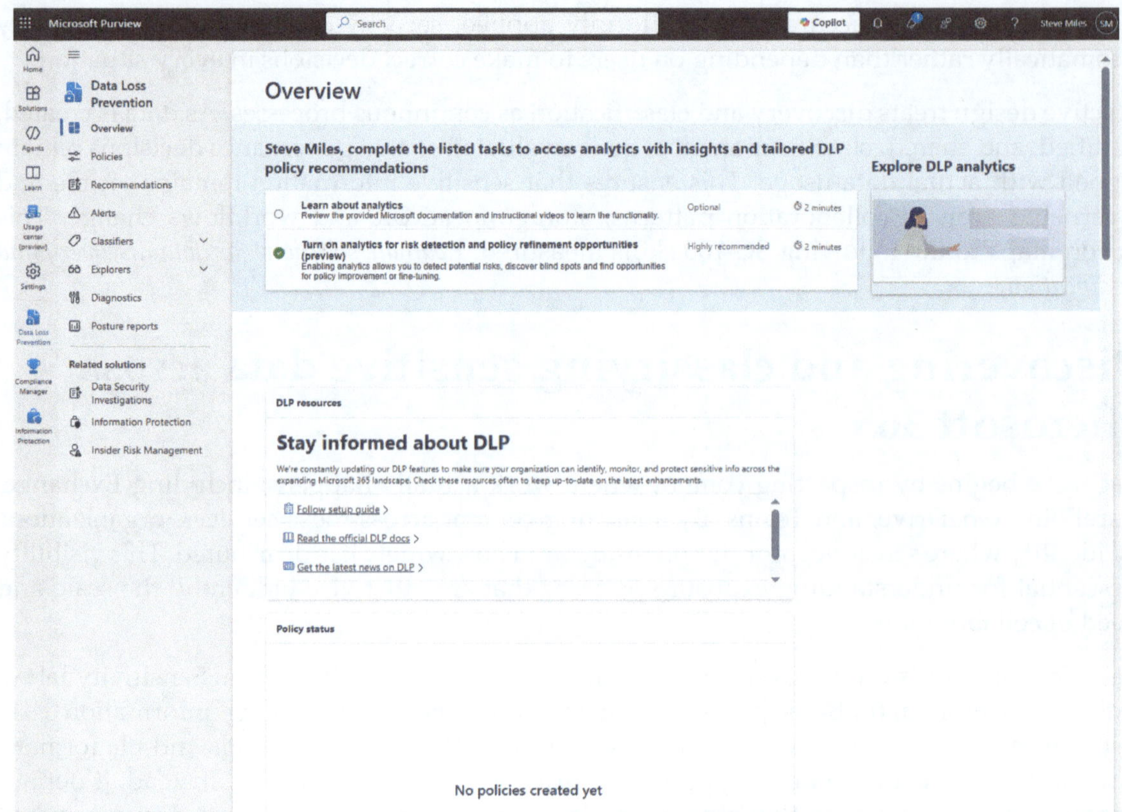

Figure 14.1: Microsoft Purview DLP overview

DLP policies are defined and managed centrally, providing the control plane through which protection rules are applied across Microsoft 365 workloads.

DLP must be distinguished from investigative and governance tooling. eDiscovery and audit capabilities are designed for after-the-fact investigation and compliance review, not for continuous identification and enforcement. DLP is the correct mechanism when the requirement is to identify sensitive information as it is being shared or moved and to take immediate action to reduce exposure. By enforcing controls based on data sensitivity rather than user intent, DLP ensures that protection follows the data wherever it appears, including across collaboration workloads and automated workflows.

With sensitive data consistently identified and labeled, the next challenge is deciding which data risks must be addressed first when controls fail.

Priorities for mitigating data threats

Data protection architecture is ultimately about making correct decisions under imperfect conditions. Organizations must assume that data will be created in unpredictable places, shared through multiple collaboration channels, and accessed by users and applications in ways that are difficult to fully control.

A common failure in data security design is treating individual controls in isolation. Classification without enforcement creates visibility without protection. Encryption without recovery planning creates confidentiality without resilience. Monitoring without prioritization generates noise without reducing impact. A coherent data protection strategy must instead be structured as a sequence of decisions that build on one another, ensuring that sensitive information remains governable, recoverable, and protected even when assumptions break down. This section maps to the following SC-100 skills measured: *Specify priorities for mitigating threats to data.*

Priorities for mitigating data threats

Mitigating threats to data requires deliberate sequencing. Modern attack scenarios, particularly ransomware, demonstrate that no preventive control can be assumed to be absolute. Credentials can be compromised, systems can be misused, and attackers can operate using legitimate permissions. Security design must therefore prioritize which failures are survivable and which are not.

Effective prioritization focuses on preserving the organization's ability to recover data under hostile conditions. When recovery paths are protected first, attackers are denied the ability to convert temporary access into permanent data loss. This approach reduces the impact of successful attacks and prevents operational disruption from becoming catastrophic.

Prioritizing recovery preparedness for ransomware mitigation

Ransomware mitigation begins with recognizing that recovery is the first critical dependency. Identity hardening, endpoint controls, and data handling policies all reduce risk, but none of them matter if data cannot be restored. Without recovery preparedness, a single successful intrusion can permanently deny access to critical information.

Designing for recovery means ensuring that restore operations remain possible even when administrators, systems, or management planes are compromised. By treating recovery planning as a foundational control rather than a contingency, organizations retain control over outcomes even when preventive defenses fail.

Protecting backups from deletion and tampering

Backups are a primary target during modern attacks. Adversaries routinely attempt to delete recovery points, disable backup services, or alter configurations before encrypting production data. Controls such as encryption, redundancy, and replication improve confidentiality and availability under normal conditions, but they do not prevent an attacker with administrative access from destroying backups outright.

Effective backup protection focuses on preventing destructive actions rather than enhancing storage characteristics. Designs that restrict or require additional authorization for high-impact operations ensure that backups cannot be silently deleted or disabled, even when privileged credentials are abused. By prioritizing protection against deletion and tampering, organizations preserve their ability to recover data without paying ransoms or accepting irreversible loss. Once recovery risks are addressed, attention can shift toward limiting data exposure through deliberate encryption design.

Data encryption at rest and in transit

Encryption is a control for reducing data exposure when systems, storage, or networks are compromised. It does not replace access control, governance, or recovery planning, and it does not prevent authorized users or services from accessing data by design. For this reason, encryption decisions must be made deliberately, based on threat models and regulatory requirements, rather than assumed to be covered by default cloud settings.

Modern cloud platforms encrypt data by default, but default encryption only addresses a narrow set of risks. Security architects must instead determine who controls encryption keys, whether service operators or administrators should ever be able to access plaintext data, and whether encryption must extend beyond the service layer into the underlying infrastructure. The effectiveness of encryption depends not on the strength of the algorithm, but on where trust boundaries are drawn and how key authority is enforced. This section maps to the following SC-100 skills measured: *Evaluate solutions for encryption of data at rest and in transit, including Azure Key Vault and infrastructure encryption.*

Designing data encryption solutions

Evaluating encryption solutions requires understanding the difference between protecting stored data and protecting data as it moves. Encryption at rest protects data from unauthorized access to storage and infrastructure, while encryption in transit protects data from interception or manipulation as it crosses network and service boundaries. Both are required, but they address different attack scenarios and rely on different control mechanisms.

Encryption decisions must also account for ownership and control of cryptographic keys. Platform-managed encryption may be sufficient for baseline protection, but regulatory, contractual, or organizational requirements often demand explicit customer control over keys. When key control is required, encryption becomes a governance decision as much as a technical one.

Evaluating encryption at rest for regulated and sensitive data

Encryption at rest ensures that stored data cannot be read without access to the appropriate cryptographic keys. While many Azure services provide service-level encryption by default, this does not grant customers control over key usage or revocation. When requirements specify customer ownership of keys, the ability to rotate or revoke keys independently of the service becomes essential.

Customer-managed keys establish a clear trust boundary by placing key authority under organizational control. This allows access to data to be effectively withdrawn by revoking key access, even if service credentials or administrative permissions are compromised. In scenarios where regulatory language requires customer control of encryption keys, platform-managed encryption is insufficient, regardless of algorithm strength.

Infrastructure encryption extends protection beyond the service layer by encrypting data at the host or hardware level in addition to service-level encryption. This additional layer is required when compliance or threat models demand protection against exposure at the underlying infrastructure level. Infrastructure encryption does not replace service encryption; it augments it to reduce exposure across a broader attack surface.

Evaluating encryption in transit

Encryption in transit protects data as it moves between clients, services, and internal components. Without transport-level encryption, sensitive information can be exposed through interception, misrouting, or compromised network paths. Encryption in transit is therefore mandatory whenever data crosses trust boundaries, whether over public networks or within distributed cloud architectures.

Effective evaluation focuses on enforcing secure protocols consistently and eliminating weaker or legacy options. Encryption in transit complements encryption at rest by protecting data during the moments when it is actively transmitted and most vulnerable, but it does not address exposure once data is stored or processed.

Applying workload-specific encryption constraints and capabilities

All Azure workloads do not support the same encryption models. Encryption capabilities, including support for customer-managed keys and additional encryption layers, vary by service and even by deployment type within a service. Encryption design must therefore account for workload-specific constraints rather than assuming uniform capability across platforms.

Evaluating encryption solutions requires confirming whether the target workload supports the required key model and encryption features. When a workload does not support a particular encryption option, alternative designs or services must be considered. Selecting an unsupported encryption model is equivalent to having no protection at all.

Protecting data using secure enclave encryption

Some scenarios require that sensitive data remain inaccessible even to database administrators. Traditional encryption models, such as transparent data encryption, protect data at rest but decrypt it in memory during processing, allowing privileged users or processes to access plaintext data.

Always Encrypted with secure enclaves addresses this limitation by keeping sensitive data encrypted even during computation. This model ensures that cryptographic operations occur within hardware-backed trusted environments, preventing administrators from accessing plaintext values while still allowing authorized queries and processing. When the requirement explicitly states that administrators must not be able to view sensitive data, enclave-based encryption is required, and service-level encryption alone is insufficient. These encryption decisions shape how data is protected, but workload characteristics determine how those protections are applied in practice.

Securing data in Azure SQL, Synapse, and Cosmos DB

Securing data in managed Azure data services is fundamentally a design decision about responsibility and trust boundaries. Unlike infrastructure-based databases, platform services place the underlying operating system, patching, and baseline hardening under Microsoft's control. The security architect's role is therefore not to secure hosts, but to deliberately choose how data is accessed, encrypted, governed, and monitored within the service boundary. When this distinction is missed, organizations often apply infrastructure-era controls to platform services and fail to reduce real risk.

Azure SQL, Azure Synapse Analytics, and Azure Cosmos DB serve different workload patterns and expose different attack surfaces. Transactional systems, analytical engines, and globally distributed databases require security designs that reflect how data is queried, who administers it, and how access is granted. A correct security solution is not one that applies the same control everywhere, but one that selects the right controls for the workload and explicitly rejects options that do not meet the stated requirement. This section maps to the following SC-100 skills measured: *Design a security solution for data in Azure workloads, including Azure SQL, Azure Synapse Analytics, and Azure Cosmos DB.*

Designing security controls for Azure data workloads

Security controls for Azure data workloads must be aligned with how the platform operates. In managed services, identity becomes the primary enforcement plane for data access, while encryption and auditing provide protection against exposure and misuse. Network isolation and host-level controls play a reduced role compared to infrastructure-based designs and cannot compensate for weak identity or data-level decisions.

Effective design assumes that administrative access exists and that services will be integrated with other workloads. As a result, controls must be explicit, enforceable, and auditable at the data layer. This ensures that sensitive information remains protected even as applications scale, access patterns change, or services are exposed through APIs and analytics pipelines.

Selecting platform-managed data services

Choosing a platform-managed data service is a security decision as much as an operational one. Services such as Azure SQL Database reduce risk by removing the need to manage operating systems, patch database engines, and secure underlying infrastructure. This directly reduces the attack surface associated with misconfiguration and delayed updates.

When the requirement is to minimize administrative overhead while maintaining strong baseline security, platform-managed services are the correct choice. Deploying databases on **virtual machines** (**VMs**) in these scenarios introduces unnecessary operational risk and expands the security surface without providing meaningful protection benefits. Selecting PaaS over IaaS is therefore a deliberate control choice, not merely a convenience.

Applying workload-specific security and encryption controls

Azure Synapse Analytics combines multiple processing models within a single service, and these models do not share identical security capabilities. Dedicated SQL pools and serverless SQL pools differ in their support for encryption options, key management, and advanced data protection features. Security design must therefore begin by identifying which pool type is being used.

When additional encryption is required beyond default service protection, customer-managed key-based encryption provides a second layer of control by placing key authority under organizational ownership. This is distinct from transport encryption or storage-level encryption and is used when regulatory or risk requirements demand explicit customer control of cryptographic keys. Selecting an encryption option that is unsupported by the chosen pool type is not a partial solution; it is a design failure that leaves data unprotected.

Protecting sensitive data from administrative access

Some data protection scenarios require that sensitive information remain inaccessible even to database administrators. Traditional encryption mechanisms, such as transparent data encryption in Azure SQL, protect data at rest but decrypt it during processing, allowing privileged users to view plaintext values. This model does not satisfy requirements where administrators must be excluded from data visibility.

Azure SQL Always Encrypted addresses this gap by ensuring that sensitive columns remain encrypted end-to-end. When data must be queried or processed while encrypted, Always Encrypted with secure enclaves enables computation within trusted hardware-backed environments without exposing plaintext data. In scenarios that explicitly require administrators to be unable to access sensitive data, enclave-based encryption is the only correct design choice.

Designing for globally distributed data

Azure Cosmos DB introduces additional security considerations due to its globally distributed architecture and flexible data models. Data may be replicated across regions and accessed through multiple APIs, increasing the importance of explicit access control and continuous monitoring. Security design must ensure that global availability does not translate into global exposure.

Effective protection for Cosmos DB emphasizes strong identity-based authorization, least privilege permissions, and monitoring of access patterns across regions and applications. Cosmos DB is designed to scale and replicate transparently; hence, security controls must be deliberate and data-centric to prevent overexposure while preserving performance and resilience. Beyond databases and analytics services, storage platforms introduce distinct exposure risks that require service-specific security decisions.

Securing data stored in Azure Storage

Securing data in Azure Storage is primarily about controlling exposure at the service boundary. Storage services are designed to be broadly consumable by applications, analytics platforms, and automation, which makes them both powerful and dangerous when access is misconfigured. Unlike compute workloads, storage is not protected by host firewalls or application gateways. Security decisions must therefore focus on how access to the storage service itself is restricted and how permissions are delegated over time.

A common design failure is assuming that network or VM controls can compensate for a weak storage configuration. Azure Storage enforces access independently of virtual networks and application tiers, and exposure at the storage account-level can bypass protections applied elsewhere. Effective security design accepts this reality and treats storage accounts as first-class security boundaries that must be explicitly governed. This section maps to the following SC-100 skills measured: *Design a security solution for data in Azure Storage.*

Designing security controls for Azure Storage

Security controls for Azure Storage revolve around two core decisions: who is allowed to reach the storage service and how access is granted once that boundary is crossed. These decisions determine whether data exposure is constrained or effectively uncontrolled. Encryption protects data from unauthorized reading, but it does not prevent access misuse. Network isolation reduces reachability, but it does not govern how credentials are used. Both must be combined with deliberate access-control choices to be effective.

Since storage is frequently accessed by automated processes and external services, security controls must support delegation without creating permanent risk. Designs that rely on long-lived credentials or implicit trust expand the attack surface over time and are difficult to revoke cleanly.

Restricting access to Azure Storage services

Restricting access to the storage service boundary is the first and most critical control. Azure Storage access is enforced at the storage account level, not through network security groups, firewalls on VMs, or application gateways. Controls applied to compute resources do not protect storage accounts, and relying on them creates a false sense of security.

Effective design explicitly limits which networks or services are permitted to reach the storage account. By enforcing access at the service boundary, organizations ensure that even valid credentials cannot be used from unauthorized locations. This containment reduces the risk of accidental public exposure and limits the blast radius of credential compromise.

Providing secure, time-limited access to stored data

There are many scenarios where temporary access to stored data is required, such as third-party integrations, automated jobs, or external collaboration. Granting permanent access in these situations introduces unnecessary risk. Account keys and broad credentials provide unrestricted access and are difficult to rotate without disrupting dependent services.

A secure design favors scoped, time-limited access mechanisms that grant only the permissions required for a specific operation. By limiting both scope and duration, access naturally expires and reduces the impact of credential leakage. This approach allows storage access to be delegated safely without permanently expanding the attack surface.

Applying granular encryption controls using encryption scopes

Encryption is enabled by default in Azure Storage, but account-level encryption can be too coarse when different data sets have different compliance or isolation requirements. In these scenarios, encrypting all data under a single key does not provide sufficient separation or control.

Encryption scopes allow encryption policies to be applied at a more granular level, enabling different containers or blobs to be encrypted with different keys. This granularity is required when regulations or organizational policies demand distinct encryption boundaries within the same storage account. When encryption requirements vary within a storage environment, encryption scopes are the correct design choice rather than account-level encryption alone.

Defender for Storage and Databases solutions

Preventive controls define what should happen in a secure system, but they do not reveal when those controls are misused, bypassed, or operating under false assumptions. Even with strong identity governance, encryption, and access restrictions in place, data services remain vulnerable to abuse through compromised credentials, excessive privileges, or insecure configurations. Defender-based protections exist to surface these conditions when they occur and to provide actionable insight before misuse becomes large-scale data loss.

Microsoft Defender for Storage and Microsoft Defender for Databases are detection and visibility controls, not enforcement mechanisms. They do not encrypt data, restrict access, or prevent configuration changes. Their purpose is to observe how storage and database services are actually being used and to identify suspicious behavior, known attack patterns, and risky configurations that preventive controls cannot reliably block. A correct security design selects Defender specifically when the requirement is to detect, alert, and investigate data-related threats rather than to enforce policy. This section maps to the following SC-100 skills measured: *Design a security solution that includes Microsoft Defender for Storage and Microsoft Defender for Databases.*

Designing threat detection for Azure data services

Threat detection for data services must assume that attackers often operate using legitimate access. Credential theft, privilege escalation, and insider misuse frequently bypass perimeter defenses and identity safeguards without triggering immediate failures. Defender-based solutions are designed to identify these scenarios by analyzing activity patterns, access behavior, and configuration drift over time.

Effective design positions Defender as a continuous monitoring layer that complements preventive controls. Encryption and access restrictions reduce exposure, but Defender provides the visibility needed to detect when those controls are abused or when risk emerges after deployment. Without this detection layer, organizations are blind to data threats that occur inside permitted access boundaries.

Detecting threats to Azure Storage using Microsoft Defender

Microsoft Defender for Storage monitors storage access patterns, configuration changes, and known threat indicators associated with blob and file services. Storage accounts are frequently accessed by applications and automation, which makes malicious activity difficult to distinguish from normal operations without behavioral analysis. Defender identifies anomalous access, suspicious operations, and indicators of compromise that signal potential misuse.

When the requirement is to identify suspicious storage activity or receive alerts about potential data exfiltration, Defender is the correct solution. Encryption and network restrictions protect data confidentiality and reachability, but they do not provide insight into how credentials are used or whether access patterns indicate malicious behavior. Defender fills this gap by surfacing actionable alerts based on observed activity.

Detecting threats to Azure SQL

Microsoft Defender for Databases analyzes activity within managed database services to identify threats such as anomalous logins, suspicious query behavior, exploitation attempts, and insecure configurations. Databases concentrate sensitive data and often operate with elevated privileges, making them high-value targets for attackers who gain legitimate access.

In scenarios where the requirement is to detect abnormal database behavior or receive alerts about potential attacks, Defender is selected over preventive controls. Access restrictions and encryption define who should access data, but Defender reveals when access is misused or when attack techniques are detected at the database layer. This distinction is critical for designing an effective monitoring strategy.

Enabling Defender plans to support visibility

Defender capabilities are only available after the relevant Defender plans are enabled. Until a plan is activated, no threat detection, alerts, or security insights exist for the service. Reviewing compliance posture, alerts, or security recommendations without first enabling the appropriate Defender plan produces no meaningful results.

A correct security solution enables Defender plans as a prerequisite step before attempting to assess data-related risk or security posture. This ordering ensures that detection and visibility are established first, allowing subsequent reviews and investigations to reflect actual runtime behavior rather than static configuration alone.

Conclusion

This chapter examined how to design data protection and governance solutions that remain effective even when assumptions fail. Rather than treating data security as a collection of isolated controls, the chapter framed protection as a sequence of deliberate architectural decisions that determine how data is identified, protected, recovered, and monitored across cloud workloads.

The chapter began by establishing threat prioritization as the foundation of data protection. By assuming credential compromise and control failure as realistic conditions, it demonstrated why recovery preparedness and backup protection must be addressed before other mitigations. This approach ensures that ransomware and destructive attacks cannot permanently deny access to critical data.

It then explored encryption as a mechanism for limiting data exposure, emphasizing that encryption decisions are fundamentally about trust boundaries and key authority. By distinguishing between platform-managed and customer-managed keys, service-level and infrastructure-level encryption, and administrator-visible versus administrator-isolated encryption models, the chapter showed how encryption choices must align with both threat models and regulatory requirements.

The chapter also examined how data security decisions differ across Azure data workloads. By contrasting platform-managed services with infrastructure-based deployments, highlighting workload-specific encryption constraints, and addressing administrative access risks, it demonstrated how security architecture must adapt to the characteristics of Azure SQL, Azure Synapse Analytics, and Azure Cosmos DB rather than applying uniform controls.

Finally, the chapter addressed data security for Azure Storage and the role of Microsoft Defender for Storage and Databases. It reinforced that storage accounts are enforced at the service boundary, that access delegation must be scoped and time-limited, and that encryption granularity matters. It also positioned Defender as the detection and visibility layer that surfaces misuse and attack behavior that preventive controls cannot stop on their own.

Together, these concepts form a cohesive data protection architecture that balances prevention, recovery, and detection. By treating data security as a designed system rather than a checklist of features, the chapter equips architects to protect sensitive information, meet compliance obligations, and respond effectively to modern data-centric threats.

The next chapter brings together the concepts, architectures, and design decisions explored throughout the book by applying them in exam-style scenarios. It provides mock tests that challenge readers to analyze requirements, evaluate trade-offs, and select appropriate security solutions in the way the exam expects.

Questions

Success on any assessment depends on understanding the underlying technologies, concepts, and principles rather than memorizing facts. The following questions help readers confirm that they can apply this chapter's ideas in realistic design scenarios, including data discovery and classification, threat prioritization, encryption strategy, workload-specific data protection, storage security boundaries, and detection of data misuse and exfiltration.

1. **An organization wants to ensure sensitive data is consistently identified across Exchange, SharePoint, OneDrive, and Teams so that protection controls can be enforced automatically. Which design approach best achieves this outcome?**

    a. Manual classification by users

    b. Enabling encryption on all storage accounts

    c. Implementing centralized data discovery and sensitivity labeling

    d. Reviewing audit logs after data exposure

2. **Why is data classification considered a foundational control rather than a protective control?**
   a. It encrypts sensitive content by default
   b. It blocks unauthorized access automatically
   c. It provides the signal that downstream controls rely on for enforcement
   d. It replaces the need for DLP
3. **Which scenario most strongly indicates a need to prioritize recovery capabilities over preventive data controls?**
   a. A single instance of unauthorized file sharing
   b. Repeated malware alerts on user endpoints
   c. The risk of ransomware encrypting and deleting critical datasets
   d. Occasional policy violations in collaboration tools
4. **Why is recovery preparedness treated as the first priority when mitigating threats to data?**
   a. Recovery eliminates the need for encryption
   b. Recovery guarantees regulatory compliance
   c. Recovery prevents attackers from converting access into permanent data loss
   d. Recovery replaces the need for monitoring
5. **An organization requires explicit control over encryption keys for regulatory reasons. Which encryption design best satisfies this requirement?**
   a. Platform-managed service encryption
   b. Transport-layer encryption only
   c. Customer-managed keys with Azure Key Vault
   d. Default storage account encryption
6. **Why is infrastructure encryption sometimes required in addition to service-level encryption?**
   a. To improve application performance
   b. To simplify key rotation
   c. To protect data at the underlying host or hardware level
   d. To replace encryption in transit

7. **A requirement states that database administrators must not be able to view sensitive column data, even during query execution. Which design choice meets this requirement?**
    a. Transparent data encryption
    b. Platform-managed encryption
    c. Always Encrypted with secure enclaves
    d. Network isolation using private endpoints
8. **Why is it architecturally incorrect to rely on network controls alone to secure Azure Storage data?**
    a. Storage accounts do not support encryption
    b. Storage access is enforced independently of compute and network controls
    c. Network controls prevent all credential misuse
    d. Storage services are isolated by default
9. **Which design best supports granting temporary, limited access to Azure Storage data without creating long-term exposure?**
    a. Sharing storage account keys
    b. Assigning permanent role-based access
    c. Using scoped, time-limited access mechanisms
    d. Allowing public access with monitoring
10. **What is the primary role of Microsoft Defender for Storage and Microsoft Defender for Databases in a data protection architecture?**
    a. Enforcing encryption and access policies
    b. Replacing identity and access controls
    c. Detecting suspicious activity and data-related threats
    d. Performing backup and recovery operations

Answers

1. c: Implementing centralized data discovery and sensitivity labeling.

   Centralized discovery and classification ensure sensitive data is consistently identified so that downstream controls such as DLP and access restrictions can be enforced automatically.

2. c: It provides the signal that downstream controls rely on for enforcement.

   Classification defines data sensitivity, enabling encryption, DLP, and monitoring controls to behave predictably.

3. c: The risk of ransomware encrypting and deleting critical datasets.

   Ransomware scenarios make recovery capability the determining factor in whether data loss is survivable.

4. c: Recovery prevents attackers from converting access into permanent data loss.

   By protecting recovery paths first, organizations retain control even when preventive defenses fail.

5. c: Customer-managed keys with Azure Key Vault.

   Customer-managed keys establish a clear trust boundary by placing key authority under organizational control.

6. c: To protect data at the underlying host or hardware level.

   Infrastructure encryption extends protection beyond the service layer when threat models or compliance requirements demand it.

7. c: Always Encrypted with secure enclaves.

   Secure enclaves ensure sensitive data remains encrypted even during processing, preventing administrator access to plaintext values.

8. b: Storage access is enforced independently of compute and network controls.

   Azure Storage security is applied at the service boundary, making network-only designs insufficient.

9. c: Using scoped, time-limited access mechanisms.

   Time-limited, scoped access reduces exposure by ensuring permissions expire automatically and cannot be reused indefinitely.

10. c: Detecting suspicious activity and data-related threats.

    Defender for Storage and Databases provides visibility and detection when preventive controls are bypassed or misused.

CHAPTER 15
Practice Exams

Introduction

The SC-100 Microsoft Cybersecurity Architect exam evaluates a candidate's ability to reason through security architecture decisions under real-world constraints. Success depends on understanding how identity, governance, threat protection, data security, and monitoring capabilities work together as a coherent design rather than as isolated technologies.

This chapter provides two full-length practice exams designed to mirror the structure, depth, and complexity of the SC-100 assessment. The questions emphasize scenario-based decision-making, trade-off analysis, and control prioritization, the same skills required of a cybersecurity architect in production environments.

Each practice exam is intended to reinforce exam readiness by highlighting common architectural patterns, exposing weak areas in understanding, and building confidence in applying Zero Trust principles and Microsoft security best practices. These exams should be used not only to test knowledge, but to refine judgment and validate architectural thinking before sitting the real assessment.

Instructions:

- Each practice exam contains 50 questions.
- Each question has one correct answer.
- Choose the option that best satisfies the requirements described.
- Correct answers and explanations are provided for each question to reinforce correct reasoning.

Practice exam 1

Questions

1. **An organization is designing a Zero Trust architecture for hybrid workloads hosted across Azure and on-premises datacenters. The security architect wants to ensure access decisions are based on identity, device health, and risk signals rather than network location. Which design principle best supports this requirement?**
    a. Enforce network perimeter security using firewalls
    b. Assume breach and continuously verify trust
    c. Segment workloads using virtual networks
    d. Use shared credentials for service access
2. **A security architect is reviewing privileged access across multiple Azure subscriptions. The organization wants to reduce standing administrative privileges while still allowing operational teams to perform elevated tasks when required. Which solution best meets this requirement?**
    a. Assign permanent global administrator roles to operations staff
    b. Use Microsoft Entra ID Privileged Identity Management
    c. Store administrator credentials in Azure Key Vault
    d. Require multi-factor authentication for all administrators
3. **An organization wants all newly deployed Azure workloads to automatically inherit security controls related to identity, logging, and network configuration. Which architectural approach best achieves this outcome?**
    a. Apply security recommendations after deployment
    b. Manually configure security settings for each workload
    c. Design landing zones aligned to the Microsoft cloud security benchmark
    d. Review Secure Score after workloads are deployed
4. **A hybrid organization wants to detect credential theft and lateral movement attacks originating from on-premises Active Directory that could impact cloud identities. Which solution best supports this requirement?**
    a. Microsoft Defender for Cloud
    b. Microsoft Defender for Identity
    c. Microsoft Defender for Endpoint
    d. Microsoft Sentinel

5. **A security architect is designing a data protection strategy for sensitive customer information stored across Microsoft 365 services and Azure data platforms. The organization requires consistent classification and policy enforcement regardless of where the data resides. Which solution best meets this requirement?**
   a. Microsoft Defender for Cloud
   b. Azure Key Vault
   c. Microsoft Purview Information Protection
   d. Microsoft Sentinel
6. **An organization is concerned about ransomware attacks that could compromise backup data. The security architect wants to ensure that backups cannot be deleted or altered even if administrative credentials are compromised. Which design decision best addresses this risk?**
   a. Store backups in the same subscription as production workloads
   b. Use immutable backup storage with role separation
   c. Rely on endpoint antivirus software to protect backups
   d. Encrypt backups using customer-managed keys only
7. **A security architect wants to reduce the attack surface of Azure workloads by ensuring that only explicitly approved services can communicate with each other. Which approach best supports this objective?**
   a. Implement network security groups with broad allow rules
   b. Use Zero Trust networking with deny-by-default segmentation
   c. Assign public IP addresses to all workloads
   d. Rely solely on perimeter firewalls
8. **An organization wants to centrally detect, investigate, and respond to security incidents across Azure, Microsoft 365, and third-party cloud platforms. Which solution best meets this requirement?**
   a. Microsoft Defender for Cloud
   b. Microsoft Entra ID
   c. Microsoft Sentinel
   d. Microsoft Purview Compliance Manager
9. **A security architect wants to ensure access decisions dynamically adapt based on real-time risk signals such as unfamiliar sign-ins and impossible travel events. Which capability supports this requirement?**
   a. Role-based access control
   b. Conditional Access

c. Network security groups

d. Azure Policy

10. **An organization wants to assess its compliance posture against regulatory standards such as ISO 27001 and GDPR, and receive guidance on how to close identified gaps. Which solution best supports this need?**

    a. Microsoft Defender for Cloud

    b. Microsoft Purview Compliance Manager

    c. Microsoft Sentinel

    d. Azure Advisor

11. **A security architect is designing access controls for Microsoft 365 and Azure resources. The organization wants to ensure users are granted only the permissions required to perform their job functions and nothing more. Which principle best supports this requirement?**

    a. Defense in depth

    b. Least privilege

    c. Assume breach

    d. High availability

12. **An organization is adopting infrastructure as code (IaC) to deploy Azure resources. The security architect wants to prevent noncomplaint configurations from being deployed in the first place. Which solution best supports this requirement?**

    a. Microsoft Sentinel

    b. Azure Policy

    c. Microsoft Defender for Endpoint

    d. Microsoft Purview Compliance Manager

13. **A security architect is reviewing identity design for a multi-cloud environment that includes Azure and third-party SaaS applications. The organization wants a centralized identity provider to enforce authentication and access controls consistently. Which solution best meets this requirement?**

    a. Azure Resource Manager

    b. Microsoft Entra ID

    c. Microsoft Defender for Cloud

    d. Azure Policy

14. **An organization wants to protect highly privileged administrative accounts from phishing attacks while maintaining usability for administrators. Which control best addresses this requirement?**
    a. Password rotation every 30 days
    b. Conditional Access policies requiring multi-factor authentication
    c. Dedicated Privileged Access Workstations
    d. Network security groups restricting admin access
15. **A security architect is designing a monitoring strategy to detect suspicious activity across Azure workloads, identities, and endpoints. The organization wants automated correlation of signals to reduce investigation time. Which solution best supports this goal?**
    a. Microsoft Defender for Cloud
    b. Microsoft Sentinel
    c. Microsoft Entra ID
    d. Azure Monitor
16. **An organization wants to reduce the risk of credential theft by isolating administrative sessions from standard user activities such as email and web browsing. Which design approach best meets this requirement?**
    a. Enforcing strong password complexity
    b. Using Privileged Access Workstation
    c. Implementing Azure Key Vault
    d. Applying Azure Policy
17. **A security architect is designing a hybrid security monitoring solution. The organization wants to collect security logs from on-premises servers and Azure resources into a single analytics platform. Which solution best meets this requirement?**
    a. Microsoft Defender for Endpoint
    b. Microsoft Defender for Identity
    c. Microsoft Sentinel
    d. Microsoft Purview
18. **An organization wants to ensure that compromised user accounts cannot automatically access all resources even after successful authentication. Which Zero Trust capability best addresses this requirement?**
    a. Network segmentation
    b. Conditional Access

c. Encryption at rest
d. Backup immutability

19. **A security architect is evaluating ransomware protection for Azure virtual machines. The organization wants visibility into missing security controls and exposure to common attack techniques. Which solution best supports this requirement?**
    a. Microsoft Defender for Cloud
    b. Microsoft Sentinel
    c. Microsoft Entra ID
    d. Microsoft Purview Information Protection
20. **An organization wants to ensure that security incidents detected across multiple platforms trigger automated response actions such as isolating devices or disabling user accounts. Which capability best supports this requirement?**
    a. Azure Policy
    b. Role-based access control
    c. Security orchestration and automated response
    d. Secure Score
21. **A security architect is designing access controls for APIs exposed by Azure-hosted applications. The organization wants to ensure that applications authenticate securely without using stored secrets. Which approach best meets this requirement?**
    a. Use shared access keys stored in configuration files
    b. Use managed identities for Azure resources
    c. Use personal user accounts for application access
    d. Store client secrets in application code
22. **An organization wants to ensure that sensitive data stored in Azure SQL Database remains protected even if the underlying storage is compromised. Which control best addresses this requirement?**
    a. Network security groups
    b. Encryption at rest
    c. Conditional Access
    d. Azure Policy
23. **A security architect is reviewing monitoring coverage for endpoints used by remote employees. The organization wants to detect advanced threats and respond quickly to suspicious activity on devices. Which solution best meets this requirement?**
    a. Microsoft Defender for Endpoint
    b. Microsoft Defender for Identity

c. Microsoft Defender for Cloud

d. Microsoft Purview

24. **An organization wants to enforce security configuration standards across Azure subscriptions while allowing limited flexibility for workload teams. Which governance approach best supports this requirement?**

a. Manual reviews of resource deployments

b. Azure Policy with initiatives

c. Microsoft Sentinel analytics rules

d. Conditional Access policies

25. **A security architect wants to ensure that only compliant devices can access Microsoft 365 services. Which capability best supports this requirement?**

a. Network security groups

b. Conditional Access with device compliance

c. Azure Policy

d. Role-based access control

26. **An organization wants to detect and investigate insider threats related to abnormal user behavior across Microsoft 365 workloads. Which solution best supports this requirement?**

a. Microsoft Defender for Endpoint

b. Microsoft Defender for Identity

c. Microsoft Purview Insider Risk Management

d. Microsoft Sentinel

27. **A security architect is designing a strategy to protect cryptographic keys used by Azure services. The organization requires hardware-backed protection and centralized key management. Which solution best meets this requirement?**

a. Azure Policy

b. Microsoft Defender for Cloud

c. Azure Key Vault with hardware security modules

d. Microsoft Sentinel

28. **An organization wants to minimize the blast radius of compromised credentials by restricting access to resources based on workload identity rather than network location. Which Zero Trust concept best addresses this requirement?**

a. Perimeter security

b. Identity as the control plane

c. Shared responsibility

d. Availability zones

29. **A security architect wants to ensure security alerts from multiple Defender products are correlated into a single incident view. Which capability best supports this requirement?**

a. Azure Monitor

b. Microsoft Sentinel

c. Microsoft Defender XDR

d. Secure Score

30. **An organization wants to evaluate how well its security controls align with recommended best practices and receive prioritized improvement actions. Which solution best supports this goal?**

a. Microsoft Defender for Cloud Secure Score

b. Azure Advisor

c. Microsoft Sentinel

d. Azure Cost Management

31. **A security architect is designing access controls for highly sensitive administrative roles. The organization wants to require additional verification only when elevated privileges are requested. Which capability best supports this requirement?**

a. Permanent role assignments

b. Privileged Identity Management with approval workflows

c. Role-based access control

d. Network security groups

32. **An organization wants to detect malicious activity targeting domain controllers in an on-premises environment that is synchronized with Azure. Which solution best supports this requirement?**

a. Microsoft Defender for Cloud

b. Microsoft Defender for Identity

c. Microsoft Defender for Endpoint

d. Microsoft Sentinel

33. **A security architect is designing a data governance strategy to ensure sensitive data cannot be shared externally without authorization. Which control best supports this requirement?**

a. Conditional Access

b. Data loss prevention policies

c. Network security groups

d. Encryption at rest

34. **An organization wants to reduce alert fatigue by grouping related security alerts into single incidents for investigation. Which solution best supports this requirement?**

a. Azure Monitor

b. Microsoft Defender XDR

c. Microsoft Purview

d. Azure Policy

35. **A security architect wants to ensure security logs from Azure workloads are retained for long-term investigations and compliance requirements. Which approach best supports this requirement?**

a. Store logs locally on each virtual machine

b. Use Azure Monitor Log Analytics with retention policies

c. Rely on real-time alerts only

d. Export logs manually when incidents occur

36. **An organization wants to enforce strong authentication for all users accessing cloud resources while allowing different access requirements based on user risk. Which capability best supports this requirement?**

a. Role-based access control

b. Conditional Access

c. Azure Policy

d. Network security groups

37. **A security architect is designing a protection strategy for APIs published through Azure. The organization wants to prevent unauthorized access and detect abuse patterns. Which solution best meets this requirement?**

a. Azure Firewall

b. Azure API management with authentication and monitoring

c. Network security groups

d. Azure Policy

38. **An organization wants to ensure that sensitive data remains protected even when accessed by authorized users from unmanaged devices. Which control best supports this requirement?**

a. Encryption at rest

b. Conditional Access with app-enforced restrictions

   c. Network security groups
   d. Azure Advisor

39. **A security architect wants to detect suspicious sign-in behavior across Microsoft Entra ID and automatically block risky sessions. Which capability best supports this requirement?**
   a. Azure Policy
   b. Identity protection risk policies
   c. Secure Score
   d. Role-based access control

40. **An organization wants to design a security monitoring strategy that supports proactive threat hunting across collected telemetry. Which solution best supports this goal?**
   a. Microsoft Defender for Cloud
   b. Microsoft Sentinel
   c. Microsoft Entra ID
   d. Microsoft Purview

41. **A security architect is designing controls to protect privileged credentials used to manage Azure infrastructure. The organization wants to prevent credential exposure during administrative sessions. Which approach best supports this requirement?**
   a. Storing credentials in password-protected documents
   b. Using Privileged Access Workstation
   c. Rotating passwords every 90 days
   d. Assigning permanent administrator roles

42. **An organization wants to ensure that security policies are consistently enforced across Azure, on-premises, and multi-cloud environments. Which solution best supports this requirement?**
   a. Microsoft Sentinel
   b. Azure Policy with Azure Arc
   c. Microsoft Defender for Endpoint
   d. Microsoft Entra ID

43. **A security architect wants to limit the impact of compromised application credentials by ensuring applications can access only the specific resources they require. Which design principle best supports this requirement?**
   a. Defense in depth
   b. Least privilege

c. High availability

d. Shared responsibility

44. **An organization wants to monitor configuration drift and security misconfigurations across its Azure subscriptions. Which solution best supports this requirement?**

a. Microsoft Defender for Cloud

b. Microsoft Sentinel

c. Azure Monitor

d. Microsoft Purview

45. **A security architect wants to prevent accidental or malicious deletion of critical security logs. Which design approach best addresses this requirement?**

a. Store logs on individual virtual machines

b. Enable immutable storage for logs

c. Rely on manual backups

d. Limit log access to administrators only

46. **An organization wants to ensure that access to sensitive applications requires stronger authentication when risk levels increase. Which capability best supports this requirement?**

a. Role-based access control

b. Conditional Access with risk-based policies

c. Network security groups

d. Azure Advisor

47. **A security architect is designing a detection strategy for suspicious PowerShell activity across endpoints. Which solution best meets this requirement?**

a. Microsoft Defender for Endpoint

b. Microsoft Defender for Identity

c. Microsoft Purview Compliance Manager

d. Azure Policy

48. **An organization wants to ensure that encryption keys used by cloud workloads cannot be accessed or exported by administrators. Which solution best supports this requirement?**

a. Software-based encryption keys

b. Azure Key Vault with customer-managed keys

c. Azure Key Vault with hardware security modules

d. Azure Storage Service Encryption only

49. **A security architect wants to improve incident response efficiency by automating common remediation tasks after an alert is triggered. Which capability best supports this goal?**

    a. Secure Score

    b. Security orchestration and automated response

    c. Azure Monitor

    d. Role-based access control

50. **An organization wants to validate that its overall security architecture aligns with Zero Trust principles and recommended Microsoft best practices. Which approach best supports this objective?**

    a. Periodic penetration testing only

    b. Reviewing Secure Score and Zero Trust assessments

    c. Relying on firewall rules

    d. Manual checklist reviews

Answers

1. **Correct answer**: b

   Explanation: Zero Trust assumes breach and requires continuous verification based on identity, device health, and risk signals rather than relying on network location. Network segmentation supports Zero Trust but does not replace ongoing trust evaluation.

2. **Correct answer**: b

   Explanation: Microsoft Entra ID Privileged Identity Management enables just-in-time privileged access with approval and auditing, reducing standing administrative privileges while maintaining operational effectiveness.

3. **Correct answer**: c

   Explanation: Landing zones aligned to the Microsoft cloud security benchmark embed security controls into the platform architecture so workloads automatically inherit identity, logging, and network protections at deployment.

4. **Correct answer**: b

   Explanation: Microsoft Defender for Identity monitors on-premises Active Directory activity to detect credential theft, lateral movement, and reconnaissance that could impact cloud-connected identities.

5. **Correct answer**: c

   Explanation: Microsoft Purview Information Protection provides consistent data classification, labeling, and policy enforcement across Microsoft 365 and Azure data services.

6. **Correct answer**: b

   Explanation: Immutable backups with strict role separation prevent backup deletion or modification even if administrative credentials are compromised, providing strong ransomware resilience.

7. **Correct answer**: b

   Explanation: Zero Trust networking enforces deny-by-default communication, allowing only explicitly approved traffic paths and significantly reducing lateral movement risk.

8. **Correct answer**: c

   Explanation: Microsoft Sentinel aggregates and correlates security alerts across Microsoft and non-Microsoft environments, enabling centralized detection, investigation, and response.

9. **Correct answer**: b

   Explanation: Conditional Access evaluates real-time risk signals such as unfamiliar sign-ins and enforces adaptive access controls rather than relying solely on successful authentication.

10. **Correct answer**: b

    Explanation: Microsoft Purview Compliance Manager maps organizational controls to regulatory standards such as ISO 27001 and GDPR and provides actionable guidance to close identified compliance gaps.

11. **Correct answer**: b

    Explanation: The principle of least privilege ensures users are granted only the permissions required to perform their job functions, reducing the impact of compromised accounts.

12. **Correct answer**: b

    Explanation: Azure Policy enforces security requirements at deployment time by blocking noncomplaint configurations, preventing insecure resources from being created.

13. **Correct answer**: b

    Explanation: Microsoft Entra ID provides centralized identity and access management for Azure and third-party SaaS applications, enabling consistent authentication and authorization.

14. **Correct answer**: c

    Explanation: Privileged Access Workstation isolate administrative sessions from common attack vectors such as email and web browsing, significantly reducing phishing risk.

15. **Correct answer**: b

    Explanation: Microsoft Sentinel correlates security signals across identities, endpoints, and workloads into unified incidents, reducing investigation time and complexity.

16. **Correct answer**: b

    Explanation: Privileged Access Workstation isolate administrative activity from standard user tasks, reducing the risk of credential theft and session hijacking.

17. **Correct answer**: c

    Explanation: Microsoft Sentinel supports centralized ingestion and analysis of security logs from on-premises servers and Azure resources, enabling unified monitoring.

18. **Correct answer**: b

    Explanation: Conditional Access ensures authentication alone does not grant access by continuously evaluating context and risk before allowing access to resources.

19. **Correct answer**: a

    Explanation: Microsoft Defender for Cloud identifies security misconfigurations, missing controls, and exposure to common attack techniques across Azure workloads.

20. **Correct answer**: c

    Explanation: Security orchestration and automated response enable automatic remediation actions such as account disablement or device isolation when incidents occur.

21. **Correct answer**: b

    Explanation: Managed identities allow Azure resources to authenticate securely to other services without storing secrets or credentials in application code.

22. **Correct answer**: b

    Explanation: Encryption at rest ensures data stored in Azure Storage remains protected even if the underlying storage infrastructure is accessed by an attacker.

23. **Correct answer**: a

    Explanation: Microsoft Defender for Endpoint provides advanced detection, investigation, and response capabilities for endpoint devices used by remote employees.

24. **Correct answer**: b

    Explanation: Azure Policy initiatives enable consistent enforcement of security requirements across subscriptions while allowing approved exceptions through scoped exemptions.

25. **Correct answer**: b

    Explanation: Conditional Access with device compliance ensures that only devices meeting defined security requirements can access Microsoft 365 services.

26. **Correct answer**: c

    Explanation: Microsoft Purview Insider Risk Management detects abnormal user behavior and insider risk scenarios such as data exfiltration across Microsoft 365 workloads.

27. **Correct answer**: c

    Explanation: Azure Key Vault with hardware security modules provides hardware-backed protection for cryptographic keys and centralized key management.

28. **Correct answer**: b

    Explanation: Zero Trust treats identity as the primary control plane, ensuring access decisions are based on verified identities rather than network location.

29. **Correct answer**: c

    Explanation: Microsoft Defender XDR correlates alerts from multiple Defender products into a single incident view, simplifying investigation and response.

30. **Correct answer**: a

    Explanation: Secure Score provides prioritized recommendations that show how improving security controls will reduce overall risk exposure.

31. **Correct answer**: b

    Explanation: Privileged Identity Management enables just-in-time privileged access with approval workflows and auditing, eliminating standing administrator privileges.

32. **Correct answer**: b

    Explanation: Microsoft Defender for Identity monitors on-premises domain controllers to detect credential theft, reconnaissance, and lateral movement attacks.

33. **Correct answer**: b

    Explanation: Data loss prevention policies prevent unauthorized external sharing of sensitive information by detecting and controlling data movement.

34. **Correct answer**: b

    Explanation: Microsoft Defender XDR reduces alert fatigue by grouping related alerts into single incidents for investigation.

35. **Correct answer**: b

    Explanation: Centralized log analytics with defined retention policies ensures security logs are retained for investigations and compliance requirements.

36. **Correct answer**: b

    Explanation: Conditional Access with risk-based policies dynamically enforces stronger authentication requirements when user risk increases.

37. **Correct answer**: b

    Explanation: Azure API management enforces authentication and monitors API usage, helping prevent unauthorized access and detect abuse patterns.

38. **Correct answer**: b

    Explanation: App-enforced restrictions through Conditional Access protect sensitive data when accessed from unmanaged devices.

39. **Correct answer**: b

    Explanation: Identity protection risk policies automatically detect and block high-risk sign-ins or require additional verification.

40. **Correct answer**: b

    Explanation: Microsoft Sentinel supports proactive threat hunting by enabling advanced queries across aggregated security telemetry.

41. **Correct answer**: b

    Explanation: Privileged Access Workstation protect privileged credentials by isolating administrative sessions from everyday user activities.

42. **Correct answer**: b

    Explanation: Azure Policy with Azure Arc enforces consistent security controls across Azure, on-premises, and multi-cloud environments.

43. **Correct answer**: b

    Explanation: Least privilege limits the blast radius of compromised service identities by ensuring applications can access only required resources.

44. **Correct answer**: a

    Explanation: Microsoft Defender for Cloud provides continuous visibility into misconfigurations and attack surface exposure across Azure workloads.

45. **Correct answer**: b

    Explanation: Immutable storage prevents security logs from being altered or deleted, preserving forensic evidence.

46. **Correct answer**: b

    Explanation: Risk-based Conditional Access adapts authentication requirements automatically when sign-in risk increases.

47. **Correct answer**: a

    Explanation: Microsoft Defender for Endpoint detects suspicious scripting activity, such as PowerShell abuse, on endpoint devices.

48. **Correct answer**: c

    Explanation: Azure Key Vault with hardware security modules prevents key export and provides hardware-backed encryption key protection.

49. **Correct answer**: b

    Explanation: Security orchestration and automated response enable automated remediation actions, improving incident response efficiency.

50. **Correct answer**: b

    Explanation: Secure Score and Zero Trust assessments validate that the security architecture aligns with Microsoft's recommended best practices.

Practice exam 2

Questions

1. **An organization is modernizing its security architecture to reduce reliance on network location as a trust signal. The security architect wants access decisions to be evaluated continuously based on identity and context. Which Zero Trust principle best supports this design goal?**
    a. Trust but verify
    b. Verify explicitly
    c. Defense in depth
    d. Perimeter isolation
2. **A security architect is reviewing authentication methods for privileged administrators. The organization wants to reduce the risk of credential replay and phishing attacks. Which authentication approach best supports this requirement?**
    a. Password-based authentication
    b. Certificate-based authentication
    c. Password rotation every 60 days
    d. Shared administrator accounts

3. **An organization wants to ensure that workloads deployed across multiple Azure subscriptions follow consistent security configurations by default. Which architectural approach best supports this requirement?**
   a. Manual configuration by application teams
   b. Secure Score reviews after deployment
   c. Landing zone design with enforced governance
   d. Post-incident remediation
4. **A hybrid organization wants to detect suspicious behavior that indicates compromised credentials being used against on-premises domain controllers. Which solution best supports this requirement?**
   a. Microsoft Defender for Endpoint
   b. Microsoft Defender for Cloud
   c. Microsoft Defender for Identity
   d. Microsoft Sentinel
5. **A security architect is designing a data classification strategy that must work across Exchange Online, SharePoint Online, and OneDrive. Which solution best supports this requirement?**
   a. Microsoft Defender for Endpoint
   b. Microsoft Purview Information Protection
   c. Azure Key Vault
   d. Microsoft Sentinel
6. **An organization wants to ensure that backup data cannot be deleted or altered by ransomware or compromised administrators. Which control best supports this requirement?**
   a. Encrypted backups
   b. Immutable backups with role separation
   c. Antivirus protection on backup servers
   d. Network isolation only
7. **A security architect wants to reduce lateral movement risk between Azure workloads by enforcing explicit communication paths. Which approach best supports this objective?**
   a. Broad allow rules in network security groups
   b. Zero Trust segmentation with deny-by-default rules
   c. Public endpoints with firewall protection
   d. Flat virtual networks

8. **An organization wants to aggregate security alerts from multiple Microsoft security services and third-party sources into a single investigation platform. Which solution best meets this requirement?**
   a. Microsoft Defender for Cloud
   b. Microsoft Entra ID
   c. Microsoft Sentinel
   d. Microsoft Purview Compliance Manager

9. **A security architect wants access policies to dynamically respond to user sign-in risk and device state. Which capability best supports this requirement?**
   a. Role-based access control
   b. Conditional Access
   c. Azure Policy
   d. Network security groups

10. **An organization wants to measure its compliance posture against regulatory standards and track improvement actions over time. Which solution best supports this goal?**
    a. Microsoft Defender for Cloud
    b. Microsoft Purview Compliance Manager
    c. Microsoft Sentinel
    d. Azure Advisor

11. **A security architect wants to ensure administrators do not retain standing privileged access and that all elevation events are auditable. Which solution best supports this requirement?**
    a. Role-based access control
    b. Privileged Identity Management
    c. Conditional Access
    d. Azure Policy

12. **An organization is adopting IaC to deploy security-sensitive workloads. The security architect wants to block deployments that violate required security configurations. Which capability best supports this requirement?**
    a. Microsoft Sentinel
    b. Azure Policy with deny effects
    c. Microsoft Defender for Endpoint
    d. Microsoft Purview

13. **A security architect is designing identity integration for multiple SaaS applications. The organization wants a single identity provider to enforce authentication and access controls. Which solution best meets this requirement?**
    a. Azure Resource Manager
    b. Microsoft Entra ID
    c. Azure Monitor
    d. Microsoft Defender for Cloud
14. **An organization wants to protect administrative accounts from phishing while allowing administrators to perform privileged tasks. Which control best supports this requirement?**
    a. Frequent password rotation
    b. Privileged Access Workstation
    c. Network security groups
    d. Secure Score reviews
15. **A security architect wants to reduce investigation time by correlating alerts across identities, endpoints, and cloud workloads. Which solution best supports this goal?**
    a. Azure Monitor
    b. Microsoft Defender XDR
    c. Microsoft Purview
    d. Azure Advisor
16. **An organization wants to prevent compromised credentials from automatically granting access to all applications after authentication. Which Zero Trust capability best supports this requirement?**
    a. Network segmentation
    b. Conditional Access
    c. Encryption at rest
    d. Backup immutability
17. **A security architect is designing centralized monitoring for on-premises servers and Azure resources. Which solution best supports unified log ingestion and analysis?**
    a. Microsoft Defender for Endpoint
    b. Microsoft Defender for Identity
    c. Microsoft Sentinel
    d. Microsoft Entra ID

18. **An organization wants to restrict external sharing of sensitive documents across Microsoft 365 services. Which control best supports this requirement?**
    a. Network security groups
    b. Data loss prevention policies
    c. Encryption at rest
    d. Azure Policy
19. **A security architect wants visibility into misconfigurations and missing security controls across Azure workloads. Which solution best supports this requirement?**
    a. Microsoft Defender for Cloud
    b. Microsoft Sentinel
    c. Microsoft Entra ID
    d. Microsoft Purview
20. **An organization wants automated response actions, such as disabling accounts or isolating devices, when high-severity incidents occur. Which capability best supports this requirement?**
    a. Secure Score
    b. Security orchestration and automated response
    c. Azure Monitor
    d. Role-based access control
21. **A security architect wants applications running in Azure to authenticate to other Azure services without managing secrets or certificates in code. Which approach best supports this requirement?**
    a. Shared access keys
    b. Managed identities
    c. Client secrets stored in Key Vault
    d. User account credentials
22. **An organization wants to ensure sensitive data stored in Azure Storage accounts remains protected even if the storage infrastructure is accessed by an attacker. Which control best supports this requirement?**
    a. Network security groups
    b. Encryption at rest
    c. Conditional Access
    d. Azure Policy

23. **A security architect is reviewing endpoint protection for remote users. The organization wants advanced threat detection and the ability to isolate compromised devices. Which solution best meets this requirement?**
    a. Microsoft Defender for Identity
    b. Microsoft Defender for Endpoint
    c. Microsoft Defender for Cloud
    d. Microsoft Sentinel
24. **An organization wants to apply consistent security requirements across subscriptions while allowing approved exceptions for specific workloads. Which governance capability best supports this requirement?**
    a. Manual deployment reviews
    b. Azure Policy initiatives with scoped exemptions
    c. Secure Score monitoring
    d. Conditional Access
25. **A security architect wants to ensure only compliant devices can access Microsoft 365 applications. Which capability best supports this requirement?**
    a. Role-based access control
    b. Conditional Access with device compliance
    c. Network security groups
    d. Azure Advisor
26. **An organization wants to detect insider risk scenarios such as data exfiltration or policy violations within Microsoft 365. Which solution best supports this requirement?**
    a. Microsoft Defender for Endpoint
    b. Microsoft Defender for Identity
    c. Microsoft Purview Insider Risk Management
    d. Microsoft Sentinel
27. **A security architect is designing cryptographic key protection for regulated workloads. The organization requires hardware-backed key protection and strict access controls. Which solution best meets this requirement?**
    a. Software-based encryption keys
    b. Azure Storage Service Encryption
    c. Azure Key Vault with hardware security modules
    d. Customer-managed keys without HSM

28. **An organization wants to minimize lateral movement by ensuring workloads authenticate using workload identity rather than network trust. Which Zero Trust concept best supports this design?**
    a. Perimeter defense
    b. Identity as the primary control plane
    c. Shared responsibility
    d. Availability zones
29. **A security architect wants alerts from multiple Defender products to be automatically correlated into a single incident for investigation. Which solution best supports this requirement?**
    a. Azure Monitor
    b. Microsoft Sentinel
    c. Microsoft Defender XDR
    d. Secure Score
30. **An organization wants prioritized recommendations that show how improving security controls will reduce overall risk exposure. Which solution best supports this goal?**
    a. Microsoft Defender for Cloud Secure Score
    b. Azure Cost Management
    c. Microsoft Sentinel
    d. Azure Advisor
31. **A security architect wants to ensure privileged access is granted only when needed and that all elevation requests are reviewed and logged. Which capability best supports this requirement?**
    a. Role-based access control
    b. Privileged Identity Management
    c. Conditional Access
    d. Network security groups
32. **An organization wants to detect attacks targeting on-premises Active Directory that could impact cloud-connected identities. Which solution best supports this requirement?**
    a. Microsoft Defender for Cloud
    b. Microsoft Defender for Identity
    c. Microsoft Defender for Endpoint
    d. Microsoft Sentinel

33. **A security architect is designing controls to prevent sensitive information from being shared externally without approval. Which control best supports this requirement?**
    a. Conditional Access
    b. Data loss prevention policies
    c. Network security groups
    d. Encryption at rest
34. **An organization wants to reduce alert fatigue by grouping related alerts from multiple security products into a single incident. Which solution best supports this requirement?**
    a. Azure Monitor
    b. Microsoft Defender XDR
    c. Microsoft Purview
    d. Azure Policy
35. **A security architect wants to retain security logs for extended periods to support investigations and regulatory requirements. Which approach best supports this requirement?**
    a. Store logs locally on each system
    b. Use centralized log analytics with defined retention policies
    c. Rely on real-time alerts only
    d. Export logs manually when required
36. **An organization wants authentication requirements to become stricter when user risk increases. Which capability best supports this requirement?**
    a. Role-based access control
    b. Conditional Access with risk-based policies
    c. Azure Policy
    d. Network security groups
37. **A security architect wants to protect APIs published in Azure by enforcing authentication and monitoring usage patterns. Which solution best supports this requirement?**
    a. Azure Firewall
    b. Azure API Management
    c. Network security groups
    d. Azure Policy

38. **An organization wants to ensure sensitive data remains protected even when accessed from unmanaged devices. Which control best supports this requirement?**
    a. Encryption at rest
    b. Conditional Access with app-enforced restrictions
    c. Network security groups
    d. Azure Advisor

39. **A security architect wants to automatically block high-risk sign-ins detected across Microsoft Entra ID. Which capability best supports this requirement?**
    a. Azure Policy
    b. Identity protection risk policies
    c. Secure Score
    d. Role-based access control

40. **An organization wants to perform proactive threat hunting across collected security telemetry. Which solution best supports this goal?**
    a. Microsoft Defender for Cloud
    b. Microsoft Sentinel
    c. Microsoft Entra ID
    d. Microsoft Purview

41. **A security architect wants to reduce the risk of privileged credential theft during administrative activities. Which design approach best supports this requirement?**
    a. Rotating administrator passwords frequently
    b. Using Privileged Access Workstation
    c. Assigning permanent administrator roles
    d. Storing credentials in encrypted files

42. **An organization wants to enforce consistent security controls across Azure, on-premises servers, and multi-cloud environments from a single control plane. Which solution best supports this requirement?**
    a. Microsoft Sentinel
    b. Azure Policy with Azure Arc
    c. Microsoft Defender for Endpoint
    d. Microsoft Entra ID

43. **A security architect wants to limit the impact of compromised service identities by ensuring applications can access only the resources they require. Which design principle best supports this requirement?**
    a. Defense in depth
    b. Least privilege
    c. Shared responsibility
    d. Availability
44. **An organization wants continuous visibility into security misconfigurations and attack surface exposure across Azure workloads. Which solution best supports this requirement?**
    a. Microsoft Defender for Cloud
    b. Microsoft Sentinel
    c. Azure Monitor
    d. Microsoft Purview
45. **A security architect wants to protect security logs from deletion or tampering by attackers. Which design decision best addresses this requirement?**
    a. Store logs on local servers
    b. Enable immutable storage for logs
    c. Limit log access to administrators
    d. Export logs manually
46. **An organization wants authentication requirements to adapt automatically when sign-in risk increases. Which capability best supports this requirement?**
    a. Role-based access control
    b. Conditional Access with risk-based policies
    c. Network security groups
    d. Azure Advisor
47. **A security architect is designing detection for suspicious scripting activity on endpoint devices. Which solution best supports this requirement?**
    a. Microsoft Defender for Endpoint
    b. Microsoft Defender for Identity
    c. Microsoft Purview Compliance Manager
    d. Azure Policy

48. **An organization requires encryption keys to be protected by hardware and not exportable by administrators. Which solution best supports this requirement?**
    a. Software-based encryption keys
    b. Customer-managed keys without HSM
    c. Azure Key Vault with hardware security modules
    d. Azure Storage Service Encryption only
49. **A security architect wants to automatically isolate compromised devices and disable accounts when confirmed incidents occur. Which capability best supports this goal?**
    a. Secure Score
    b. Security orchestration and automated response
    c. Azure Monitor
    d. Role-based access control
50. **An organization wants to validate that its security architecture aligns with Zero Trust principles and Microsoft's recommended best practices. Which approach best supports this objective?**
    a. Firewall rule reviews
    b. Secure Score and Zero Trust assessments
    c. Manual compliance checklists
    d. Periodic penetration testing only

Answers

1. **Correct answer**: b

   Explanation: Verify explicitly is a core Zero Trust principle that requires access decisions to be continuously evaluated based on identity, device state, and contextual risk rather than implicit trust.
2. **Correct answer**: b

   Explanation: Certificate-based authentication removes reliance on reusable secrets and is resistant to phishing and credential replay attacks compared to password-based methods.
3. **Correct answer**: c

   Explanation: Landing zone design with enforced governance ensures security controls are embedded into the platform architecture and inherited automatically by deployed workloads.
4. **Correct answer**: c

Explanation: Microsoft Defender for Identity monitors on-premises Active Directory to detect credential theft, abnormal authentication patterns, and lateral movement in hybrid environments.

5. **Correct answer**: b

   Explanation: Microsoft Purview Information Protection provides consistent data classification and labeling across Exchange Online, SharePoint Online, and OneDrive.

6. **Correct answer**: b

   Explanation: Immutable backups with role separation prevent deletion or modification of backup data even if ransomware or compromised administrators are present.

7. **Correct answer**: b

   Explanation: Zero Trust segmentation enforces deny-by-default communication and allows only explicitly approved traffic paths, reducing lateral movement risk.

8. **Correct answer**: c

   Explanation: Microsoft Sentinel aggregates and correlates alerts from Microsoft and third-party sources into a centralized SIEM and SOAR platform.

9. **Correct answer**: b

   Explanation: Conditional Access dynamically evaluates user risk and device state to enforce adaptive access controls.

10. **Correct answer**: b

    Explanation: Microsoft Purview Compliance Manager assesses regulatory compliance and tracks improvement actions over time.

11. **Correct answer**: b

    Explanation: Privileged Identity Management enables just-in-time privileged access with approval and auditing, eliminating standing administrator privileges.

12. **Correct answer**: b

    Explanation: Azure Policy with deny effects blocks noncomplaint deployments at creation time, enforcing security requirements proactively.

13. **Correct answer**: b

    Explanation: Microsoft Entra ID provides centralized identity management and access control for Microsoft and third-party SaaS applications.

14. **Correct answer**: b

    Explanation: Privileged Access Workstation isolate administrative sessions from common attack vectors such as email and web browsing.

15. **Correct answer**: b

    Explanation: Microsoft Defender XDR correlates alerts across identities, endpoints, and workloads into unified incidents, reducing investigation time.

16. **Correct answer**: b

    Explanation: Conditional Access ensures authentication alone does not grant access and evaluates context and risk before allowing application access.

17. **Correct answer**: c

    Explanation: Microsoft Sentinel supports unified log ingestion and analysis across on-premises servers and Azure resources.

18. **Correct answer**: b

    Explanation: Data loss prevention policies prevent unauthorized external sharing of sensitive information across Microsoft 365 services.

19. **Correct answer**: a

    Explanation: Microsoft Defender for Cloud provides visibility into misconfigurations, missing controls, and security posture gaps across Azure workloads.

20. **Correct answer**: b

    Explanation: Security orchestration and automated response enable automatic remediation actions such as account disablement or device isolation.

21. **Correct answer**: b

    Explanation: Managed identities allow Azure applications to authenticate securely without storing secrets or credentials in code.

22. **Correct answer**: b

    Explanation: Encryption at rest protects stored data even if the underlying storage infrastructure is accessed by an attacker.

23. **Correct answer**: b

    Explanation: Microsoft Defender for Endpoint provides advanced endpoint threat detection, investigation, and response capabilities, including device isolation.

24. **Correct answer**: b

    Explanation: Azure Policy initiatives enable consistent enforcement of security requirements while allowing approved deviations through scoped exemptions.

25. **Correct answer**: b

    Explanation: Conditional Access with device compliance ensures only compliant devices can access Microsoft 365 applications.

26. **Correct answer**: c

    Explanation: Microsoft Purview Insider Risk Management detects insider risk scenarios such as data exfiltration and policy violations.

27. **Correct answer**: c

    Explanation: Azure Key Vault with hardware security modules provides hardware-backed cryptographic key protection and strict access controls.

28. **Correct answer**: b

    Explanation: Zero Trust treats identity as the primary control plane rather than relying on network-based trust.

29. **Correct answer**: c

    Explanation: Microsoft Defender XDR automatically correlates alerts from multiple Defender products into single incidents.

30. **Correct answer**: a

    Explanation: Secure Score provides prioritized recommendations showing how security improvements reduce overall risk exposure.

31. **Correct answer**: b

    Explanation: Privileged Identity Management supports time-bound elevation with approval workflows and full auditing.

32. **Correct answer**: b

    Explanation: Microsoft Defender for Identity detects malicious activity targeting on-premises domain controllers in hybrid environments.

33. **Correct answer**: b

    Explanation: Data loss prevention policies control sensitive data movement and prevent unauthorized external sharing.

34. **Correct answer**: b

    Explanation: Microsoft Defender XDR reduces alert fatigue by grouping related alerts into unified incidents.

35. **Correct answer**: b

    Explanation: Centralized log analytics with retention policies supports long-term investigations and regulatory compliance.

36. **Correct answer**: b

    Explanation: Risk-based Conditional Access dynamically enforces stronger authentication as sign-in risk increases.

37. **Correct answer**: b

    Explanation: Azure API management enforces authentication, authorization, and monitoring for APIs, helping detect abuse patterns.

38. **Correct answer**: b

    Explanation: App-enforced restrictions limit data actions when accessed from unmanaged devices, reducing data leakage risk.

39. **Correct answer**: b

    Explanation: Identity protection risk policies automatically block or challenge high-risk sign-ins.

40. **Correct answer**: b

    Explanation: Microsoft Sentinel enables proactive threat hunting across aggregated security telemetry.

41. **Correct answer**: b

    Explanation: Privileged Access Workstation reduce the risk of credential theft by isolating administrative activities.

42. **Correct answer**: b

    Explanation: Azure Policy with Azure Arc enforces consistent security controls across Azure, on-premises, and multi-cloud environments.

43. **Correct answer**: b

    Explanation: Least privilege ensures service identities can access only the resources required, limiting blast radius.

44. **Correct answer**: a

    Explanation: Microsoft Defender for Cloud provides continuous visibility into security misconfigurations and attack surface exposure.

45. **Correct answer**: b

    Explanation: Immutable storage prevents security logs from being deleted or tampered with, preserving forensic evidence.

46. **Correct answer**: b

    Explanation: Conditional Access with risk-based policies adapts authentication requirements automatically as risk increases.

47. **Correct answer**: a

    Explanation: Microsoft Defender for Endpoint detects suspicious scripting activity, such as PowerShell abuse, on endpoint devices.

48. **Correct answer**: c

    Explanation: Azure Key Vault with hardware security modules prevents key export and provides hardware-backed key protection.

49. **Correct answer**: b

    Explanation: Security orchestration and automated response enable automated remediation actions, improving response speed.

50. **Correct answer**: b

    Explanation: Secure Score and Zero Trust assessments validate alignment with Microsoft's recommended security best practices.

Index

A

B

C

D

E

G

H

I